Neither Separate nor Equal

Perspectives on the History of Congress, 1789–1801

Kenneth R. Bowling and Donald R. Kennon, Series Editors

Inventing Congress: Origins and Establishment of the First Federal Congress

Neither Separate nor Equal: Congress in the 1790s

Neither Separate nor Equal

Congress in the 1790s

Edited by Kenneth R. Bowling and Donald R. Kennon

PUBLISHED FOR THE
UNITED STATES CAPITOL HISTORICAL SOCIETY
BY OHIO UNIVERSITY PRESS • ATHENS

Ohio University Press, Athens, Ohio 45701
© 2000 by Ohio University Press
Printed in the United States of America
All rights reserved

Ohio University Press books are printed on acid-free paper ∞

09 08 07 06 05 04 03 02 01 00   5 4 3 2 1

Library of Congress Cataloging-in-Publication Data

Neither separate nor equal : Congress in the 1790s / edited by
Kenneth R. Bowling and Donald R. Kennon.
        p. cm. — (Perspectives on the history of Congress, 1789–
1801)
    Includes bibliographical references and index.
    ISBN 0-8214-1327-9 (alk. paper)
    1. United States. Congress — History — 18th century.
    2. Legislators — United States — History — 18th century.
    3. United States — Politics and government — 1789–1797.
    I. Bowling, Kenneth R. II. Kennon, Donald R., 1948– III. United
States Capitol Historical Society. IV. Series.
    JK1041 .N45 2000
    328.73'09'033 — dc21
                                                00-024185

Contents

III. Congress and the Executive and Judicial Branches in the 1790s

Preface

The United States Capitol Historical Society has sponsored an annual conference on American history since 1978. The more than 140 published papers delivered between then and 1993 dramatically altered in both depth and breadth the way we understand the American Revolution. In 1993 the society decided to hold two annual conferences, one focusing on congressional history and the other on the art and architectural history of the Capitol. Kenneth R. Bowling of the First Federal Congress Project at The George Washington University was asked to chair the first series, "Perspectives on the History of the United States Congress, 1789–1801." Thus was born the society's 1994–2000 conference series on Congress before it moved to Washington, D.C., in 1800. The first volume of papers, covering the 1994 conference — "Inventing Congress" — and the 1995 conference — "A Vessel Just Launched: The First Federal Congress" — was published in 1999.

Entitled "Neither Separate nor Equal: Congress and the Executive and Judicial Branches in the 1790s," the 1996 conference was held in the Rayburn House Office Building on April 12. The American Revolution was predicated on legislative supremacy; the federal government existed prior to 1789 with only a very dependent executive and virtually no judiciary. The Constitution created a supreme court and the offices of president and vice president but otherwise left to Congress the configuration of the executive and judicial branches. How did the three branches interact during the precedent-setting first decade of the federal government under the Constitution? How did presidents Washington and Adams compare and contrast in the style of their relationships with Congress? What was the relationship between Secretary of the Treasury Alexander Hamilton and Congress? These and other issues were addressed in five papers.

Professor Wythe Holt of the University of Alabama Law School opened the conference with "Separation of Powers? Relations between the Judiciary and the Other Branches of the Federal Government before 1803." Modern historians find the origins of a "wall of separation" among the three branches of the federal government in Hayburn's Case in 1792 and in the refusal of the justices of the Supreme Court to give the president and his cabinet an opinion about international law in a political crisis in 1793. Holt demonstrates, however, that members of the three branches interacted frequently in the 1790s, especially including the judges of the Supreme Court. Rather than an absolute wall dividing the judges from the other branches, in the 1790s the judges understood "separation of powers" to require each branch to oppose any branch's encroachment upon the exercise of independent judgment by another of the three branches.

Professor William R. Casto of Texas Tech University School of Law looked at the issue of separation of powers and foreign policy. "French Cruisers, British Prizes, and American Sailors: Coordinating American Foreign Policy in the Age of Fighting Sails," a case study of the neutrality crisis of 1793, argues that the Supreme Court acted as a virtual arm of the executive, while Congress — not in session — played almost no role. To those who see the event as a strong indication of separation of powers based on the justices' refusal to provide formal answers to queries submitted by President Washington, Casto maintains that it was the executive branch — in the form of Secretary of the Treasury Alexander Hamilton — which lobbied them not to reply. The less restrictive view of separation of powers held by the Supreme Court justices of the 1790s, all appointed by the same president and uniquely in agreement with each other, changed forever in 1801 with the election of Thomas Jefferson to the presidency.

Jack D. Warren, Jr., an editor of the papers of George Washington at the University of Virginia, spoke on " 'The Line of My Official Conduct': George Washington and Congress, 1789–1797." Warren argues that Washington as president was assertive rather than passive with Congress: a president who, although keenly aware of revolutionary America's distrust of executive power, established an energetic and effective presidency. Further, Warren maintains that Washington achieved most of his goals: the establishment of a strong federal government, presidential leadership in foreign affairs and the appointment process, and the location of the federal city on the Potomac River.

Professor John Ferling of West Georgia College entitled his paper "'Father and Protector': President John Adams and Congress in the Quasi-War Crisis," arguing that Adams's overriding concern as president was to be "father and protector" of the many against the malevolence of the few. In the Quasi-War Crisis, Adams successfully exercised his presidential powers to stanch what he saw as an oligarchic plot to fundamentally alter American politics and society. He considered this achievement "the most splendid diamond in my crown."

Professor Joanne B. Freeman, a graduate student at the University of Virginia and now a member of Yale University's department of history, delivered the final paper of the day: "'The Art and Address of Ministerial Management': Secretary of the Treasury Alexander Hamilton and Congress." Freeman writes about how politicking between Congress and executive branch officials—Hamilton in particular—actually worked. She does this by getting at the roots of Hamilton's political method, proving that Secretary of State Thomas Jefferson had legitimate complaints when he accused his colleague of widespread influence and "corruption," and in the process pointing out that Jefferson's political method gave Hamilton legitimate concern as well.

Entitled "The Social and Political Lives of Members of Congress at Philadelphia," the 1997 conference was held in the Rayburn House Office Building on April 11. This conference looked at the neighborhood in which congressmen spent most of their time and how they spent it, the role of the congressional wife at home, and the congressional careers of a senator and two representatives.

Anna Coxe Toogood of Independence National Historical Park opened the program with a slide description of the State House Square neighborhood during the 1790s entitled "Philadelphia as the Nation's Capital, 1790–1800." Many of the images she shared are printed with her chapter in this volume.

Elizabeth M. Nuxoll, editor of the papers of Robert Morris at Queens College of the City University of New York, spoke on Morris's six-year tenure as a senator from Pennsylvania. In "The Financier as Senator: Robert Morris of Pennsylvania, 1789–1795," she examines his role in light of his term as superintendent of finance from 1781 to 1784, emphasizing the continuities between the confederation period and the early national period. She also discusses legislation more closely tied to Morris's personal interests, particularly the seat of government issue, duties protecting America's Asiatic trade, and a policy of non-involvement in European wars. Nuxoll challenges Gordon Wood's assertion that during the 1790s Morris abandoned trade and aspired to become a disinterested "classical republican aristocrat." Instead, she argues, Morris's business choices were determined by economic circumstances, while his fabled hospitality was directed to the achievement of concrete objectives. Finally, Nuxoll analyzes the controversies over the settlement of Morris's public accounts.

Mary A. Giunta of the National Historical Publications and Records Commission entitled her paper "In Opposition: The Congressional Career of William Branch Giles, 1790–1798." She focused on Giles's role as a vigorous opponent of the policies of George Washington and Alexander Hamilton and as an ally of James Madison and Thomas Jefferson, exploring his role in the political debates and conflicts that occurred in the House. In the process she provides details about the beginnings of the first political party system.

John D. Gordan III, an attorney with Morgan, Lewis and Bockius, spoke on a representative of a decidedly different political persuasion: "Egbert Benson: A Nationalist in Congress, 1789–1793." Gordan explores Benson's role in the crafting of the Fourth Amendment to the Constitution, in asserting the importance of a federal judiciary separate and independent from the states, and in the adoption of the fugitive slave act of 1793, when Benson voted against his conscience.

William C. diGiacomantonio's article, "A Congressional Wife at Home: The Case of Sarah Thatcher, 1781–1792," illuminates a silent, hidden corner of the traditional congressional biography. Old school scholarship typically celebrated that silence: one biographer thought that the lack of letters between Sen. Oliver Ellsworth and his wife "happily spared [the historian] the temptation to stimulate the interest of his readers with any parade of family skeletons" (William G. Brown, *The Life of Oliver Ellsworth* [New York, 1905], p. 24). This approach lumps the public and private content of congressional spouses' letters into a single domestic significance and then robs it of all but prurient interest. DiGiacomantonio seeks to restore balance and perspective to the multidimensional life of early members of Congress by reviewing the largest extant correspondence between a member of the First Federal Congress and his wife, George and Sarah Thatcher of Maine.

Kenneth R. Bowling, conference chair, delivered the final paper: "The Federal Government and the Republican Court Move to Philadelphia, November 1790–March 1791." He discusses the physical move of the members and their attendants, describes the social and cultural activities of the members, and argues that the "republican court" did not arise in Philadelphia but moved there from New York City, where it had been established and evolved in 1789 and 1790.

Kenneth R. Bowling
Donald R. Kennon

I. The Physical and Social Context

Kenneth R. Bowling

The Federal Government and the Republican Court Move to Philadelphia, November 1790–March 1791

ON JULY 16, 1790, President George Washington signed the Residence Act, locating the permanent capital of the United States a few miles north of Mount Vernon on the Potomac River. The act's provisions called for the federal government to settle at Philadelphia until 1800. Congress previously had resided there from its inception in August 1774 until the Continental Army mutiny in June 1783, except for two occasions when it fled to avoid the British army. It left for the third time when the government of Pennsylvania refused to knuckle under to federal pressure during the mutiny.[1] Speaker of the Pennsylvania Assembly Frederick Augustus Muhlenberg observed then that, should Congress return, it would be the eighth wonder of the world if it

Unless otherwise noted, sources dated July through December are from 1790; those dated in the months of January through June are from 1791. The author wishes in particular to acknowledge Nola Kotter, a former employee of the Commission on the Bicentennial of the United States Constitution, whose research in the Philadelphia newspapers yielded much new information about the city's social life. The author's colleagues at the First Federal Congress Project, Charlene Bickford, Helen Veit, and William C. diGiacomantonio, provided valuable comments and editorial revision. John Alviti, formerly of the Museum of the City of Philadelphia, gave the manuscript a critical reading.

[1]For Congress at Philadelphia during the Revolutionary War and the passage of the Residence Act in 1790, see Kenneth R. Bowling, *The Creation of Washington, D.C., The Idea and Location of the American Capital* (Fairfax, Va., 1991).

FIG. 1. "Cong_ss Embark'd on board the Ship Constitution of America bound to Conogocheque by way of Philadelphia." This cartoon was hawked on the streets of New York City late in July 1790 after President George Washington had signed the Residence Act. It showed Sen. Robert Morris directing the ship *Constitution* over a waterfall to Philadelphia en route to the permanent capital on the Potomac River. *(Courtesy Library of Congress)*

ever mustered the votes to leave again.[2] In the wake of the 1790 act, many of the politically aware in America feared his prediction would prove true and that Philadelphia would become the permanent capital despite George Washington's machinations for the Potomac (fig. 1). Congress would be happy to stay at Philadelphia, a newspaper writer concluded, because the city had long enjoyed superior cultural and social activities, and unlike New York City, her eyes were "not dazzled by ostentatious splendor, her ears not deadened by the clamor of revelry, her mind not distracted by (what may be called) genteel dissipation." Such talk elicited a letter to a Philadelphia newspaper urging that no official of the state ever stain its honor by acting in any way to prevent removal to the Potomac in 1800. Nevertheless, members of Pennsylvania's congressional delegation observed privately that

---

[2]Frederick Augustus Muhlenberg to Richard Peters, Aug. 30, 1783, Peters Papers, Historical Society of Pennsylvania (hereafter PHi).

a lot could happen in ten years, and many Philadelphians hoped a way would be found to retain the federal government in 1800.[3]

Philadelphia was certainly the most attractive, materially comfortable, populous, and ethnically and religiously diverse city in the United States. Its accommodations, fine dining, cultural resources, and international tone contributed to its reputation. By 1790 it was known as the Athens of America, the financial, commercial, manufacturing, political, publishing, intellectual, and cultural capital of the young nation. Including the suburbs of Southwark and the Northern Liberties, the city ran for more than two miles along the Delaware River and housed 43,000 residents, while the second and third largest cities in the nation, New York and Boston, had 33,000 and 18,000 residents respectively. Straight, often tree-lined and pebble-paved streets were separated from raised brick sidewalks by gutters and protective posts. Along them stood numerous imposing public buildings and houses of red brick appointed with white marble.[4] This contrasted with chaotic, unplanned New York City, with its narrow pedestrian-unfriendly streets and rainbow of painted buildings. Westward toward the Schuylkill River, Philadelphia's 7,000 buildings thinned out after State House Square between Fifth and Sixth, and beyond Twelfth Street the planned city remained pasture (fig. 2).[5]

---

[3]Bowling, *The Creation of Washington, D.C.,* chaps. 7–8; *Federal Gazette* (Philadelphia), Nov. 23.

[4]On Philadelphia in the 1790s see Clement Biddle, *Philadelphia City Directory* (Philadelphia, 1791); the several articles, two cited elsewhere in these notes, in *Historic Philadelphia, Transactions of the American Philosophical Society* 43, pt. 1 (1953); Ed Riley, "Philadelphia: The Nation's Capital, 1790–1800," *Pennsylvania History* 20 (1953):357–79; Roland D. Baumann, "The Democratic-Republicans of Philadelphia: The Origins, 1776–1797," Ph.D. diss., Penn State University, 1970; Ethel Rasmusson, "Capital on the Delaware: The Philadelphia Upper Class in Transition, 1789–1801," Ph.D. diss., Brown University, 1962. Russell F. Weigley, ed., *Philadelphia: A 300-Year History* (New York, 1982) contains two relevant chapters: Theodore Thayer, "Town into City, 1746–1765," pp. 68–108, describes the city and its economy on the eve of the American Revolution, while Richard G. Miller, "The Federal City, 1783–1800," pp. 155–207, details its local, state, and federal politics.

[5]For New York as the federal capital see Kenneth R. Bowling, "New York City, Capital of the United States, 1785–1790," in *World of the Founders: New York Communities in the Federal Period,* ed. Stephen L. Schechter and Wendell Tripp (Albany, 1990); Thomas E. V. Smith, *The City of New York in the Year of Washington's Inauguration, 1789* (1889; reprint ed., Riverside, Conn., 1972); Robert I. Goler, "Traveler's Guide to Federal New York: Visual and Historical Perspectives," in *Federal New York: A Symposium,* ed. Robert I.

Vice President John Adams, who was familiar with Paris, Amsterdam, and London, described Philadelphia in December 1790 as a great city of science, literature, wealth, and beauty. Rep. Fisher Ames of Boston considered it magnificent and its citizens advanced in public spirit, enterprise, and institutions. South Carolina Sen. Pierce Butler found the city large and handsome and credited the Quakers for a city plan that imposed order and regularity. Comptroller of the Treasury Oliver Wolcott, Jr., like many of the newcomers, thought Philadelphia large and elegant, but not quite as astonishing as its citizens had promised. "Like the rest of mankind the Philadelphians judge favorably of their city and themselves, and their representations are to be admitted with some deductions." This was a gentler way of saying what a visitor had noted twenty years earlier: "The almost universal topic of conversation among [Philadelphians] is the superiority of Philadelphia over every other spot on the globe. All their geese are swans."[6]

Rep. Theodore Sedgwick of western Massachusetts shared his friend Ames's view. He recognized the pride Philadelphians took in their city and lavished praise on its plan and the "universal appearance of richness. . . . They seem in their city improvements to have got the start on any other place on the continent." His comments were made to his wife, Pamela, in one of the many letters in which he described Philadelphia during the winter of 1790–91. Had the Pennsylvanians been aware of what he wrote, at least on this occasion, they would have been pleased, for he was among the congressional leaders whom they hoped would assist in keeping Congress at Philadelphia after 1800.[7]

Goler (New York, 1990), pp. 6–12; and Sidney I. Pomerantz, *New York, An American City, 1783–1803* (2d ed., Port Washington, N.Y., 1965).

[6]John Adams to John Quincy Adams, Dec. 13, Adams Family Manuscript Trust, Massachusetts Historical Society (hereafter MHi); Fisher Ames to Thomas Dwight, Dec. 12, Ames Papers, Dedham Historical Society; Pierce Butler to John Leckey, Feb. 11, Butler Letterbook, South Carolina Historical Society; Oliver Wolcott, Jr., to Mrs. Oliver Wolcott, Sept. 7, George Gibbs, *Memoirs of the Administrations of Washington and John Adams*, 2 vols. (New York, 1846), 1:57; Jonathan Boucher, *Reminiscences of an American Loyalist* (New York, 1925), p. 101.

[7]Theodore Sedgwick to Pamela Sedgwick, Dec. 26, Sedgwick Papers, MHi. Sedgwick was one of ten high-level federal officeholders who served during the entire decade that Congress met in Philadelphia. Their papers, most of which are extant in non-Philadelphia repositories, provide untapped information about the social history of the federal government during its years in Philadelphia. Nine members of the First Federal Congress served in Congress continuously until 1800: John Langdon and Samuel Liver-

Proper accommodation for Congress was the first challenge Philadelphia faced when it again became the seat of federal government in 1790. New York City had provided elegant Federal Hall, an effort that Rep. George Thatcher of Maine believed had slowed down Philadelphia's effort to lure Congress southward: Philadelphians knew that whatever they did would be compared to it.[8] A newspaper writer recommended that the state build lavish garden-enhanced quarters on the still-rural central square at the intersection of Broad and Market. Such facilities would take the pressure off existing public buildings and undercut the effort to move the state capital westward and the federal capital southward. Whether old or new, another newspaper writer stressed the importance of a cupola on the building where Congress met in order to shed light on its proceedings. Time, more than anything, forced a decision in favor of existing buildings, at least for the moment. Pennsylvania suddenly found the State House, home to the Revolutionary Congress and the Federal Convention, indispensable and reneged on its earlier offers. Upon the advice of the Pennsylvania members of Congress who happened to be in town and able to visit potentially available buildings, the recently completed Philadelphia County Courthouse at Sixth and Chestnut was chosen. Renaming it Congress Hall, the city quickly remodeled and fitted it out to match Federal Hall as closely as possible. A few yards to the east stood the State House. The proposal to enclose the buildings with an iron railing and evergreens and to lay marble or freestone between them was not implemented. Serpentine, graveled walks with elms and shrubs lay behind the buildings (fig. 3).[9]

---

more of New Hampshire; George Thatcher, Benjamin Goodhue, and Theodore Sedgwick of Massachusetts; Theodore Foster of Rhode Island; Josiah Parker of Virginia; and James Gunn and Abraham Baldwin of Georgia. The most important executive branch official to serve throughout the decade was John (and Abigail) Adams. In addition, the papers of dozens of officials who served at Philadelphia for less than a decade have not yet been explored.

[8]George Thatcher to Sarah Thatcher, Sept. 29, 1788, Thatcher Papers, MHi; Thomas Fitzsimons to Miers Fisher, July 16, Fisher Papers, PHi; "A. B.," *Pennsylvania Gazette* (Philadelphia), Sept. 2.

[9]Extract of Philadelphia letter dated Sept. 29, *Massachusetts Spy* (Worcester), Oct. 14; "A Citizen," "Another Citizen," *Federal Gazette*, July; Thomas Affleck to Tench Coxe, Sept. 16, Coxe Papers, PHi; Tench Coxe to Richard Varick, Sept. 7, Miscellaneous American Autographs, Pierpont Morgan Library; Bowling, *The Creation of Washington,*

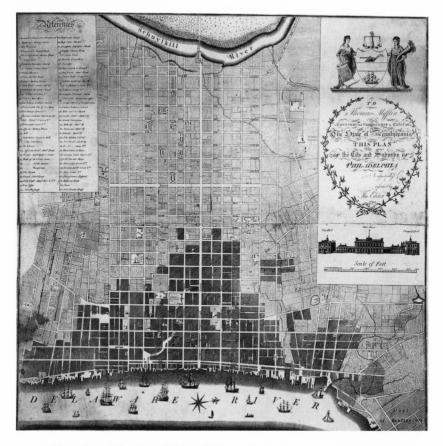

FIG. 2. This plan of the city of Philadelphia and suburbs by geographer A. P. Folie was presented to Gov. Thomas Mifflin in 1794. *(Courtesy New York Public Library)*

Sedgwick found Congress Hall "neat, elegant, & convenient," but, unlike Federal Hall, "not of the splendid grandeur of federal stile." Others were less generous. The building's perimeter lacked trees to cool it in summer and became muddy after inclement weather. The tiny second-floor Senate chamber provided no room for a gallery if that body decided to open its debates to public scrutiny, and the steep

---

D.C., p. 212; *Federal Gazette,* Oct. 20; Memorial of the Philadelphia Common Council to the State Legislature, Dec. 28, 1790, Fisher-Warner Papers, Friends Library, Swarthmore College. For a detailed description of the area around Congress Hall, see Anna Coxe Toogood, "Philadelphia as the Nation's Capital, 1790–1800," this volume.

FIG. 3. *Back of the State House*, by William Birch, 1799. With its serpentine graveled walks and tree-lined promenade, the yard behind the State House was a popular social setting. *(Courtesy Independence National Historical Park)*

stairs to it must have challenged many senators, especially the elderly and gout-ridden. Most dramatically, the entire building could almost fit within the chamber allocated to the House of Representatives alone at New York. The House's two committee rooms and its clerk's office had to be located on the second floor of the west wing of the State House.[10]

Philadelphia felt the impact of its new status by early November, when the city was so full that even bachelors found it hard to secure lodging. Like camp followers, but in this case preceding federal officials, came tailors, milliners, shoemakers, hair and wig dressers, teachers, musicians, artists, actors, shopkeepers, clerks, printers, and shorthand writers. Applicants for office, petitioners, and speculators were

---

[10]Theodore Sedgwick to Pamela Sedgwick, Jan. 9, Feb. 17, Sedgwick Papers, MHi; New York Letter dated Feb. 20, *Dunlap's American Daily Advertiser* (hereafter *Dunlap's Daily Advertiser*), Mar. 4; "Uncle Gwynn's Oddities Exposed," *Independent Gazetteer* (Philadelphia), Mar. 5.

not far behind. While the new arrivals hailed from several parts of the nation (and even Europe), the majority came from New York: these included printers John Swaine and John Fenno; congressional debate recorder Thomas Lloyd; dance instructor James Robardet; artificial flower arranger John Vache, who sold ribbons and feathers as a sideline; dry goods merchant and stationer Michael Roberts; merchant tailor John Shepperd; and even A. A. Van Ottingen with his rheumatism cure. Artists who followed Congress included the portraitist Joseph Wright, the miniaturist Samuel Folwell, and, near the end of the session, John Trumbull; they joined the three resident Peales, Charles Willson, James, and Rembrandt. The musicians Alexander Reinagle and Henry Capron and the Old American Company of actors moved the seat of performing arts from New York to Philadelphia. Others thought of moving with Congress but did not. Included in this group was a Mrs. Loring, who had moved her boardinghouse from Boston to New York in 1789.[11] Among the new residents was former Postmaster General Ebenezer Hazard, a native Philadelphian who had left for New York before the Revolutionary War and who now felt that the need of a job forced his return. He became a documentary editor, reviving his prewar dream of publishing an edition of American state papers. Hazard secured a subscription list that stands as a who's who of federal officialdom in early 1791. It included twenty-one senators, thirty-five representatives, the president, the vice president, the attorney general, and Assistant Secretary of the Treasury Tench Coxe.[12]

As if trying to prove that Philadelphia was a better location for the seat of government than New York, the First Federal Congress achieved a quorum only one day late for its third session on Decem-

---

[11]*Federal Gazette*, Nov. 6, 8, 26, Dec. 10; *Pennsylvania Packet* (Philadelphia), Nov. 3, 23; William Loughton Smith to Edward Rutledge, Nov. 24, Smith Letters, South Carolina Historical Society; Alexander Hamilton to Tobias Lear, Oct. 29, 1790, Harold Syrett and Jacob E. Cooke, eds., *The Papers of Alexander Hamilton*, 27 vols. (New York, 1961–87), 7:132; Solomon Drowne to Theodore Foster, July 25, Drowne Papers, Brown University; *General Advertiser* (Philadelphia), Dec. 10, Jan. 1, 6, 18; Kenneth Silverman, *A Cultural History of the American Revolution* (New York, 1976), pp. 471–72, 554–56, 592–98; George Thatcher to Sarah Thatcher, Jan. 6, Thatcher Letters, Library of Congress (hereafter DLC); Theodore Sedgwick to Pamela Sedgwick, Aug. 20, 1789, Sedgwick Papers, MHi.

[12]Ebenezer Hazard to Jeremy Belknap, Oct. 3, Belknap Papers, MHi; Proposals for a Collection of State Papers, Feb. 24, Hazard Papers, PHi.

ber 6. On the other hand, the disasters several members experienced en route gave credence to the argument that Philadelphia was difficult to reach by water. Rep. Thomas Tudor Tucker of South Carolina endured a sixteen-day storm-filled journey on the Atlantic. At least he fared better than fellow South Carolina Rep. Aedanus Burke, whose ship went aground at the mouth of Delaware Bay during a violent night storm. Georgia representatives James Jackson and George Mathews escaped shipwreck, but after being buffeted by repeated storms at sea, they left ship at Cape May and continued to Philadelphia by wagon. During one of the storms Jackson had resigned himself to death, a fate not even Sedgwick, who loathed Jackson's passionate and populist rhetoric on the House floor, would have wished. Land carriage proved only slightly less disastrous. A stagecoach transporting Sen. Tristram Dalton and representatives Elbridge Gerry, George Partridge, and Jonathan Grout of Massachusetts overturned near New Brunswick, New Jersey. Partridge could not proceed because of bruised ribs. Gerry, also badly bruised, had to wear an enormous black patch on his "skinned face." Dalton and Grout suffered less, but to add insult to injury the former was robbed of forty dollars and a dozen shirts within minutes of his arrival at Philadelphia. Maryland Rep. Joshua Seney suffered a similar but apparently less severe accident. Massachusetts Sen. Caleb Strong was so fatigued by his journey that it took him a month to throw off the cold that struck him.[13]

Several members arrived in the wake of personal tragedy. The wives of Connecticut Rep. Benjamin Huntington and North Carolina Rep. Hugh Williamson died in October, and in November, just as Senator Butler prepared to leave New York, his wife died. Butler's arrival at Philadelphia with his daughters did not improve his emotional state. They discovered that housing arrangements made through Tench Coxe had not been completed, but the matter was quickly resolved and the furniture he had shipped from New York found a new

[13]*Federal Gazette*, Dec. 8; Aedanus Burke letter dated Nov. 27, *Pennsylvania Gazette*, Dec. 8; William L. Smith to Gabriel Manigault, Dec. 19, *American Historical Review* 14 (1909):779; James Jackson to John Milledge, as quoted in William O. Foster, *James Jackson* (Athens, Ga., 1960), p. 70; Theodore Sedgwick to Williams, Jan. 27, 1791, Sedgwick Papers, MHi; Joshua Seney to Frances Seney, Dec. 9, Gratz Collection, PHi; Fisher Ames to Thomas Dwight, Dec. 12, Ames Papers, Dedham Historical Society; Caleb Strong to David Sewall, Jan. 17, Miscellaneous Manuscripts, DLC.

home. Perhaps the misunderstanding arose because Coxe had overextended himself to accommodate various members, particularly the Philadelphia-loathing South Carolinians. He found lodging for the families and furniture of Rep. William Loughton Smith and his father-in-law, Sen. Ralph Izard, who had stables and a coach house built to store his coach, post chaise, and one-horse chair.[14]

Not every member of Congress needed or could afford to rent an entire house. Philadelphia's private homes, boardinghouses, and taverns provided accommodations and meals for most (fig. 4). New Hampshire Sen. Paine Wingate resided with Connecticut Rep. Roger Sherman and Massachusetts Rep. Benjamin Goodhue at the home of William Smith, former president of the College of Philadelphia. Six members lodged at John Francis's hotel. Pennsylvania Sen. William Maclay chose a room at William Ogden's Second Street tavern. Rhode Island Sen. Theodore Foster at first resided at James Thompson's Indian Queen Tavern, but then moved into the home of Samuel Bayard on Third Street, where Delaware Sen. Richard Bassett roomed. Sedgwick also resided at a tavern when he first arrived, but, finding the numerous guests very unpleasant, he moved to a boardinghouse with a "motly mixture" of five other representatives. Beginning in February, City Tavern, which had advertised itself as a hotel since 1789, promised that private dinners could be ordered at any hour by members of Congress. Philadelphia means varied from the simple to the exotic ones for which it had long been famous. Washerwomen were available to care for the clothing of visitors, and Senator Butler spent about twenty-five dollars for four months of washing.[15]

---

[14]*Federal Gazette*, Oct. 18; *Daily Advertiser* (New York), Nov. 15; William L. Smith to Edward Rutledge, Nov. 24, Smith Papers, South Carolina Historical Society; William Smith to Tench Coxe, Oct. 20, Pierce Butler to Tench Coxe, [n.d.]; Ralph Izard to Tench Coxe, Sept. 6, Oct. 14, 26, Coxe Papers, PHi. Pennsylvania Sen. Robert Morris assisted his friend New Hampshire Sen. John Langdon in finding housing (Morris to Langdon, Oct. 6, Alfred Elwyn, ed., *Letters to John Langdon* [Philadelphia, 1880], pp. 74–75).

[15]Theodore Sedgwick to Pamela Sedgwick, Dec. 26, Jan. 5, Sedgwick Papers, MHi; *Dunlap's Daily Advertiser*, Feb. 16, Mar. 8; Robert Graham, "Taverns of Colonial Philadelphia," *Historic Philadelphia*, pp. 323–24; Charles E. L. Wingate, *Life and Letters of Paine Wingate*, 2 vols. (Medford, Mass., 1930), 1:379–80; Theodore Foster to Dwight Foster, Jan. 8, Dwight Foster Papers, MHi; Kenneth R. Bowling and Helen E. Veit, eds., *The Diary of William Maclay and Other Notes on Senate Debates* (Baltimore, 1988), vol. 9 of

FIG. 4. *State House with a View of Chestnut Street*, by William Birch, 1798. Philadelphia was a walking city, where members of Congress could readily come and go from their nearby residences to Congress Hall. *(Courtesy Independence National Historical Park)*

Many congressmen already had some connection with Philadelphia. Including the Pennsylvanians, all of whom had lived in the city while holding state elective office, forty of the ninety-one members had served in Congress before it left in 1783 or had attended the Federal Convention in 1787. Representative Goodhue had married a Philadelphia resident when he was a merchant in the city for a decade before the Revolutionary War. Three New Jersey members maintained close ties to the city: Rep. Lambert Cadwalader, who attended college there, had several relatives in the city; Sen. Philemon Dickinson owned an elegant mansion; and Rep. Elias Boudinot moved in with his

Documentary History of the First Federal Congress, 14 vols. to date (Baltimore, 1972–), p. 343; James McHenry to William Hindman, July 19, 1783, McHenry Papers, Maryland Historical Society; *General Advertiser,* Nov. 13; Butler Receipt Book, Mar. 1791, Butler Papers, PHi.

daughter and son-in-law, William Bradford, attorney general of Pennsylvania. Virginia Sen. Richard Henry Lee probably lived with his sister Alice, wife of Dr. William Shippen. Several members of Congress had business connections in Philadelphia, including Maryland representatives Benjamin Contee and Michael Jenifer Stone, both tobacco planters. Their House colleague Joshua Seney and North Carolina Representative Williamson, a Pennsylvania native, had graduated from the College of Philadelphia.

Several congressmen brought family members to Philadelphia. Ruth Dalton joined her husband; their daughter was already living there. New Hampshire Sen. John Langdon brought his wife, Elizabeth, and their only child, a daughter. Delaware Rep. John Vining married two weeks before the session opened, but it is uncertain if his wife, Mary, accompanied him. Frances Seney, a New York native, joined husband Joshua. Newly appointed Virginia Sen. James Monroe and his wife, Elizabeth, arrived on December 17. She remained several weeks — long enough to get a smallpox inoculation for their daughter before journeying on to her parents in New York. Monroe then joined Rep. James Madison at Elizabeth House's, a boardinghouse long favored by Virginia congressmen; North Carolina Sen. Benjamin Hawkins also boarded there. Several members invited relatives to experience Philadelphia's social and cultural life. Vice President Adams persuaded his son, John Quincy, to visit. Representative Stone entertained some of his nieces for the winter while Faith Trumbull and Harriet Wadsworth, daughters of the Connecticut representatives, joined their fathers. Faith found it hard to return to Lebanon, Connecticut, for "I believe I had always a little sneaking partiality for a City life & City air always agreed with me very much & I love Society very well."[16]

President Washington, who arrived on November 28, must have worn out his secretary, Tobias Lear, and his agent, Clement Biddle,

[16]*Gazette of the United States* (Philadelphia), Nov. 24; Elbridge Gerry to Ann Gerry, Dec. 2, Mundlein College; *Federal Gazette,* Nov. 27; Jacob Cox Parsons, ed., *Extracts from the Diary of Jacob Hiltzheimer of Philadelphia* (Philadelphia, 1893), p. 165; John Adams to John Quincy Adams, Dec. 13, 17, Adams Family Manuscript Trust, MHi; Michael Jenifer Stone to Walter Stone, Dec. 24, Stone Papers, DLC; [Faith Trumbull] to [Catherine (Caty) Wadsworth], Feb. 13, Wadsworth Family Papers, Connecticut Historical Society.

during September and October as he micromanaged his housing preparations as if planning a military campaign.[17] At first he considered renting or even purchasing an estate in the suburbs, but finally he accepted the city council's offer of the mansion at 190 Market (near Sixth), built in 1761 and reconstructed in 1785, when senator-to-be Robert Morris purchased it. Into it moved the Washingtons, two of Martha's grandchildren, about twenty servants and slaves, and several presidential aides, including Lear and his pregnant wife. Washington's nephews George and Lawrence, who had come to Philadelphia to study at the new law department of the College of Philadelphia, were often about the house as well. Once his new home was altered to his specifications, Washington admitted that, despite its inadequacies, which included all varieties of urban street noise, it was the best house in the city for his needs. The president preferred to suffer the inconveniences of the Morris house rather than give Pennsylvania any excuse to build a presidential mansion, which, once constructed, might discourage Congress from moving to the Potomac in 1800. Later, when Pennsylvania built a mansion anyway, both Washington and his successor, John Adams, refused to live in it.[18]

Vice President Adams and his wife, Abigail, rented Bush Hill, an estate on the west side of the Schuylkill, two miles from the city, for four hundred dollars a month. While beautiful, it lacked not only a garden but also the grandness and sublimity of their Manhattan Island domicile and easily became isolated in winter when the mile-and-a-half-long road turned to mud. Moving into Bush Hill proved difficult for Abigail, already unsettled by family illness and the loss of her best gowns, ruined when the ship carrying family possessions from New York

---

[17]The correspondence among the three can be found primarily in the Washington Papers, DLC, and the Washington-Biddle Collection, PHi. When Washington's letters to Lear, of which the writer claimed to have kept no copies, were sold on the autograph market, most were purchased by the Henry E. Huntington Library. On the mansion see Harold D. Eberlein, "190 High Street: The Home of Washington and Adams, 1790–1800," *Historic Philadelphia*, pp. 161–78.

[18]Various documents dated 1790, "Independence Hall," Etting Collection, PHi; Robert Morris and Charles Jarvis statement, Oct. 1, Logan Papers, PHi; Tobias Lear to Tench Coxe, Oct. 3, 1790, Coxe Papers, PHi; *Daily Advertiser*, Sept. 7, 1790; Stephen Decatur, Jr., *Private Affairs of George Washington* (Boston, 1933), pp. 158–64; Riley, "Philadelphia," p. 369.

sprang a leak. She and John had to bear the considerable cost of keeping at least four horses in order to be prepared to go into the city two or three times a day. Philadelphia servants proved no more reliable than those in New York. One lasted only three days before she got so drunk that she had to be carried to bed; once there, she became so indecent that the male servants fled the house. Free blacks made far superior servants than foreigners from Europe, Abigail concluded.[19]

Executive departments, federal courts, and diplomats also had to be accommodated. Secretary of the Treasury Alexander Hamilton took the house at 79 South Third. The auditor's office was nearby at number 44. The department's main offices were at 100 Chestnut, with the treasurer at number 71.[20] Secretary of State Thomas Jefferson rented a house at 274 Market, which he filled with books and furniture just arrived from France, but he resided at Elizabeth House's until renovations on the rented house had progressed far enough for him to move in. Even then he continued to take meals at Mrs. House's until January. Jefferson's office was at 307 Market on the northwest corner of Eighth.[21] Secretary of War Henry Knox, the only high executive official who had not previously served in Congress at Philadelphia, ran his department from Carpenter's Hall, off Chestnut between Third and Fourth. The secretary's wife, Lucy, was so dissatisfied with Philadelphia's efforts to accommodate federal officials that she threatened to live in a tent as she and her equally corpulent husband had during the Revolutionary War. But with the arrival of her furniture, at first feared lost at sea, she once again became the hostess who had made her

---

[19]Abigail Adams to Abigail Smith, Nov. 21–28, Charles F. Adams, ed., *Letters of Mrs. Adams, the Wife of John Adams* (Boston, 1840), pp. 207–9; Abigail Adams to Mary Cranch, Jan. 9, Stewart Mitchell, ed., *New Letters of Abigail Adams* (Boston, 1947), pp. 67–68; Abigail Adams to Cotton Tufts, Oct. 3, Miscellaneous Manuscript Collection, New-York Historical Society.

[20]Riley, "Philadelphia," p. 370 n; Hamilton to Walter Stewart, Aug. 27, Hamilton to Thomas Fitzsimons, Sept. 1, 15, Syrett and Cooke, *Hamilton Papers,* 7:572, 8:5, 34–35; Tench Coxe to Samuel Meredith, Aug. 26, Independence National Historical Park; Benjamin Rush to Tench Coxe, Sept. 13, Coxe Papers, PHi; and Coxe to Rush, Sept. 10, Rush Papers, Library Company of Philadelphia collections at PHi.

[21]Riley, "Philadelphia," p. 370 n. Correspondence between Jefferson, Thomas Leiper, and William Temple Franklin regarding housing for the former can be found in volume 17 of Julian Boyd, ed., *Papers of Thomas Jefferson* (Princeton, 1965). Dumas Malone, *Jefferson and the Rights of Man* (Boston, 1951), pp. 321–23, details the move and house renovations.

parties famous at New York.[22] Supreme Court justices, often absent riding circuit through the states, stimulated less interest than did members of Congress and executive officials. When the Court convened in February 1791, it sat in the State House, pending the completion of the new city hall to the east. With the exception of British Consul John Temple, the diplomatic establishment moved to Philadelphia. Temple remained at New York, claiming that he was unable to find a suitable house. It took French chargé d'affaires Louis-Guillaume Otto a month to complete the move.[23]

Just as Philadelphia's accommodations were compared with New York's, so too was its social and cultural life. Between 1785 and 1790 post–British occupied New York had rebuilt its society around the federal government, creating what would become known as the Republican Court. Senator Maclay, no fan of New York, nevertheless considered it five times more attractive than the capital of his own state. "I know no so unsocial a city as Philadelphia," he confided to his diary. "The gloomy severity of the Quakers has proscribed all fashionable dress and amusement. Denying themselves these enjoyments, they as much as in them lies, endeavour to deprive others of them also. While at the same time there are not in the world more scornful nor insolent characters than the wealthy among them."[24]

Philadelphians recognized the problem and set about to change their city's reputation. The annual return of the upper class from their summer estates outside the city occurred just before the federal government arrived. Invitations rained upon federal officials for dinners and especially routs, a function at which guests ate and drank lightly while playing and gambling at card games, the favorite being loo. Dancing was popular at parties given by such prominent families as the Chews, McKeans, Clymers, Dallases, and Binghams. Unlike New Yorkers, Philadelphians entertained on Saturday nights as well as weeknights. Tobias Lear described the entertainment as frenzied and the

---

[22]Riley, "Philadelphia," p. 370 n; Lucy Knox to Mrs. Ogden, Aug. 19, Knox Papers, MHi; Abigail Adams to Abigail Smith, Nov. 21–28, Adams, *Letters of Mrs. Adams*, p. 210; Rasmusson, "The Capital on the Delaware," p. 53.

[23]John Temple to Duke of Leeds, Sept. 2, Apr. 21, Louis-Guillaume Otto to Comte de Montmorin, Mar. 4, Henry Adams Transcripts, DLC.

[24]Bowling and Veit, *Maclay Diary*, p. 331.

inhabitants as half mad since the city became the seat of government. He found no limit to their prodigality and profligacy.[25] Too many invitations could complicate life. The most important dinner invitation was to one of the president's Thursday state dinners; perhaps less solemn than the ones at New York, the meal was served at four, and afterward the women and men separated for conversation. John Quincy Adams had to decline an invitation to one state dinner. This was because Vice President Adams had invited guests to dinner previous to the invitation to the Adamses from the president. Consequently, the vice president asked his son to stay home and entertain his guests.[26]

Some Philadelphians feared that the arrival of Congress would introduce luxury and dissipation. But the city already offered a rich variety of cultural and social activities. Senator Foster promised his brother Dwight, newly elected to the Senate from Massachusetts, that the theater, concerts, and dancing assemblies made Philadelphia life highly gratifying. While including a formulaic condemnation of dissipation, the Rhode Islander confided that it was inevitable — one might as well try to stop the course of the sun as to prevent these entertainments from appearing in a city once they had been legalized. Representative Gerry failed to convince his old friend Samuel Adams in the summer of 1790 that allowing theater in Boston could improve public morals. Supporters of the theater were more successful in Philadelphia. The actors John Henry and Lewis Hallam the younger, who managed the Old American Company at New York, had spearheaded the fight for legalized theater in Philadelphia after the Revolutionary War. They were unsuccessful until the autumn of 1788, when, after the Confederation Congress rejected a motion to convene the First Federal Congress at Philadelphia, Pennsylvania took several actions designed to render the city more appealing. Once again theater was legal.[27]

---

[25]Eberlein, "190 High Street," *Historic Philadelphia*, pp. 169–70; Abigail Adams to Abigail Smith, Jan. 8, Adams, *Letters of Mrs. Adams*, p. 213; [Tobias Lear] to David Humphreys, [n.d.], as quoted in Decatur, *Private Affairs*, p. 195.

[26]John Quincy Adams to Tobias Lear, Feb. 2, Jonathan Bayard Smith Family Papers, DLC.

[27]Philadelphia letter dated Dec. 6, *Columbian Centinel* (Boston), Dec. 18; Susanna Dillwyn to William Dillwyn, Mar. 3, 1790, Dillwyn Papers, Library Company of Philadelphia collections at PHi; Benjamin Rush to Jeremy Belknap, Nov. 19, Belknap Papers,

In the fall of 1790 the Old Southwark Theater at Cedar (now South) Street, between Fourth and Fifth, was remodeled. No one seemed upset that opening night, set for the evening of the day Congress was to convene, had to be postponed two days. From December 8 until Congress adjourned in March, every Monday, Wednesday, and Friday, and sometimes on Saturday, the theater opened its doors at 5:15 P.M. and raised its curtain an hour later. Henry and his wife, Maria Storer Henry, Hallam, Thomas Wignell, Stephen Wools, and Mr. and Mrs. Owen Morris were the leading actors in the company.[28] The Old American's first production was David Garrick's comedy, *The Clandestine Marriage*. Later productions included Shakespeare's *Richard III, Julius Caesar, Henry IV, The Tempest, Romeo and Juliet*, and *The Taming of the Shrew;* Henry Fielding's *Miser;* Oliver Goldsmith's *She Stoops to Conquer;* Richard Sheridan's *School for Scandal;* and *The Father,* written by William Dunlap, an American artist and playwright. Even the comedies were generally accompanied by a short farce such as John O'Keeffe's *Poor Soldier* or Samuel Foote's *Mayor of Garratt*. On January 5 the Washingtons, with eleven people in their party, and the Adamses, among others, saw *The School for Scandal* and *The Poor Soldier*. This was the same bill Washington had seen on his first trip to the theater as president in May 1789. Sedgwick informed his wife, Pamela, that he looked forward to attending *The Taming of the Shrew,* observing that he chose the play for purposes of entertainment, not instruction. On January 24 a delegation of visiting Seneca Indian leaders attended *Richard III* and *The Mayor of Garratt*. A newspaper writer hoped that the visitors would absorb the plays' moral lessons: blood can be expiated only by blood, honesty is the best policy, and nations wanting to be known as good should select only leaders lacking avarice and ambition.[29] One viewer

---

MHi; A Citizen of Philadelphia [Pelatiah Webster], *An Essay on the Seat of the Federal Government* (Philadelphia, 1789), pp. 29–30; Theodore Foster to Dwight Foster, Jan. 8, Dwight Foster Papers, MHi; Elbridge Gerry to Samuel Adams, July 17, Aug. 7, 1789, Samuel Adams Originals, New York Public Library; Samuel Adams to Elbridge Gerry, July 29, 1789, Miscellaneous Manuscript Collection, DLC; Silverman, *Cultural History,* pp. 592–98.

[28]*General Advertiser,* Nov. 24, Dec. 10; *Pennsylvania Gazette,* Nov. 24.

[29]The *General Advertiser* and *Independent Gazetteer* contain advertisements announcing the productions. Decatur, *Private Affairs,* p. 186; Abigail Adams to Abigail Smith, Jan. 8, Adams, *Letters of Mrs. Adams,* pp. 213–14; Theodore Sedgwick to Pamela Sedgwick, Jan. 16, Sedgwick Papers, MHi; *Federal Gazette,* Jan. 24.

that she had never seen such a "parcel of ugly women" as those at Martha Washington's reception of January 7. Faith Trumbull gloated that a Connecticut friend whom she took to the February 11 reception was better dressed and looked better than any woman there, quite outshining even "our high mightynesses." Harriet Wadsworth's brother was not surprised that Martha Washington treated Harriet and Faith with so much civility because "surrounded as she is by the affected and the vain of both sexes (as no doubt the greater part of her visitors are of that character) I think she must feel much pleasure in seeing two young Ladies from a small country Town, who appear to have minds of their own, and minds not trained up to folly, or infected with it from their change of situation." Less delighted with the First Lady's receptions was Sedgwick, who one Friday in January "saw assembled all the beauties of Philadelphia. I staid about an hour and returned home satiated with the stupid formality of a great number of well dressed people assembled together for the unmeaning purpose of seeing and being seen."[33]

Abigail Adams and Frances Seney were particularly struck by Anne Willing Bingham, the daughter of Philadelphia's most prominent banker and wife of the Speaker of the Pennsylvania House of Representatives, who as a congressman had spearheaded Philadelphia's unsuccessful attempt in 1788 to move Congress back to the city of brotherly love. The vice president's wife credited her with setting the style for fashion and elegance, an observation confirmed by her influential role in the Republican court during the decade ahead. Seney described her as "a shewy woman." John Adams believed the Binghams lived in a style of pomp and splendor almost unknown in the United States. Completed in 1788, their house at Third and Spruce was modeled after that of the duke of Manchester in London. With its circular driveway, landscaped grounds, and greenhouse with exotic plants, it covered almost an entire square block. Inside, replicas of the old masters lined the marbled entrance hall and wide staircase. The Binghams

---

[33]Eberlein, "190 High Street," *Historic Philadelphia*, pp. 168–69; Decatur, *Private Affairs*, pp. 145, 177; Frances Seney to Hannah Nicholson, Jan. 12, Albert Gallatin Papers, New-York Historical Society; Faith Trumbull to Catherine (Caty) Wadsworth, Feb. 7, Daniel Wadsworth to Harriet Wadsworth, Jan. 15, Wadsworth Family Papers, Connecticut Historical Society.

entertained in a second-floor drawing room with large pier mirrors, French wallpaper, fine rugs, and furniture in the style fashionable in London at the time.[34]

Celebrations were held on special days. On New Year's Day both President Washington and Gov. Thomas Mifflin held receptions. On March 4, 1791, to celebrate the conclusion of the momentous First Federal Congress on the previous day, Philadelphia merchants and citizens gave an elegant entertainment for the vice president and other members of Congress. The gala also was attended by the three departmental secretaries, the congressional chaplains, the diplomatic corps, and a great number of citizens and foreigners. The most spectacular celebration was in honor of the president's fifty-ninth birthday on February 22 and consciously mimicked those held in London for the king. The city's artillery and light infantry corps paraded, a salute was fired at noon, and Washington received the compliments of Congress. A dinner and ball, rated the most brilliant ever held in Philadelphia, took place at the New Rooms on Chestnut. After the playing of the president's march, guests gave three huzzahs. Toasts were offered at dinner to the king and National Assembly of France, as well as to other nations in alliance with the United States. Washington attended in his military uniform, complementing a painting of him so dressed while trampling the British standard. Several British officers in attendance were not amused. Sedgwick, despite his devotion to Washington and his support for a strong executive, found the ceremony of huzzahing the president "more proper . . . for savages than first citizens of the first city in America."[35]

Lectures also attracted public audiences. On March 1 Congress attended a eulogy for Benjamin Franklin at the German or Zion Lutheran Church. A eulogy for George Bryan, author of the state's

[34]Abigail Adams to Abigail Smith, Nov. 21–28, Dec. 26, Adams, *Letters of Mrs. Adams,* pp. 209, 211; Frances Seney to Hannah Nicholson, Jan. 12, Albert Gallatin Papers, New York Historical Society; Theodore Sedgwick to Pamela Sedgwick, Jan. 28, Sedgwick Papers, MHi; Abigail Adams to Cotton Tufts, Feb. 6, 1790 [1791], John Adams to John Quincy Adams, Dec. 13, Adams Family Manuscript Trust, MHi; Rasmusson, "The Capital on the Delaware," pp. 52, 72–73.

[35]Bowling and Veit, *Maclay Diary,* p. 354; *Federal Gazette,* Feb. 22, 23, 24, Mar. 5; Decatur, *Private Affairs,* p. 202; Theodore Sedgwick to Pamela Sedgwick, Feb. 23, Sedgwick Papers, MHi.

abolition law and a justice of its supreme court, also was open to the public. The most widely hailed lecture of the winter occurred at the December 15 commencement of the College of Philadelphia. Supreme Court Justice James Wilson spoke on the law. Then, following a commencement address by Benjamin Rush, the college conferred two Doctor of Medicine and three Doctor of Laws degrees. The president and Mrs. Washington, both houses of Congress, and the Pennsylvania legislature attended.[36] "MIRA," purportedly written by a woman, declined to comment on Wilson's speech itself, but observed pointedly that the speaker's language was "pure, chaste and elegant, his s[i?]miles sublime and beautiful."[37]

A variety of daytime attractions existed in Philadelphia. In November a Philadelphia visitor observed that "there is nothing new stirring and probably there will not be until the Congress meets, and by their witty Repartees, entertain the audience in the Gallery, who will have no occasion to draw on the Theatre for Diversion." But Congress Hall never matched the magnetism of Federal Hall. Neither its architecture nor the House debates within attracted visitors in the same way. One auditor of the debates complained about Quakers and others who wore their hats in the gallery, blocking the view below. On the other hand, John Quincy Adams so enjoyed himself that he spent part of five days listening to the national bank debate. When congressional debates proved uninteresting, visitors had the opportunity of walking next door to the State House to listen to Pennsylvania's House of Representatives. The accessibility of Congress Hall to tourists so pleased "A Foreigner" that he sent a letter to a newspaper complimenting congressional officials on their graciousness.[38]

No hot air balloon launches occurred after the first week of November. But on any day, for twenty-five cents, one could visit Charles Willson Peale's Repository for Natural Curiosities at Third and Lombard.

---

[36]*General Advertiser*, Mar. 1; George Nelson Diary, Mar. 1, PHi; Bowling and Veit, *Maclay Diary*, p. 372; *Federal Gazette*, Oct. 28, Dec. 16; *Gazette of the United States*, Dec. 1.

[37]*General Advertiser*, Dec. 23.

[38]*Federal Gazette*, Dec. 20; John Randolph to St. George Tucker, Nov. 17, St. George Tucker Papers, DLC; John Quincy Adams Diary, Feb. 2–8, Adams Family Manuscript Trust, MHi; "Z," *General Advertiser*, Dec. 11.

There, the artist, at great personal expense, had assembled an eclectic collection of artifacts including coins, a shark's jawbone, various animal and bird skins, minerals, fossils, shells, insects, and pieces of moss and soil. Added during the winter of 1790–91 were a live bear from Georgia, a piece of the oak tree in which Charles II had hidden when he fled London, a feather cloak from the South Seas, and a chicken with four legs. Sedgwick had to admit that even he, who held in light estimation the "business and learning of the virtuosi," found the visit gratifying; particularly moved by the almost one hundred portraits of heroes of the American Revolution, he had never until that moment so well understood the value of portraits.[39]

Bowen's Waxworks on Third just below Market housed a likeness of Benjamin Franklin in his own clothes and one of George Washington "supporting the union of liberty, justice, peace, and plenty." Bowen offered to execute wax likenesses or miniature portraits of anyone. Other curiosities that winter included a ventriloquist whose "Speaking Figure," a beautiful young woman, answered questions; a model of the city of Jerusalem; and a live red lion, or cougar, from the Spanish colonies. For a more practical outing, one could go to the Wigwam Baths and Tavern on the east bank of the Schuylkill at Race Street for a plunging bath or a shower—those with health problems who were too poor to pay were invited to use the baths free of charge. Gray's Gardens, where the public could enjoy various activities including concerts and illuminations, apparently closed for the winter.[40]

Residents of the city could avail themselves of classes in a variety of subjects and skills. James Smither ran a drawing school for young gentlemen five nights a week. Language classes were available in Spanish and French. George Holland taught shorthand. Mr. McDougall, Mr. Sicard, and James Robardet offered dancing lessons, as did Mr. Duport, who promised to perfect any pupil in three months. One could

---

[39]*Dunlap's Daily Advertiser,* Jan. 14, Feb. 7; Theodore Sedgwick to Pamela Sedgwick, Jan. 9, Sedgwick Papers, MHi; *The Selected Papers of Charles Willson Peale,* 4 vols. (New Haven, 1983–96), vol. 2, *The Artist as Museum Keeper, 1791–1810,* Lillian B. Miller and Sidney Hart, eds.

[40]*Freeman's Journal* (Philadelphia), Nov. 3, 29; *Dunlap's Daily Advertiser,* Jan. 15, Feb. 26; *General Advertiser,* Mar. 5; *Independent Gazetteer,* Nov. 6; *Federal Gazette,* Nov. 1, 13.

learn fencing from Mr. Lemaire at his academy, or just come for the monthly General Assault Day, when anyone could participate.[41]

While federal officeholders did not generally participate in local civic activities, they could not help but be struck by the dozens of associations existing in Philadelphia. These included societies promoting the abolition of slavery, Sunday schools, poor relief, inland navigation, useful arts and manufactures, prison reform, "political inquiries," the availability of fresh fish, the concerns of such ethnic groups as the Germans, the Scots, the English, and the Irish. Philadelphia also hosted a Masonic lodge. Federal officials benefited from the numerous publications: in addition to ephemera and pamphlets, the city's printers published two magazines and eleven newspapers, including one in German and three dailies.[42]

The two most established associations in the city were the American Philosophical Society and the Library Company of Philadelphia. Thomas Jefferson was a member of the former and devoted some of his time during the winter to its committee on the Hessian fly. Alexander Hamilton and Atty. Gen. Edmund Randolph were admitted to membership not long after Congress returned to the city. The Philosophical Society's recently completed hall on State House Square housed its "cabinet of curiosities," Charles Willson Peale's copy of a portrait of Benjamin Franklin, and a library. Federal officials sometimes used the books, but since there was no staff, the society mainly served its members. Given the proper introduction, these members would gladly show visitors through the hall.[43] Most beneficial to federal officials was the Library Company of Philadelphia. At the end of the year it moved into a new home on Fifth, across from Philosophical Hall. The striking brown brick and white marble building was large enough to hold a collection six times as large as the eight thousand volumes it owned in 1790. Consequently, Sedgwick and others were struck by the look of emptiness in the book room. It was open to

---

[41] *Independent Gazetteer,* Nov. 6; *Freeman's Journal,* Nov. 3; *General Advertiser,* Dec. 8, 10, 11, Jan. 4, 6.

[42] *Independent Gazetteer,* Feb. 26; *Pennsylvania Mercury* (Philadelphia), Dec. 4, 30, Jan. 15, 18; *General Advertiser,* Nov. 30, Jan. 3; Bowling and Veit, *Maclay Diary,* p. 374.

[43] *Federal Gazette,* Nov. 20, Dec. 17, Jan. 7, 21, 26; Whitfield J. Bell, Jr., "The Cabinet of the American Philosophical Society," *A Cabinet of Curiosities* (Charlottesville, 1967), pp. 1–34.

members from 1:00 P.M. until sunset, Monday through Saturday. On January 18 its board of directors granted the president and members of Congress full use of the library's books just as if they were members of the corporation.[44]

Philadelphia was hard pressed to match "Calypso's Island," as New York City was sometimes known. The Quaker City lacked its readily available prostitutes; nevertheless, at least one city doctor advertised that he offered anonymous treatment for venereal disease. It did attempt to compete as a marriage mart, an amateur poet urging the city's "maids" to "put on your best; In all the colors of the bow be drest. Procure clean linen — if you can — For every maid shall have her man."[45]

Considering the bitterness of the seven-year fight over the location of the federal seat of government, the sometimes unhappy legacy of the decade when Congress had last met at Philadelphia, the hostility of some congressmen and others toward the city in 1790, and the logistics of accommodating the large number of new residents who arrived at nearly the same time, complaints about the new capital were astonishingly few, generally inconsequential, and fleeting. A newspaper letter purportedly written by a congressman who arrived in mid-November laid out most of them: the low, thick morning and evening fogs, which hung over the flat city, had to be unhealthy; the cost of living was high, and certain items, particularly lobsters and fish, were scarce; the Philadelphians were avaricious; and, of course, the building provided for Congress was inadequate.[46]

The winter of 1790–91 in Philadelphia was dry and cold, the most severe in years.[47] Representative Thatcher found it as cold as Maine and colder than the last two winters in New York, but for the most part

[44]*General Advertiser,* Jan. 1, 27; *Federal Gazette,* Jan. 19; Theodore Sedgwick to Pamela Sedgwick, Jan. 9, Sedgwick Papers, MHi; Resolution of the Directors of the Library in Philadelphia, Jan. 18, Senate Records, 1A–F4, Record Group 46, National Archives and Records Administration.

[45]Goler, *Federal New York,* pp. 7–8; *Daily Advertiser,* July 16, 1790; *General Advertiser,* Nov. 13; William Grayson to James Madison, Mar. 22, 1786, Robert A. Rutland and William M. E. Rachal, eds., *The Papers of James Madison,* 17 vols. to date (Chicago and Charlottesville, 1962–), 8:510; "On the expected arrival of Congress," *Independent Gazetteer,* Nov. 20.

[46]Letter from a member of Congress dated Nov. 17, *Federal Gazette,* Nov. 27.

[47]Weather summaries can be found in the George Nelson Diary, PHi, and the *Pennsylvania Mercury,* Dec. 21, Jan. 1, 18, Feb. 1, 15, Mar. 1, 19.

newcomers accepted the situation without complaint. The Delaware River froze early in December; although it thawed in January, the port was again closed by ice on February 18. Abigail Adams noted that the January thaw gave everyone colds and that by the time the harsh arctic air of mid-February arrived with a new winter, she had used forty cords of wood at Bush Hill. At the end of January, Representative Gerry reported that flu was common.[48] Enough snow had fallen by December 2 to cause a resident to urge the city corporation to undertake yet another civic improvement: clearing the brick sidewalks after snow-falls. This would prevent colds resulting from wet feet and injuries from slipping on the ice. Alluding to the issue that was never far below the surface, the author went on to suggest that uncleared walks were particularly hard on members of public bodies and urged remedial action in particular for the sake of members of Congress, their attendants, and foreigners, as well as the disabled. On December 27, as he was leaving Congress Hall, Rep. Thomas Hartley of Pennsylvania slipped on the icy steps and broke his arm. He was unable to write for two weeks or to return to Congress Hall for three. The incident motivated one newspaper writer to suggest that Philadelphians follow the European practice of spreading ashes on the snow in front of their homes.[49]

Dismay over the weather, scarcity of coaches, seafood, and housing disappeared as the weeks passed. It took longer to adjust to the higher cost of living, a complaint congressmen had made about most of the places that had served as the seat of federal government. A newspaper suggested to its readers in mid-November that "one mark of kindness to strangers is less equivocal than any other, and that is, moderate rents and a moderate price for the necessaries of life." Readers apparently

---

[48]Jonathan Trumbull to William Williams, Jan. 10, Jonathan Trumbull Papers, Connecticut Historical Society; George Thatcher to Sarah Thatcher, Dec. 9, 20, Thatcher Letters, DLC; *Federal Gazette,* Jan. 5, Feb. 18; Abigail Adams to Mary Cranch, Jan. 9, Mitchell, *New Letters of Abigail Adams,* pp. 67–68; Abigail Adams to Abigail Smith, Feb. 21, Adams, *Letters of Mrs. Adams,* p. 355; Caleb Strong to Benjamin Lincoln, Feb. 21, Lincoln Papers, MHi; Elbridge Gerry to Ann Gerry, Jan. 27, as quoted in Parke-Bernet Catalog 4179 (1978):item 560.

[49]*General Advertiser,* Dec. 2; Bowling and Veit, *Maclay Diary,* p. 348; Thomas Hartley to Tench Coxe, Jan. 11, Coxe Papers, Hartley to Jasper Yeates, Jan. 20, Yeates Papers, PHi; *Pennsylvania Packet,* Dec. 29.

failed to heed this advice. Rents allegedly doubled. The price of every-thing else also seemed to jump. When someone wondered publicly why the price of grain rose when congressmen did not eat it, he was informed that their horses did.[50] As it had been during the war, the avarice of Philadelphians once again became the object of complaint. "People have an exalted idea of their present envied situation, and omit no opportunity in making the most of it," complained a letter to the newspapers. "Their avarice, respecting their rents and boards is unparalleled, and extravagantly extravagant." The cost of living was al-leged to be one-third higher than New York. Representative Thatcher, who thought himself not so well accommodated as in New York, esti-mated room and board at seven dollars a week, probably a dollar higher than it turned out to be.[51]

More important than Philadelphia's ability to provide accommoda-tions at a reasonable price was whether the city would match New York's hospitality and social amenities. Despite the city's cosmopolitan nature, several newcomers at first echoed Senator Maclay's description of it as unsocial. Thatcher did not enjoy himself as much. Neither did Sedgwick, who was still complaining in January that in New York he had seen friends and acquaintances every day but that he was alto-gether among strangers in Philadelphia. Taking private delight in the grumblings that winter from those who had insisted on leaving New York, he reported that other members of Congress and federal officials felt the same lack of hospitality. But by the end of the month the situation must have improved, for he insisted that "since I have been in this city I have been treated with more politeness & attention than ever I was in New York."[52] Getting adjusted to a new place of residence is

---

[50]*Gazette of the United States,* Jan. 12; Michael Price to David Daggett, Aug. 18, Daggett Papers, Beineke Library, Yale University; *Federal Gazette,* Nov. 15, Dec. 4; Oliver Wolcott, Jr., to Oliver Wolcott, Sr., Sept. 6, Gibbs, *Memoirs of the Washington and Adams Administra-tions,* 1:59; *Daily Advertiser,* Oct. 13; *New York Daily Gazette,* Aug. 18, Nov. 25.

[51]Letter from a member of Congress dated Nov. 17, *Federal Gazette,* Nov. 27; *Federal Gazette,* Nov. 29; Abigail Adams to Abigail Smith, Nov. 21–28, Adams, *Letters of Mrs. Adams,* p. 209; Abigail Adams to Mary Cranch, Jan. 9, Mitchell, *New Letters of Abigail Adams,* pp. 67–68; Abigail Adams to Cotton Tufts, Mar. 11, Miscellaneous Manuscript Collection, New-York Historical Society; George Thatcher to Sarah Thatcher, Nov. 28, Jan. 6, Thatcher Letters, DLC.

[52]Oliver Wolcott, Jr., to Oliver Wolcott, Sr., Jan. 1, Gibbs, *Memoirs of the Washington and Adams Administrations,* 1:62; George Thatcher to Sarah Thatcher, Jan. 6, Thatcher

seldom easy, and many of the newcomers probably shared Sedgwick's experiences. Abigail Adams certainly did, although she was always less critical of Philadelphia than Sedgwick. It was not New York, she rue-fully told her daughter after two months in the city, but soon thereafter she admitted that, despite her attachment to New York, Philadelphia had an agreeable, if inbred, society.[53]

While newcomers tolerated the weather, accepted their accom-modations and the cost of living, and adjusted their thinking about Philadelphia's social and cultural life, the old fear of the influence of the city's politically sophisticated citizenry and press on Congress re-mained. During its five years at New York, Congress had been virtually free from jurisdictional conflicts with its host state. Attempts to influ-ence its proceedings — other than when the question of Congress's leaving the city arose — were essentially nonexistent. Well aware of the jurisdictional conflicts that had plagued Pennsylvania's relationship with Congress before it left in 1783, and perhaps hoping to give the federal government every reason to make its stay in Philadelphia per-manent, Gov. Thomas Mifflin called on the Pennsylvania legislature to "pursue the most effectual measures for removing every ground, on which their interest or their plans might possibly appear to clash with that of federal government." Aware also of the frequent expressions of concern by congressmen from the Lower South, particularly the South Carolinians, about the antislavery climate of the Quaker city, Mifflin recommended exempting anyone coming into the state to transact business with the federal government from the state's abolition law, which granted freedom to any slave who remained in Pennsylvania for one year. Previously exemptions had been extended to federal offi-cials. Nevertheless, President Washington would send his own slaves out of the state at least once each year, if only for a few hours, in order to avoid any entanglement with Pennsylvania's judicial system.[54]

Some thought it more likely that President Washington would clash

---

Letters, DLC; Theodore Sedgwick to Pamela Sedgwick, Dec. 26, Jan. 1, 27, Theodore Sedgwick to Ephraim Williams, Jan. 24, Aaron Burr to Theodore Sedgwick, Jan. 7, Sedgwick Papers, MHi.

[53]Abigail Adams to Abigail Smith, Jan. 8, 25, Adams, *Letters of Mrs. Adams,* pp. 213, 215–16.

[54]*Pennsylvania Archives (Series 1),* 112:37; Tobias Lear to George Washington, Apr. 24, June 5, Washington Papers, DLC.

with Governor Mifflin. Both men had large egos and enjoyed center stage, and they had been political and personal enemies since early in the Revolutionary War. Gov. George Clinton, a good friend of the president's, had readily yielded in matters of protocol when Congress resided in New York, and Washington had successfully demanded the same of Gov. John Hancock when touring Massachusetts. Would Mifflin do the same? He took to heart his own advice to the legislature, and the two men managed to be as civil to each other as they had been when Mifflin, as president of the Confederation Congress, accepted Washington's resignation as commander in chief of the Continental Army. Mifflin, however, disputed rank with the vice president while Elizabeth Powel, wife of Philadelphia's state senator and the former mayor, got into a dispute with Lucy Knox over the same issue.[55]

No one could stop attempts to influence congressional proceedings. Connecticut Rep. Jonathan Trumbull rightly labeled them Philadelphia's "old teasing tricks."[56] Another observer complained that "the Philadelphians ask everything of Congress, and already begin to look upon them as their own." Some of the pressure was subtle, such as the existence of an antislavery press. But much was direct and open, as residents lobbied members for contracts and jobs and sought to influence legislation through petitions and political maneuvers. Most annoying were the petitions. Citizens condemned excise laws. The state's public creditors condemned the Funding Act of 1790. Merchants wanted piers built on the Delaware River at Chester and special tariff duties on certain imports from the Orient—then other merchants wanted different piers and different tariffs. The College of Physicians called for excises on domestically distilled liquors as a means of diminishing alcohol abuse. An interstate meeting of Quakers at Philadelphia called for militia exemptions on religious grounds.[57] Other groups

---

[55]Otto to Montmorin, Nov. 15, Correspondance-Politique, Etats-Unis, 35, Archives Nationales, France (microfilm at DLC); William North to Benjamin Walker, Jan. 15–Feb. 4, Miscellaneous Manuscripts, New-York Historical Society.

[56]Jonathan Trumbull to William Williams, Dec. 18, Jonathan Trumbull Papers, Connecticut Historical Society; William North to Benjamin Walker, Jan. 15–Feb. 4, Miscellaneous Manuscripts, New-York Historical Society.

[57]William Symmes to George Thatcher, Feb. 10, Thatcher Papers, Boston Public Library; Henry Marchant to John Adams, Feb. 19, Adams Family Manuscript Trust, MHi; Oliver Wolcott, Jr., to Oliver Wolcott, Sr., Feb. 12, Gibbs, *Memoirs of the Washington*

held meetings to consider demands, including militia exemptions for minors and apprentices. The situation was well enough known to lend itself to such parodies as one in which "10,000 Federal Maids" demanded the right to combat service.[58]

The most serious crisis arose when the Pennsylvania House of Representatives, meeting next door to Congress, condemned the proposed federal excise as subversive of the peace, liberty, and rights of the citizens of Pennsylvania. Although some local newspaper writers complained about the legislature's action, criticism outside the state was widespread, compounding the preexisting opinion that Pennsylvania had a proclivity to intrude into federal affairs. This belief was so strong that when Virginia called on the other states to instruct their senators to vote in favor of opening the Senate's doors to the press and public, South Carolina state senator Charles Cotesworth Pinckney argued against the proposal on the grounds that Pennsylvania already had too much influence with the doors closed. Opening them would only give it more; indeed, he expressed a wish that the doors of the House of Representatives would be closed as well.[59]

Nevertheless, while Philadelphia would prove to be a turbulent seat for the federal government as political tensions mounted during the 1790s, there were fewer complaints during the early months about the city as a seat of government than there had been when Congress sat there during the Revolutionary War. As early as 1792 George Washington correctly concluded that opposition to the coming move had disappeared everywhere except among Philadelphians. Prominent among those who hoped to fulfill Frederick Muhlenberg's 1783 pledge that, once back, Congress would never leave again, were two friends of Washington: Philadelphia's state senator, Samuel Powel, and the Speaker of the Pennsylvania House of Representatives, William Bingham. Shortly after the First Congress adjourned in March 1791, the Pennsylvania legislature took up the question of permanent buildings for Congress

---

and Adams Administrations, 1:62–63; *Documentary History of the First Federal Congress,* vol. 3 (Linda Grant DePauw, Charlene Bangs Bickford, and LaVonne Siegel Hauptmann, eds.), pp. 635, 637, 649, 662, 664, 674, 679, 725.

[58]*Dunlap's Daily Advertiser,* Jan. 15; *Gazette of the United States,* Jan. 26.

[59]"Civis," *Dunlap's Daily Advertiser,* Feb. 1, 12; *Federal Gazette,* Feb. 1; *Daily Advertiser,* Jan. 26; *American Mercury* (Hartford), Feb. 17; *City Gazette* (Charleston, S.C.), Mar. 24.

and the president. Bingham declared his support for appropriations because Congress might decide in 1800 that it was in the interest of the union for Congress to reside in a populous and monied place. Powel argued that, because of events yet in the womb of time, it was impossible to say what Congress would do in ten years. On the other side, state senator John Smilie was convinced that Congress would move in 1800 if only because of "the situation of the person entrusted with making the necessary arrangements." He complained that the bill was an interference in federal affairs that looked like a bribe. Most important, the "federal court" would outshine Philadelphia's magnificence and impose its more decadent manners and morals. This had not happened during the winter of 1790–91; indeed, Smilie thought, the plain manners of Philadelphia had toned down those that Congress had brought from New York. But it was only a matter of time, and the federal government should not be encouraged to stay after 1800. Smilie proved correct. Congress left Philadelphia in 1800 not because it disliked the city, but because participants in the Compromise of 1790, except perhaps some of the Pennsylvanians, held it to be sacrosanct, and because of George Washington's obsession with an American capital on the Potomac River.[60]

---

[60] *General Advertiser,* Apr. 6–13. The Fisher-Warner Papers, Friends Library, Swarthmore College, contains many documents related to the debate in Pennsylvania over the construction of federal buildings.

Anna Coxe Toogood

Philadelphia as the Nation's Capital, 1790–1800

PENNSYLVANIA'S STATE HOUSE SQUARE — today's Independence Square — suffered years of abuse and neglect during the
Revolutionary War (fig. 1). Having served as a government center, a
place for military training, artillery storage, munitions production, and
a temporary jail for prisoners of war, the yard and its buildings needed
much attention. With peace in 1783, the state assembly launched a
program to restore the structures and their furnishings and to trans-
form the large walled lot behind the State House into a stylish garden.
This landscaping finally carried out a long-anticipated improvement:
in 1732 the Provincial Assembly had discussed leveling the grounds,
planting trees, and laying out walks in the State House yard to render it
"more beautiful and commodious"; in 1736 it had passed an act to set
aside the yard as "a public open greene and walks forever."[1]

The landscape design followed a naturalistic or Romantic style with
serpentine paths and a variety of plantings. Samuel Vaughan (fig. 2), a
recent British immigrant, designed and laid out the plan for the state
between 1784 and 1787. Although a newcomer, Vaughan mixed easily
with Philadelphia's leading citizens during his brief stay. His election to

---

[1]Gertrude MacKinney, ed., *Pennsylvania Archives, Eighth Series*, 18 vols. ([Harrisburg,
Pa.,] 1931), 3:2163; *Statutes at Large of Pennsylvania, 1682–1801* ([Harrisburg, Pa.,]
1897), 4:301.

FIG. 1. *View of State House in Philadelphia,* 1778, by Charles Willson Peale. Detail from copperplate engraving of 1790 by James Thachara. This Revolutionary War–era view of the State House shows the long wooden sheds on either corner used for artillery storage by the Continental Army. *(Courtesy Independence National Historical Park)*

FIG. 2. *Samuel Vaughan,* by Robert Edge Pine, circa 1787. *(Courtesy American Philosophical Society)*

FIG. 3. *The State House Garden,* by William Birch, 1798. Birch's print indicates the various people who enjoyed the public garden — Native Americans, children, even pets. After 1797 the legislators and visitors also could buy ice cream, a novel addition to Philadelphia's culinary taste, sold by a French émigré vendor. *(Courtesy Independence National Historical Park)*

the American Philosophical Society and the Society for the Promotion of Agriculture put him in contact with some of the best minds in the city, as well as the nation. In such circles he met Gen. George Washington in 1783, just months before launching the landscape project. Washington, a passionate gardener himself, may have influenced Vaughan's design for the State House grounds, as it and Mount Vernon showed strikingly similar plans and plantings when completed in 1787.

Vaughan's final product, as one admiring reporter recorded in 1790, must have posed a welcome sight for the U.S. Congress, which returned late that year for its first session in Philadelphia since 1783:

> [The State House yard] consists of a beautiful lawn, interspersed with little knobs or tufts of flowering shrubs and clumps of trees well disposed. Through the middle of the gardens runs a spacious gravel walk,

lined with double rows of thriving elms and communicating with serpentine walks which encompass the whole area. The surrounding walks are not uniformly on a level with the lawn, the margin of which, being in some parts a little higher, forms a bank which in fine weather affords pleasant seats. When the trees attain to a larger size it will be proper to place benches under them, in different situations, for the accommodation of persons frequenting the walks.[2]

Throughout the 1790s the State House yard (fig. 3) drew admiration from many city visitors. Such notice is not surprising, considering that other than New York's Bowling Green park, Philadelphia probably boasted the only public gardens in the nation's several urban centers.[3] As citizens of the largest, richest, and most populated port in the nation, Philadelphians took pride in their pioneering spirit. During the decade they pursued groundbreaking social reforms, as well as the frontiers of science, medicine, and the arts. What follows is a piece of the Philadelphia story during the decade when the State House Square (fig. 4) stood at the epicenter of such cultural ferment as well as of the new federal government.

Congress Moves to Philadelphia

On July 16, 1790, the U.S. Congress (then seated in New York City) finally agreed on the Potomac River as the site for the nation's capital and designated Philadelphia as the temporary capital for ten years while federal buildings were under construction at the permanent site. The Residence Act set off a phenomenal real estate boom and population explosion in Philadelphia and brought the State House

---

[2] *Columbian Magazine* (1790):25–26. Anna Coxe Toogood, "Cultural Landscape Report, Independence Square," draft (Independence National Historical Park, 1996), develops the theory about Washington's possible influence. After Vaughan visited Mount Vernon in 1787, he drew up a plan of Mount Vernon that Washington critiqued. Vaughan and his wife returned to London in 1790.

[3] New York Parks and Recreation Department, *Three Hundred Years of Parks: A Timeline of New York City Park History* (New York, 1987). New York set aside this half-acre plot "for the Beauty and ornament of the Said Street as well as for the Recreation & Delight of the Inhabitants" in 1733, but did not landscape it until later that century. Other urban centers in early America had little planned open space except commons for public display and livestock grazing.

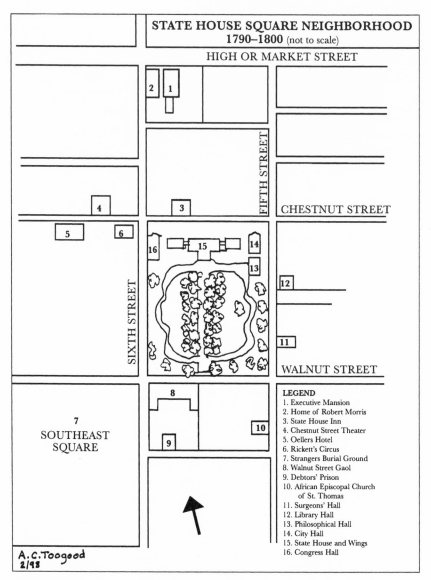

STATE HOUSE SQUARE NEIGHBORHOOD
1790–1800 (not to scale)

HIGH OR MARKET STREET

FIFTH STREET

CHESTNUT STREET

SIXTH STREET

WALNUT STREET

SOUTHEAST
SQUARE

LEGEND
1. Executive Mansion
2. Home of Robert Morris
3. State House Inn
4. Chestnut Street Theater
5. Oellers Hotel
6. Rickett's Circus
7. Strangers Burial Ground
8. Walnut Street Gaol
9. Debtors' Prison
10. African Episcopal Church
  of St. Thomas
11. Surgeons' Hall
12. Library Hall
13. Philosophical Hall
14. City Hall
15. State House and Wings
16. Congress Hall

A.C.Toogood
2/98

FIG. 4. State House Neighborhood, 1790–1800, based on historical research,
1998.

Square to a new level of importance. Massachusetts Rep. Theodore Sedgwick reported at the close of 1791 that at least five hundred houses had been built in the previous six months. During the 1790s the city, county, state, and federal governments all shared the square and its garden, bringing a layering of political authority on one piece of urban real estate never repeated in the nation's history.[4]

The State House, except for the committee rooms of the federal House of Representatives, was reserved for Pennsylvania's new bicameral state legislature, state supreme court, and state administrative offices. When the new city hall reached completion in August 1791 on the corner of Fifth and Chestnut Streets, finally culminating the long-desired master plan for the State House Square, the Supreme Court of the United States sat biannually in its mayor's courtroom. The federal circuit and district courts for Pennsylvania met upstairs in the city and county council chambers and the city surveyor's office.[5] The State House stood at the hub of the city's busy life. The president lived only a block away, at 190 High (Market) Street, in the former home of Sen. Robert Morris of Pennsylvania. Federal government departments bordered the square — Treasury two blocks east on Chestnut Street, War at Carpenters Court and then at Fifth and Chestnut Streets, and State a short two blocks northwest on Market Street — and legislators boarded or rented homes within an easy walk from the square.[6]

Beginning December 6, 1790, at the opening of the third session of the First Federal Congress, the members occupied the new and

---

[4]Theodore Sedgwick to Pamela Sedgwick, Nov. 6, 1791, Theodore Sedgwick Papers, Massachusetts Historical Society (hereafter MHi); *Portfolio* (Philadelphia), Apr. 6, 1805, p. 2.

[5]See the following staff reports prepared for Independence Hall National Historical Park: David Kimball, "Independence Hall Historic Structure Report, Part II, Appendices A–I, Independence Hall Room Use, 1732–1792" (draft 1992), p. 5; "Furnishing Plan for the Mayor's Court, Old City Hall, Part B: Historical Narrative" (August 1959); David Kimball, "Old City Hall, Historic Structure Report, Part II" (1961), p. 1; Sidney Bradford, Jr., and Franklin R. Mullaly, "Old City Hall, Historic Structure Report, Part I: Historical Data" (1959), chap. 2. See also Robert P. Reeder, "The First Homes of the United States Supreme Court," *Proceedings of the American Philosophical Society* 76 (1936):551–53.

[6]Harold Donaldson Eberlein, "190 High Street (Market Street below Sixth) — The Home of Washington and Adams, 1790–1800," *Historic Philadelphia from the Founding until the Early Nineteenth Century: Papers Dealing with Its People and Buildings with an Illustrative Map, Transactions of the American Philosophical Society* 43, pt. 1 (1953):161–78.

elegant county courthouse, called Congress Hall, at the corner of Sixth and Chestnut Streets on State House Square (fig. 5). The representatives sat in a refitted courtroom (figs. 6, 7) on the ground floor, while senators climbed the steep stairs to the second floor, where a former courtroom (fig. 8) and the four large rooms on either side of the central hall accommodated their sessions, staff, law books, and committee meetings.[7]

The House chamber (fig. 6), with its two rows of semicircular desks, almost immediately felt crowded, even though on any one day some of the sixty-five members were absent from the hall. When the census of 1790 increased the number of representatives to 106, Pennsylvania began to debate whether to build a new and elegant hall or to expand the courthouse. Finally, in the spring of 1793, the contentious legislature agreed to enlarge the existing building an additional twenty-six feet to the south. The state also constructed a portico for the legislators between Congress Hall and the west wing of the State House. Representatives then could assemble in the portico before a session and proceed with ceremony into the hall and down the central aisle to their seats. They could also attend House committee meetings upstairs in the west wing of the State House without braving the elements.[8]

The 1793 enlargement provided two doors into the State House yard on either side of an eight-foot bay on the south wall (fig. 7). Many a legislator passed through these doors to stroll the graveled walks in conference, or to find a spot for quiet contemplation on one of the garden benches. Others needed to visit the privies or simply retire to rest from the often raucous debates during this decade of heightened political animosities.[9]

People from all parts of the city came to the State House complex to record their real estate and business transactions, to participate in trials, to see the public buildings and gardens, to enjoy Peale museum and art exhibits, to hear lectures or attend meetings at Philosophical

---

[7] *Historic Philadelphia,* p. 28.

[8] See Independence Hall National Historical Park staff report, "Historic Structure Report, (HSR), Part I, on Congress Hall" (May 1959); and "HSR, Part II, Congress Hall" (February 1960), chap. 4, for information on the portico.

[9] Theophilus Bradbury to Harriet Bradbury, Dec. 26, 1795, *Pennsylvania Magazine of History and Biography* 8 (1884):226.

FIG. 5. Congress Hall, or County Courthouse, as restored by the National Park Service. Photograph by Richard Frear. *(Courtesy Independence National Historical Park)*

FIG. 6. House of Representatives chamber (looking north) restored by National Park Service, circa 1985. The first-floor chamber included a balcony to accommodate five hundred spectators. Photograph by Tom Davies. *(Courtesy Independence National Historical Park)*

FIG. 7. Restored House of Representatives chamber (looking south), showing two doors opening to the State House yard. *(Courtesy Independence National Historical Park)*

FIG. 8. Restored Senate chamber. The second-floor Senate chamber was smaller but more ornate than the House chamber. Red Morocco leather upholstered seats, a specially made Axminster carpet, and drapes behind the president's seat accented the dignified setting. Photograph by Tom Davies. *(Courtesy Independence National Historical Park)*

Hall, to witness the highly charged political debates at Congress Hall and the State House, to petition the various governments, to cast votes at elections, and to demonstrate their political views. Philadelphia, a city of more than forty thousand, including its suburbs to the north and south, appeared "to be in a constant hurry of business and amusements," Charles Willson Peale noted early in 1791.[10]

A Center for Politics

The State House yard was often the scene of mass political meetings and raucous mob rallies. Philadelphia's lower and middling classes turned out in numbers to protest city, state, and federal laws, and international treaties, and to demand their rights. Political parties had formed by 1793 — pro-French Republicans and pro-British Federalists — and it was the Republicans who rallied the masses with cries of liberty and self-determination. That year a rally welcomed the new French minister, Edmond Genêt; soon thereafter, another rally supported American sailors held captive in Algeria. Benjamin Franklin's grandson, Benjamin Franklin Bache, publisher of the *Aurora,* the leading Republican newspaper, led the charge in 1795 when he called his readers to the State House yard to protest a state law banning construction of wooden buildings in the city. The law was designed to prevent the city's many disastrous fires, but Bache wrote, "ALARM!" because he saw the act as unconstitutional and "oppressive to the mechanic and poor man." Such rallies had their impact; in this case, the protest won enough support to secure modifications to the legislation.[11]

On July 23 that year, a town meeting was called to protest Jay's

[10]Charles Willson Peale to Rachael Leeds Bozman Kerr, Jan. 1, 1791, in *The Selected Papers of Charles Willson Peale and His Family,* ed. Lillian B. Miller, 3 vols. (New Haven, 1983–88), 1:611. Bureau of Census, *Heads of Families at the First Census of the United States Taken in the Year 1790: Pennsylvania* (Washington, 1908), p. 10. The count includes the three city districts and Southwark along its southern line, and the Northern Liberties along its northern line, totaling 44,095. Recent historians consider these census figures for the city conservative because often runaways and the poor were not counted.

[11]*General Advertiser* (Philadelphia), May 7, 1795; George Thatcher to John Hobby, Mar. 19, 1794, Thatcher Papers, MHi; *Gazette of the United States* (Philadelphia), May 22, 1793, Mar. 22, 1794; *Hazard's Register* (Philadelphia) 3 (1829):3; James Hutchinson to Albert Gallatin, Aug. 19, 1792, Gallatin Papers, New-York Historical Society.

Treaty with the British government. John Beckley, clerk of the House of Representatives, reported that five thousand people attended and "utterly condemned" the treaty. Treasury Secretary Oliver Wolcott, who witnessed the event, told President Washington that no more than twelve hundred people turned out, and that half did not participate in the demonstration. Dr. William Shippen chaired the event, joined by other prominent Philadelphians on the temporary stage set up in the yard behind the State House. A copy of the treaty was tossed out to the crowd, who stuck it on a pole and proceeded some three-hundred-strong to the French minister's house and then to both the British minister's and consul's houses, where the treaty was burned with "hurrahs and acclamations."[12]

In 1798, when the United States was on the brink of war with France, ten to fifteen thousand young patriotic demonstrators, according to the local press, marched to President John Adams's house to show their support. The crowd then proceeded before a "vast crowd of admiring, wondering spectators" to the State House, where the president's reply was read to those who had followed them into the yard. The very next day, some young men — "the Butcher's boys," as one observer called them — mocked the young volunteers by giving their own display in the yard, clearly wearing their tricolor cockades in support of France. Angry members of the anti-French youth corps descended on them, a brawl ensued, the police interceded, and several of the combatants were sent to the Walnut Street jail.[13]

Great crowds also assembled in the State House yard to watch the inaugurations of Presidents Washington and Adams in March 1793 and March 1797. On at least one occasion, Gov. Thomas Mifflin called out militia troops to stand guard at the buildings, perhaps anticipating

[12]John Beckley to DeWitt Clinton, July 24, 1795, Clinton Letters, Columbia University; Oliver Wolcott, Jr., to George Washington, July 26, 1795, George Gibbs, ed., *Memoirs of the Administrations of Washington and John Adams*, 2 vols. (New York, 1846), 1:217–18; Frank M. Etting, *An Historical Account of the Old State House of Pennsylvania Now Known as Independence Hall* (Boston, 1876), pp. 197–98.

[13]*Connecticut Courant* (Hartford), May 14, 1798; Henry Tazewell to unknown, May 9, 1798, Henry Tazewell Papers, Library of Congress; Samuel Sewall to his brother, May 9, 1798, Robie-Sewall Papers, MHi; George Thatcher to Sarah Thatcher, May 12, 1798, Thatcher Papers, MHi.

possible damage from political protestors. More routine gatherings included elections at the State House or political committee meetings to select candidates for legislative seats. Processions and militia parades through the city regularly started at the State House. In 1796 a convention of the nation's abolition societies met in the common council's chambers in city hall. The State House square and its yard hardly ever had a moment when people were not milling around for one reason or another. It was an interesting place to be, where state and federal governments fashioned the future and great minds studied the meaning of man and nature. All those participating fed off each other's intensity and excitement.[14]

A Center for Culture

As the national capital, Philadelphia experienced an irrepressible burst of growth and development. Real estate speculation and construction reached new heights, and the cost of housing for legislators and other newcomers skyrocketed. Turnpike companies formed to link the city with outlying farm settlements, a canal connected the Delaware and Schuylkill Rivers, and stage companies expanded to provide or improve regular public transportation between Philadelphia and New York, Trenton, Bristol, Elizabethtown, Princeton, Harrisburg, Lancaster, Reading, and Bethlehem. Immigration picked up, placing a burden of additional poor on the city. Philadelphians responded, as English observer Henry Wansey noted in 1794, with a "vast number of charitable organizations."[15]

Philadelphians, as well as the city's temporary residents, recognized

[14]For an account of Washington's inauguration, see Arthur J. Stansbury, "Recollections and Anecdotes of the President of the United States," in Thompson Westcott, *A History of Philadelphia*, 3 vols. (Philadelphia, 1886), 3:605; Gov. Thomas Mifflin to President of the United States, Apr. 14, 1794, Executive Correspondence, Apr. 8–14, 1794 (Record Group 26), Department of State Public Records Office; Mifflin to Josiah Harmar, Secretary of Commonwealth's Letterbook, vol. 3, Mar. 10, 1794–Oct. 18, 1799, Pennsylvania State Archives. Minutes of Common Council, Dec. 31, 1795, microfilm copy in Independence National Historical Park.

[15]David John Jeremy, *Henry Wansey and His American Journal* (Philadelphia, 1970), p. 102; Russell F. Weigley, ed., *Philadelphia: A 300 Year History* (Philadelphia, 1982), p. 238.

FIG. 9. *Library and Surgeons' Hall,* by William Birch, 1799. Across Fifth Street from the State House Square, the Library Company of Philadelphia offered their fine collection of books for the use of members of Congress. Founded by Benjamin Franklin in 1743 as the first circulating library in the colonies, the Library Company became the model for the Library of Congress. Surgeons' Hall, down the street, was built by the University of Pennsylvania for its medical school. *(Courtesy Independence National Historical Park)*

FIG. 10. Philosophical Hall, after restoration, circa 1965. The American Philosophical Society's Philosophical Hall was the only private building constructed on the State House Square. *(Courtesy Independence National Historical Park)*

that the world was watching the American experiment in republican government for the first signs of failure. The tension and excitement that international scrutiny generated, particularly after France declared war on England in spring 1793, contributed to a passionate pursuit of knowledge as well as to the often violent party politics of the decade.[16] Leading Philadelphians, like many Americans, aspired to see the United States excel in social and political reform, education, the arts and sciences. This was particularly evident in the State House neighborhood during the capital city decade. In 1791 the Library Company of Philadelphia — called by some the City Library and today the oldest subscription library in the country — completed its new building on Fifth Street across from the State House Square (fig. 9). By act of the legislature that year, the Library Company merged with the Loganian Library on Sixth Street. According to the terms of the agreement, James Logan's fine collection of scholarly works, deeded to the city in 1760 as a gift by his heirs, retained its separate identity by being housed in a special room added to Library Hall.[17] Just down the street on the same block, the University of Pennsylvania in 1791 completed construction of an "elegant and spacious anatomical theater and chemical elaboratory," where Dr. Shippen lectured on anatomy and surgery in the theater. Across the street, on the second floor of the newly completed Philosophical Hall (fig. 10) on State House Square, the College of Physicians, thought to be the nation's most prestigious assemblage of medical seers, held courses on "Chemistry, Institutes of Medicine and Clinical Cases, Materia Medica and Practice of Physic."[18]

Charles Willson Peale, portrait painter and enthusiastic student of nature, moved his family and his novel museum into Philosophical Hall in June 1794 after the American Philosophical Society hired him

---

[16]For a good study of the politics of the decade, see Richard G. Miller, *Philadelphia the Federalist City: A Study of Urban Politics, 1789–1801* (Port Washington, N.Y., 1976).

[17]Charles E. Peterson, "Library Hall: Home of the Library Company of Philadelphia, 1790–1880," *Historic Philadelphia*, pp. 50, 136–37; "A Short Account of the City of Philadelphia," in James Hardie, *The Philadelphia Directory and Register* (Philadelphia, 1794), p. 220.

[18]*Dunlap's American Daily Advertiser* (Philadelphia), Sept. 24, 1791, Nov. 7, 1791, Nov. 5, 1792; quote on College of Physicians from Hardie, *Philadelphia Directory and Register*, pp. 191–92. Julie S. Berkowitz, *The College of Physicians of Philadelphia Portrait Catalogue* (Philadelphia, 1984), p. vii.

as its assistant curator, librarian, and custodian. Since opening his natural and historical museum at his home at Third and Lombard Streets in 1791, Peale had been struggling to make it a success but finally had agreed with a friend's advice that the "situation on the statehouse square would be much more advantageous" for its future.[19] Peale's large family must have made quite an impression on the State House Square. After his first wife, Rachael Brewer, died in 1790, Peale remarried in May 1791 to Betsy DePeyster, and together they added three more children — Charles Linnaeus in March 1794, Benjamin Franklin in October 1795, and Sybilla Miriam in October 1797 — while in residence at Philosophical Hall. Peale instructed his older children — Raphaelle, 20 in 1794; Angelica, 18; Rembrandt, 16; Titian, 14; Rubens, 10; and Sophonisba, 8 — in the art of painting, and eventually set aside space in their quarters to tutor Charles and Benjamin in the art of taxidermy.[20]

Smitten by "the bewitching study of Nature" and blessed with phenomenal energy and enthusiasm, Peale aimed to make his museum "an instrument for rational pleasure and the instruction of the public." In 1792 he invited a cadre of the nation's wealthiest and most prominent men — Secretary of State Thomas Jefferson, Secretary of the Treasury Alexander Hamilton, Atty. Gen. Edmund Randolph, Rep. John Page of Virginia, Bishop William White, Senator Morris, and Governor Mifflin among the list of twenty-seven — to advise him on the birth of his visionary national museum. The prospect, which called for state or federal underwriting of the museum, failed to go anywhere.[21] Although mortified by the lack of support, Peale found comfort in the fact that most of the men, nearly all members of the Philosophical Society, still found his museum worthy of their private backing. In an age when few museums were known or accessible in the Western

[19]Quoted in Miller, ed., *Selected Papers of Charles Willson Peale*, 1:93; Lillian B. Miller and David C. Ward, eds., *New Perspectives on Charles Willson Peale* (Pittsburgh, 1991), pp. 5–6.

[20]Miller, *Selected Papers of Charles Willson Peale*, 2:xxxviii; idem, *New Perspectives*, p. 5; Charles Coleman Sellers, *Charles Willson Peale* (New York, 1969), p. 262; idem, *Mr. Peale's Museum* (New York, 1980), pp. 50–51; Charles H. Elam, comp., *The Peale Family: Three Generations of American Artists* (Detroit, 1967), genealogical chart.

[21]Edgar P. Richardson, Brooke Hindle, and Lillian B. Miller, *Charles Willson Peale and His World* (New York, 1982), p. 87; Sellers, *Charles Willson Peale*, p. 258.

world — the British Museum had opened in 1759 but with very limited public admission, and the Louvre, a newcomer, opened in 1793 with similar restrictions — Peale's Museum at Philosophical Hall made its wide-ranging collections available to all citizens for a small fee. Peale also offered lectures, concerts, and a printed guide to the collections. His effort to make the museum a place for popular education was a century ahead of its time.[22]

Situated on the square, Peale's Museum readily drew on the prominent body of legislators and government officials as visitors and subscribers. George Washington led Peale's annual subscription drives for many years. In 1787 he contributed two golden pheasants, gifts from the Marquis de Lafayette, to its collections, and in 1795 he sat for Peale so he could paint the first president's portrait. An inveterate collector, Peale received additions to his museum wherever and whenever he could, from explorers, sea captains, friends, and family. Henry Wansey admired the breadth of Peale's exhibits in 1794, naming birds' nests, tiny four-inch Chinese women's slippers, huge Chinese fans six feet tall, and many "curious and rare Birds preserved in their plumage" — such as manakins, birds of paradise, toucans, and spoonbills. Wansey marveled even more at the portraits of all the leading men from the "late revolution," which he rightly estimated would "be very valuable in the eyes of posterity."[23]

Other leading Philadelphians led the effort to bring penal reform to the Walnut Street Prison (fig. 11) across from the State House Square. In 1791 a new "penitentiary house" with sixteen cells, each eight by six feet and furnished with flush toilets, was added to the prison grounds. This innovation was designed to provide solitary confinement for inmates so they could find inner reflection and, in turn, personal reform. The concept won universal praise from enlightened visitors, even though the cells never actually achieved their intent. Real change came in 1794 when the Pennsylvania Assembly abolished the death penalty for all crimes except first-degree murder. Progress also came in the improvement of inmates' cleanliness and physical needs,

---

[22]Jeremy, *Wansey and His American Journal,* p. 104.
[23]Richardson, *Peale,* pp. 80–81; Sellers, *Peale,* p. 277; Jeremy, *Wansey and His American Journal,* p. 105.

FIG. 11. *Gaol in Walnut Street, Philadelphia,* by William Birch, 1799. The Walnut Street prison across from the State House Square, designed by Robert Mills, was considered a showpiece of Philadelphia architecture. To the right of the picture, opposite the prison, the city's Southeast Square served as a potter's field. *(Courtesy Independence National Historical Park)*

as well as in disseminating the new concepts to other states. These efforts won Philadelphia a widespread reputation for penal reform. Accounts of the Walnut Street prison once again praised it as "elegant," rather than a source of alarming social disgrace.[24]

A more self-determined social reform took root in the neighborhood in 1792, when the Free African Society purchased a lot of ground half a block south of the square, on the west side of Fifth Street, and broke ground on a pioneer black church. The location, only one block from the potter's field at Southeast Square (today's Washington

---

[24]Thorsten Sellin, "Philadelphia Prisons of the Eighteenth Century," *Historic Philadelphia,* pp. 329–30; quotations from *Philadelphia Monthly Magazine* (1798):338. See also Negley K. Teeters, *The Cradle of the Penitentiary: The Walnut Street Jail at Philadelphia, 1773–1835* (Philadelphia, 1955), pp. 36–63.

Square), where the city's poor and African Americans were buried, must have been an important factor in selecting the site. In 1790 black leaders had petitioned the city to lease part of Southeast Square to enclose their burial ground but presumably had been turned down. They likely aimed to deter the grave robbing practiced by those needing corpses for anatomical lectures at the nearby medical school. With the creation of the African church, free blacks planned an adjoining burial ground where their dead would have better protection.[25]

White clergy and city leaders at first opposed the Free African Society's church plan. Through the careful campaigning of Free African Society leaders Richard Allen and Absolom Jones, however, the church effort found supporters among some of the city's most prominent citizens—outstanding among them, Dr. Benjamin Rush and state Comptroller General John Nicholson—so that the African Episcopal Church of St. Thomas reached completion in 1794. Jones took the pulpit for this congregation, while the same summer, Allen, a former slave and well-known Methodist preacher, founded Bethel African Methodist Episcopal Church (today known as Mother Bethel), in a carpenter's shop on land he purchased a few blocks to the south at Sixth and Lombard Streets. As the African American population in Philadelphia more than tripled during the decade to more than six thousand, the two churches filled many social needs for their rapidly expanding congregations. Moreover, the presence of the churches marked the neighborhood adjoining the State House as a destination for African American migration well into the twentieth century.[26]

The Yellow Fever Epidemic of 1793

Allen and Jones also proved themselves as community leaders in the summer and fall of 1793 during the worst yellow fever epidemic the city had ever seen. Although Congress was in recess, word of the fatal epidemic spread quickly throughout the nation. Many fled the city, businesses closed, and government was at a standstill. Jones and Allen,

---

[25]Gary B. Nash, *Forging Freedom: The Formation of Philadelphia's Black Community, 1720–1840* (Cambridge, 1988), p. 109.

[26]Ibid., pp. 119, 133, 137, 143.

at Dr. Benjamin Rush's urging, recruited a cadre of African Americans to help nurse the sick and bury the dead in an atmosphere of widespread panic and fear. Rush had mistakenly assured Jones and Allen that African Americans were immune to the disease, but they succumbed nearly as often as whites. In the potter's field at Southeast Square, 1,334 poor and African American dead were buried, first in graves and then, as the numbers mounted, in trenches. In apparent recognition of the assistance provided by African Americans during the epidemic, the local community finally gave up resistance to the African church on Fifth Street.[27]

The epidemic of 1793 created the first major crack in the confidence of Philadelphians in their remarkable progress as a capital city. Some thought the epidemic was the destroying angel sent from God to punish the city for its luxury and dissipation, especially since the arrival of the federal government. Yellow fever touched families across all social lines — two-time mayor Samuel Powell, ten doctors, ten ministers, four members of the mayor's committee, and scores of others among the leading citizens died, contributing to a total death toll of nearly five thousand, almost one-fifth the city's estimated population.[28]

Many hard lessons were learned that year, and measures were immediately launched to protect the city from future attacks. Although medical doctors could not agree on the source of yellow fever, the city set about to improve sanitation in case the mysterious disease emanated from the city's filth. Five water carts were procured to clean the streets, and sheds to house three of the carts were erected on the

---

[27]Ibid., pp. 127–132; Benjamin Rush to John Nicholson, Aug. 12, 1793, L. H. Butterfield, ed., *The Letters of Benjamin Rush*, 2 vols. (Princeton, 1951), 2:636.

[28]Philadelphia suffered through earlier but less severe yellow fever outbreaks in 1693, 1741, and 1762. Cecil Kent Drinker, *Not So Long Ago: A Chronicle of Medicine and Doctors in Colonial Philadelphia* (New York, 1937), p. 112; John Harvey Powell, *Bring Out Your Dead: The Great Plague of Yellow Fever in Philadelphia in 1793* (New York, 1949), pp. 13–16; Isaac Heston to Abraham Heston, Sept. 19, 1792, Independence National Historical Park Museum Collection; Benjamin Rush, *An Account of the Bilious Remitting Yellow Fever as It Appeared in the City of Philadelphia in the Year 1793* (Philadelphia, 1794), pp. 317, 322–23; A[bsolom] Jones and R[ichard] Allen, *A Narrative of the Proceedings of the Black People during the Late Awful Calamity in Philadelphia in the Year 1793* (Philadelphia, 1794), p. 4; Mathew Carey, *A Short Account of the Malignant Fever* (Philadelphia, 1793), app.; Elaine Forman Crane, ed., *The Diary of Elizabeth Drinker,* 3 vols. (Boston, 1991), 1:510; Butterfield, *Letters of Benjamin Rush,* 2:722; Julie Winch, *Philadelphia's Black Elite* (Philadelphia, 1988), p. 16.

northeast corner of Southeast Square. The city also closed Southeast Square as a potter's field and added two more rows of trees around its perimeter, a measure, it seems, to mask the hideous memory of the mass burials.[29]

Taking their improvements one step further, the city decided to lay out Southeast Square as a public walk. In 1797 geographer Jedidiah Morse anticipated that when the trees grew up and the ground was leveled, the square would be a pleasant promenade. Real estate development on the west side of the square followed, culminating in 1799 with "Sansom's Row" of stately Federal-style houses on Walnut above Seventh, designed by prominent architect Benjamin Henry Latrobe. The advertisement for their rental noted that the houses faced the public square and that the site's advantages were "obvious, combining vicinity to the trading parts of the city, with a pure air, and an open prospect interspaced with trees and herbage, resembling a country retreat." The notice failed to mention, however, either the city's cattle market on Seventh Street from Walnut south to Prune Street or the fact that Seventh Street ran right through the square; nevertheless, the new horticultural improvements to the Southeast Square by the close of the decade gave incentive for developers to expect the interest and investments of the gentry class.[30]

Even with measures to clean up the city, yellow fever reappeared every year, and in 1797 and 1798 the death tolls rose to alarming levels in spite of huge tent cities set up for the poor along the banks of the Schuylkill. In 1797 the mayor and his committee once again met the challenge, and "a large and respectable committee of citizens" distributed relief supplies "from the State House on fixed days of the week." In spite of these efforts the epidemic caused "much suffering in middle and lower classes of the inhabitants." At the first sign of yellow fever in 1798, the city set up tent encampments, one on the Schuylkill River and another on Germantown Road, as places of escape for the

[29]Benjamin Johnson, *An Account of the Rise, Progress, and Termination of the Malignant Fever* (Philadelphia, 1793), p. 3; Carey, *Short Account of the Malignant Fever,* p. 11; Benjamin Rush to Julia Rush, Sept. 29–30, 1793, Butterfield, *Rush Letters,* 2:686; Powell, *Bring Out Your Dead,* pp. 234, 255, 301–2.

[30]Jedidiah Morse, *American Gazetteer* (Boston, 1797); Westcott, *History of Philadelphia,* 3:123; Denise Rabzak, "Washington Square: A Site Plan Chronology, 1683–1984" (Independence National Historical Park, 1987), pp. 3, 7.

poor. Even so, yellow fever caused so many deaths that year that at its recurrence in 1799, the federal government moved its offices across the Delaware River and north to Trenton, New Jersey.[31]

Arenas of Amusement

In spite of such dreaded epidemics, Philadelphians lived in spirited times, full of the bustle of an expanding economy and population. Throughout the State House neighborhood the presence of French immigrants contributed to the area's cultural development. The Reign of Terror in France beginning in 1793 and bloody slave revolts in the French colony of Haiti brought many refugees to Philadelphia. The French Benevolent Society held meetings at Anatomical Hall, across from the State House yard, and erudite French refugees were inducted as members of the American Philosophical Society. France and all things French came into full fashion in clothes, food, education, and entertainment. French émigrés taught children and adults the language, fencing, and dancing. Through need, talent, and preference, these immigrants found social venues and work in the State House neighborhood.[32] Beginning in 1791, Jean Legay secured the contract from the state government to set off fireworks annually for the Fourth of July celebrations. Jean Blanchard rose from the Walnut Street prison yard in a hot air balloon in January 1793, creating a spectacle many came to witness. President Washington and members of his admin-

---

[31]Quotes from Eliza Cope Harrison, *The Diary of Thomas Cope, 1800–1850* (South Bend, Ind., 1978), pp. 302, 303, 337. *Connecticut Courant*, Nov. 13, 1797, Nov. 26, 1798; James McHenry to John Adams, Aug. 4, 1798, McHenry Papers, Library of Congress; Samuel Powel Griffiths, manuscript Diary of the Epidemic of Yellow Fever in 1798, College of Physicians, Philadelphia; Timothy Pickering to Richard O'Brien, Nov. 10, 1798, Pickering Papers, MHi; *Massachusetts Spy* (Worcester), Sept. 4, 1799; Timothy Pickering to John Adams, Sept. 11, 1799, Charles Francis Adams, ed., *The Works of John Adams*, 10 vols. (Boston, 1850–56), 9:23.

[32]Figures vary on the number of French West Indian refugees. Martin S. Pernick, "Politics, Parties, and Pestilence: Epidemic Yellow Fever in Philadelphia and the Rise of the First Party System," *William and Mary Quarterly*, 3d ser. 29 (1972):561, notes more than two thousand French refugees arrived from Haiti. Pernick's figures are contradicted by Nash, *Forging Freedom*, pp. 125, 141, and Mulford Stough, "The Yellow Fever in Philadelphia, 1793," *Pennsylvania History* 6 (1939):6, who cite only 750 arrivals from Santo Domingo.

istration watched from within the prison yard while "several thousand spectators, many of whom had come from New York, Baltimore, and other distant parts," crowded the streets and windows of the city, filled the Southeast Square, and climbed into the trees in the State House yard to watch the balloon take to the sky. Another French émigré, Bernard Desaa from Haiti, began selling ice cream in the State House yard in 1797, and Charles Willson Peale selected Palisot de Beauvois to publish a catalog of his museum in Philosophical Hall.[33]

Probably Philadelphia's enthusiasm for the French people and French fashion was nowhere more evident than at Oellers Hotel on Chestnut Street, half a block west of the State House, in the large new Episcopal Academy building, which James Oellers purchased in 1791 from the financially strapped school. The Republicans often chose Oellers as the scene for elaborate pro-French political receptions, especially at the arrival of Citizen Genêt in spring 1793. The hotel turned into the foremost political and social gathering place in the city. Henry Wansey wanted to stay there during his 1794 visit but found it full. Many members of Congress took up residence at Oellers during sessions, attracted by its convenience and gracious accommodations. In the heat of summer the hotel served refreshing cold punch, a specialty made possible by the huge forty-foot-thick block of ice in the icehouse behind the kitchen. In April 1792 the governor gave a dinner for the representatives of the Six Nations (the Five Nations of the Iroquois confederacy and the Tuscarora), who were in town to negotiate with the government. Ninety-two people consumed ninety-five bottles of Madeira, twenty-seven bottles of porter, twenty-one double bowls of punch, and five glasses of brandy, and smoked one hundred cigars at the meal. In 1798 a reception honored John Marshall upon his triumphant return from negotiations in France. Such lavish receptions took place in the assembly room, which Wansey described as

---

[33]George W. Corner, ed., *The Autobiography of Benjamin Rush . . . together with his Commonplace Book for 1789–1813* (Westport, Conn., 1970), p. 304; Westcott, *History of Philadelphia*, 3:609; Nov. 22, 1790, in "Day Book, Nov. 1, 1790–Sept. 30, 1791," RG 24, Pennsylvania State Archives; *Independent Gazetteer* (Philadelphia), May 25, June 8, 1793; Powell, *Bring Out Your Dead*, p. 1; Richardson, *Peale*, p. 117; Petition of Joseph Marie Thomas, July 2, 1799, State House Papers, Public Records Office, Harrisburg; Emily V. Smith, "The French in Philadelphia with Especial Reference to the Period 1783 to 1793," M. A. thesis, Teachers College, 1938, pp. 34–36.

FIG. 12. *Congress Hall and the New Theater,* by William Birch, 1800. *(Courtesy Independence National Historical Park)*

wallpapered "after the French taste," with classical figures, festoons, and pillars, all fashions he had lately seen "in the most elegant houses in London." Philadelphia's high society held their exclusive Dancing Assembly balls there as well, and invited many of the legislators as guests.[34]

The neighborhood played host to other amusements geared to please the sophisticated visitors to the nation's capital. In April 1794 the new and elegant Chestnut Street Theater opened its doors across the street from Oellers Hotel and immediately was a great success. It was the first theater permitted within the city limits — Quakers finally had lost their hold — and President Washington was among its most enthusiastic patrons. William Birch's print (fig. 12) of the theater from

---

[34]Jeremy, *Wansey and His American Journal,* pp. 103–4; Warrant Book, 1789–92, RG 24, Office of the Register General, Pennsylvania State Archives; Register of Accounts, 1790, p. 255, Records of Sec. of Commonwealth, Division of Public Records; *Massachusetts Spy,* Apr. 12, 1792; *Gazette of the United States,* June 23, 25, 1798.

the State House Square shows its dignified classical facade and its architectural harmony with the buildings that made up the seat of government across the street.[35]

Scottish equestrian John Bill Ricketts, long a popular attraction at his circus arena at the edge of town, opened the new Pantheon Circus and Amphitheater in 1795 across from the Chestnut Street Theater, at the southwest corner of Sixth and Chestnut. The next year another circus, Laison's, opened on Fifth Street near St. Thomas African Episcopal Church, but it lasted only a year because its dome collapsed. Rickett's, too, suffered a disaster on December 17, 1799, when the building went up in flames, taking with it Oellers Hotel and six new houses on Sixth Street across from the State House Square. The fire came at the close of an era, when both the state and federal governments were departing the city, a fact that evidently deterred any initiative to rebuild the popular Rickett's Circus or Oellers Hotel. And so it was logical and even inevitable that in 1800 the square would slide into decline when Philadelphia's decade as the nation's capital came to an end.[36]

---

[35] *Public Ledger Almanac, 1874–1880* (Philadelphia, 1880), p. 1875; Jeremy, *Wansey and His American Journal*, pp. 101–2.

[36] For a colorful advertisement for Rickett's, see *Aurora General Advertiser* (Philadelphia), Apr. 19, 1796; for an account of the fire, see ibid., Dec. 19, 1799; George Thatcher to Sarah Thatcher, Dec. 17, 1799, Thatcher Papers, MHi.

II. The Social and Political Lives of Members in Philadelphia

John D. Gordan III

Egbert Benson

A Nationalist in Congress, 1789–1793

W̶E ARE FORTUNATE in Egbert Benson's friends. He was eclipsed by the luster of other Federalist Founding Fathers of the first rank—George Washington, Alexander Hamilton, and John Jay; yet Benson's friendships with Jay, which Benson described as "as close for sixty-five years as between brothers,"[1] and with that giant of nineteenth-century New York jurisprudence, James Kent, who was apprenticed to Benson in the 1780s, generated a rich and accessible store of materials from which to fashion a fairly complete picture of Benson as an individual. The reconstruction is aided by two Gilbert Stuart portraits of Benson, one (fig. 1) painted in 1794 for John Jay's home in Katonah, New York, and the other painted in Benson's old age, now at the New-York Historical Society, of which Benson was a founder in 1804 and first president.

Born in 1746, Benson lived to the age of eighty-seven. Following his death in 1833, Kent wrote: "This great and good man lived to survive all his contemporaries, and seems to have died almost unknown and forgotten by the profession which he once so greatly

I would like to thank Charlene Bangs Bickford, Kenneth R. Bowling, Kathryn Preyer, and Wythe Holt for the improvements and corrections they suggested.

[1] *Reminiscences of Egbert Benson* in the hand of Henry C. Van Schaack, Van Schaack Collection, Columbia University.

FIG. 1. *Egbert Benson*, by Gilbert Stuart. Believed to have been commissioned by John Jay in 1794, the portrait has been in the possession of the Jay family since its completion and hangs at the John Jay Homestead in Katonah, New York. *(Courtesy John Jay Homestead, New York State Office of Parks, Recreation and Historic Preservation)*

adorned."[2] The obscurity surrounding Benson deepened in the next century and a half, but the bicentennials of the Revolution, the Constitution, and the First Federal Congress have reminded historians of Benson's importance and have rekindled scholarly interest in his multifaceted activities.[3] His range was very wide indeed, for he served New York State in all three branches of government — as its first attorney general, as a member of the assembly, and as a justice of the supreme court. He served the nation as a member of Congress under

[2]James Kent, "Egbert Benson," in Benjamin F. Thompson, *History of Long Island* (New York, 1839), pp. 408–10.

[3]Until ten years ago the only significant biographical essays about Benson were those by James Kent in the various editions of Thompson, *History of Long Island* (1839, 1843, 1849, and 1918) and in William Kent, *Memoirs and Letters of James Kent, LL. D.* (Boston, Mass., 1898). The Benson "renaissance" began with the publication by the Second Circuit Committee on the Bicentennial of the *Constitution of Egbert Benson, First Chief Judge of the Second Circuit, 1801–1802* (New York, 1987), containing two essays by Wythe Holt and one by David A. Nourse. Holt wrote a further biographical essay on Benson published in Stephen L. Schechter, ed., *New York and the Union* (Albany, N.Y., 1990), pp. 377–84. Biographical essays about Benson also appear in Margaret C. S. Christman, *The First Federal Congress 1789–1791* (Washington, D.C., 1989), pp. 228–31, and *Documentary History of the First Federal Congress*, 14 vols. to date (Baltimore, 1972–),

the Articles of Confederation and, most pertinently, as the representative from Dutchess and northern Westchester Counties in the First and Second Congresses under the U.S. Constitution, completing his public career with a seventeen-month tenure as chief judge of the U.S. Circuit Court for the Second Circuit under the short-lived Judiciary Act of 1801, popularly called the Midnight Judges Act. Kent wrote further of Benson that "he took a zealous part in the adoption of the constitution of the United States, on which, as he uniformly thought and declared, rested all his hopes of American liberty, safety and glory. No person could be more devoted to its success."[4]

The relationship between Benson's career in public service up to his election to Congress and his more striking activities in the First and Second Congresses illustrate the political attitudes of one of that group of early congressional leaders who fought for a strong central government and serve as a reminder of a hardly remembered individual whom Kent described at the end of his life as "a venerable monument of the wisdom, the integrity, the patriotism and the intrepidity of the sages of the Revolution."[5] But, although he was venerable, Benson was not boring. Here is Kent's description of Benson:

> He remained through life an invincible bachelor, but there was nothing morose nor ascetic about him. No one was more fond of society; no one enjoyed more, but always in an innocent and decorous degree, the pleasures of the table. It was a jubilee to the children and a pleasure to the parents, when, on a summer afternoon, the Judge was seen to drive up to the door of a friend, . . . announcing his intention of passing a few days, and carefully dislodging from his carriage a fine fish, or a pair of canvas-back ducks, or some other epicurean rarity, which he delivered over to the cook, with some skillful suggestions as to the dressing. Then would follow a season of liveliness and gayety, — of thronging visitors, disputations, dinners, conversations, in which the old gentleman would display all his peculiarities, all his pertinacity and disputatiousness;

---

vol. 14 (Charlene B. Bickford, Kenneth R. Bowling, Helen E. Veit, and William C. diGiacomantonio, eds.), pp. 710–13, hereafter cited as *DHFFC*. At the June 1996 New York State History Conference at SUNY New Paltz, Robert Ernst delivered a comprehensive paper entitled "Egbert Benson, Forgotten Statesman of the Revolutionary War."

[4]Kent, "Egbert Benson," in Thompson, *History of Long Island*, p. 409.

[5]Kent, *Memoirs of Kent*, p. 290.

keep the table in a roar, while he never for a moment forgot that he was a Federalist and a gentleman.[6]

Benson graduated from King's College, now Columbia University, in 1765. His classmates included John Jay; Gouverneur Morris, one of the principal drafters of the Constitution; and Robert R. Livingston, the chancellor of New York from 1777 to 1801. He studied law in the offices of John Morin Scott, a future radical in the Revolution, and was admitted to the bar in 1769. Even then New York City had too many lawyers, and so in 1772 Benson moved north to Red Hook in Dutchess County and began a practice there.[7]

Not long afterward he became involved in revolutionary activity. In 1773 he began his service on the Dutchess County Committee of Safety; in 1775 he was a Dutchess County representative to the New York State Provincial Congress. In early 1777, as "chairman of Dutchess County," he began his participation on the Committee for Detecting and Defeating Conspiracies in the State of New York, chaired by John Jay, and, later, the commission that succeeded it.[8] Benson and Jay were active in rooting out Loyalist sympathizers, even among the gentry, and forcing them out of their homes to exile behind British lines in the southern portion of the state.[9] Kent reports that "as president of the board of commissioners in Dutchess County for detecting and defeating conspiracies," Benson sent "William Smith, the historian of New-York, into the British lines; and who did not fail to complain severely of the stern and inflexible manner" in which Benson treated him.[10] In May 1777 the state convention held at Kingston named Benson the first attorney general of New York, a position he held until his election to the First Federal Congress more than a decade later. In October 1777 Benson also began four years of service as representative of Dutchess County in the New York Assembly. In 1783 New York

---

[6]Ibid., pp. 21–22.

[7]Holt, "Egbert Benson" in Schechter, *New York and the Union*, p. 377.

[8]Ernst, "Egbert Benson," pp. 4–6; John D. Gordan, III, "Introduction," *Benson, First Chief Judge*, pp. 2–3.

[9]Richard B. Morris, *John Jay, The Making of a Revolutionary: Unpublished Papers, 1745–1780* (New York, 1975), pp. 345–51.

[10]Kent, "Egbert Benson" in Thompson, *History of Long Island*, p. 409.

Gov. George Clinton sent Benson to negotiate the evacuation of New York City with the departing British commander, Sir Guy Carleton.[11]

Although highly energetic at the local level, Benson seems to have had little use for the Congress organized under the Articles of Confederation, which was finally ratified in 1781. Elected to Congress in that year, Benson did not bother attending. Even though reelected several times in subsequent years, Benson's appearance was infrequent. His absence was not, however, for want of attachment to national goals; as one of New York's delegates to the Hartford Convention in 1781 Benson strongly supported increasing the powers of the national government.[12] Benson's emerging nationalism was probably the consequence of the political frustration of the New York conservatives, whom he led in the state assembly, by the ascendancy of the radical yeomanry led by Abraham Yates, Jr., of Albany. Staughton Lynd, in a chapter aptly titled "A Governing Class on the Defensive," argues that "it was only as the New York conservatives lost control of state government to their upstart opponents, that the thought of the conservatives turned clearly in a centralist direction."[13] In this context, *centralist* means both nationalistic at the expense of state sovereignty and, ultimately, antidemocratic.[14]

For Benson the defining moment may have been the bitter battle leading to the Confiscation Act of 1779, a bill of attainder that provided for the forfeiture of Loyalist estates; he was ultimately reduced to drafting the legislation he opposed in order to mitigate the excesses of his radical opponents. The 1780 legislative session saw the sale of the confiscated estates, again over Benson's initial opposition but with his ultimate capitulation; open warfare between factions in the legislature; and attacks on Benson in the newspapers of Dutchess County. In the elections in 1781, Benson lost his seat and did not return to the assembly until 1788. Similarly, men like his former classmates Jay, Livingston, and Morris found their way into high posts at the national

---

[11]John P. Kaminski, *George Clinton: Yeoman Politician of the New Republic* (Madison, Wis., 1993), p. 54.

[12]Ernst, "Egbert Benson," pp. 13–15; *DHFFC*, 14:710–11.

[13]Staughton Lynd, *Class Conflict, Slavery, and the United States Constitution* (Westport, Conn., 1967), p. 116.

[14]Thornton Anderson, *Creating the Constitution: The Convention of 1787 and the First Congress* (University Park, Pa., 1993), pp. 43–44.

level, leaving New York in the control of the radicals.[15] Hamilton, however, stayed behind and mobilized the commercial interests in newly liberated New York City. Class distinctions blurred in the common pursuit of financial success by merchants and artisans alike, and in the mid-1780s New York City emerged as a strong counterweight to the agrarian radicalism upstate.[16]

By this time, also, Benson had experienced firsthand the possibilities of higher authority as a check on what he perceived as the unbridled radicalism of the New York legislature. While still attorney general of New York, Benson served as counsel to his aunt, the plaintiff, in the case of *Rutgers* v. *Waddington.* Mrs. Elizabeth Rutgers had owned a brewery in New York City that she had abandoned during the British occupation. Joshua Waddington, a British merchant, used the brewery for five years—for the first two years with the permission of the British commissary general and thereafter by permission of the British commander in chief. Two days before the British evacuation on November 25, 1783, the brewery burned to the ground. Mrs. Rutgers brought suit for eight thousand pounds against Waddington in the mayor's court for the City of New York under the Trespass Act of 1783, which prohibited any reliance on military orders as a justification. The case was argued before Mayor James Duane on June 29, 1784, with Benson appearing as one of the counsels for the plaintiff and Alexander Hamilton for Waddington. The case turned on the extent to which the law of nations or the recently concluded Treaty of Paris protected Waddington and whether their application was precluded by the prohibitions of the Trespass Act. While counsel for Rutgers advanced various subsidiary arguments, their basic point was that neither the law of nations nor Congress, exercising its power to make treaties under the Articles of Confederation, could interfere with an enactment of the state legislature. Hamilton argued the contrary. Mayor Duane found that the law of nations protected the period of Waddington's possession of the brewery under the authority of the British commander in chief and refused to conclude that the legislature in-

---

[15]Lynd, *Class Conflict*, pp. 25–61; Edward Countryman, *A People in Revolution: The American Revolution and Political Society in New York* (New York, 1981), pp. 204–20.

[16]Lynd, *Class Conflict*, pp. 122–32.

tended that the Trespass Act should apply where that would lead to the opposite result.[17]

While Julius Goebel suggests that Mayor Duane's decision must have been "disappointing, even shocking to plaintiff's counsel . . . [who] had argued the case on the assumption that it involved a direct conflict between the State and national governments . . . and that the authority of the state legislature was supreme," it seems to me more likely that, apart from his feelings for his aunt, Benson must have been thrilled. Benson; his co-counsel, John Laurance, who would join him in the House of Representatives and later serve as U.S. district judge and U.S. senator; Alexander Hamilton, future first secretary of the Treasury; and James Duane, future first U.S. district judge for the New York District, were all ardent nationalists. Indeed, Richard Morris, a leading historian of the period, traces to a letter from Hamilton to Duane in 1780 an early statement of Hamilton's centralist position.[18] Duane's opinion in *Rutgers* strongly supported the supremacy of the Confederation Congress in the exercise of its powers against any encroachment "by the authority of a single state." The trouble was that in too many ways the authority of the central government under the Articles of Confederation was inadequate. Hamilton called it "a want of power in Congress" in his 1780 letter to Duane: its fiscal powers were limited, and its ability to act required unanimity of the states. In addition, the central government's judicial function was limited to appeals in prize cases, and its executive powers were weak.[19]

In early 1786 the Virginia legislature proposed a convention of the states to consider the regulation of interstate trade and to make proposals on that subject to the Confederation Congress. Of the commissioners named by the New York legislature only Benson and Hamilton attended the meeting, which was held at Annapolis, Maryland, in September 1786; their goal, as Benson later recorded, was "to revise the whole of the Articles of Confederation, as a Mode or System of Government." Benson served as secretary of the convention, and its report,

---

[17] *The Law Practice of Alexander Hamilton*, 5 vols. (New York, 1964–81), vol. 1 (Julius Goebel, Jr., ed.), pp. 282–419.

[18] Richard B. Morris, *The Forging of the Union, 1781–1789* (New York, 1987), p. 245.

[19] Stanley Elkins and Eric McKitrick, *The Age of Federalism* (New York, 1993), pp. 100–101.

which was drafted by Hamilton, proposed a convention be called for the spring of 1787 in Philadelphia "to take into Consideration the Situation of the United States, and to devise such further Provisions as should appear to them necessary to render the Constitution of the federal government adequate to the Exigencies of the Union."[20] That convention in Philadelphia drafted the Constitution of the United States. Hamilton was one of three delegates from New York; the other two were Antifederalists, one a nephew of Benson's old foe in the legislature, Abraham Yates; Hamilton's signature alone appears for New York on the Constitution.

It was on Benson's motion in the New York legislature on January 31, 1788, that the New York ratification convention was summoned. Benson did not attend, because, residing in largely Antifederalist Dutchess County, he was defeated in the election of delegates.[21] Nevertheless, New York City returned many of his closest associates as delegates, including Jay, Hamilton, Duane, and another of Benson's Federalist friends, Judge John Sloss Hobart. On July 26, New York ratified the Constitution by a narrow vote, accompanied by a circular letter recommending consideration of amendments proposed by state ratification conventions, including New York's.[22]

In the elections for the House of Representatives for the First Congress under the U.S. Constitution, Benson proved more successful than he had for the ratification convention. Opposed by an Antifederalist lawyer for the Third Congressional District formed by Dutchess and northern Westchester Counties, Benson prevailed by a slim margin after some of the votes for his opponent were rejected for irregularity.[23] Benson took his seat in the House on April 9, 1789,[24] and re-

---

[20]Gordan, "Introduction," *Benson, First Chief Judge*, p. 4.

[21]John P. Kaminski, "New York: The Reluctant Pillar," in *The Reluctant Pillar: New York and the Adoption of the Federal Constitution*, ed. Stephen L. Schechter (Albany, N.Y., 1987), pp. 49, 73–74, 88–91.

[22]Ibid., pp. 110–14. These proposals are collected in Helen E. Veit, Kenneth R. Bowling, and Charlene Bangs Bickford, eds., *Creating the Bill of Rights* (Baltimore, 1991), pp. 14–28.

[23]Margaret Beekman Livingston, mother of the chancellor, Robert R. Livingston, and grande dame of Dutchess County, "boasted that 'I have been the means of getting in Benson by my exertions'" (Alfred F. Young, *The Democratic Republicans of New York : The Origins, 1763–1797* [Chapel Hill, 1967], pp. 135–36).

[24]*DHFFC*, 14:711.

mained there until the conclusion of the Second Congress in 1793.[25] He was not a vocal figure on the floor of the House, but his role in the adoption of the Bill of Rights, the Judiciary Act, the acts establishing the executive departments, and the debate on slavery leave no doubt that his central purpose remained the establishment of a strong national government.

Egbert Benson and the Fourth Amendment

In retrospect the most important work of the first session of the First Congress was the enactment of the amendments to the Constitution that have come to be known as the Bill of Rights. James Madison, a representative from Virginia who appears to have done more talking at the first session of Congress than anyone else, was their draftsman and sponsor in the House of Representatives, where they originated. Madison's purpose, shared by his Federalist supporters in the House, including Benson, was to neutralize Antifederalist criticism of the Constitution and avoid the perils of a second constitutional convention.[26] With the exception discussed below, Egbert Benson's role was not a visible one; his occasional comments about double jeopardy and conscientious objection have had no lasting impact, although his brief exposition on the First Amendment is quoted by Justice Stanley Reed in his 1943 dissent in *Murdock* v. *Pennsylvania (City of Jeannette).*[27]

The continuing importance of Benson's role in the adoption of the Bill of Rights arises from the not very flattering suspicion on the part of some scholars — and it is only that — that he took advantage of his position on the committee of arrangement to alter the provisions of what is now the Fourth Amendment in a way that the House of Representatives had expressly rejected when he had proposed it in debate a week earlier. The record reflects that, as first proposed by Madison on

---

[25]Benson was defeated in the assembly in the January 1791 U.S. senatorial election in which Aaron Burr captured the seat that had been held by Philip Schuyler, Alexander Hamilton's father-in-law. See Alfred F. Young, *The Democratic Republicans,* pp. 188–92.

[26]Kenneth R. Bowling, *Politics in the First Congress, 1789–1791* (New York, 1990), pp. 121–51.

[27]319 U.S. 105, 125 (1943).

June 8, 1789, what became the Fourth Amendment read as follows: "The rights of the people to be secured in their persons, their houses, their papers, and their other property from all unreasonable searches and seizures, shall not be violated by warrants issued without probable cause, supported by oath or affirmation, or not particularly describing the places to be searched, or the persons or things to be seized."[28] Madison's proposal was referred to a select committee, which included Benson, on July 21. The committee's report on July 28 did little to Madison's text on this proposal except to compress it: "The right of the people to be secure in their person, houses, papers and effects, shall not be violated by warrants issuing, without probable cause supported by oath or affirmation, and not particularly describing the places to be searched, and the persons or things to be seized."[29] When the amendment was debated in the House on August 17, 1789, two changes were proposed. The first, which carried, substantially restored language in Madison's original proposal by inserting the words "against unreasonable seizures and searches" after the word "effects." The second motion would have substituted the words "and no warrants shall issue" for "by warrants issuing," described by the proponent of the motion as "good as far as it went" but "not sufficient." This second motion "lost by a considerable majority," according to the *Congressional Register*, although the reason is unknown.[30] Two sources are primarily relied upon by scholars for the debates in the House of Representatives at the first session of the First Congress — Thomas Lloyd's *Congressional Register* and John Fenno's *Gazette of the United States*. These sources agree on the motions that were made on August 17, 1789, and on the action taken on each by the House, but differ as to whether Benson made the first or the second. Because Lloyd's publication was used for volume 1 of the *Annals of Congress*, his attribution to Benson of the second, losing motion is the one commonly accepted.

No further action was taken by the House on the language of this amendment. On August 22, 1789, Benson and two other representa-

---

[28]Veit, *Creating the Bill of Rights*, pp. 11–13.

[29]*DHFFC*, vol. 3 (Linda G. DePauw, Charlene Bangs Bickford, and LaVonne Siegel Hauptman, eds.), p. 117; Veit, *Creating the Bill of Rights*, pp. 29, 31.

[30]*DHFFC*, vol. 11 (Charlene Bangs Bickford, Kenneth R. Bowling, and Helen E. Veit, eds.), pp. 1284, 1291.

tives were appointed to a committee to "prepare and report a proper arrangement of, and introduction to the articles of amendment to the Constitution of the United States, as agreed to by the House."[31] However, what this committee reported the following day, and what the House, and later the Senate, and finally the state legislatures all adopted, and is the Fourth Amendment today, is *not* the Fourth Amendment "as agreed to by the House." It is instead the Fourth Amendment as modified by the motion attributed to Benson, which the House had expressly rejected "by a considerable majority": "The right of the people to be secure in their persons, houses, papers, and effects, against unreasonable searches and seizures, shall not be violated, and no warrants shall issue, but upon probable cause, supported by oath or affirmation, and particularly describing the place to be searched, and the persons or things to be seized."[32] This curious parliamentary anomaly has become one of the artillery shells lobbed or dodged by every side in the ceaseless academic and judicial war over the meaning of the Fourth Amendment. The two major camps seem to be, on the one hand, those who argue that the second, or "warrant," clause defines the limit of permissible searches carved out of the general prohibition of the first, or "reasonableness," clause; and on the other hand, those who treat the two clauses as entirely separate, limiting the scope of the second clause to warrants and treating the first as justifying the ever-expanding categories of warrantless searches if they are "reasonable."

Most scholars are prepared to conclude, on no evidence beyond his original motion and his presence on the committee of arrangement, that Benson tampered with the language of the Fourth Amendment before the House passed it.[33] Tracey Maclin, while citing earlier scholarly treatises that take differing positions, says that the final version of the amendment, which he ascribes to Benson's misbehavior, does seem "to provide for 'two constitutional mandates where only one had existed before.'" Marco Caffuzzi argues that the final revision not only "limit[s] the issuance of warrants, but arguably, it creates a broader right as well. Parsing the text like this shows more clearly the establishment of

---

[31]*DHFFC*, 3:165.

[32]Veit, *Creating the Bill of Rights*, pp. 3, 4, 37, 39, 48.

[33]Nelson B. Lasson, *The History and Development of the Fourth Amendment to the United States Constitution* (New York, 1970), pp. 101–3.

a general right to privacy which is the underpinning of the Fourth Amendment." Phyllis Bookspan, relying on earlier scholarship, treats the clandestine activities she convicts Benson of as vitiating any meaningful determination of the House's intentions. Tony Freyer takes the darkest view: "Congressman Egbert Benson altered the final draft so that instead of probable cause being 'universally required for any search or seizure, regardless of the circumstances,' the 'tampered text . . . seemed expressly to require probable cause only in cases involving warrants.' The Rehnquist Court has exploited this ambiguity to erode the Court's earlier strong adherence to probable cause in determining whether a search or seizure was 'reasonable.' "[34]

Quite another point of view is taken by Prof. Akil Reed Amar, a leading constitutional scholar at the Yale Law School.[35] He embraces the narrow interpretation of the Fourth Amendment that Professor Freyer decries and buttresses his position by blasting as a "triply troubling canard" any suggestion that Egbert Benson slipped one by the House, arguing instead that Thomas Lloyd, who was drunk much of the time, probably misrecorded the vote on Benson's August 17 motion to alter the amendment, that the House and Senate "treated the final wording of their proposed amendments with great care," and that the text of the Bill of Rights "was adopted by supermajorities of both houses and ratified by a supermajority of states." Professor Amar's analysis does not address the absence of evidence that the representative of the *Gazette of the United States,* who reported the vote on Benson's August 17 motion the same way Lloyd did, was also intoxicated.

Depending on one's resolution of the textual and factual underpinnings of this debate, Benson's proposed amendment, and the text of the Fourth Amendment, may demonstrate an unwillingness to hobble the national government with too rigorous a warrant requirement.

---

[34]Marco Caffuzzi, "Private Police Power and Personal Privacy: Who's Guarding the Guards," *New York Law School Law Review* 40 (1995):225, 238; Tony A. Freyer, "A Precarious Path: The Bill of Rights after 200 Years," *Vanderbilt Law Review* 47 (1994):757, 787–88; Tracey Maclin, "The Central Meaning of the Fourth Amendment," *William and Mary Law Review* 35 (1993):193, 208–10; Phyllis T. Bookspan, "Reworking the Warrant Requirement: Resuscitating the Fourth Amendment," *Vanderbilt Law Review* 44 (1991):517–18.

[35]Akhil Reed Amar, "Fourth Amendment First Principles," *Harvard Law Review* 107 (1994):774–75.

How different the substance is from the text Madison originally proposed, or from that reported by the select committee of the House, seems highly debatable; perhaps that is why no one noticed. In any event, Benson's centralist tendencies and his parliamentary adroitness shine in a clearer light in other aspects of the important work of the First Congress.

The Judiciary Act of 1789

No issue displayed Benson's belief in the importance of a strong national government more clearly than the debates surrounding the establishment of the federal judiciary. This was an issue of no little sensitivity, particularly for a New York representative, because the constitutional amendments proposed by the state's ratification convention, apart from those which became part of the Bill of Rights, were primarily addressed to limiting the judicial power of the United States.[36] The Judiciary Act originated in the Senate, and its bill did not reach the House until late July 1789.[37] The debates did not begin for another month, after the House had completed its work on the Bill of Rights. The Senate bill was itself a compromise engineered by Oliver Ellsworth of Connecticut, its principal author. As it arrived in the House, the bill by no means occupied the full expanse of jurisdiction that the Constitution had granted to the federal judiciary. Rather, the Senate bill curtailed the jurisdiction of the federal courts in many ways to placate those who feared a strong national judiciary and, particularly, its potential impact on the power and role of the state courts.[38]

Not much actually happened to the Senate bill in the House of Representatives, but much of the ground was gone over once again. Samuel Livermore of New Hampshire was particularly vocal in objecting to the creation of any lower federal courts, repeating the claim that their establishment would lead to repeated jurisdictional clashes between them and the state courts.[39] Benson came out strongly against

---

[36]Veit, *Creating the Bill of Rights*, pp. 23–24.

[37]*DHFFC*, 3:115.

[38]Wythe Holt, " 'To Establish Justice': Politics, the Judiciary Act of 1789, and the Invention of the Federal Courts," *Duke Law Journal* (1989):1421, 1478–94.

[39]*DHFFC*, 11:1324, 1329, 1330–32, 1366–67.

those who grounded their opposition to federal courts in a deference to state court jurisdiction:

> The honorable gentleman had observed that difficulties would arise out of the proposed establishment; but these difficulties or embarrassments are not to be charged to the house, they grow out of the constitution itself. The gentlemen suppose that two sovereign and independent authorities can never be exercised over the same territory but this was not the business of the committee, they could not get rid of these difficulties by retrenching their powers; they must carry the constitution into effect. The gentleman has stated a case, in supposing that process shall issue from the state and continental courts, and both be served upon the defendant at the same time, and then asks what is to be done? Is the man to be divided? Now, in return, he would ask the same question, is the United States to abandon all its powers and jurisdiction, because the exercise of it may be attended with some inconvenience? As well might we ask individual states to abandon theirs, because there is some clashing with the federal judiciary. He apprehended that neither were to be abandoned, but that they should endeavor to administer both with as little inconvenience to either as was practicable.[40]

The passage of the Judiciary Act, and its approval by President Washington in late September 1789, merely closed the first chapter of the debate on the appropriate scope of the federal judicial power. It was revived in the second session when, in response to a request by the House of Representatives, Atty. Gen. Edmund Randolph, on December 31, 1790, filed his report commenting on the operation of the Judiciary Act and proposing a fully articulated bill reenacting a federal judicial system with substantial variations from the existing one.[41] The impact of the report and the ingenious tactic adopted by Benson, which stopped it in its tracks, were ably explored a decade ago by Wythe Holt, to whose article the reader is referred.[42] In brief, Ran-

---

[40]Ibid., 11:1368.

[41]The report is reprinted in *Documentary History of the Supreme Court of the United States,* 5 vols. to date (New York, 1985–), vol. 4 (Maeva Marcus, James C. Brandon, Robert P. Frankel, Stephen Tull, and Natalie Wexler, eds.), pp. 122–67, hereafter cited as *DHSC.*

[42]Wythe Holt, "'Federal Courts as the Asylum to Federal Interests': Randolph's Report, the Benson Amendment, and the 'Original Understanding' of the Federal Judiciary," in *Benson, First Chief Judge,* reprinted in expanded form in *Buffalo Law Review* 36 (1987):341.

dolph's report sought to avoid the clash of state and federal jurisdiction. His proposal identified a narrow group of categories that were to be subject exclusively to federal jurisdiction, but otherwise provided for concurrent state court jurisdiction over federally created rights; the opportunity to transfer claims based on federally created rights from state to federal court before trial was to replace the appellate jurisdiction of the Supreme Court of the United States to review state court judgments; and federal jurisdiction under the "all writs" provision of the Judiciary Act was to be abolished.

Benson countered Randolph's proposals on the last day of the First Congress by offering a lengthy, detailed amendment to the Constitution, which in part was a reductio ad absurdum of Randolph's restructuring of the federal court system.[43] Benson's amendment would have created a "General Judicial Court" in each state, which could have been fashioned from the existing state trial courts of general jurisdiction, and vested such courts with original jurisdiction "in all cases to which the judicial power of the United States doth extend" and exclusive immediate appellate jurisdiction over all other state courts. The catches were that the general judicial courts were to be subject to congressional regulation and their judges to hold their commissions during good behavior, be paid by the federal government, and be impeachable in the House of Representatives. In addition, to the extent that Congress chose to replace the existing federal district courts by the general judicial courts, the federal judges were to be transferred to the new courts. Finally, although the states were authorized to establish appellate courts of last resort to hear appeals from the general judicial courts, that jurisdiction would be limited to cases to which the existing jurisdiction of the Supreme Court of the United States did not extend.

Benson's amendment thus accepted the premise of Randolph's report — that the clash of state and federal jurisdiction must be avoided — and then took it to the logical extreme of creating a single, unified court system exercising both state and federal jurisdiction. To protect federal interests, however, Benson postulated, in Professor Holt's words, "a degree of supervision by the Supreme Court (via

---

[43]*DHSC,* 4:168–72.

appeals) and by Congress (via legislation regulating State judges and judicial officials) which would amount to a conversion of the State judiciaries into subordinate adjuncts of the national. . . . Benson's amendment would have been a giant step along the path toward consolidation of the States into the federal government."[44] The supporters of proposals similar to Randolph's report understood Benson's warning and stepped back. Randolph's report and the Benson amendment were quietly buried by the Second Congress, together in an unmarked grave.

Egbert Benson and the Trial of President Andrew Johnson on Articles of Impeachment

The first order of business of the House of Representatives at the first session of the First Congress was to create a source of national revenue by establishing a system of import duties. Upon substantial completion of that task, the House moved on, beginning on May 19, 1789, to a series of bills to establish the executive departments of the federal government. No sooner had these discussions begun than the House found itself seriously embroiled in the first full-scale debate on the meaning of the Constitution — the existence and scope of the presidential power of removal. James Madison's role in those debates was probably the most prominent, as it usually was, but otherwise the most active and steadfast of the Federalist leaders for a strong and streamlined executive in general, and for a constitutionally mandated presidential removal power in particular, was Benson; after winning Madison's support on the latter point, his was the position that prevailed. Its consequences would be vital to the outcome of the impeachment trial of President Andrew Johnson nearly eighty years later.

Madison's proposal for the creation of the three executive departments — Foreign Affairs, Treasury, and War — concluded with a clause authorizing the removal of the heads of those departments by the president. An immediate Antifederalist objection was that the only constitutional means for such removal was by congressional impeachment. Both Madison and Benson promptly spoke out against this inter-

---

[44]Holt in *Benson, First Chief Judge*, p. 51.

pretation. But a second constitutional argument—that the "constitution declares, that the president and the senate shall appoint, and it naturally follows, that the power which appoints shall remove also"— drew from Benson a statement of position more extreme than Madison's proposal: according to Benson, no legislative provision was necessary "because the power [of removal] was given to the president by the constitution."[45]

In May and again for a week in mid-June 1789, the House engaged in intense debate on this subject, with Madison moving toward Benson's construction of the Constitution in strongly worded addresses on June 16 and 17 that emphasized the distinctness of the legislative and executive branches.[46] Benson weighed in against the argument that the Senate should participate in removals and an alternative suggestion that would have granted the president the power to suspend, but not to remove, without the concurrence of the Senate.[47] Perhaps most dramatic was the presentation on June 19 by Abraham Baldwin of Georgia, a member of the Federal Convention, who decried the accusation that those who did not agree that the Senate should participate in removals, as in appointments, were violating the Constitution. Baldwin continued, "the mingling of the powers of the president and senate was strongly opposed in the convention. . . . Some gentlemen opposed it to the last; and finally it was the principal ground on which they refused to give it their signature and assent. One gentleman called it a monstrous and unnatural connection; and did not hesitate to affirm, it would bring on convulsions in the government."[48] On June 22, after several days of more debate, Benson proposed two amendments to the Department of Foreign Affairs bill that were expressly intended to recognize the power of removal he believed the Constitution vested in the president and to strike from the pending legislation the words "removable by the President of the United States" to avoid any suggestion that the removal power was congressionally granted. Both motions carried, Madison expressly adopting the reasons stated by Benson.[49] Much of the same ground was covered in understandably melodramatic debates

---

[45]*DHFFC*, 10:718–40.
[46]Ibid., 11:866, 895, 921.
[47]Ibid., 11:902, 931.
[48]Ibid., 11:1003–4.
[49]Ibid., 11:1026–36; 3:91–96.

when this legislation went in July to the Senate, whose equal division was resolved by the tie-breaking vote of Vice President John Adams.[50] This action by Congress not only strengthened the presidency, it also was an intentional and significant curtailment of the power of the Senate and of the state legislatures for which the Senate was a surrogate in our original bicameral national legislature.

As significant as the merits of the debate that Benson and Madison led was the perception repeatedly articulated by Madison that Congress was engaged in giving a binding construction of the meaning of the Constitution and that it had the power and the right to do so:

> [June 17, 1789] I feel the importance of the question before us, as our decision will be a permanent exposition of the constitution in this point, and as on this decision will depend, in a great degree, the genius and character of our government. On the determination which will now take place, will depend perhaps the preservation of the government on that equal balance which the constitution designed. It is therefore of the utmost importance that we weigh the subject with the most cautious deliberation.
>
> [June 18, 1789] Nothing has yet been offered to invalidate the doctrine, that the meaning of the constitution may as well be ascertained by the legislative as by the judicial authority. When a question emerges as it does in this bill, and much seems to depend upon it, I should conceive it highly proper to make a legislative construction.[51]

The debates of the First Congress on the removal power, its decision — elevated, as a lawyer would say, from dictum to holding by the approval of Benson's motions on June 22, 1789 — that the Constitution vested that power solely in the president, and the deference to be accorded that decision as precedent would all figure largely in the impeachment trial of President Andrew Johnson in the U.S. Senate in the winter and spring of 1868.[52]

---

[50]See Bowling, *Politics in the First Congress*, pp. 98–100; Charlene Bangs Bickford and Kenneth R. Bowling, *Birth of the Nation: The First Federal Congress, 1789–1791* (New York, 1989), pp. 37, 41–42; Anderson, *Creating the Constitution*, pp. 185–90.

[51]*DHFFC*, 11:895 (June 17, 1789) and 987 (June 18, 1789). See Jack N. Rakove, *Original Meanings: Politics and Ideas in the Making of the Constitution* (New York, 1977), pp. 347–50.

[52]See, generally, John Niven, *Salmon P. Chase* (New York, 1995), pp. 415–26; William H. Rehnquist, *Grand Inquests* (New York, 1992), pp. 143–261.

In brief, the formal charge against President Johnson was that he had violated the Tenure of Office Act of 1867 by removing Edwin Stanton as secretary of war after the Senate had overridden Johnson's exercise of his power under the act to suspend Stanton during its recess. The Tenure of Office Act provided that cabinet officers were "subject to removal by and with the advice and consent of the Senate."

On April 9, 1868, after two weeks of trial, President Johnson's counsel, Benjamin Robbins Curtis, a former associate justice of the Supreme Court who had dissented and then resigned because of the Court's decision in the *Dred Scott* case, opened the case for the defense. Not long into his speech, Curtis framed the constitutional defense that was advanced for the president — that the Tenure of Office Act was an unconstitutional infringement on his powers. For support, Curtis turned first to the debates in the First Congress and to Benson's resolutions specifically:

> Now, it is a rule long settled, existing, I suppose, in all civilized countries, certainly in every system of law that I have any acquaintance with, that a contemporary exposition of a law made by those who were competent to give it a construction is of very great weight; and that when such contemporary exposition has been made of a law, and it has been followed by an actual and practical construction in accordance with that contemporary exposition, continued during a long period of time and applied to great number of cases, it is afterwards too late to call into question the correctness of such a construction. . . . I desire to bring before the Senate in this connection, inasmuch as I think the subject has been frequently misunderstood, the form taken by that debate of 1789 and the result that was attained. In order to do so, and at the same time to avoid fatiguing your attention by looking minutely into the debate itself, I beg leave to read a passage from Chief Justice [John] Marshall's Life of Washington: . . . "To obviate any misunderstanding of the principle on which the question has been decided, Mr. Benson moved in the House, when the report of the Committee of the Whole was taken up, to amend the second clause in the bill so as clearly to imply the power of removal to be solely in the President. He gave notice that if he should succeed in this he would move to strike out the words which had been the subject of debate. If those words continued, he said, the power of removal by the President might hereafter appear to be exercised by virtue of a legislative grant only, and consequently be

subjected to legislative instability; when he was well satisfied in his own mind it was by fair construction fixed by the Constitution. The motion was seconded by Mr. Madison, and both amendments were adopted. As the bill passed into a law, it has been considered as a full expression of the sense of the legislature on this important part of the American Constitution."[53]

This argument was repeated again and again by President Johnson's defenders.[54] The whole sorry spectacle of the consequences of the Tenure of Office Act had been foretold in the 1789 debates, not only by Madison, but also by Benson:

I will not repeat what has been said to prove that the true construction is, that the president alone has the power of removal; but will state a case to shew the embarrassment which must arise by a combination of the senatorial and legislative authority in this particular. I will instance the officer to which the bill relates. To him will necessarily be committed negociations with the ministers of foreign courts. This is a very delicate trust. The supreme executive officer, in superintending this department, may be entangled with suspicions of a very delicate nature, relative to the transactions of the officer; and such as from circumstances would be injurious to name; indeed he may be so situated that he will not, cannot give the evidence of his suspicion. Now, thus circumstanced, suppose he should propose to the senate to remove the secretary of foreign affairs, are we to expect the senate will, without any reason being assigned, implicitly submit to his proposition? They will not. Suppose he should say he suspected the man's fidelity, they would say we must proceed farther, and know the reasons for this suspicion; they would insist on a full communication. Is it to be supposed that this man will not have a single friend in the senate who will contend for a fair trial and full hearing? The president then becomes the plaintiff, and the secretary the defendant. The senate are sitting in judgment between the chief magistrate of the United States, and a subordinate officer. Now, I submit to the candor of the gentlemen, whether this looks like good government?[55]

---

[53] *Trial of Andrew Johnson, President of the United States, on Impeachment for High Crime and Misdemeanors,* 3 vols. (Washington, D.C., 1868), 1:388–89. For an interpretation at odds with Chief Justice Marshall's, see David P. Currie, *The Constitution in Congress: The Federalist Period, 1789–1801* (Chicago, 1997), pp. 36–41.

[54] *Trial of Andrew Johnson,* 2:155–56, 202–4, 315–18.

[55] *DHFFC,* 11:931–34.

The Fugitive Slave Act of 1793

The Second Congress had several noisy and rancorous disputes: in its first session, on the apportionment of representation among the states in the House of Representatives, and in its second, on "the unsuccessful Republican effort in the House of Representatives to censure Alexander Hamilton's administration as Secretary of the Treasury and bring about his removal from office."[56] In the former controversy Benson was active in the debates, but he seems to have left visible leadership on the floor in opposing William Branch Giles's censure resolutions to John Laurance, another of Hamilton's staunch political allies in the New York delegation. From the vantage point of the historian at the end of the twentieth century, however, neither of these controversies touches in significance a piece of legislation, originating in the Senate, which passed the House by nearly unanimous concurrence, including Benson's, on February 5, 1793, after a brief debate the day before merely noted in the *Annals:* the four-section "Act respecting Fugitives from Justice, and Persons escaping from the Service of their Masters," which was signed into law a week later by President George Washington.[57]

The legislative history of this statute, which has come to be known as the Fugitive Slave Act of 1793, was recounted in *Prigg v. Pennsylvania,*[58] in which its constitutionality was sustained, and most recently by historian Paul Finkelman.[59] The act, as its title suggests, separately addressed the apprehension and removal of fugitives either from justice or from slavery and had its origins in a dispute between Virginia and Pennsylvania. In brief, in 1788 John Davis, a slave who had earned his freedom from his master's failure to comply with Pennsylvania's 1780 emancipation statute, was taken by his master to Virginia and put out for hire. Abolitionists rescued him and brought him back to Pennsylvania. The Virginian to whom he had been hired out then arranged to

---

[56] *The Papers of Thomas Jefferson,* 27 vols. to date (Princeton, 1950–), vol. 25 (John Catanzariti, Eugene R. Sheridan, and J. Jefferson Looney, eds.), p. 280.

[57] U.S., *Statutes at Large,* 1:302. On Giles's resolutions, see the article by Mary A. Giunta in this volume.

[58] *Prigg v. Pennsylvania,* 41 U.S. 539 (1842).

[59] Paul Finkelman, *Slavery and the Founders: Race and Liberty in the Age of Jefferson* (Armonk, N.Y., 1996), pp. 81–98.

have Davis kidnapped in Pennsylvania and forcibly returned to Virginia. Indictments were returned in Pennsylvania against the kidnappers, and in June 1791 Thomas Mifflin, the governor of Pennsylvania, requested the assistance of the governor of Virginia to extradite the accused and to free Davis. The sophistry of the attorney general of Virginia and the claim that Davis was a fugitive slave led its governor to refuse Pennsylvania's request, and Governor Mifflin laid the dispute before President Washington, who in turn referred it to Congress in October 1791. An initial fugitive slave bill in the House never reached a vote, and it was not until a year later that a series of three bills was considered by the Senate, varying in the protections to be accorded alleged slaves in the state where found and in the role imposed on local authorities in the process of arrest and removal. The changes in the bills reflect serious disagreements in the Senate, whose debates were closed to the public; by the time the measure reached the House for concurrence, the balance had been struck and the action by the House was pro forma.

The Fugitive Slave Act of 1793 generated far fewer reported proceedings than its relatively short-lived successor, the Fugitive Slave Act of 1850, technically an amendment and supplement of the 1793 statute but in fact legislation that created a broader, national enforcement system. The 1793 act was before the Supreme Court a second time in *Jones* v. *Van Zandt*, 46 U.S. 215 (1847), a proceeding which occupied the U.S. Circuit Court for the District of Ohio between 1843 and 1851. In that case, the Supreme Court sustained against constitutional and other challenges the award of the statutory penalty prescribed by the 1793 act against a farmer on his way home from market who had given a lift in his wagon in broad daylight to a group of fugitive slaves, one of whom was able to escape when the wagon was overtaken by their pursuers.[60] The decisions of the Supreme Court in *Prigg* and *Jones*, to-

---

[60]Paul Finkelman, *Slavery in the Courtroom* (Washington, D.C., 1985), pp. 71–74; see also Robert M. Cover, *Justice Accused: Antislavery and the Judicial Process* (New Haven, Conn., 1975), pp. 243–49; Niven, *Salmon P. Chase*, pp. 76–84; John Niven, ed., *The Salmon P. Chase Papers*, 3 vols. to date (Kent, Ohio, 1993–), 2:134–54. (Chase wrote to Charles Sumner that, upon being informed of the Supreme Court's decision affirming the judgment against him, Van Zandt said to Chase that " 'if a single word could restore the man who escaped and save me from all sacrifice, I would not utter it.' And such I believe is the universal spirit of those who have aided the oppressed in regaining their freedom.")

gether with several decisions by Justice John McLean on circuit in *Jones*,[61] form the bulk of the accessible published materials about proceedings brought under the 1793 act, a collection which is dwarfed by the reports of the many hotly contested removal proceedings and criminal prosecutions under the 1850 act, particularly in abolitionist Boston.[62] The enforcement of the 1850 Fugitive Slave Act was one of the major points of friction between North and South in the decade before the Civil War.

Benson's vote for the Fugitive Slave Act of 1793 was not the only occasion on which he was confronted in Congress with the issue of slavery. Indeed, many of the issues faced by members of the First and Second Congresses—from import duties to representation—had a significant slavery component. But nothing that came before the First Congress was as incendiary as the memorials against slavery and the slave trade, including one signed by Benjamin Franklin.[63] The memorials were referred to a committee, which in substance reported that Congress was powerless, until 1808, to do much about slavery other than to impose the importation tax authorized by the Constitution. Nevertheless, the debate, which began on March 16, 1790, with Benson presiding as chairman of the Committee of the Whole House, was ugly from the moment it started.[64] William Smith of South Carolina referred to the Quakers in the gallery of the House as "evil spirits hovering over our heads."[65] James Jackson of Georgia demanded to know: "Who's to pay me? Are these good people, the Friends, going to pay me? I presume not. In proportion as you injure me in regard to my slaves, in that proportion will (to me) fall—Is not my property as dear

---

[61] 13 F. Cas. 1040 and 1047 (C. C. D. Ohio 1843) (Nos. 7,501 and 7,502); 13 F. Cas. 1054 and 1056 (C. C. D. Ohio 1849) (Nos. 7,503 and 7,504); 13 F. Cas. 1057 (C. C. D. Ohio 1851) (No. 7,505). See also Cover, *Justice Accused*, pp. 159–74. The trial of *Daggs* v. *Frazier*, an action for the statutory penalty under the 1793 act brought in the U.S. District Court for Iowa, is reported in a pamphlet published in 1850 and reprinted in Paul Finkelman, ed., *Fugitive Slaves and the American Courts*, 4 vols. (New York, 1988), 1:495–534.

[62] Reprints of these pamphlets may be found in Finkelman, *Fugitive Slaves*, vols. 2–4.

[63] See William C. diGiacomantonio, "'For the Gratification of a Volunteering Society': Antislavery and Pressure Group Politics in the First Federal Congress," *Journal of the Early Republic* 15 (1995):169.

[64] *DHFFC*, vol. 12 (Helen E. Veit, Charlene Bangs Bickford, Kenneth R. Bowling, and William C. diGiacomantonio, eds.), p. 718.

[65] Ibid., 12:719.

to me as a man's person is to him?"[66] He pointed out that "the Union had received the different states with all their ill habits about them. This was one of these habits established long before the constitution, and could not now be remedied." He concluded by claiming that the Quakers "came forward to blow the trumpet of sedition, and to destroy that constitution, which they had not in the least contributed by personal service or supply to establish."[67]

The agony continued for a second day. Aedanus Burke of South Carolina assured the House that slaves were housed more comfortably than poor whites and that families were not broken. He heaped scorn on the Quakers, questioning their motives and patriotism.[68] Smith of South Carolina relied on Jefferson's *Notes on the State of Virginia* to establish the natural inferiority of blacks and argued that slavery had been accepted from antiquity. He then proceeded to disparage the patriotism of the Quakers and argued that "he could not help observing that this squeamishness was very extraordinary at this time. The Northern states knew the Southern states had slaves before they confederated with them. If they had such an abhorrence for slavery, why . . . did they not cast us off and reject our alliance?" Smith argued that the Northern states knew that slavery could not be eradicated in the South and had accepted the South with its slaves, just as the South accepted the North with its Quakers.[69] A voice raised against the criticisms of the Quakers' motives toward the end of the day was quickly met with the retort that Congress should not "gratify people who had never been friendly to the independence of America."[70]

Early the next day Benson rose to try to stop the carnage. He moved to discharge the committee of the whole and to recommit the bill "to strike out every word of it as not material." Echoing the committee report, he argued that the debate was "a perfect waste of time" and that "it does not appear that Congress can make any law."[71] He was seconded by others who pointed out that all other businesses had

---

[66]Ibid., 12:720.
[67]Ibid., 12:734.
[68]Ibid., 12:738.
[69]Ibid., 12:749–61.
[70]Ibid., 12:762.
[71]Ibid., 12:763.

ground to a halt and that the Quakers' proposals had already been rejected by the Senate unanimously.[72] But both sides were too inflamed
to heed the voice of reason, and Benson's motion lost.[73] The Southerners then began introducing resolutions of their own for acknowledgment of constitutional limitations on congressional powers over
the slave trade and emancipation.[74] The debates finally burned themselves out on March 23 in an astute compromise sponsored by Madison. Benson never spoke again. In a letter written at the close of these
debates Fisher Ames of Massachusetts spoke of:

> the violence, personality, low wit, violation of order, and rambling
> from the point, which have lowered the House extremely in the debate
> on the Quaker memorial. . . . The Quakers have been abused, the
> eastern states inveighed against, the chairman rudely charged with par-
> tiality. . . . The southern gentry have been guided by their hot tempers,
> and stubborn prejudices and pride in regard to southern importance
> and negro slavery; but I suspect the wish to appear in the eyes of their
> own people, champions for their black property, is influencial — an
> election this year makes it the more probable.[75]

At the outset of the Second Congress further Quaker memorials were
presented on the subject of slavery. On December 8, 1791, the memorials were referred to a committee chaired by Benson and never heard
of again.[76]

Benson's apparently unresisting support for such iniquitous legislation as the Fugitive Slave Act and his effort to stifle the Quaker protests
appear paradoxical in light of the evidence that he was personally
opposed to slavery. First, John Jay, the patriarch of a veritable tribe
of abolitionists, counted Benson as a trusted and intimate personal
friend and, while on a diplomatic mission to Spain in 1780, confided
to him in a letter: "An excellent law might be made out of the Pennsylvania one for the gradual abolition of slavery. Till America comes into

---

[72]Ibid., 12:773–76.

[73]Ibid., 12:767.

[74]Ibid., 12:769.

[75]Seth Ames, ed., *Works of Fisher Ames*, 2 vols. (1854, reprint ed., Indianapolis, 1983),
1:729–31.

[76]Joseph Gales, Jr., and William W. Seaton, comp., *Annals of the Congress of the United
States*, 42 vols. (Washington, D.C., 1834–56), 2:241.

this measure, her prayers to Heaven for liberty will be impious. This is a strong expression but it is just. Were I in your legislature, I would prepare a bill for the purpose with great care, and I would never leave moving it till it became a law or I ceased to be a member. I believe God governs this world, and I believe it to be a maxim in His as in our court, that those who ask for equity ought to do it."[77] It is improbable that Jay would have written this to someone who was not at least sympathetic with his views. It seems clear that Benson was, for, after New York enacted a comprehensive antislavery statute in February 1788,[78] the first person in Poughkeepsie, where he lived, to record a manumission in conformity with the law was Egbert Benson.[79]

After completion of his service in Congress in 1793 and his elevation to the Supreme Court of the State of New York in 1794, Benson was called upon to construe the 1788 New York antislavery statute and refused to join his fellow judges, including James Kent, in creating an exception into the act's prohibition of the sale of slaves. That case, *Sable* v. *Hitchcock,* involved the sale of a slave by an executor. Under the statute, sale of the slave by the deceased while living would have been prohibited, but a majority of the court held that the act would not apply to sales by persons, like executors, on whom the duty to marshal and sell assets devolved by law. Application of the statute in such a case, said Justice Jacob Radcliff, "would be highly injurious to creditors . . . and extremely embarrassing to persons acting in these capacities." Benson, the sole dissenter, would have none of it. His solution was to treat the deceased's ownership interest in the slave as terminating when the owner died; otherwise, said Benson, "there may be a sale of a slave, as a slave, and neither the seller be liable to the penalty, nor the slave be free, which is contrary to the express provision of the act."[80] Benson would have awarded judgment to the plaintiff—her freedom.

Finally, in the notes to the second edition of his *Memoir Read before the Historical Society of the State of New-York, December 31, 1816,* Benson

---

[77]Henry P. Johnston, ed., *The Correspondence and Public Papers of John Jay,* 4 vols. (New York, 1890–93), 1:406–7.

[78]"An Act Concerning Slaves," 11th Sess., chap. 40 (Feb. 22, 1788), *Laws of the State of New York* (1792), 2:85.

[79]Edmund Platt, *The Eagle's History of Poughkeepsie from the Earliest Settlements, 1683 to 1905* (Poughkeepsie, N.Y., 1905), p. 63.

[80]*Sable* v. *Hitchcock,* 2 Johnson's Cases (1800), pp. 79, 84, 88.

added the following passage: "*Negro* slavery, common, at the time, to all the colonies on our continent, whichsoever of the European States the metropolitan — so far, perhaps, in extenuation. A milder form of it than among the Dutch of New-Netherland, scarcely to be imagined. . . . Still he was a slave, *subject* to the *will* of *another*, his fellow-man; and assignable, as the 'beast, born to bear labour;' and surely not among the least of the mercies calling for praise; it has been given to us in these latter days to see the injustice of the bondage."[81] The absence of any explanation from the lips or pen of Benson himself relegates to informed surmise resolution of the seeming paradox between his personal beliefs and his public behavior. That it is a paradox at all may be in fact only in its appearance to us at the end of the twentieth century, not to him two hundred years ago. Benson was probably simply demonstrating the Federalist willingness to pay the price of slavery as part of a larger potential compromise for an invigorated national government under the Constitution.[82]

The immorality of slavery and particularly the slave trade was squarely presented at the Philadelphia Convention in 1787. Its apologists were the Federalists, especially those in the delegation from Connecticut; the most outspoken opponent was a Southerner, George Mason of Virginia. The following exchange on August 22, 1787, between Mason and Oliver Ellsworth, a future chief justice of the Supreme Court, is illustrative:

[Mason] Every master of slaves is born a petty tyrant. They bring the judgment of heaven on a Country. As nations can not be rewarded or punished in the next world they must be in this. By an inevitable chain of causes & effects providence punishes national sins, by national calamities. He lamented that some of our Eastern brethren had from a lust of gain embarked in this nefarious traffic. As to the States being in possession of the Right to import, this was the case with many other rights, now to be properly given up. He held it essential in every point of view that the Genl. Govt. should have power to prevent the increase of slavery.

[Ellsworth] As he had never owned a slave could not judge of the

---

[81]Egbert Benson, *Memoir Read before the Historical Society of the State of New-York, December 31, 1816* (Jamaica, N.Y., 1825), pp. 105–6.

[82]Lynd, *Class Conflict*, pp. 185–213.

effects of slavery on character: He said however that if it was to be considered in a moral light we ought to go farther and free those already in the Country. — As slaves also multiply so fast in Virginia & Maryland that it is cheaper to raise than import them, whilst in the sickly rice swamps foreign supplies are necessary, if we go no farther than is urged, we shall be unjust towards S. Carolina & Georgia. Let us not intermeddle. As population increases poor laborers will be so plenty as to render slaves useless. Slavery in time will not be a speck in our Country. Provision is already made in Connecticut for abolishing it. And the abolition has already taken place in Massachusetts. As to the danger of insurrections from foreign influence, that will become a motive to kind treatment of the slaves.[83]

The same argument continued in the ratification debates. James Wilson, the future associate justice of the Supreme Court, argued to the delegates to the Pennsylvania ratification convention:

Under the present confederation, the states may admit the importation of slaves as long as they please; but by this article after the year 1808, the Congress will have power to prohibit such importation, notwithstanding the disposition of any state to the contrary. I consider this as laying the foundation for banishing slavery out of this country; and though the period is more distant than I could wish, yet it will produce the same kind, gradual change, which was pursued in Pennsylvania. It is with much satisfaction I view this power in the general government, whereby they may lay an interdiction on this reproachful trade; but an immediate advantage is also obtained, for a tax or duty may be imposed on such importation, not exceeding ten dollars for each person; and this, sir, operates as a partial prohibition. It was all that could be obtained, I was sorry it was no more.[84]

James Madison, facing another blast from George Mason about "this detestable kind of commerce" at the Virginia ratification convention, defended the constitutional clause extending the slave trade to 1808: "I should conceive this clause to be impolitic, if it were one of those things which could be excluded without encountering greater evils.

---

[83]Max Farrand, ed., *The Records of the Federal Convention of 1787*, 4 vols. (New Haven, 1911), 2:370–71.

[84]Merrill Jensen, ed., *The Documentary History of the Ratification of the Constitution*, 13 vols. to date (Madison, 1976–), 2:463.

The Southern States would not have entered into the union of America, without the temporary permission of that trade. . . . Great as the evil is, a dismemberment of the union would be worse."[85] Similarly, *Federalist* no. 38 argued: "Is the importation of slaves permitted by the new Constitution for twenty years? By the old, it is permitted for ever."[86]

The Fugitive Slave Act of 1793 merely implemented Article IV, section 2, paragraph 3 of the Constitution, which required the return of fugitive slaves.[87] Justice Story wrote of that paragraph in *Prigg*:

> Historically, it is well known, that the object of this clause was to secure the citizens of the slaveholding states the complete right and title of ownership in their slaves, as property, in every state in the Union into which they might escape from the state where they were held in servitude. The full recognition of this right and title was indispensable to the security of this species of property in all the slaveholding states; and, indeed, was so vital to their domestic interests and institutions, that it cannot be doubted that it constituted a fundamental article, without the adoption of which the Union could not have been formed.[88]

By the time the fugitive slave bill reached the House in February 1793, the debate was over. The issue had been settled, for the time being, with the ratification of the Constitution.

Conclusion

This brief examination of Egbert Benson's congressional career illustrates his Federalist convictions — that is, his unwavering support of a strong national government. Passing the ambiguities of the Fourth Amendment, he stands out, just as Kent said, for the steadfastness of his efforts to maximize the powers of the executive branch and to protect the national judiciary against encroachments urged by those who wished to defer to state sovereignty. In addition, although Kent never mentions it, Benson demonstrated time and again an amazing

---

[85]Ibid., vol. 10 (John P. Kaminski, Gaspare J. Saladino, Richard Leffler, Charles H. Schoenleber, et al., eds.), p. 1339.

[86]Benjamin F. Wright, ed., *The Federalist* (Cambridge, Mass., 1961), pp. 272, 278.

[87]See generally Finkelman, *Slavery and the Founders*, pp. 1–33, 80–104.

[88]U.S., *Statutes at Large*, 41:611.

parliamentary adroitness. But in their single-mindedness to promote a union with a strong central government, Benson and his fellow Feder-alists were prepared to implement legislatively the compromise on slavery made by the Founding Fathers at the Philadelphia Convention, despite the warnings of the Quakers. The terrible consequences of their impotence to confront as statesmen the wrong most of them rec-ognized as people — indeed, their willingness to collaborate with it — tarnishes their otherwise brilliant and lasting record of achievement.

Elizabeth M. Nuxoll

The Financier as Senator

Robert Morris of Pennsylvania, 1789–1795

THE FIRST U.S. SENATE was Robert Morris's last hurrah. When he entered office on March 4, 1789, at the age of fifty-four, he had been a merchant for nearly forty years and a politician for fourteen. As a partner in firms in Philadelphia, Baltimore, Richmond, New York, and Charleston, with affiliates or "friends" throughout the United States, Europe, Asia, and the West Indies, he was at the center of a global commercial network. He had served in the Continental Congress, the Pennsylvania Assembly, and the Federal Convention and had held executive office for four years (1781–84) as superintendent of finance of the United States, in which post he was popularly referred to as "The Financier." He was one of only two men who signed the Declaration of Independence, the Articles of Confederation, and the Constitution. Morris (fig. 1) was regarded as the leader of Pennsylvania's Republican or Anti-Constitutionalist party and of the nationalist movement seeking to strengthen the union and develop greater

This paper is derived in part from project research of The Papers of Robert Morris, 1781–1784, at Queens College of the City University of New York and reflects the efforts of all staff members. The project is supported by grants from the National Endowment for the Humanities and the National Historical Publications and Records Commission, and by matching funds from various private foundations, organizations, and individual contributions. In citations below, *Morris Papers* refer to E. James Ferguson, John Catanzariti, Elizabeth M. Nuxoll, and Mary A. Gallagher, eds., *The Papers of Robert Morris, 1781–1784*, 9 vols. (Pittsburgh, 1973–99).

FIG. 1. *Robert Morris,* by Gilbert Stuart, circa 1795. *(Courtesy Smithsonian Institution)*

centralized power. He was a close friend of George Washington and was well acquainted with most of the other congressmen and public officials with whom he served. He was thus a man of enormous influence and prestige.[1]

Yet, at the time he took office, he also was both financially and politically beleaguered. He had suffered financial reverses under a

---

[1]For an overview of Morris's administration as superintendent of finance, see Clarence L. Ver Steeg, *Robert Morris, Revolutionary Financier, with an Analysis of his Earlier Career* (Philadelphia, 1954); E. James Ferguson, *The Power of the Purse: A History of American Public Finance, 1776–1790* (Chapel Hill, 1961); idem, "The Nationalists of 1781–1783 and the Economic Interpretation of the Constitution," *Journal of American History* 56 (1969):241–61; Jack N. Rakove, *The Beginnings of National Politics: An Interpretive History of the Continental Congress* (Baltimore, 1979), pp. 297–329, 337–42; and [Robert Morris], *A Statement of the Accounts of the United States of America . . . 1784* [Philadelphia, 1785]. For general biographies of Morris, see Ellis Paxson Oberholtzer, *Robert Morris, Patriot and Financier* (1894; reprint ed., New York, 1968); William Graham Sumner, *The Financier and the Finances of the American Revolution,* 2 vols. (1892; reprint ed., New York, 1970); Eleanor Young, *Forgotten Patriot: Robert Morris* (New York, 1950); and Frederick Wagner, *Robert Morris, Audacious Patriot* (New York, 1976). These works should be consulted for additional information on the topics discussed in this chapter. On Morris's business network, see also Robert A. East, *Business Enterprise in the American Revolutionary Era* (New York, 1938), pp. 126–48, 285–91; and Thomas M. Doerflinger,

tobacco contract with the French Farmers General,[2] and he had been publicly embarrassed when a fearful partner in England allowed a large number of his bills of exchange to return protested (in effect, his checks bounced).[3] His political enemies gleefully reported his difficulties in the press. Opponents of the Constitution also were exploiting longstanding charges related to his failure to settle his public accounts with the secret and commercial committees of Congress early in the Revolutionary War, and they alleged he had thwarted efforts of the Confederation Congress to create an independent commission to inquire into his administration and investigate his accounts as superin-

---

A Vigorous Spirit of Enterprise: Merchants and Economic Development in Revolutionary Phila-delphia (Chapel Hill, 1986), pp. 163, 212–14, 236–41, 291–92. On Morris as a leader of the Republican or Anticonstitutionalist party of Pennsylvania, see Roland M. Baumann, "The Democratic-Republicans of Philadelphia: The Origins, 1776–1797," Ph.D. diss., Pennsylvania State University, 1970, pp. 30–32, 56–57; Robert L. Brunhouse, *The Counter-Revolution in Pennsylvania, 1776–1790* (Harrisburg, Pa., 1942), pp. 20–30, 60–61, 89–112, 131–35, 167–96, 216, 222–23 passim; and Douglas McNeil Arnold, "Political Ideology and the Internal Revolution in Pennsylvania, 1776–1790," Ph.D. diss., Princeton University, 1976, pp. 63, 200–208, 216–20, 318–19.

There are many portraits of Robert Morris (hereafter RM) and his family. Those dating from the period of his service in the Senate include a portrait by Edward Savage, circa 1790, now at the Historical Society of Pennsylvania, and "Congress Voting Independence" by Robert Edge Pine and Edward Savage, in which a similar portrait of RM is included. Remaining in family hands are miniatures of RM and Mary White Morris by John Trumbull, 1790, and portraits of RM and his daughters Esther (Hetty) and Maria, done by Gilbert Stuart in the 1790s. Copies of portraits and etchings based on them done by H. B. Hall and Albert Rosenthal are also extant. RM is also included in "The Declaration of Independence, Philadelphia, July 4, 1776," by John Trumbull (1786 to before 1797), now in the Yale University Art Gallery, the enlarged version of which is installed in the rotunda of the Capitol in Washington, D.C. Though purporting to show RM in the Continental Congress, the image presented is of Morris in the 1790s.

[2]See Agreement with William Alexander and Jonathan Williams, Jr., March 2, 1784, and notes, *Morris Papers*, 9:150–59; Jacob M. Price, *France and the Chesapeake: A History of the French Tobacco Monopoly, 1674–1791, and of Its Relationship to the British and American Tobacco Trades* (Ann Arbor, Mich., 1973), pp. 738–87; and Frederick L. Nussbaum, "American Tobacco and French Politics, 1783–1789," *Political Science Quarterly* 40 (1925):497–516, and "The Revolutionary Vergennes and Lafayette versus the Farmers General," *Journal of Modern History* 3 (1931):592–604. See also the documents on the tobacco contracts, the efforts to implement them, and the subsequent disputes found in the Arents Collection, the Constable-Pierrepont Papers, and the Robert Morris Papers, all New York Public Library, and in the Tilghman Papers and Account Books, Maryland Historical Society. On RM's positive attitude toward Thomas Jefferson despite the problems caused him by Jefferson's role in promoting the Berni decision limiting his tobacco contract, see RM to Gouverneur Morris, Jan. 3 and Feb. 1, 1790, Gouverneur Morris Papers, Columbia University (NNC).

[3]See RM to John Rucker, June 18, 1784, and notes, *Morris Papers*, 9:407–19.

tendent of finance.[4] His term as senator marked the fulfillment of many of the goals he had developed as superintendent of finance, yet it simultaneously saw him marching inexorably to ultimate bankruptcy and imprisonment for debt.

The story of Morris's Senate career has elements of comedy and tragedy, and more than a little soap opera. But, for the most part, it is a story told by an "unreliable narrator," his fellow senator from Pennsylvania, William Maclay. Maclay's portrait is the fullest and most detailed description available of Morris in action.[5] But it is marred by Maclay's previous unfamiliarity with Morris, by his outsider status that often kept him in the dark about the inner workings of political intrigues

---

[4]For RM's response to attacks on him as a public defaulter, see his letter to the editor, printed in the *Independent Gazetteer* (Philadelphia), Apr. 8, 1788 [*Morris Papers*, 9:630–32], and reprinted in the *Freeman's Journal* (Philadelphia), Apr. 9, the *Pennsylvania Mercury* (Philadelphia), Apr. 10, the *Federal Gazette* (Philadelphia), Apr. 15, and the *Carlisle Gazette*, Apr. 23, 1788. He was probably responding to "A Friend to the People," published in the *Freeman's Journal* of March 12 and the *Independent Gazetteer* of March 13. For other attacks, see "Centinel," X (*Independent Gazetteer*, Jan. 12, 1788), XVI (Feb. 26, 1788), XVII (Mar. 24, 1788), XXIII (Nov. 20, 1788), and XXIV (Nov. 24, 1788), all reprinted in John Bach McMaster and Frederick D. Stone, eds., *Pennsylvania and the Federal Constitution, 1787–1788*, 2 vols. (1888; reprint ed., New York, 1970), 2:630–33, 657–64, 691–98, 787–89; "One of the People," cited by "Centinel" (XXIII) as also written by himself, and "Public Justice," *Independent Gazetteer*, Apr. 17 and Nov. 26, 1788; Edward Fox to Andrew Craigie, Nov. 30, 1789, Craigie Papers, American Antiquarian Society; *The Documentary History of the Ratification of the Constitution*, 15 vols. to date (Madison, Wis., 1976–), vol. 2 (Merrill Jensen, ed.), p. 643, and microform supplement; vol. 13 (John P. Kaminski and Gaspare J. Saladino, eds.), pp. 326–28; vol. 16 (Kaminski and Saladino, eds.), pp. 217–20, 475–77; *The Documentary History of the First Federal Elections, 1788–1790*, 4 vols. (Madison, Wis., 1976–89), vol. 1 (Merrill Jensen and Robert A. Becker, eds.), pp. 350–53, 358–60, 367–68, 377. For defenses of RM, see "Z," *Independent Gazetteer*, Mar. 8 and 15, 1788; RM's letter of November 21, 1788, printed in the *Independent Gazetteer*, Nov. 22, 1788; and "Justice," "A Philadelphian," and "Civis," *Federal Gazette*, Nov. 25, 1788, Dec. 11 and 12, 1789; and *Documentary History of the First Federal Elections*, 1:354, 361. "Centinel" 's writings, originally ascribed to Pennsylvania's Constitutionalist party leader George Bryan, were subsequently attributed to his eldest son, Samuel Bryan (1759–1821); his attacks on Morris primarily repeated charges long raised by Arthur Lee of Virginia. See Herbert J. Storing, ed., *The Complete Anti-Federalist*, 6 vols. (Chicago, 1981), 2:130.

[5]See Kenneth R. Bowling and Helen E. Veit, eds., *The Diary of William Maclay and Other Notes on Senate Debates* (Baltimore, 1988), vol. 9 of *Documentary History of the First Federal Congress of the United States of America, March 4, 1789–March 3, 1791*, 14 vols. to date (Baltimore, 1972–), hereafter cited as *DHFFC*. This volume supersedes the earlier edition of the diary: Edgar S. Maclay, ed., *The Journal of William Maclay, United States Senator from Pennsylvania, 1789–1791* (1890; reprint ed., with an introduction by Charles Beard, New York, 1927 and 1965).

and the motives of those involved, and by personal and ideological biases that affected the ways he interpreted the behavior he observed. Furthermore, Maclay's comments are selective and often in a terse, choppy style, leaving his remarks open to many interpretations. Nevertheless, when combined with other documents and viewed in the light of what we have learned about other stages of Morris's career, they provide great insight into the role of one of the first Senate's dominant figures.

Maclay presents varied and often contradictory images of Morris as senator: Morris is a supremely clear, focused, well-informed speaker who can mow down opponents when provoked;[6] he is restless, impatient, reluctant to enter into close reasoning on a new subject;[7] he refuses to speak on most topics, preferring to leave the presentation of ideas and policies to others, whenever possible;[8] he walks out on debates, arrives late, or refuses to attend at all, preferring to spend his time writing letters, organizing his public accounts, or huddling in caucuses negotiating compromises or bargaining for votes;[9] he is frank, confiding, and open with his colleagues;[10] he is sly, wary and secretive, a poker player refusing to reveal his hand;[11] and, in fact, at various times, Morris is all these things, depending on the circumstances and the issues. Which Morris comes to the fore can often be predicted or explained in light of Morris's overall career. I will comment on these various aspects of Morris's modus operandi in the course of the issues in which they emerge, but first I wish to highlight the issues with which Morris was most concerned and emphasize the continuities with his former goals and policies as superintendent of finance and nationalist leader.

In office from 1781 to 1784 and aided by his assistant Gouverneur Morris and other nationalist leaders, Morris had proposed a political and financial agenda that consisted of the following: creation of a national bank to make public loans and create a stable national money

---

[6]Bowling and Veit, *Maclay Diary*, pp. 50, 55, 263–64, 67.
[7]Ibid., p. 50.
[8]Ibid., pp. 48–50, 191, 384.
[9]Ibid., pp. 134–35, 162, 188, 271–72, 282, 297, 330, 342, 357, 361.
[10]Ibid., pp. 56, 357–58.
[11]Ibid., pp. 56, 191, 320.

supply;[12] establishment of an American mint and national coinage;[13] settlement of wartime accounts with various public creditors, including the unpaid army and the civil servants;[14] settlement of accounts between the federal government and the various states, in part to offset each state's conviction it had done more than its share and need contribute little more;[15] adoption of a national funding plan for paying off the public debt, which he believed necessitated a federal right not only to levy taxes but also to collect them under its own authority; state ratification of an amendment to the Articles of Confederation that would permit the U.S. government to levy and collect tariffs on imports as the first and most important revenue for paying its debts; and ratification of an amendment to allow other federal taxes, including excise and land taxes, to cover the remainder of the debt.[16]

As the Revolutionary War came to an end, Morris added some other objectives: obtaining an amendment to allow federal regulation of interstate and international commerce;[17] creating a nationwide common market for goods and financial instruments;[18] retaining access to the various French and Spanish West Indian ports opened to the United States during the war and regaining access to the British West Indies;[19]

---

[12]On RM's plan for the bank and the bank's subsequent evolution, see *Morris Papers*, 1:66–74, 7:795–824, 9:639–85; Elizabeth M. Nuxoll, "The Bank of North America and Robert Morris's Management of the Nation's First Fiscal Crisis," *Business and Economic History* 13 (1984):159–70; George David Rappaport, *Stability and Change in Revolutionary Pennsylvania: Banking, Politics, and Social Structure* (University Park, Pa., 1996), pp. 137–58, and idem, "The Sources and Early Development of the Hostility to Banks in Early American Thought," Ph.D. diss., New York University, 1970, pp. 12–50; and Doerflinger, *Spirit of Enterprise*, pp. 296–310.

[13]*Morris Papers*, 1:304, 4:25–40, 7:737–43.

[14]RM to the President of Congress, Feb. 18, 1782, *Morris Papers*, 4:250–53; Ferguson, *Power of the Purse*, pp. 188–93.

[15]RM to the President of Congress, Aug. 28, 1781, *Morris Papers*, 2:124–39; and Ferguson, *Power of the Purse*, pp. 143–45, 203–19, 306–25, 332–33.

[16]On the impost of 1781 and subsequent funding plans, see RM to the President of Congress, July 29, 1782, and Mar. 8, 1783, and notes, *Morris Papers*, 1:xxii–xxiv, 395–402, 6:36–84, 113–15, 123–26, 7:513–38; and Ver Steeg, *Robert Morris*, pp. 122–31, 174–75, 184–86. On the other federal taxes RM proposed, see *Morris Papers*, 4:356, 603, 604, 616, 618; 6:35, 40, 48, 49, 55–56, 65–66, 91, 206.

[17]*Morris Papers*, 8:66, 543–46; and Frederick W. Marks III, *Independence on Trial: Foreign Affairs and the Making of the Constitution* (Baton Rouge, La., 1973), pp. 72–80, 84–85, 92–93, 146–51, 216–17.

[18]RM to [unknown], Apr. 10, 1783, *Morris Papers*, 7:695.

[19]Ibid., 8:510–11, 542–50, 552–53, 558–59, 681–98; and Marks, *Independence on Trial*, pp. 52–95, 109–12.

opening up new areas of commerce throughout the world and promoting American economic growth generally, especially by encouraging foreign investment;[20] redeveloping a strong national defense system, particularly a navy, once financial circumstances permitted — primarily to defend American commerce and ensure "respect" abroad;[21] and last, but by no means least, returning the seat of Congress to Philadelphia temporarily and securing a permanent residence nearby or at a site along the Delaware River, preferably at the falls near Trenton.[22] By the time Morris entered the Senate on March 4, 1789, he had created the Bank of North America as a national bank but had seen it return to essentially local and private status at war's end.[23] He had presented a plan for a mint and produced sample coins, but had to abandon coinage for lack of resources, and saw his plan substantially modified under Thomas Jefferson's leadership. The money supply remained inadequate, and merchants and foreigners involved in business with the United States were terrified of the reintroduction of state paper money they were sure would depreciate.[24] The navy was dismantled and its

---

[20]Oberholtzer, *Robert Morris*, pp. 315–17, 321–23, 329–30; Matthew Carey, ed., *Debates and Proceedings of the General Assembly of Pennsylvania on the Memorials Praying a Repeal or Suspension of the Law Annulling the Charter of the Bank* (Philadelphia, 1786), p. 55.

[21]On RM's effort to rebuild the American navy in 1782, see *Morris Papers*, 6:94–95, 101–3. For his continued belief in the importance of the navy, but argument that it could not be sustained until the public was willing and able to support it, see RM to [unknown], Apr. 10, to the President of Congress, May 3 and July 10, and to John Jay, Nov. 27, 1783, and RM's report to Congress of July 31, 1783, *Morris Papers*, 7:694–95, 790, 8:265, 361, 786. On RM's prior role in establishing the American navy and patronizing its heroes, see Samuel Eliot Morison, *John Paul Jones: A Sailor's Biography* (Boston, 1959), pp. 59, 66–67, 87, 91, 180, 181, 297, 318; and Charles Oscar Paullin, *The Navy of the American Revolution: Its Administration, Its Policy, and Its Achievements* (1906; reprint ed., New York, 1971), pp. 90, 173–76, 182–83. On the dismantling of the Continental navy, see William M. Fowler, Jr., *Rebels Under Sail: The American Navy during the Revolution* (New York, 1976), pp. 84–86, 89–91; and Stephen T. Powers, "Decline and Extinction of American Naval Power," Ph.D. diss., University of Notre Dame, 1965, pp. 162–87, 194–97. On subordination of the army's needs to finance during RM's term as financier, see William Johnson, *Sketches of the Life and Correspondence of Nathanael Greene, Major General of the Armies of the United States*, 2 vols. (Charleston, S.C., 1822), 2:253–56; and E. Wayne Carp, *To Starve the Army at Pleasure: Continental Army Administration and American Political Culture* (Chapel Hill, 1984), pp. 214–16.

[22]On RM's early involvement in the residence issue, see *Morris Papers*, 8:665.

[23]On the return of the bank to private status, see *Morris Papers*, 7:654–55, 798–99, 818, 819; and Rappaport, *Stability and Change*, pp. 150–51, and idem, "Hostility to Banks," pp. 34–40.

[24]On the modification of RM's monetary proposals and termination of his efforts to

ships sold (mostly to Morris and his associates), and the army was minuscule. The country was largely defenseless and subject to occasional attack by Indians. Algerian corsairs threatened American shipping and minimized American trade with the Mediterranean.[25] American trade with the West Indies remained shut with the Spanish islands, limited to British vessels for the British islands, and elaborately restricted in the case of the French islands. The Mississippi River was closed to American ships and the northwestern posts were still in the hands of the British. Efforts to negotiate a commercial treaty with Britain had failed. A constitutional amendment to give Congress the right to regulate commerce had been thwarted by variations among the measures approved by the different states. Specie was draining out of the country to pay for imports and was not being adequately replaced by the proceeds of American exports. The country had undergone a severe postwar recession, from which it was only beginning to emerge. Ratification of the funding plan adopted in 1783 and with it approval of federal taxes had been blocked first by Rhode Island, then ultimately by New York. States routinely failed to make payments on congressional requisitions, and, despite its drastic downsizing of government, the United States had defaulted on some of its foreign loans. Public creditors were compensated, if at all, by state payments or by certificates of interest receivable for taxes.[26] In short, much of Morris's

---

open a mint, see *Morris Papers*, 7:739, 743, 9:285–87, 299–302, 614–17; and *The Papers of Thomas Jefferson*, 27 vols. to date (Princeton, 1950–), vol. 7 (Julian P. Boyd, ed.), pp. 150–60, 189–93; and Elizabeth M. Nuxoll, "A Generation of Numismatic Cooperation: Findings on the Notes and Coins of the Confederation through the Papers of Robert Morris," *American Journal of Numismatics*, 2d ser. 9 (1997):60–73. On the monetary problems of the 1780s, see Richard B. Morris, *The Forging of the Union, 1781–1789* (New York, 1987), pp. 154–59.

[25] On the perception of weakness and its role in the adoption of the U.S. Constitution and creation of a stronger central government, see Marks, *Independence on Trial*, pp. 36–51, 207–19; Powers, "Decline and Extinction of American Naval Power," pp. 235–57; Marshall Smelser, *The Congress Founds the Navy, 1787–1798* (South Bend, Ind., 1959), pp. 37, 44; and Craig L. Symonds, *Navalists and Antinavalists: The Naval Policy Debate in the United States, 1785–1827* (Newark, Del., 1980), p. 23. On the threat of corsairs to American trade with the Mediterranean, see *Morris Papers*, 8:548, 550 n, 558, 560 n; Marks, *Independence on Trial*, pp. 36–45; Ray Watkins Irwin, *The Diplomatic Relations of the United States with the Barbary Powers, 1776–1816* (Chapel Hill, 1931), pp. 1–54; and James A. Field, Jr., *America and the Mediterranean World, 1776–1882* (Princeton, 1969), pp. 27–67.

[26] On the restrictions on commerce and the postwar depression, see Morris, *Forging*

agenda was left unfulfilled, and some of his achievements had been dismantled. But the Federal Convention opened up new possibilities.

The new Constitution gave Congress the right to tax and regulate commerce and created a stronger, more balanced central government. Morris had a new opportunity to advance his agenda, and he chose to do so in a legislative rather than an executive capacity. Although there is no contemporary evidence extant for the assertion that Washington offered Morris the post of secretary of the Treasury,[27] it seems probable that the president did so, but it may have been merely a formality, an offer that Washington knew his friend would reject. Morris was the most politically controversial leader of his time; he was still in the process of settling some of his public accounts; and his business affairs were entangled and in need of attention. Moreover, as secretary of Treasury, most of his business would undoubtedly be limited or barred by conflict of interest regulations against commercial pursuits similar to those adopted for the Board of Treasury after Morris resigned as superintendent of finance; and Morris could not, or would not, withdraw from business.[28] Hence, Morris accepted the office of

---

of the Union, pp. 30, 152, 159–61. On the failure of the funding plan, state assumption of debts, and resort to certificates of interest, see *Morris Papers,* 6:82–83, 7:525, 536; and Ferguson, *Power of the Purse,* p. 223, idem, "Nationalists of 1781–1783," pp. 251–53, and idem, "State Assumption of the Federal Debt during the Confederation," *Mississippi Valley Historical Review* 38 (1951):403–24.

[27]For assertions that Washington offered RM the post of secretary of the Treasury, see the sketch of RM published in various newspapers in 1825, including the *Kentucky Gazette* of Sept. 9, 1825 (brought to my attention by Burnet Outten, Jr., of Orlando, Fla.); and George Washington Parke Custis, *Recollections and Private Memoirs of Washington, by His Adopted Son, George Washington Parke Custis, with a Memoir of the Author, by His Daughter; and Illustrative and Explanatory Notes, by Benson J. Lossing* (New York, 1860), pp. 349–50. Custis's material on Washington's relationship with Morris was first published in the *National Gazette* (Philadelphia), June 29, 1826. As early as May 1, 1789, a well-informed John Doughty reported to Josiah Harmar that the new "financier . . . will not be Morris" (Harmar Papers, William L. Clements Library, University of Michigan). The story that RM nominated Hamilton for the post also appeared in Custis, *Recollections,* pp. 349–50. See also RM to Mary Morris, Sept. 6, 1789 (in which Morris reports that Hamilton's appointment would soon be announced), in *DHFFC,* vol. 16 (forthcoming).

[28]The act of May 28, 1784, establishing the board of Treasury stipulated that no commissioner would be permitted to engage, "either directly or indirectly, in any trade or commerce whatsoever, on pain of forfeiting his Office." The conflict of interest regulations included in the act creating the U.S. Treasury Department in September 1789 banned members of the department from engaging in trade, owning a sea vessel, dealing in public securities or public lands, and profiting in any way from office. See *Journals of the Continental Congress, 1774–1789,* 34 vols. (Washington, D.C., 1904–37),

senator and set to work to accomplish what he could, well aware that expectations were so high that they were bound to be dashed, and that the conflicting personal, sectional, state, and local interests and attachments that had bedeviled the politics of the Confederation would soon reemerge.[29] It should be emphasized that for Morris most of what went on in the U.S. Congress was not new. It was old wine in a new bottle, an old agenda in a new institutional framework that made success more likely.

During the First Federal Congress, the only period for which we have Maclay's testimony as guide, Morris remained for the most part the nationalist leader he had always been. As one of the first Senate's "six-year men," he was relatively free from short-term political considerations and more able to follow his own conscience without immediate political repercussions than were those with only two-year terms like Maclay and the members of the House of Representatives. Morris objected to the idea that federal legislators should be bound by state instructions or work exclusively for the interests of their own constituents. He argued that, once elected, a senator should seek the larger good of the nation as a whole; state legislatures were merely the mechanisms by which senators were chosen, and they had no more right to give instructions than presidential electors had to direct the president. Despite such assumptions, Morris proved mindful of state interests on certain key issues.[30]

Morris's philosopher-king perception of his role as senator was augmented by his disregard for actions designed to seek "popularity" with the public, an effort he perceived as populist demagoguery aiming to appeal to public prejudices and resentments. When he did bow to the importance of public opinion, he sought to make his views popular, rather than adopt views that were already popular. He lamented and mocked as timid "poor [James] Madison['s]" sudden turn from na-

---

vol. 27 (Gaillard Hunt, ed.), pp. 469–70; *DHFFC,* 6:1975–77; E. James Ferguson and Elizabeth Miles Nuxoll, "Investigation of Government Corruption during the American Revolution," *Congressional Studies* 8 (1981):34.

[29]For RM's expectations when entering the Senate, see RM to Gouverneur Morris, Mar. 4, 1789, *DHFFC,* vol. 16 (forthcoming).

[30]On RM's independence, disdain for "popularity," and opposition to state instructions to its delegates, see Bowling and Veit, *Diary of William Maclay,* pp. 156, 159, 388–89. For an earlier comment on popularity, see RM to Horatio Gates, Oct. 28, 1784, *Morris Papers,* 9:577–78.

tionalist policies after his near defeat for Congress in Virginia.[31] He viewed amendments to the Constitution — the Bill of Rights — as a waste of time. He opposed efforts to open Senate debates to the public, arguing that it would lessen decorum in the Senate and lead to frequent grandstanding and playing to the audience.[32] He seemed to regard human nature and society as fundamentally immutable, frequently quoting one of Gouverneur Morris's favorite sayings "Whatever is, is."[33] Yet he believed in the inevitability of American economic growth and never doubted that such growth would be good for all Americans, and indeed for much of the world.[34] Despite his disdain for "democracy" as he saw it, he also retained an optimistic faith that people individually and as a group could learn from experience, and that if they did not back wise measures initially, the harsh consequences of their errors would ultimately bring them around. Hence he felt free to fight hard for measures he believed in, occasionally taking inflexible political stances, but once a decision had been made and he had lost, he acquiesced, made the best of things, and moved on.[35]

As a senator, Morris was a master of parliamentary procedure and,

---

[31]On RM's criticism of Madison, see RM to James Wilson, Aug. 23, 1789, *DHFFC*, vol. 16 (forthcoming); and Gouverneur Morris to RM, May 3, 1790, Gouverneur Morris Commercial Letterbooks, Library of Congress (DLC).

[32]On RM's opposition to open debates in the Senate, see Bowling and Veit, *Diary of William Maclay*, pp. 388–89, 463.

[33]"Whatever is, is," is apparently a variation on "Whatever is, is right," or "Whatever is, is for the best," which are concepts used by Alexander Pope in his *Essay on Man* (Epistle 1, line 293), by Leibnitz in his *Théodicé*, and by Bernard Mandeville in his *Fable of the Bees*, and satirized by Voltaire in *Candide*. RM quoted Gouverneur Morris's use of the expression "Whatever is, is" in his letter to William Constable of May 6, 1794, Jay Papers, NNC. Both RM and Gouverneur Morris applied the idea to the notion that one cannot fundamentally change things, but only adapt to or turn to advantage what exists. See, for example, Gouverneur Morris to John Jay, Jan. 10, and RM to Jefferson, Feb. 25, 1784, *Morris Papers*, 9:17–18, 136.

[34]On the inevitability and benefits of U.S. economic growth and power, see, for example, RM to George Washington, July 2, 1781, the notes to RM to the President of Congress, July 29, 1782, RM to [unknown], Apr. 10, 1783, and to the President of Congress, Sept. 30, 1784, *Morris Papers*, 1:214–15, 6:41–42, 77, 7:693–95, 9:536–37.

[35]On the view that people and legislatures could and would learn from experiencing the consequences of bad actions, see, for example, Gouverneur Morris to John Jay, Jan. 1, 1783, Observations on the Present State of Affairs, [ca. Jan. 13,] 1783, RM to the President of Congress, July 10, 1783, to the Willinks, van Staphorsts, and de la Lande and Fynje, Dec. 12, 1783, and to John Wendell, Apr. 8, 1784, *Morris Papers*, 7:257, 305–6, 307, 8:265, 808, 9:242; and Mary Jo Kline, "Gouverneur Morris and the New Nation, 1775–1788," Ph.D. diss., Columbia University, 1970, pp. 183–84, 259–60, 266, 270, 309, 345.

as he had been in the Continental Congress, a committeeman par excellence. He served on forty-one committees during the First Congress, more than any other senator, and reported for fifteen. For the most part these committees dealt with trade or with the unfulfilled aspects of Morris's earlier agenda. He served on the committees dealing with the impost and the means of regulating and enforcing it; with every aspect of Alexander Hamilton's financial plan — including the bank, the mint, and the funding plan — and with all other bills relating to commerce, including ones on tonnage duties, coastal trade, merchant seamen, West Indian trade, consuls, weights and measures, creation and management of lighthouses, and responses to the depredations of the Algerian corsairs.[36] On many of the important bills he worked closely with his longtime political allies, fellow Philadelphians Thomas Fitzsimons and George Clymer, now members of the House of Representatives. Their coordinated efforts, rather than Morris's alone, are largely responsible for the victories of the policies they favored.[37] It is not possible to trace Morris's actions on all these measures, but for those subjects in which Maclay was especially interested and which he therefore covered extensively, the varieties of Morris's political style can be followed.

Morris's involvement with the impost bill is a good opportunity to see him in action. At first he tried to be the silent, observant Morris previously seen at the Federal Convention. He adopted the strategy he had explained in 1784 to Dutch visitor Gisbert van Hogendorp: "When I was in that Assembly (of Pennsylvania) some members used to come to my house and asked me, what is your opinion on such a matter. I told them, when I come to the house I'll hear what they have to say and I'll determine. Do you the same. Keep yourselves open as I

---

[36]See the sketch of Morris in *DHFFC,* 14:766–73. For RM's committee assignments, see generally the Senate Legislative Journal, and the Senate Executive Journal, *DHFFC,* vols. 1 and 2. In letters to RM, Gouverneur Morris called the foreign intercourse bill "your" bill, although RM had no formal role in the handling of the bill. See the letters dated July 31 and August 31, 1790, in the Gouverneur Morris Commercial Letterbooks, DLC.

[37]RM to Tench Coxe, Sept. 2, 1789, *DHFFC,* vol. 16 (forthcoming); Bowling and Veit, *Diary of William Maclay,* pp. 55–56; Jack N. Rakove, "The Structure of Politics at the Accession of George Washington," in *Beyond Confederation: Origins of the Constitution and American National Identity,* ed. Richard Beeman, Stephen Botein, and Edward C. Carter II (Chapel Hill, 1987), pp. 281–83.

do. If I had given them my opinion, and any circumstance had brought me to a change, they would not have known how to reconcile it to my honesty, and would no more have trusted me." Morris at first refused to commit himself or to take the floor on controversies related to the ways specific tariff rates would impact various states. He told Maclay he would listen carefully, then decide. However, when a New England senator ranted that the proposed tariff on molasses represented an attempt by Pennsylvanians to rig tariffs so as to put the burden of taxation on New England, Maclay saw Morris's "[n]ostrils widen, and his nose flatten out like the head of a Viper." Enraged, Morris took the floor, and "charmingly did he unravel all their Windings." He was "clear strong and conclusive." This was the forcefully eloquent Morris who had previously dominated banking debates in the Pennsylvania Assembly in 1785 and 1786.[38]

During most of the elaborate bargaining over tariff rates, tonnage duties, and similar measures, Morris seems to be playing an honest broker, gathering the needed data, favoring less protectionism than Maclay, and accommodating the interests of the various regions, but battling for those rates deemed essential by Pennsylvanians.[39] On only one aspect was his own interest directly involved — that of tariffs on tea and other East India goods. Morris personally had opened trade with China by sponsoring the voyage of the *Empress of China* in 1784 and continued to be among those actively involved in trade with India and China. Indeed, the China trade had produced some of Morris's most significant postwar commercial successes. Morris and his allies considered it essential to keep U.S. trade with East Asia directly in American

[38]On RM's role in the assembly, see Maxims, Mar. 4, 1784, G. K. van Hogendorp Papers, 36:44, Algamien Ryksarchief, The Hague. For the tariff debates, see Maclay, *Journal*, pp. 56–57, 63–67. On RM's effective speaking in the Pennsylvania Assembly, see Carey, *Debates and Proceedings*, pp. 37–38, 42, 80–81, 91; Rappaport, *Stability and Change*, pp. 206–7, and idem, "Hostility to Banks," pp. 168–76, 183–85, 191–92, 218–19, 224–27; and William Pierce's character sketch, published in Max Farrand, ed., *The Records of the Federal Convention of 1787*, 4 vols. (1937, reprint ed., New Haven, 1966), 3:91.

[39]On the tariff and tonnage bills, see Bowling and Veit, *Diary of William Maclay*, pp. 56–60, 63–69, 72, 84, 89, 90, 383, 452, 453; RM to Gouverneur Morris, May 15, 1789, RM to Coxe, Sept. 2, 1789, *DHFFC*, vol. 16 (forthcoming). On RM's opposition to tariff discrimination against nations not having commercial treaties with the United States, see Bowling and Veit, *Diary of William Maclay*, p. 50.

hands, rather than allowing it to fall back into the prewar American pattern of purchasing Asian goods through Europe. Hence, with the support of an appeal from Philadelphia's China traders, he proposed a high duty on tea imported via Europe and backed a measure to confine the direct trade between the United States and India and China to American-owned vessels. But after his opponents objected to the latter, Morris appeared to concede, saying that since it would not meet with approbation, he would not second the motion, but would "leave the matter until experience would show the necessity of it." Richard Henry Lee of Virginia and Oliver Ellsworth of Connecticut, possibly now perceiving the measure as not essential to Morris, immediately rose and supported the motion, despite having condemned it the week before. Maclay immediately identified their inconsistency as the result of "cabal." Presumably, personal enmity to Morris and long-standing factionalism had in this instance played a role in the stand Lee and Ellsworth originally had taken. Morris, by not fighting for the measure, got what he wanted. After these protective measures were adopted, foreign involvement in the trade between the United States and Asia quickly faded.[40]

Even better case studies are the related questions of the residence of Congress and the assumption of the state debts. In these instances we see an assertive wheeler and dealer, a consummate bargainer, acting on issues as closely related to personal and local self-interest as to national well-being. How skillfully Morris played his hand over the course of the two years of maneuvering that took place before the question of the federal seat of government was resolved is highly debatable, as is the extent to which he was important to the ultimate outcome. The story of the endless rounds of maneuvering over placement

---

[40]On the questions of duties on East Asian goods, see Bowling and Veit, *Diary of William Maclay*, p. 63; *DHFFC*, 1:60–67, 537–38; Constable to James Chalmers, Apr. 14, 1789, Constable Letterbooks, Constable-Pierrepont Papers, New York Public Library; and William A. Davis, "William Constable: New York Merchant and Land Speculator, 1772–1803," Ph.D. diss., Harvard University, 1955, pp. 209–10. On RM's role in the evolution of the China trade, see *Morris Papers*, 8:857–82; Mary A. Y. Gallagher, "Charting a New Course for the China Trade: The Late Eighteenth Century American Model," *American Neptune* 57 (1997):201–15; Jonathan Goldstein, *Philadelphia and the China Trade 1682–1846* (Philadelphia, 1978), pp. 8–9, 25–35; Philip Chadwick Foster Smith, *The Empress of China* (Philadelphia, 1984), pp. 18–20, 43–44, 46–47, 49, 51–52, 55–56, 72–73; and Clarence L. Ver Steeg, "Financing and Outfitting the First United States Ship to China," *Pacific Historical Review* 22 (1953):1–12.

of both the temporary and permanent seats is too long to discuss here and has been covered very effectively in published works, most notably by Kenneth Bowling. Only a quick overview of Morris's role can be presented here.

Morris entered Congress seeking placement of the permanent residence near Philadelphia, or at a site on the Delaware River, preferably at the falls, where he had acquired property. Securing the temporary residence for Philadelphia was also desirable and might lead Congress in fact to stay on permanently at nearby Germantown once Congress experienced the benefits of the location. The economic advantages to himself and to Philadelphia, and no doubt the personal convenience for his participation in government with minimal damage to his business or social interests, seem to have been his primary motives. His goals placed him at odds both with Maclay, who wanted the residence on the Susquehanna River, preferably near his own lands, and with Washington, who favored placement on the Potomac River near Mount Vernon. The selection of either alternate would tend to direct economic growth away from Philadelphia toward the Chesapeake and promote settlement westward from those areas.

The bargaining with the other delegates to obtain either the permanent or temporary seats for the Delaware was complicated by the fact that there were few examples of what was once described as an honest politician — that is, one who when bought, *stayed* bought. Pacts were made and as quickly unmade, and Morris was frequently outmaneuvered. But, in what proved to be the final stage of horse-trading, Morris, Fitzsimons, and Clymer agreed with Hamilton, Jefferson, Madison, and Washington that in exchange for enough Southern votes to assure temporary residence of the federal government in Philadelphia for ten years followed by permanent placement of the capital on the Potomac, they would obtain the votes needed for the passage of the assumption of state debts, the one aspect of the funding plan Hamilton had thus far failed to secure of his own.[41] In this instance the bargain

---

[41]Bowling and Veit, *Diary of William Maclay*, pp. 135, 136, 138, 144–67 passim; RM's correspondence with Mary Morris, 1789–90, Morris Papers, Henry E. Huntington Library; RM to Wilson, Aug. 23, 1789, *DHFFC*, vol. 16 (forthcoming); and, for general discussions, Kenneth R. Bowling, *The Creation of Washington, D.C.: The Idea and Location of the American Capital* (Fairfax, Va., 1991), pp. 99–105, 127–207; and idem, "Politics in the First Congress, 1789–1791," Ph.D. diss., University of Wisconsin, 1968, pp. 152–

FIG. 2. "View of Con__ss on the Road to Philadelphia." This cartoon was sold on the streets of New York City early in July 1790. Morris is carrying the fourteen senators who voted for the Residence Act on a ladder of preferment and pulling the twelve members of the minority along by strings through their noses. *(Courtesy Historical Society of Pennsylvania)*

held, and in August 1790 Congress departed for Philadelphia. New Yorkers blamed Morris for their loss and caricatured him in poems and cartoons that depicted "Bobby the Cofferer" in league with the devil in luring Congress to Philadelphia (fig. 2). In "The Removal," poet and polemicist Philip Freneau proclaimed:

> Such thankless usage much we fear'd
> When Robert's coach stood ready geer'd
> And he, the foremost on the floor
> Sat pointing to the Quaker shore.
>
> So long confin'd to little things
> They now shall meet where *Bavius* sings:
> Where *Mammon* guilds his walls in style
> And B-b-'s *bawdy* seasons smile.

99; T. L. Loftin, *Contest for a Capital: George Washington, Robert Morris, and Congress, 1783–1791 Contenders* (Washington, D.C., 1989), pp. 12–20, 63, 77, 117–27, 130–32, 135–37, 148–51, 154–60, 170, 172–73, 178, 191–92, 203–6, 220–21, 223–24, 227–30, 300–301, 306–8, 323–24; and Jacob E. Cooke, "The Compromise of 1790," *William and Mary Quarterly*, 3d ser. 27 (1970):523–45.

Another poem, however, challenged this view, asserting that Fitzsimons had more influence "whenever he wills" than "bawdy Bob" with his "noted long bills," and that it was Fitzsimons, not Morris, who was responsible for the bargain's success.[42]

The financial part of this bargain was equally complex. Morris and his allies had backed most of Hamilton's funding plan. In particular, they had agreed with Hamilton in opposing a discrimination among public creditors in favor of original certificate holders as opposed to later investors, whom many disdained as predatory speculators. Echoing the views of Pennsylvania's well-organized public creditors, Morris had staunchly opposed Hamilton's scaling down of interest payments, but in the end had acquiesced, acknowledging that "half a Loaf is better than no bread."[43]

Among the Pennsylvanians in Congress, the assumption of state debts was strongly backed by Morris, Fitzsimons, and Clymer, and bitterly opposed by Maclay as contrary to the interests of Pennsylvania and conducive to speculation. Many leaders of the Pennsylvania public creditors also opposed assumption because the Pennsylvania debt was satisfactorily covered by the state government and/or because the creditors were using state certificates to buy land from the state land office. Morris, however, swore "it must be done," and was much chagrined when the assumption plan was first defeated. He continued to fight for its passage. Maclay's allegation that Morris's backing of assumption was based on his speculation in state securities is partly true; Morris's associates abroad were attempting to market blocks of

---

[42]Copies of the cartoons can be found in Bowling and Veit, *Diary of William Maclay*, p. 331; and Bowling, *Creation of Washington*, between pp. 160 and 161. Freneau's "The Removal" was published in the *New York Daily Gazette*, Aug. 10, 1790, and reprinted in Freneau's *Poems* (1795); see Judith R. Hiltner, ed., *The Newspaper Verse of Philip Freneau: An Edition and Bibliographical Survey* (Troy, N.Y., 1986), pp. 404–5. For discussions of the press coverage regarding RM's role, see also Bowling, *Creation of Washington*, pp. 198–201, 271 n. Maclay's horrified response to RM's bawdy speech was recorded in his *Diary* of May 17, 1790 (p. 270), but it is not known if he influenced the newspaper references to RM's bawdiness.

[43]See *Morris Papers*, 6:77; RM to Gouverneur Morris, Dec. 11, 1789, Gouverneur Morris Papers, NNC; Bowling and Veit, *Diary of William Maclay*, pp. 183–84, 295; Pieter J. van Winter, *American Finance and Dutch Investment, 1780–1805, with an Epilogue to 1840*, rev. ed., trans. with the assistance of James C. Riley (New York, 1977), pp. 345–46. On RM's support for assumption but initial threat to oppose it if Hamilton scaled down the interest on the public debt, see Bowling and Veit, *Diary of William Maclay*, pp. 207, 300, 318, 319; and Bowling, "Politics in the First Congress," pp. 224–25.

securities to foreign investors, and his recurring financial difficulties added urgency to the success of such efforts.[44] However, assumption was also consistent with Morris's hopes for a national marketplace and for substantial foreign investment in the United States, both of which were often blocked by state preferences for paying only their own citizens and other state regulations that discriminated against foreigners. Furthermore, Morris believed assumption would enable the country to bypass the complicated and divisive problems that arose during efforts to settle state accounts with the union.[45] Still, winning support in Pennsylvania for assumption was by no means assured and only the tying together of the residence and assumption issues gave Morris enough bargaining power to accomplish his objectives.[46]

On the other items on Morris's decade-old agenda, far less is known about his role. Hamilton conferred with Morris on the details of the bank bill during the third session of the First Congress, but Morris's exact contributions to the discussion are unidentified. Morris backed the bill, and his longtime partner, Thomas Willing, ultimately became

---

[44]On RM's involvement in speculation in debt certificates, though on a relatively small scale, see Ferguson, *Power of the Purse,* pp. 258, 328; Bowling and Veit, *Diary of William Maclay,* p. 327; Gouverneur Morris to William Constable, Aug. 25, and to RM, Aug. 26, 1789, Gouverneur Morris Commercial Letterbooks, DLC. However, as Forrest McDonald has noted, Morris was also a land speculator, an activity conducted largely with depreciated state certificates, and stood to lose by measures that would raise the price of the certificates used to purchase land from state land offices; see Forrest McDonald, *Alexander Hamilton: A Biography* (New York, 1979), p. 176.

[45]RM had himself proposed the assumption of state debts in 1783. See RM to Elbridge Gerry, Aug. 26, 1783, *Morris Papers,* 8:453; Ferguson, *Power of the Purse,* pp. 209–10, and idem, "Nationalists of 1781–1783," pp. 251, 257–59; and Ver Steeg, *Robert Morris,* p. 175. On the crucial importance of foreign investment to RM's land speculations and other ventures, see van Winter, *Dutch Investment,* 2:622–24, 703, 705–6.

[46]On the views of Pennsylvania's public creditors, see Bowling and Veit, *Diary of William Maclay,* pp. 344–45; Hamilton to RM, Nov. 9, 1790, and Tench Coxe to Hamilton, Dec. 31, 1790, Harold Syrett and Jacob E. Cooke, eds., *The Papers of Alexander Hamilton,* 26 vols. (New York, 1961–79), 7:146, 396; and Roland M. Baumann, "'Heads I Win, Tails You Lose': The Public Creditors and the Assumption Issue in Pennsylvania, 1790–1802," *Pennsylvania History* 44 (1977):195–232.

On RM and Hamilton's funding plan, see also RM to Tench Coxe, Sept. 2, 1789, Mar. 25, 1790, May 2, 1790, Coxe Papers, PHi; to Gouverneur Morris, Apr. 4, Dec. 21, 1790, and to Daniel Garesché, Dec. 7, 1790, Gouverneur Morris Papers, NNC; to Walter Stewart, July 28, 1790, Boston Public Library; Gouverneur Morris to RM, July 31, 1790, in Jared Sparks, *The Life of Gouverneur Morris, with Selections from His Correspondence and Miscellaneous Papers* (Boston, 1832), 3:10–15; and Hamilton to RM, Nov. 9, 1790, Syrett and Cooke, *Hamilton Papers,* 7:146.

the new bank's president, leaving his post as president of the Bank of North America in order to do so.[47] However, according to Madison, both Morris and Fitzsimons were among those whose efforts to obtain significant amounts of national bank stock were frustrated when the subscription was immediately oversubscribed. Morris was reportedly so angry he wanted to sue the directors, and Fitzsimons threatened to take the issue of the distribution of shares up in the House of Representatives, but nothing seems to have come of it.[48] The wild speculation in bank stock and debt certificates that followed, and the devastating stock market crash that came in 1792, did much to discredit both the bank and the Federalists who backed it, but neither seems to have been anticipated by Hamilton, Morris, or any of the plan's originators. As Morris had previously predicted when discussing speculative activities occurring during his administration, speculation did indeed cure itself—but in this case only after producing severe economic hardship in Philadelphia, New York, and elsewhere.[49]

In the Second Congress Morris chaired the Senate committee responsible for drafting the bills for establishing a mint and coinage. He is believed to have been involved in the planning and production of controversial sample coins featuring the bust of George Washington for the consideration of Congress. After heated debate in the House of Representatives, the concept of placing the head of the incumbent president on coins was rejected as excessively monarchical, and the liberty motif was adopted instead. The Senate fought stubbornly for

----

[47]On RM and the bank bill, see *DHFFC*, 1:516, 536; 4:171; Bowling and Veit, *Diary of William Maclay*, pp. 361–64; Syrett and Cooke, *Hamilton Papers*, 6:281n–82n, 7:146. For a recent discussion of Thomas Willing's role as president of the Bank of the United States, see Robert E. Wright, "Thomas Willing (1731–1821): Philadelphia Financier and Forgotten Founding Father," *Pennsylvania History* 63 (1996):545–47.

[48]See *The Papers of James Madison*, 17 vols. (Chicago and Charlottesville, 1962–91), vol. 14 (Robert A. Rutland, ed.), pp. 41–42; Baumann, "Democratic-Republicans of Philadelphia," pp. 305–15.

[49]On speculation curing itself, see RM to the President of Congress, July 29, 1782, and to William Churchill Houston, Mar. 3, 1783, *Morris Papers*, 6:69–70, 7:487; for the impact of the stock speculation of the early 1790s, see Ferguson, *Power of the Purse*, pp. 326–30; Doerflinger, *Spirit of Enterprise*, pp. 310–14; and Robert F. Jones, "The Public Career of William Duer: Rebel, Federalist Politician, and Speculator, 1775–1792," Ph.D. diss., University of Notre Dame, 1966, pp. 193–96, 201–2, 205–21, 245–97, and idem, *King of the Alley: William Duer, Politician, Entrepreneur and Speculator, 1768–1799* (New York, 1992).

the original design but was ultimately forced to relent. Also arising in the Senate during debates over the mint was a proposed amendment to put a justice figure on a coin, a thematic echo of Morris's earlier liberty and justice coin proposal. The suggestion was immediately rejected, possibly because the idea of justice was by then too closely associated with the polemics over debt funding.[50]

In foreign policy Morris adhered strongly to the concept of American neutrality among the various European powers and to the maintenance of peace if at all possible. Peace was crucial to his hopes for foreign investment and to the safety of the western lands in which he was speculating on a large scale. In 1793 Morris was among those who advocated the sending of a special envoy to England to resolve the growing tensions between Britain and the United States, and Senate Federalists persuaded him to discuss the subject with the president. Once Washington eliminated from consideration Hamilton, the Federalists' favorite candidate for the post, Morris supported the appointment of John Jay, rather than Jefferson or John Adams, and expressed high hopes for the success of his mission.[51] Morris was out of office when the time came for the Senate to vote for ratification of Jay's

---

[50]*Morris Papers*, 7:743; *DHFFC*, 6:2072; *Madison Papers*, 14:188, 262, 263, 269–70, 278; Don Taxay, *The U.S. Mint and Coinage: An Illustrated History from 1776 to the Present* (New York, 1966), pp. 51, 57–59; Walter Breen, "The United States Patterns of 1792," *Coin Collector's Journal* 21 (1954):10–13; and George Fuld, "Coinage Featuring George Washington," in Philip L. Mossman, *Coinage of the American Confederation Period* (New York, 1996), pp. 166–259, esp. pp. 183–90. On the use of a justice motif on a 1779 continental currency note and on RM's proposed coin designs of 1783, see Eric P. Newman, *The Early Paper Money of America* (Iola, Wis., 1990), p. 44; on its proposal and rejection in 1792, see Taxay, *U.S. Mint and Coinage*, pp. 59–60.

[51]On RM's support of neutrality and the negotiations of John Jay, see Charles R. King, ed., *Life and Correspondence of Rufus King*, 6 vols. (1894–1900; reprint ed., New York, 1971), 1:517–19; Constable to RM, Aug. 26, 1793, Constable Letterbooks, Constable-Pierrepont Papers, New York Public Library; RM to Constable, Nov. 27, 1793, private collection of John Constable of Watertown, New York; RM to Thomas Morris, Mar. 30, May 20, and June 1794, and to William White Morris, June 1794, all Morris Papers, Henry E. Huntington Library; to Constable, May 6, 1794, and [ca. May 1795?] [June 9, 1794], Jay Papers, NNC. On RM's involvement in the neutral trade, his early profits, and his later problems with both French and British restrictions and depredations, see Thomas Fitzsimons and RM to Sylvanus Bourne, June 29, 1793, in extra-illustrated Washington Irving, *Life of George Washington*, Cornell University Library; RM to Daniel Garesché, Nov. 11, 1794, to John Parish and Company, Mar. 16 and Nov. 12, to Mordecai Lewis, Mar. 24, and to John Richard, Apr. 7, 1795, Morris Private Letterbook 1, DLC; and Davis, "William Constable," pp. 189–251.

Treaty in a special session held in June 1795, but he unofficially gave it his support. He had the usual Federalist reservations, particularly to the clause limiting American ships trading with the British West Indies to seventy tons and specifying the articles of tropical produce that could not be reexported from the United States. He approved of the Senate's resolution that the clause be suspended. Morris informed his mercantile associates abroad that he was basing his commercial measures on peace and neutrality and advised them to do likewise. Peace, he argued, was more central to American interests than any benefits that could be obtained from a wartime neutral trade (in which he and his partners were participating). Violations of American neutrality and other offenses could be arbitrated or compensated for at a later date. Force should be used only as a last resort.[52] Yet, at the same time, he penned strong hints to his influential British and European correspondents of the inadvisability of Britain's more arrogant and inflexible stands, and of the dangers inflammatory British actions presented to American intent to preserve peace and neutrality.

Making clear that American patience was not inexhaustible, Morris's private statements, unlike Hamilton's, supported rather than undermined Jay's mission. For example, to William Constable, he proclaimed in June 1794:

> Our Government is really disposed to preserve a strict Neutrality as I have always told you they were, and if Peace can be preserved (with honor) it will be preserved, but should we be forced into Hostile measures, farewell to British Connection & Commerce forever, for one of the first steps will be to prohibit the Consumption in this Country of British manufactures, thereby to force forward the manufacturing for ourselves, it is indeed wonderful to behold the progress we are making in this way. In short it is decided by Fate that America must take the lead

---

[52]For RM's reservations about the Jay Treaty, but continued hopes for peace, see RM to Jefferson, June 1, to William White Morris, June 28, and to Messrs. J. H. Cazenove, Nephew and Co., Nov. 13, 1795, Morris Private Letterbook 1, DLC. On the importance RM attached to the Jay Treaty for the peace with the Indians necessary for the success of his land speculations, see RM to Charles Williamson, Jan. 31, and to Anthony Wayne, Mar. 27, 1795, and to Thomas Morris, Mar. 26, 1796, all Morris Private Letterbook 1, DLC. The furor over the Jay Treaty had bad consequences for RM's land speculations for it obstructed passage in the various states of "alienage laws" permitting the sale of land to foreigners. See RM to Gouverneur Morris, Oct. 1, 1795, Morris Private Letterbook 1, DLC.

amongst Nations & every step they take in Europe to retard, only has-
tens her progress.[53]

In making such a statement, Morris was reiterating a belief he often
expressed while superintendent of finance — that British offenses ultimately aided the United States by promoting strength and unity.[54]

Morris was less critical in letters to his French correspondents, but
after one of his ships delivering flour to France was long detained in
port, he reported to a French affiliate American irritation with such
detentions and the likelihood that Americans would refuse to continue
to send supplies to Europe if such problems continued. Although
the French invasion of Holland and the subsequent revolution there
ended his chances for the Dutch investment that was the last hope for
keeping his land speculation schemes afloat, Morris wrote admiringly
of French military victories, hoped they would induce the opposing
allies to seek peace, and argued that in the end the French must be
allowed to choose their own form of government. Tired of the consequences of war and revolution, but mindful of abuses within England,
he exclaimed, "I pray to God to spare mankind & let us have no more
Revolutions, except in those Countries where the oppressions of the
Powerfull and Rich over the Middling & poor are more intolerable
than Revolutionary Evils."[55]

In short, Morris's foreign policy views were similar to those of most
Federalists, but like most Philadelphians he did not adopt the pro-

---

[53]For RM's warnings about the consequences of British behavior, see RM to Con-
stable, May 6, 1794, and [ca. May 1795?] [June 9, 1794], Jay Papers, NNC; to Samuel
Bean, June 1, 1795, to Messrs. Bourdieu, Chollet, and Bourdieu, and to J. H. Cazenove,
Nephew and Co., both Oct. 7, 1795, all in Morris Private Letterbook 1, DLC.

[54]For earlier comments by both RM and Gouverneur Morris about British intran-
sigence and arrogance promoting American unity, see Gouverneur Morris to John Jay,
Sept. 25, 1783, Jan. 10, 1784, and RM to Matthew Ridley, Nov. 5, and to Jay, Nov. 27,
1783, *Morris Papers*, 8:543–44, 546, 549, 731, 9:17.

[55]For RM's positive statements about French victories and the French right to self-
determination, see RM to Daniel Garesché, Apr. 6, and to William White Morris,
June 28, 1795, Morris Private Letterbook 1, DLC. RM may have been somewhat influ-
enced in these views by letters received from his son William who was then traveling in
Europe (see William White Morris's letters to Mary Morris of Feb. 28, June 16, and
Dec. 6, 1794, Morris Papers, Henry E. Huntington Library). For the impact of the
French invasion of Holland on RM's prospects for Dutch investment in his land spec-
ulations, see RM to John Swanwick, Jan. 12, and to Benjamin Harrison, Jr., July 1, 1795,
Morris Private Letterbook 1, DLC.

British bias, hostility to the French, or intense fear of revolution common to his more extreme colleagues. He never got caught up in the furies over the Jay Treaty, depicting it as merely a partisan battle between the "Ins and the Outs," and expressing regret that the treaty had become the "Touch stone" of party politics. What remains unclear with regard to Federalist foreign policy is the extent to which Morris was influencing its course. Did he help shape the views of Washington, Jay, or other officials, or did he merely share their ideas and loyally support their measures? The record on this is largely silent.[56]

Despite, or perhaps because of, his desire for peace, Morris advocated the revival of the American navy, favoring a bill calling for the building of naval vessels that was adopted in 1794 in response to Algerian depredations. He submitted the ideas of shipbuilder Joshua Humphreys, and no doubt others, for the construction of the ships that ultimately became such gems as the *Constitution* and the *Constellation*. The fact that Morris and his allies backed the long, time-consuming process of building solid new ships implies that the ships were not intended for immediate action, but for deterrence and for developing the American infrastructure necessary to produce a stronger defense in the long run. Typically, patronage concerns and a need to distribute the economic benefits among the states shaped the way the ships were built, but their size and design were similar to what Morris was considering at the end of his administration as agent of marine, a post he had held concurrently with that of superintendent of finance.[57]

---

[56]For a comparison of RM's views on the Jay Treaty with that of other Philadelphia merchants, see Jacob E. Cooke, *Tench Coxe and the Early Republic* (Chapel Hill, 1978), pp. 274–79; and Roland M. Baumann, "John Swanwick: Spokesman for 'Merchant Republicanism' in Philadelphia, 1790–1798," *Pennsylvania Magazine of History and Biography* 97 (1973):156, and idem, "Democratic-Republicans of Philadelphia," pp. 465–68, 512–41. For RM's downplaying of the significance, and bemoaning, of the partisan bickering following the Jay Treaty, see RM to Patrick Colquhoun, Oct. 10, 1795, and to George C. Fox and Sons, Nov. 5, 1795, Morris Private Letterbook 1, DLC. While there is little evidence regarding the question of RM's influence over Washington's foreign policy, French minister Edmond Genêt claimed that upon his arrival in 1793, Jefferson "did not at all conceal from me that Senator Morris and Secretary of the Treasury Hamilton, attached to the interests of England, had the greatest influence over the President's mind, and that it was only with difficulty that he [Jefferson] counterbalanced these efforts" (Genêt to the Minister of Foreign Affairs, Oct. 7, 1793, quoted in Stanley Elkins and Eric McKitrick, *The Age of Federalism* [New York, 1993], p. 344).

[57]On RM's involvement in calls for a naval revival as soon as "the state of public

Morris's work in 1789 on the Judiciary Act, the one major bill he contributed to that was unrelated to his earlier mission, is one of the few cases in which we have Morris's insights to complement the depiction given by Maclay. Both men had sought the advice of prominent lawyers in Pennsylvania on what should be included in the measure determining the shape of the federal judiciary. Many of the replies were addressed to Morris personally, and when Maclay asked to see them, Morris was evasive, delayed showing him some letters, and, in the case of Francis Hopkinson, never showed him the letter at all, despite the fact that Maclay knew that Morris had showed Hopkinson's opinions to other senators. Maclay was baffled and offended by Morris's behavior.[58]

Morris's explanation of at least part of this mystery is amusingly revealed in his letters to Hopkinson, in which he complained that the always impecunious Hopkinson had written his appeals for Morris's support for his appointment to a judicial post on the back of the letter giving his views on the Judiciary Act. Morris teasingly cited Hopkinson's action as evidence for his belief that men of "wit, Humour, Superior Genius, or great Talents" lacked the "same degree of discretion and judgment" in their management of "the ordinary occurances and business of life" that ordinary mortals had. "A common man" writing such a letter would make it easy to keep his confidences, Morris as-

---

finances will admit," see Joshua Humphreys to RM, Jan. 6, 1793 [1794?], *Journal of American History* 10 (1916):52–53; *DHFFC*, 2:114–15, 425–49; Syrett and Cooke, *Hamilton Papers*, 16:308 n; Tyrone G. Martin, "The USS Constitution: A Design Confirmed," *American Neptune* 57 (1997):257, 261; Symonds, *Navalists and Antinavalists*, p. 28; L. H. Bolander, "An Incident in the Founding of the American Navy," *United States Naval Institute Proceedings* 55 (June 1929):491–94; and, for Maclay's opposition, see Bowling and Veit, *Diary of William Maclay*, pp. 77, 373. The continuities between RM's naval objectives in the 1780s and the creation of the U.S. Navy in the 1790s are further discussed in my unpublished paper, "The Naval Movement of the Confederation Era," presented at the conference of the North American Society for Oceanic History, Boston, April 1996, and scheduled for publication under the auspices of the Naval History Center, Washington, D.C.

[58]See Bowling and Veit, *Diary of William Maclay*, pp. 78–79, 100, 102; RM to James Wilson, Aug. 23, 1789, *DHFFC*, vol. 16 (forthcoming); RM to Edward Tilghman, Jr., June 21, 1789, Tilghman Collection (MS 2821), Maryland Historical Society; Edward Shippen to RM, July 13, 1789, Autograph Collection, PHi; and Wilfred J. Ritz, *Rewriting the History of the Judiciary Act of 1789: Exposing Myths, Challenging Premises, and Using New Evidence* (Norman, Okla., 1990), pp. 73–75, 183, 214 n, 215 n, 226 n, 233 n.

serted. "But the man of talents, first writes Remarks on a public business knowing they are intended for the inspection of other people, and then on the back of one of the pages so written he writes his confidential letter — it cannot be separated and those who read one must have the opportunity of seeing the other. Thus your Friend is reduced to a dilemma. He must either suppress the remarks, expose the private letter, or be at the trouble to Copy over the remarks." In his next letter to Hopkinson, Morris admitted the work of recopying had not been all that arduous and reported that he had shown Hopkinson's remarks to some senators, who then incorporated Hopkinson's arguments into their statements during debate. What he did not say was that he had not shown Hopkinson's remarks to Maclay. It seems probable that, knowing that his colleague would be suspicious if shown only an extract and not Hopkinson's original letter, Morris elected not to show Maclay anything at all.

Morris's correspondence with Hopkinson places a less sinister face on his unwillingness to share data with his colleague, and reveals how Morris's propensity to have others put forward ideas he wanted disseminated makes it difficult to trace or evaluate the full measure of his influence on the measures of Congress. It also well reveals the mixture of admiration and exasperation that he, who saw himself as a practical man of affairs, felt for men of "genius." Remarks later in the letter show an even greater impatience with the lawyers by whom he was surrounded in Congress. He notes that the judiciary bill had been "severely handled" and amended and was soon to be sent to the House of Representatives, where "as there is no less than Two & twenty lawyers in that House I expect they will turn and twist this poor bill until they send it back to its parents as unlike the Original as Law Language will permit of."[59]

The perils of interpreting Maclay's comments without any equivalent explanation by Morris are revealed in a discussion Gordon Wood included in his Pulitzer Prize–winning book, *The Radicalism of the*

---

[59]On Hopkinson's letter on the judiciary bill and a hoped-for appointment, see RM to Hopkinson, July 3 and Aug. 15, 1789, *DHFFC*, vol. 16 (forthcoming). On Hopkinson's nomination as a district judge, see RM to Mary Morris, Sept. 11, 1789, ibid.

American Revolution. Morris, Wood contends, unlike many of his fellow merchants, long resisted the common practice of successful merchants to seek "ennoblement" by withdrawing from business, investing in proprietary wealth, adopting an aristocratic lifestyle, and seeking high public office. However, he alleges, by the late 1780s and 1790s, the lure of office was too great and Morris succumbed to the aristocratic notions of republican virtue. According to Wood, Morris then

> shifted all his entrepreneurial energy and much of his capital into the acquisition of speculative land — something that seemed more respectable than trade — and tried to set himself up as an aristocrat. He acquired a coat of arms, patronized artists, and hired [Pierre] L'Enfant to build him a huge marble palace [on Chestnut Street] in Philadelphia. He surrounded himself with the finest furniture, tapestry, silver, and wines and made his home the center of America's high social life. Like a good aristocrat, . . . he maintained . . . "a profuse, incessant and elegant hospitality," and displayed a luxury that was to be found nowhere else in America.

Wood, working mostly from Maclay's comments, then applied his argument to Morris's senatorial career, asserting, "When he became a United States senator in 1789, he [Morris] was edgy and anxious to prove himself a disinterested aristocrat. When informed that the public were alarmed at the extent of 'commercial influence' in the Congress, he supposed 'they blame me.'" Morris seemed, Wood asserts, "almost desperate" to win the approval of the South Carolina "nabobs" Pierce Butler and Ralph Izard, who had "a particular antipathy" to him. "When the Carolina senators haughtily expressed their contempt for vulgar moneymaking, Morris, to the astonishment of listeners, did 'likewise.'" According to Maclay, Morris gave himself "Compliments on his manner & Conduct of life . . . and the little respect he paid to the common Opinions of People." Like the "classical republican aristocrat he aspired to be," Wood proclaims, Morris was proud of "his disregard of money." But, adds Wood, "for Morris to disregard money was not only astonishing, it was fatal. We know what happened, and it is a poignant, even tragic story. All his aristocratic dreams came to nothing; the marble palace on Chestnut Street went unfinished; his dinner parties ceased; his carriages were seized; and he ended in debtors' prison. That Morris should have behaved as he did says something about the power of the classical aristocratic ideas of disinterestedness in post-revolutionary America."[60]

However, the events Wood describes, and Maclay's statements in particular, bear other explanations. Morris, in fact, did not withdraw from commercial pursuits any more than conditions and his financial circumstances dictated. At the end of the Revolutionary War, he had created a series of new partnerships, placing active management in the hands of younger men, as was common for merchants of his age and stature. What comments he made about his urge to withdraw from personal activity in trade were associated with his stage in life, not with status considerations or an urge for political office. And whatever he may have said about retirement, especially when things went wrong, he could not refrain from delving into new fields of commercial endeavor. Only gradually did he withdraw from his numerous partnerships. He declined to renew his partnership in William Constable and Company when it expired in 1791, alleging the need to wind up his tangled affairs. He sold his stake in Willing, Morris and Company to John Swanwick, probably for financial reasons, in 1794. Other partnerships and affiliations remained in place throughout Morris's term in the Senate, and ships and cargoes in which he had a stake continued to come and go on as extensive a scale as the availability of credit permitted. Morris's land investments were not a leisurely gentlemanly pursuit or an attempt to live off the income obtained from landed estates. Rather, land was just another commodity that could be marketed to European investors, one that Morris asserted might, if successfully sold, have made him the richest man in America. In sum, Morris had not lost his interest in money, or come to see its pursuit as beneath him.[61]

---

[60]Gordon S. Wood, *The Radicalism of the American Revolution* (New York, 1992), pp. 211–12, 266, and idem, "Interests and Disinterestedness in the Making of the Constitution," in *Beyond Confederation*, pp. 96–100.

[61]The accounts of RM's investments and expenditures for the 1790s can be found in Robert Morris Business Records, PHi. For further evidence of RM's continued interest not merely in trade but in technology and manufacturing in the 1790s, see Charles E. Peterson, "Morris, Foxall, and the Eagle Works: A Pioneer Steam Engine Boring Cannon," *Canal History and Technology Proceedings* 7 (March 1988):207–40, especially pp. 208–18; and RM to David Ramsay, Dec. 7, 1795, in Robert L. Brunhouse, ed., *David*

How then are we to interpret his statements to Maclay boasting of his disregard for money? The remarks must be seen in context. They appear in the course of a discussion of the salaries of public officials, which Morris believed should be generous, while Maclay thought they should be Spartan. Also involved in the discussion were Pierce Butler and Ralph Izard, two Southern aristocrats arguing for very high salaries—which they said should be spent to demonstrate the high status and lifestyle appropriate for senators. Faced with Maclay's disapproval and belief that high salaries were disliked by his constituents, Morris appears to be arguing, as he always had, that good salaries were necessary to permit appropriate and honest candidates to take public positions and to enable them to cover the costs of social obligations expected of them, but that he himself was not motivated by the size of the salary attached to office. Similarly, Maclay next reports that Morris went on to expostulate on his disregard for "popularity," no doubt a reflection of Morris's belief that politicians' calls for low salaries were one of those appeals to the prejudices of the public rather than the real needs of good government that were common to electioneering demagogues. Morris's denial that he took office for his own financial benefit in the face of long-term allegations that he always had done so should not be construed as a belief that he had rejected the private pursuit of wealth outside of public office. The cause of his loss of wealth must be sought elsewhere.[62]

Furthermore, there is no evidence Morris was seeking the social approval of Butler and Izard; more likely he was seeking their votes. He was well aware of the longstanding hatred and suspicion of both him and Philadelphia in certain circles in South Carolina. In the instance of his support for high salaries, and on another occasion when Morris refused to speak in favor of antislavery petitions from Pennsylvania so as not to antagonize the South Carolinians over what he no doubt perceived as a lost cause, the desire to tone down their hostility to the point

---

Ramsay, 1749–1815: Selections from His Writings, American Philosophical Society, *Transactions,* n.s. 55, pt. 4 (Philadelphia, 1965), p. 142.

[62]For RM's stance on salaries and the sort of statements about his disinterestedness on the subject that he probably made during the discussion recorded by Maclay, see Bowling and Veit, *Diary of William Maclay,* pp. 133–34, 138, 143–44, 155; and RM to the President of Congress, July 28, 1783, and to Jefferson, Feb. 25, 1784, *Morris Papers,* 8:353, 9:133–43.

that they could be bargained with on measures of importance seems more likely than any misguided attempt to make them like him.[63]

Morris's lifestyle had been lavish and his hospitality legendary as early as the 1770s and 1780s, and he used such aristocratic trappings for the entertainment and cultivation of potential investors, partners, and customers, as well as for those he wished to impress for political or social reasons. His entertaining was conducted partly for the sheer fun of it, for Morris was a gregarious, ebullient man who liked people, however much he disdained "the People." But it was also purposeful, and usually tied to the facilitation of more concrete goals than the achievement of aristocratic status. As an import/export merchant, Morris was constantly exposed to material goods, and perhaps it was inevitable he would want to possess some of the best for himself. Many luxuries were also a means of indulging the fine tastes of his beloved wife, Mary White Morris (fig. 3), and, to some extent, her desire to remain "the hostess with the mostest" when challenged by the rise of her younger, more beautiful, and more extravagant rival Ann Willing Bingham. In the case of his notorious marble Chestnut Street mansion, known as "Morris's Folly," Morris, who initiated its construction in 1793, at a time he believed his financial difficulties had been resolved, was in part the victim of his self-indulgent architect, Pierre L'Enfant, but probably also of his own wounded ego.[64]

---

[63]On RM's opponents in South Carolina, see, for example, Nathanael Greene to RM, Mar. 17, 1783, and to Gouverneur Morris, Apr. 3, 1783, *Morris Papers,* 7:598–99, 670–71; Alexander Gillon to Nathanael Greene, Apr. 11, 1783, Greene Papers, William L. Clements Library, University of Michigan; David Ramsay to Nathanael Greene, Sept. 10, 1782, and to Benjamin Rush, July 11, 1783, Brunhouse, *Ramsay Writings,* pp. 71, 75; and Bowling and Veit, *Diary of William Maclay,* p. 73. For RM's refusal to speak on the slavery petitions, see Bowling and Veit, *Diary of William Maclay,* pp. 202. RM did, however, cooperate with Maclay in support of liberal naturalization laws and the rights of Quakers (Bowling and Veit, *Diary of William Maclay,* pp. 88, 89, 214).

[64]On RM's hospitality and luxurious living throughout his career, and his use of such hospitality for both political and business purposes, and on Mary Morris's role as hostess, see, for example, John Adams to RM, Nov. 6, 1782, and "Lucius" to RM, Apr. 9, 1783, *Morris Papers,* 7:20, 687; Marquis de Chastellux, *Travels in North America in the Years 1780, 1781, and 1782,* trans. and ed. Howard C. Rice, Jr., 2 vols. (Chapel Hill, 1963) 1:135, 136, 164, 301, 303; Jay to RM, Dec. 26, 1777, in Richard B. Morris, ed., *John Jay, The Making of a Revolutionary: Unpublished Papers, 1745–1780* (New York, 1975), p. 460; Catharine W. Livingston to Jay, Aug. 12, 1782, in Richard B. Morris, ed., *John Jay, The Winning of the Peace: Unpublished Papers, 1780–1784* (New York, 1980), pp. 459–60; Bowling and Veit, *Diary of William Maclay,* p. 74; and Ethel Elise Rasmusson,

A few other important aspects of Morris's senatorship require comment: namely his role as "first friend," and the unusual case of the
ongoing investigations into his public accounts throughout his term in
office.

Morris's close friendship with Washington was widely recognized by
early observers but has confused some later biographers, who tend to
disregard or deny it. Once Washington's image as "Cincinnatus," the
disinterested, unambitious public servant, and Morris's as a "Founding Finagler" became entrenched, the legendary friendship seemed
inexplicable, though it was still sometimes used to tear down Washington's monumental status. Marvin Kitman, for example, in his satirical
The Making of the President 1789, compares the friendship to that between Richard Nixon and Bebe Rebozo, with Morris positioned as
corrupt presidential crony. But many reasons can be advanced for
the friendship between these two men of affairs, hardworking since
youth, less philosophically inclined and less formally educated, and of

---

"Capital on the Delaware: The Philadelphia Upper Class in Transition, 1789–1801,"
Ph.D. diss., Brown University, 1962, pp. 48–52, 70, 73, 74, 77, 137, 213. On "Morris's
Folly," see Oberholtzer, *Robert Morris,* pp. 297–99, 331–32; Sumner, *Financier and the
Finances of the Revolution,* 2:228–29; and Young, *Forgotten Patriot,* pp. 214–17. For the
argument that RM's motivations were "modern" and "bourgeois," rather than "aristocratic," see John F. Walsh, " 'Men of Property and Understanding': The Pennsylvania
Republican Party, 1776–1790," Ph.D. diss., Claremont Graduate School, 1992, pp.
282–88. Although they noted his expensive furnishings, European visitors commented
on the simplicity of RM's dress and demeanor. See, for example, van Hogendorp's story
of RM's placing on a table next to a piece of Sèvres porcelain a hat of a shape and
quality that would not even have suited the style of a European laborer (quoted in van
Winter, *Dutch Investment,* 1:145); van Hogendorp's sketch of RM printed in *Brieven en
Gedenkschriften van Gijsbert Karel van Hogendorp* (The Hague, 1866), 1:348–49; and
Chastellux, *Travels in America,* 1:136, 301 n.

On the social tension Mary Morris experienced after the return of the Binghams
from Europe and their initiating an unprecedentedly lavish lifestyle in Philadelphia at
the time RM's bills had bounced, see RM to Mary Morris, Dec. 27, 1787, and Jan. 9,
1788, and Mary Morris to RM, Jan. 13, 1788, Morris Papers, Henry E. Huntington
Library. RM's letters to his wife indicate a cutback in expenditures from 1787 until at
least 1790. RM was declared free of debt as of February 1793, but soon afterward
suffered major losses from the collapse of the London stock market and bankruptcy of
two of his banking houses there. For Gouverneur Morris's repeated (but disregarded)
advice that RM settle his business affairs and retire from commercial endeavors, but not
from politics because "your mind is too active to be without pursuits and too great to be
satisfied with small objects," see his letters to RM of Feb. 14 and June 25, 1792, Feb. 14,
1793, May 26, and Dec. 28, 1794, and Dec. 7, 1795, Gouverneur Morris Commercial
Letterbooks, DLC.

FIG. 3. *Mary Morris,* by Gilbert
Stuart, circa 1795. *(Courtesy
New York Public Library)*

somewhat lower status than many of those with whom they were surrounded. They had supported each other's struggles to sustain the war
effort over a seven-year period. Both were men of strong passions that
they worked hard to control, and both sought "to rule with their reason, not with their blood," as Nelson Mandela reportedly characterized his own moderate stance. Morris and his wife therefore held
prominent positions on all social occasions in which Washington was
involved, and Morris's influence over Washington was widely known,
though usually undocumented.[65]

But the friendship did not prevent the two men from differing over
policy on occasion or following their own interests. Washington continued his quest for the capital on the Potomac, and Morris continued

[65]On RM's friendship with Washington, see Marvin Kitman, *The Making of the President 1789* (New York, 1989), pp. 212–14; *Life and Correspondence of Rufus King,* 1:622;
Oberholtzer, *Robert Morris,* pp. 273–78, 351; and Rasmusson, "Capital on the Delaware," pp. 49–50. For RM's classification as a founding finagler, see Nathan Miller, *The
Founding Finaglers* (New York, 1976), pp. 79–83, 100, 103–4.

to fight for the Delaware, but it is perhaps not mere coincidence that in the end each got some of what he wanted, while others lost out. When Washington came before the Senate for advice and consent on an Indian treaty, expecting a rubber stamp, it was Morris who spoke for the senators in their insistence on reviewing the issue carefully, conceding only that they would give an answer within three days.[66] Moreover, Washington remained careful about appearances. He no longer stayed at Morris's home once elected president, and although he took over Morris's house when Philadelphia provided it once Congress moved there, he insisted on a fair-market rent of three thousand dollars a year.[67] Nor could Washington's accommodation of Morris's patronage requests be taken for granted. Benjamin Rush quoted the following Thomas Fitzsimons anecdote as an example of Washington's penchant for secrecy. Morris had approached Washington seeking an appointment for George Clymer as inspector of excise; Washington listened but gave no answer. Morris stopped in to ask a second time while en route to the Senate, but again Washington was silent. As soon as Morris reached the Senate, he heard the announcement of Clymer's nomination for the post. Washington had submitted the nomination two hours earlier, but had not felt free to tell Morris so.[68]

Even before he took his seat in the Senate, Morris was working to resolve the politically damaging question of the settlement of his accounts with the secret and commercial committees. He dealt first with Washington's former aide Benjamin Walker, who had been assigned the task by the Board of Treasury. With the creation of the new government, auditor Nicholas Eveleigh and comptroller Oliver Wolcott, Jr., took over the settlement, and Morris spent long hours acquiring and presenting additional documentation for all his claims. Morris believed the settlement was close to completion in 1790, but in fact things dragged on until his term ended. Maclay believed that Hamil-

---

[66]On the advise and consent issue, see Bowling and Veit, *Diary of William Maclay,* pp. 80, 127.

[67]RM to Jay, Apr. 20, 1789, Jay Papers, NNC; Leonard D. White, *The Federalists: A Study in Administrative History* (Westport, Conn., 1948), pp. 490–91; Douglas Southall Freeman, *Patriot and President,* vol. 6 of *George Washington: A Biography* (New York, 1954), pp. 285–86.

[68]Rush to John Adams, Aug. 22, 1806, Lyman H. Butterfield, ed., *The Letters of Benjamin Rush,* 2 vols. (Princeton, 1951), 2:925–26.

ton used the settlement process as a way to put Morris in his power and thereby ensure Morris's support for his measures, but no evidence of this has been found. In the final settlement made in 1795, Morris and his partners were held to owe $93,312.63 on the commercial transactions they conducted for these congressional committees. Morris signed bonds for payment of this sum but soon went bankrupt. As he explained the situation in the printed account of property he produced while in debtors' prison, "Mr. [John] Ross, and Willing, Morris and Co., made certain contracts, and the latter transacted much business for the old Congress. And upon a settlement of the accounts by officers who meant Fairness, but who, I ever thought, did not truly understand mercantile method and principle, and who, by charging depreciation which I objected to upon principles that I thought right, altho over-ruled by them, brought a Balance in favour of the United States, to which I at last submitted." He claimed "the former Balance will be considerably reduced by objects of Credit I have discovered that were not at the former settlement brought into view," but that he gave "Security on Lands," and when those proved deficient, assigned all his claims on Ross and on Thomas Willing to the government. "I expect there will from these two Sources be sufficient to extinguish that debt to the United States, my part as well as theirs." But, if such payments were ever made, no record has been found.[69]

---

[69]On the settlement process, see RM to Mary Morris, Apr. 25, June 19, Aug. 1, 1790, Morris Papers, Henry E. Huntington Library; and RM to Tench Coxe and Richard Harison, and to John Ross, both Jan. 12, 1795, Robert Morris Private Letterbook 1, DLC. For the final settlement of RM's secret and commercial committee accounts, see Robert Morris, *In the Account of Property* (Philadelphia, n.d. [ca. 1801]), pp. 29–30; Balances due to and from Willing, Morris and Company, and RM and John Ross, Sept. 22, 1795, and A. Brodie to John Davis, Oct. 26 and Dec. 1, 1795, Manuscript File, nos. 29585 and 29304, War Department Collection of Revolutionary War Records, RG 93, and Willing, Morris and Company accounts, Oct. 1–6, 1795, accounts with RM, Silas Deane, John Alsop, Philip Livingston, and Francis Lewis, June 29, 1796, RM's account dated July 13, 1796, and his bonds dated May 24, 1796, and John Steele to Joseph Nourse, July 12, 1796, in Treasury Journal K (Old Government), Nov. 29, 1794–May 3, 1799, Central Treasury Records of the Continental and Confederation Governments, 1775–1789, RG 217, National Archives; the copies of the accounts as settled Sept. 22, 1795, with RM, Deane, Alsop, Livingston, and Lewis, in Miscellaneous Manuscripts, Robert Morris, New York Historical Society; RM to Willing, Mar. 1 and May 10, 1796, and to Ross, Feb. 22 and Mar. 28, 1796, Robert Morris Private Letterbook 1, DLC; Bowling and Veit, *Maclay Diary*, pp. 193, 194, 199, 208, 227, 269, 300; Ferguson, *Power of the Purse*, pp. 199–202; and, for examples of the complexities which made settlement

A different solution was needed to answer newspaper charges regarding Morris's accounts as superintendent of finance. At the close of his administration in 1784, Morris had printed up an account of his entire administration and submitted it to Congress for distribution to the states and other interested parties. However, rather than accepting his resignation with a resolution of thanks for services performed, as had been done with other retiring executive officers, Morris's accounts were referred to a committee dominated by his opponents. In response to its report, Congress had in June 1785 authorized the appointment of a three-person commission to "inquire into the receipts and expenditures of public Monies" and "to examine and adjust the accounts of the United States with that department, during his administration, and to report a state thereof." However, finding suitable candidates for the commission deemed to be beyond Morris's "influence" proved difficult, and none was ever appointed. This inaction left Morris politically vulnerable. Morris's opponents alleged he had blocked the appointments, and they charged that he was a defaulter on both his secret and commercial committee and finance office accounts. In an effort to discredit the Constitution they alleged that the ban on ex post facto laws was placed in it to prevent the prosecution of those who, like Morris, were indebted to the public prior to the onset of the new government. The subject was extensively and vitriolically debated in Pennsylvania in 1788 and 1789, and Morris, who was being considered for many high offices, vowed to settle his accounts and get rid of all the "dirt" that had been flung on his good name. Believing the secret and commercial committee accounts were nearly settled, in February 1790 he petitioned the president and both houses of Congress to appoint a commission to examine his accounts as superintendent of finance. In the Senate, the memorial was referred to a committee that recommended the president appoint a three-man commission; the Senate agreed and authorized a five-dollar-a-day salary for each commissioner.

After the Senate's resolution was received and debated, Madison presented the House committee report, which asserted that a regular

---

of these accounts so difficult, Elizabeth M. Nuxoll, *Congress and the Munitions Merchants: The Secret Committee of Trade during the American Revolution, 1775–1777* (New York, 1985), pp. 149–51, 153–56, 159–60, 187–88, 373–74, 399–400, 432–33.

official examination had already been made into Morris's transactions and that it was inexpedient to incur the expense of a reexamination by commissioners. After further debate the House resolved to appoint a committee to inquire into the receipts and expenditures and report the results to Congress. The committee obtained relevant statements of the accounts from Joseph Nourse, longtime register of the Treasury. In February 1791 Madison presented the committee's report with supporting papers, stating that it was "evidently impossible" for the committee to examine the accounts in detail and "unnecessary" because they had been examined and passed in the proper offices. Consequently, the committee had obtained Nourse's statement and printed enough copies to furnish to each member of Congress "the best practicable means of appreciating the Service of the Superintendant, and the Utility of his Administration."[70] And there the controversy was allowed to stand.

Morris's term ended in March 1795 and he declined renomination.[71] At about that time he received a letter from the recently resigned secretary of state, Thomas Jefferson, who expounded on his happiness in retirement, adding: "I am *told* it is in the newspapers, (for I make a point to read none of them) that you also are retiring. I congratulate you on the sensations you experience, though I doubt whether you can enjoy them fully, residing as you do at the very fountain-head of torment's[;] associating as you must daily with those who are broiling on the public gridiron, you cannot avoid participating in their pains."[72] On June 1, 1795, Morris responded to Jefferson's comments on retirement:

---

[70]On RM's memorial, copies of which were enclosed in letters to the president of the United States, to John Adams as vice president, to Frederick Muhlenburg as Speaker of the House, all dated Feb. 8, 1790, see *Morris Papers*, 9:633–37; Bowling and Veit, *Diary of William Maclay*, pp. 199, 200, 205; *DHFFC*, 1:237–41, 8:663–75; Joseph Nourse, *Statements of the Receipts and Expenditures of Public Monies during the Administration of the Finances by Robert Morris;* Nourse's supportive report of Mar. 4, 1790, to the committee of the House of Representatives appointed to consider RM's memorial, in the John H. Hazelton Collection, DLC; RM to Walter Stone, Mar. 21, 1790, Stone Family of Maryland Papers, DLC; and Madison to RM, Mar. 24, 1790, Bortman Collection, Boston University.

[71]On RM's retirement, see RM to Wilhem and Jan Willink, Mar. 8, and to Anthony Wayne, Mar. 27, 1795, Morris Private Letterbook 1, DLC.

[72]Jefferson to RM, Feb. 19, 1795, Brooklyn Naval Lyceum Collection, U.S. Naval Academy, Annapolis.

I have no doubt of the enjoyments you find in Retirement. You are a philosopher as well as a practical Planter. These pursuits will occupy body and mind and when that is the case happiness is generally attendant. With respect to yourself, to retire was to act wisely, but as your Retirement regards the United States, the Public have to lament the loss of Abilities and Talents which have been eminently useful & which no doubt would have Continued to be so. . . . I think however that it is not improbable that you will again be drawn forth into public life. I have Retired from Public service & will never resume it, and I am trying to clear myself of a vast load of private business, in order to enjoy if I can what will remain of life when my work is accomplished in quiet and Calm.[73]

But as Morris's financial situation grew even worse over the next few years, he found quiet and calm, if at all, only within the walls of debtors' prison. Morris's investment in Washington, D.C., lots proved disastrous. Peace did not arrive in Europe and the violations of American neutrality escalated. Money remained tight. Morris's frantic efforts to raise funds at home and abroad failed, and he was forced to hide out from his creditors at his country estate, "The Hills," while more and more of his property was seized and sold at auction. Once imprisoned for debt in 1798, his usual equanimity returned and he bore his misfortune with dignity. He worked away at his financial records, took his daily exercise, aided some of his fellow prisoners, evaded the epidemics plaguing Philadelphia, and welcomed the visits of family and friends. Released from prison in 1801 after the passage of a federal bankruptcy law, Morris lived modestly until 1806 on the fruits of a pension his friend and former colleague Gouverneur Morris had obtained for Mary Morris from a land company, but he was never again to engage in public or private business.[74] Yet even then not all confidence in his

---

[73]RM to Jefferson, June 1, 1795, Morris Private Letterbook 1, DLC.

[74]On RM's bankruptcy and its impact, see Oberholtzer, *Robert Morris,* pp. 335–57; Sumner, *Financier and the Finances of the Revolution,* 2:279–92; Young, *Forgotten Patriot,* pp. 238–60; and Elizabeth M. Nuxoll, "Illegitimacy, Family Status, and Property in the Early Republic: The Morris-Croxall Family of New Jersey," *New Jersey History* 113 (1995):6–14. For a comprehensive discussion of RM's land speculation and its relationship to RM's fall, see Barbara Ann Chernow, *Robert Morris, Land Speculator, 1790–1801* (New York, 1978). For an analysis of land speculation generally during that period, its connection with foreign investment, and RM's relationship to the overall trends, see Doerflinger, *Spirit of Enterprise,* pp. 314–29.

abilities was gone. When Jefferson, as Morris had predicted, returned to office as president in 1801, he looked around for someone to manage the navy. If only Morris could be released from confinement, and public confidence in him regained, he would have been Jefferson's choice for secretary of the navy.[75]

---

[75]Jefferson to Madison, Mar. 12, 1801, Robert J. Brugger, Robert A. Rutland, J. C. A. Stagg et al., eds., *The Papers of James Madison: Secretary of State Series*, 4 vols. to date (Charlottesville, 1986–), 1:12.

Mary A. Giunta

In Opposition

The Congressional Career of William Branch Giles, 1790–1798

T HE FOLLOWING ACCOUNT focuses on the role of Virginia Republican William Branch Giles as an ally of James Madison and
Thomas Jefferson in vigorously opposing the Federalist policies of
George Washington and Alexander Hamilton during the first decade
under the Constitution of 1787. Giles, from Amelia County in the
eastern Piedmont south of the James River, served in the U.S. House
of Representatives from 1790 to 1798 and from 1801 to 1803. He
later served in the U.S. Senate, 1804–15, and as governor of Virginia,
1827–30. He was an early supporter of the Constitution; however,
throughout his political career Giles was a strict constructionist who
sought to protect the rights of the states against the imposition of
federal power. An examination of his early career and actions in the
House of Representatives provides an opportunity to explore the
political debates and conflicts of the early years of the federal government and the beginnings of the first political party system of Federalists and Democratic-Republicans, also known as Jeffersonian Republicans, or Republicans.

This essay is dedicated to the memory of Eugene R. Sheridan, senior associate editor of
The Papers of Thomas Jefferson. The author wishes to draw attention to Mr. Sheridan's
article, "Thomas Jefferson and the Giles Resolutions," *William and Mary Quarterly,*
3d ser. 49 (1992):589–608, and to acknowledge the editing skills of Kenneth R. Bowling that reflect his knowledge of the period.

FIG. 1. *William Branch Giles,*
1762–1830, by an unknown
artist. *(Courtesy National Portrait*
Gallery, Smithsonian Institution)

Giles's immediate forebears came to America from England in the
seventeenth century. Christopher Branch, the great-great-great-grand-
father of William Branch Giles, settled at Arrowhattocks, Henrico
County, in the area that later became Chesterfield County, Virginia.
Branch's grandson, also named Christopher, had several children,
one of whom fathered a daughter, Ann. She married William Giles,
the father of William Branch Giles. Ann Branch and William Giles
had four daughters and two sons; William Branch was the third child
and youngest son. He was born on August 12, 1762, in rural Amelia
County, Virginia.[1] As a young man he attended the newly established
Hampden-Sydney College in nearby Prince Edward County before
transferring in 1779 to the Presbyterian college at Princeton, New

---

[1]Giles's birthplace is uncertain. In his will he requested that he be buried "in the
family burying ground at the old place formerly the residence of my father." Giles is
buried in Amelia County, Virginia. See Giles Family Papers, University of Virginia, and
Dice Robin Anderson, *William Branch Giles: A Study in the Politics of Virginia and the Nation
from 1790 to 1830* (Gloucester, Mass., 1965), pp. 1–2. See also Blanch Baldridge, *My
Virginia Kin* (Strawberry Point, Iowa, 1968), pp. 58–60.

Jersey, where he received his bachelor of arts degree two years later. Giles next studied law at William and Mary College under the tutelage of George Wythe. After receiving his license to practice in 1786, he became a successful lawyer in and around Petersburg, Virginia.[2]

Many of Giles's earliest cases involved claims by British merchants against Virginia planters and businessmen. Prior to 1790, when the British "suited for payment" in federal court, debt cases were settled in state courts. Part of Giles's task was to represent British merchants in an indebted society with a limited amount of gold and silver and a depreciated currency in circulation. He was an effective litigator; he wrote Jefferson that "in all cases within my recollection in which the debts were established by competent testimony, judgements were rendered for the plaintiff [the British merchants]."[3] His legal practice also entailed other property and financial transactions and lawsuits, including those involving Robert Randolph, Benjamin Harrison, Peyton Randolph, Joseph Jones, and lesser known persons. Many relied upon him to look after their business interests.[4] In contrast to the harsh political relationship that prevailed between them later, Giles and future Chief Justice John Marshall exchanged information about the fine points of cases in which one or both were involved. Evidently Giles was also a close friend of James Marshall, John's brother.[5]

Like many other Virginia planters, Giles acquired large tracts of

---

[2]Giles's name, along with others who attended the College of William and Mary between 1776 and 1781, is listed in a school catalogue. The exact dates of his stay are not known, although it followed his graduation from the College of New Jersey. See *Catalogue of the College of William and Mary* (1859), p. 44. No record is available of Giles's education either at the College of New Jersey or at William and Mary. See Anderson, *Giles*, p. 5.

[3]Anderson, *Giles*, p. 7. See also Isaac S. Harrell, "Some Neglected Phases of the Revolution," *William and Mary Quarterly*, 2d ser. 5 (1925):167–70; William Branch Giles to Thomas Jefferson, May 6, 1792, Miscellaneous Letters, RG 59 (Records of the U.S. Department of State), National Archives and Records Administration (NARA).

[4]John Lewis to Giles, Sept. 19, 1789, Robert Randolph to Giles, Apr. 15, 1787, David Mason to Giles, Oct. 6, 1789, Giles to Henry Heth, Aug. 3, 1814, David Meade to Giles, Dec. 8, 1815, Giles Papers, Virginia Historical Society; Giles to Richard Archer, Nov. 8, 1791, Archer Family Papers, Virginia Historical Society; Giles to Littleton Dennis, May 1787, Maryland Historical Society; John Randolph to Giles, Boston Public Library; Samuel Shepard to Giles, Dec. 11, 1790, Princeton University Library; Thomas Jefferson to Giles, Dec. 12, Dec. 13, 1789, and Giles to Jefferson, Dec. 13, 1789, all in *The Papers of Thomas Jefferson*, 25 vols. to date (Princeton, 1950–), vol. 16 (Julian P. Boyd, ed.), pp. 280–96.

[5]John Marshall to Giles, n.d., Special Collections, University of Minnesota; Marshall to Giles, Sept. 22, 1786, John Marshall Papers, College of William and Mary.

land during his lifetime. One of Giles's early land purchases was recorded on January 1, 1790, when he and his father agreed to an
indenture for four hundred acres.[6] On his land Giles planted a variety
of crops, including wheat, corn, and hemp, as well as tobacco. His
extensive involvement in agriculture soon earned him the sobriquet
"Farmer Giles."[7]

Prior to holding elected federal office, in addition to his professional status as a successful lawyer and planter, Giles gained societal position in a manner often recorded in early Virginia history. He courted
Mary Jefferson, daughter of Thomas Jefferson. When he married Martha Peyton Tabb in 1797, he became associated with two of the most
prominent and wealthy families of Virginia's aristocracy. Their life
at the "Wigwam," in addition to operating large landholdings with a
number of slaves, consisted of entertaining family members and visitors, including overnight guests. As a man of his station, Giles accepted
the prevailing idea that landed aristocracy and democracy were "not
mutually exclusive and that both of these can and ought to be used by a
self-governing people." He performed his private and public duties
with a sense of responsibility typical of others in similar positions in
Virginia society.[8]

Giles traveled to Richmond in the early summer of 1788 during the
debates of Virginia's convention to ratify the Federal Constitution.
While he did not participate in the formal debates, Giles had ample
opportunity to express his views at social gatherings. The Antifederalist leader, George Mason, praised the intelligence of the young man
and observed "there was a stripling of a lawyer at the Hotel this morning who has as much sense as one-half of us, though he is on the wrong
side."[9] Giles's interest in the affairs of government soon became that of
an elected official.

Following the death of Rep. Theodorick Bland, Giles was elected in

---

[6]Amelia County Deed Book, no. 19, p. 34, microfilm, Virginia State Library.

[7]"Memoirs of a Monticello Slave," *William and Mary Quarterly,* 3d ser. 8 (1951):576 n.

[8]Charles S. Sydnor, *American Revolutionaries in the Making: Political Practices in Washington's Virginia* (New York, 1962), p. 116. For a study of the intellectual side of Virginia
society, see Richard Beale Davis, *Intellectual Life in Jefferson's Virginia, 1790–1830* (Knoxville, 1972). An unknown diarist wrote that he had "spent many happy times" in Giles's
home in Petersburg (Diary, July 23, 1804–Sept. 29, 1804, p. 38, Virginia Historical
Society).

[9]*Richmond Enquirer,* Dec. 16, 1830.

July 1790 to fill the remainder of Bland's term in the House of Representatives.[10] Elections to and service in the federal government would occupy much of his life for the next twenty-five years. Giles took his House seat on the first day of the third session of the First Congress on December 7, 1790, even though he had been bedridden that fall. He was a societal and political leader and a Federalist, but one dedicated to the republican principles of the "spirit of '76." Throughout his career, though there were some exceptions, he sought to protect the rights of states and individuals against the encroachment of a strong federal government. He was especially leery of a government dependent on "stock jobbers" and financial speculators. Accordingly, he did not believe that the policies of Secretary of the Treasury Alexander Hamilton were compatible with the designs of the Revolutionary generation or of the Framers and their plan for the new government. Representing a predominantly rural region, he followed republican principles against the monarchical tendencies he found prevalent in the administration's actions, especially Hamilton's financial system. It was not long before he was in opposition to President George Washington as well.

Giles had letters of introduction to James Madison and Secretary of War Henry Knox among others. John Marshall provided a letter to Madison informing him that Giles was "particularly desirous of being known to you." On December 25, 1790, Edward Carrington, the U.S. marshal for Virginia, told Madison that although Giles was "yet a very young man he has acquired high reputation in both the superior & inferior Courts of this State. You will find him upon trial to possess real genius, acquired knowledge, & solid honesty such as will make him a valuable Co-adjutor in our representation." Carrington urged Giles to "form as close an acquaintance [with Madison] as possible, I doubt not your striking his mind to advantage, in which case you will find it easy to gain his confidence, and you will always find that circumstance greatly to your benefit in your political walks."[11]

---

[10]Giles represented the counties of Amelia, Brunswick, Cumberland, Dinwiddie, Greenville, Lunenburg, Mecklenburg, Powhatan, Prince George, and Sussex.

[11]John Marshall to James Madison, Nov. 29, 1790, Edward Carrington to James Madison, Carrington to Giles, Dec. 25, 1790, all in *The Papers of James Madison,* 27 vols. to date (Chicago and Charlottesville, 1962–), vol. 13 (C. F. Hobson and Robert A. Rutland, eds.), pp. 309, 335–36 n.

Virginians were not the only ones to take note of Giles. Pennsylvania Sen. William Maclay was "attentive to" Giles during a dinner at President Washington's home in January 1791, and his description of the young congressman helps to complete the picture of the legislator:

> I saw a Speech of his in the papers which read very Well, and they said he delivers himself handsomely. . . . Canvas-backs ham & Chickens Old Maderia, the Glories of the Ancient Dominion, all *amazing* fine were his constant Themes. boasted of personal Prowess, *more manual Exercise than any man in New England*. fast but fine living in his Country, Wine or Cherry bounce from 12 O'clock, to night, every day. he seemed to practice on these principles too, as often as the Bottle passed him. . . . he is but a Young man. and seemed as if he always would be so.[12]

Giles's earliest speeches in Congress reflected his states' rights and sectional interests. This pattern is seen in his position on several subjects, including the discussions on a national militia bill. On December 16, 1790, he opposed an amendment to the bill to oblige state governments to furnish the militia with weapons and related supplies on the ground that "to lay an obligation on the state government to furnish their militia with arms, was to lay a tax on them, which was by no means authorized by the constitution." He also objected to exemptions of government officials from militia service on the ground that "the law-giver be made to feel the influence of the law he has had a hand in framing," although state legislators might exempt these officials, and if Congress "had had it in their power to exempt themselves from the weight of the militia law, they had the power to do the same in all cases"; furthermore, the exemption was unconstitutional as "the privileges [of members] . . . were defined in the constitution, and this was not made one."[13] These early appearances on the floor of the House established Giles as an ardent debater, one with a watchful eye

---

[12]For Maclay's description, see Kenneth R. Bowling and Helen E. Veit, eds., *The Diary of William Maclay and Other Notes on Senate Debates* (Baltimore, 1988), vol. 9 of *Documentary History of the First Federal Congress*, 14 vols. to date (Baltimore, 1972–), p. 365.

[13]For the third session of the First Congress, quotations are from *Documentary History of the First Federal Congress*, 14 vols. to date (Baltimore, 1972–), 14:50, 51, 53, 66–67, 70, 75, 78, 100, 108, 109, 112, 121, 128, 129, 131, 133–34, 153–55, 159, 163, 180, hereafter cited as *DHFFC*. Another source for the debates of Congress are *Annals of Congress: Debates and Proceedings in the Congress of the United States, 1789–1824*, 41 vols. (Washington, D.C., 1834–56), hereafter cited as *Annals*. No militia bill was passed in the First Congress.

on the growing powers of the federal government. When Hamilton's financial policies came under debate, this watchfulness turned to action.

Hamilton's financial plan included the assumption into the federal debt of much of the debt incurred by the states in fighting the Revolutionary War. Although assumption helped to establish the public credit of the United States, it had met with powerful opposition, especially from Southerners, earlier in 1790 before Giles joined the Virginia delegation. However, a compromise was reached: in exchange for a permanent capital on the Potomac River — the exact area to be selected by Washington — Congress agreed to assumption.[14] As a follow-up measure, in order to raise revenue to pay the interest on the assumed debt, Hamilton recommended an excise on liquor. After he initially supported the excise, Giles joined other Southerners in an attempt to defeat its passage. He believed that the tax was unfair because it placed a disproportionate burden on the South. His brief support of the measure may have been the result of the influence of Madison, who as part of the deal that located the capital on the Potomac had committed himself to support the taxes necessary to finance assumption.[15]

Another example of Giles's voting prior to the drawing of formal party lines was the debate on the establishment of a national bank. A bill to establish the Bank of the United States, as proposed by Hamilton, passed the Senate on January 20, 1791. When debate began in the House on January 31, Giles attacked the constitutionality of the bill, contending that the establishment of a bank usurped powers that rightfully belonged to the states. He further argued that expediency was no reason to violate the powers reserved to the state governments or to increase the powers of the national government.[16] In spite of Giles's opposition, the bill passed the House on February 8 by a vote of 38 to 20. Thirty-three of the yea votes were from north of Maryland,

---

[14]For compromise on location of the capital, see Charlene Bangs Bickford and Kenneth R. Bowling, *Birth of the Nation: The First Federal Congress, 1789–1791* (New York, 1989), pp. 67–75, and Stanley Elkins and Eric McKitrick, *The Age of Federalism: The Early American Republic, 1788–1800* (New York, 1993), pp. 133–34, 156–61, 226.

[15]*DHFFC*, 14:228, 235–36, 261–64, 339, 345–46; Kenneth R. Bowling, *The Creation of Washington, D.C.: The Idea and Location of the American Capital* (Fairfax, Va., 1991), p. 197.

[16]For text of Giles's speeches, see *DHFFC*, 14:376–77, 447–51, 462–70.

while all but one of the nays were from Maryland, Virginia, the Carolinas, and Georgia. All Virginia members voted against the bill.

Issues other than arguments against the constitutionality of the bank influenced opposition to the bill. According to some scholars, while opponents used arguments based on constitutionality, the main reason for the opposition of Southern members was "their belief that the agricultural interests would derive no benefits from a national banking institution." Another issue related to the location of the federal capital on the Potomac: Southerners feared that the bank and federal government would become "so entwined" that Congress would not leave Philadelphia in 1800, despite the compromise reached in 1790.[17] Washington shared this fear even though he supported the bank in general. He had asked Congress for a special act to allow him to include Alexandria, Virginia, just north of Mount Vernon, within the federal district. While the president considered his decision on the bank bill, a vote on altering the capital location was postponed until the very day he had to either sign or veto it. He signed, and the Senate immediately passed the bill granting Washington's request regarding the capital.[18] Although the issue of the capital's location influenced Washington's decision to sign the bank bill, he signed primarily because he supported Hamilton's program to place the United States on a stronger financial footing.[19]

It was becoming obvious to members of Congress who opposed Hamilton's policies that a concerted effort was needed to present a "meaningful opposition."[20] The leader of this opposition in Congress was Madison; Giles, who had been outspoken on the excise and bank

---

[17]Congressional Republicans opposed this bill more intensely than did members of the Virginia legislature. The bank bill helped the commercial segment in Virginia without affecting those who "did not benefit from it" (Richard R. Beeman, *The Old Dominion and the New Nation, 1788–1801* [Lexington, 1972], pp. 116–17). The Bank of the United States was contrary to the wishes of "non-mercantile interests." See Harry Ammon, "The Republican Party in Virginia, 1789–1824," Ph.D. diss., University of Virginia, 1948, p. 122; Bowling, *Creation of Washington, D.C.*, pp. 215–19; Bickford and Bowling, *Birth of the Nation*, pp. 73–75.

[18]Bickford and Bowling, *Birth of the Nation*, pp. 73–75.

[19]Bray Hammond, *Banks and Politics in America from the Revolution to the Civil War* (Princeton, 1957), pp. 116–18.

[20]Irving Brant, *James Madison: Father of the Constitution, 1787–1800* (Indianapolis, 1950), pp. 328–33.

issues, also assumed an important role.[21] The opposition soon unified into a political party with Jefferson at its head. For Jefferson, Madison, Giles, and others, Hamilton's advocacy of a funded debt, a national bank, an excise, and other plans for the federal government represented a direct threat to their vision of a democratic republic. Moreover, Hamilton's ability to influence House and Senate members, some of whom supported him because of their own financial interests, caused concern for the independence of the legislature from executive control. Jefferson and others believed that Hamilton, through his financial program, had made Congress "subservient to the supposed Federalist design to restore monarchy in America."[22]

As opposition to Hamilton deepened, Republicans, perhaps encouraged by their success in the 1792 congressional elections, sought not only to undermine Hamilton's influence with the people and with Washington but also to force the secretary to resign. Giles became a leading participant in this plan. Hamilton provided a reason to investigate his activities by recommending that the federal government repay the national bank for a two-million-dollar bank loan that had enabled the government to "subscribe to an equivalent amount of bank stock." In order to make this repayment, Hamilton suggested that funds borrowed to repay Revolutionary War loans from France be used to pay the bank loan instead. The proposal raised Republican fears that the secretary favored the bank at the expense of France at a time when that nation was at war.

In December 1792 Giles proposed one of three House resolutions regarding Hamilton's activities in carrying out his official duties. Giles's resolution called for President Washington to send the House a statement of the loans made under his authority with an account of their interest rates and the balance remaining in each case. On January 23, 1793, dissatisfied with the report Hamilton sent to Congress, Giles, with the almost certain knowledge, if not assistance, of Jefferson and Madison, demanded a more detailed accounting. In five resolutions presented to the House, Giles asked for: (1) copies of the authorities

---

[21]Sheridan, "Jefferson and the Giles Resolutions," pp. 595–97, and Noble E. Cunningham, *Jeffersonian Republicans: The Formation of Party Organization, 1789–1801* (Chapel Hill, 1957), p. 51.

[22]Sheridan, "Jefferson and the Giles Resolutions," p. 591.

under which loans had been negotiated under the Funding and Sinking Fund Acts of 1790; (2) the names of the persons by whom and to whom French, Dutch, and Spanish debts had been paid; (3) a statement showing the semimonthly balances between the federal government and the Bank of the United States to the end of 1792; (4) a full account of the Sinking Fund; and (5) a report on all unapplied revenue and money from loans to the end of 1792.[23] In effect Giles called for a comprehensive accounting of Hamilton's administration of the Department of the Treasury. The Virginia congressman justified the resolutions on the ground that the House lacked the complete information on the nation's finances it needed in order to exercise its constitutional role of originating revenue and appropriation bills. The House unanimously approved the resolutions the same day they were introduced because both Republicans and Federalists felt their positions would be supported; the information either would discredit Hamilton or vindicate his fiscal administration.

During the first three weeks of February 1793, Hamilton provided Congress with seven voluminous reports. In addition to responding to Giles's resolutions, Hamilton prepared reports to answer similar Senate resolutions.[24] The reports disputed any misconduct on Hamilton's part while providing Congress with a detailed account of the activities of his department. He defended his handling of foreign loans and denied any impropriety in his relations with the Bank of the United States. Hamilton was clearly aware that Giles's resolutions were politically motivated. The "resolutions to which I am to answer," he wrote, "were not moved without a pretty copious display of the reasons, on which they were founded. These reasons are before the public through the channel of the press. They are of a nature, to excite attention to beget alarm, to inspire doubts. Deductions of a very exordinary complexxion may, without forcing the sense be drawn from them."[25]

With the information provided by Hamilton, some congressmen,

---

[23]See "Report on the Balance of All Unapplied Revenues at the End of the Year 1792 and on All Unapplied Monies Which May Have Been Obtained by the Several Loans Authorized by Law (February 4, 1793)," in *The Papers of Alexander Hamilton,* ed. Harold C. Syrett and Jacob E. Cooke, 27 vols. (New York, 1961–87), 13:542–79.

[24]For additional reports see *Hamilton Papers,* 14:2–6, 17–80, 93–133.

[25]Ibid., 13:542.

including Giles, still wanted to censure him, even though Hamilton had strongly defended his actions and disputed accusations of misconduct. Madison believed the timing of new resolutions so close to the end of the Second Congress affected the outcome. "The other inquiry [into the Treasury Department] was suggested by some casual light on certain pecuniary operations which were unknown & unsuspected by the body of the [House] of Representatives," he wrote. "The Session was too near its close for a proper discussion [and] it is very unfortunate that they were offered."[26] However, Madison clearly believed there was reason to pursue the subject further. Earlier he had written Edmund Pendleton that "there has been at least a very blameable irregularity & secrecy in some particulars of it, and many appearances which at least require explanation."[27] The Third Congress, which held the possibility of a Republican majority, Madison believed, would be a better forum in which to pursue efforts to find Hamilton guilty of malfeasance and possibly drive him from the cabinet. While Madison was cautious, Jefferson was not. Sometime between February 21 and 27, 1793, the date Giles presented censure resolutions, Jefferson drafted ten of his own.[28] These resolutions accused Hamilton of exceeding his authority and not properly carrying out his duties as treasury secretary and, where he did carry them out, of disregarding the laws.

The wording of Giles's censure resolutions was similar to Jefferson's, though significantly modified. Questions have arisen as to whether Jefferson did indeed draft the resolutions.[29] No conclusive proof can be given; however, it is possible that Giles presented his resolutions after Jefferson had written them, and Madison, perhaps in an effort to prevent their defeat, had modified them. But without evidence, it is best to conclude that Giles presented resolutions similar to those drafted by Jefferson.

The resolutions were handily defeated, in part because "Republican leaders failed to rally the wavering ranks of their followers . . . [reveal-

[26]James Madison to George Nicholas, Mar. 15, 1793, *Madison Papers*, 14:472.

[27]James Madison to Edmund Pendleton, Feb. 23, 1793, ibid., 14:452; Cunningham, *Jeffersonian Republicans*, p. 51.

[28]Sheridan, "Jefferson and the Giles Resolutions," p. 528, 600–601; see *Jefferson Papers*, 25:280–96.

[29]Anderson, *Giles*, p. 22 n; *Hamilton Papers*, 13:539.

ing] a striking lack of party discipline." The only members who voted consistently with Giles and Madison on the resolutions were William Findley (Pennsylvania), John F. Mercer (Maryland), Josiah Parker (Virginia), Nathaniel Macon and John Baptista Ashe (North Carolina), and Abraham Baldwin (Georgia).[30] The defeat was humiliating for the Republicans. In "Notes on the Giles Resolutions" and in a letter to his son-in-law, Thomas Mann Randolph, Jr., Jefferson sought to give the impression that Giles had been "the sole author" of the resolutions:

> You have for some time past seen a number of reports from the Secretary of the Treasury on enquiries instituted by the H. of representatives. When they were all come in, a number of resolutions were prepared by Mr. Giles, expressing the truths resulting from the reports. . . . Mr. Giles and one or two others were sanguine enough to believe that the palpableness of the truths rendered a negative of them impossible, and therefore forced them on. Others contemplating the character of the present house, one third of which is understood to be made up of bank directors and stockjobbers who would be voting in the case of their chief; and another third of persons blindly devoted to that party, of persons not comprehending the papers, or persons comprehending them but too indulgent to pass a vote of censure, foresaw that the resolutions would be negatived by a majority of two to one. Still they thought that the negative of palpable truth would be of service, as it would let the public see how desperate and abandoned were the hands in which their interests were placed. The vote turned out to be what was expected, not more than 3 or 4 varying from what had been conceived of them.[31]

The resolutions — regardless of who wrote them — and their defeat show Giles working on the front line of political battle. The timing of the first set of five resolutions introduced on January 23, 1793, may indicate that he and other congressional Republicans believed that Hamilton would be unable to prepare the necessary reports before Congress adjourned in early March. This would leave the voters with the impression that Hamilton was guilty of the allegations. Moreover,

---

[30]Cunningham, *Jeffersonian Republicans,* pp. 53, 54; Sheridan, "Jefferson and the Giles Resolutions," p. 606.

[31]Thomas Jefferson to Thomas Mann Randolph, Jr., Mar. 3, 1793, *Jefferson Papers,* 25:311, 313–14.

the nine censure resolutions that were based on Hamilton's reports were introduced so late in the session that, if they passed, Hamilton would not have time to reply, therefore casting an even darker shadow over the secretary of the treasury. This seemed a gamble worth taking. The strategy failed when Hamilton drew up the necessary reports and accounted for his actions in such a manner as to defeat further attack on him. There is yet another possible reason for the introduction of the resolutions: their potential influence on the elections scheduled for March in Virginia and other states. A month after the Virginia elections, Madison summarized the results. He noted that Samuel Griffin's votes on Giles's resolutions "had nearly turned the scale agst. him." Of the six resolutions voted on, Griffin "voted against two, favored one, and abstained on three." The effect of voting for and against the resolutions was felt outside Virginia. Madison reported that John Breckenridge of Kentucky had "adverted to [Christopher] Greenup's late vote with indignation and dropped threats of its effects on his future pretensions." Greenup had voted against two and abstained on four resolutions. Jefferson himself recognized the influence of Giles's resolutions on the elections:

> The public will see from this the extent of their danger, and a full representation at the ensuing session will doubtless find occasion to revise the decision, and take measures for ensuring the authority of laws over corrupt maneuvres of the heads of departments under the pretext of exercising discretion in opposition to revise the law. The elections have been favorable to the republican candidates every where south of Connecticut; and even in Massachusetts there is a probability that one republican will be sent [to Congress].[32]

Hamilton's actions with regard to the nation's finances had violated the letter of the law. He had used monies specifically designated for the foreign debt for the payment of the domestic debt. This action and opposition to his financial program precipitated Giles's resolutions.

---

[32]James Madison to Thomas Jefferson, Apr. 12, 1793, *Madison Papers*, 15:7–8. See Norman K. Risjord, *Chesapeake Politics, 1781–1800* (New York, 1978), p. 422. See also Jefferson to George Washington, May 23 and Sept. 6, 1792; Jefferson to Thomas Mann Randolph, Jr., Nov. 16, 1792, and Mar. 3, 1793; and "Notes on Giles Resolutions," Mar. 2, 1793, all in *Jefferson Papers*, 25; and Elkins and McKitrick, *Age of Federalism*, pp. 295–96.

Underlying causes included both irreconcilable ideological differences and personal animosity toward Hamilton — dislike for him on the part of Jefferson and members of Virginia's congressional delegation bordered on hatred. Republicans truly believed the secretary of treasury carried out public financial matters for the benefit of the commercial class and speculators. Hamilton, closely associated with financial and banking interests, also was vulnerable to charges of using his connections and position to benefit these groups. His personal integrity in this instance was demonstrated to the overall satisfaction of Congress, but to Giles, Jefferson, Madison, and others, it was still in doubt. Had there been greater evidence of misconduct, the calling for the reports and the subsequent censure resolutions might have been a victory rather than a defeat for the Republicans.

Throughout the remainder of the Second Congress and the ensuing Third Congress, Giles worked effectively for the Republican party. During the Third Congress, the legislative issues of the previous two sessions were set aside as members turned their attention to foreign affairs, in particular the relationship of the United States with France and England. Following the French Revolution and the declaration of war between France and Great Britain in early 1793, the divisions between Federalists and Republicans grew. Although Washington declared the nation's neutrality, the House debated Republican resolutions that specifically targeted Great Britain. In lengthy speeches on the floor, Giles supported Madison's resolutions for higher tonnage duties against countries having no commercial treaty with the United States.[33] He denounced Great Britain and its commercial restrictions while praising France. On January 23, 1794, Giles spoke in House debate to attack the mercantile interests and those who would vote against the tonnage resolutions based on British opposition to them. He enumerated the "injuries" inflicted by Great Britain and accused that country of being "the instrument of letting loose the pirates of the Barbary states upon our commerce." He praised France for "a renewal of the existing commercial treaty upon the most liberal policy." He answered those who asked what "advantages have the United States received from the French treaty?" by reminding Congress that in 1778,

---

[33]*Annals,* 3d Cong., 1st sess., Jan. 3, 1794, pp. 155–56.

France "acknowledged our right to trade as a nation!" He also pointed out the presence of British mercantile capital and commercial agents from the "extremes of New Hampshire to the extremes of Georgia." These agents formed "intimate connexions" with American citizens. For him "insensible foreign influence was operating, at this moment upon our councils." Again Giles was in the forefront of congressional action, supporting Madison in an attempt to punish Great Britain for offenses against American commerce. He rose again, using many of the same arguments in support of a resolution calling for the sequestration of debts owed to the British by Americans. He accused Great Britain of committing acts that "constitute injuries which amount to war." The United States "possessed the right, consistently with the Law of Nations, to exercise any act against Great Britain which would be justified in a state of war." As for neutrality, it was Great Britain that violated the principle.[34]

During the second session of the Third Congress, Giles opposed a motion to condemn the democratic societies. Earlier, Washington, in his annual address to Congress, criticized these "self-created societies" for their opposition to the excise tax.[35] Giles responded that "there was not an individual in America, who might not come under the charge of being a member of some one or another self-created society. Associations of this kind, religious, political, and philosophical, were to be found in every quarter of the Continent." Condemnation of the societies meant censure, which could lead to the infringement of the protesters' constitutional rights of freedom of speech and assembly. When Giles saw "the House of Representatives about to erect itself into an office of censorship, he could not sit silent."[36] The furor in the House over the democratic societies continued for several days. Part of

---

[34]Ibid., Jan. 23, 1794, pp. 274–90, Mar. 28, 1794, pp. 542–44, 547. Giles also was influenced by his friend John Taylor of Caroline, who published "An Examination of the Late Proceedings in Congress Respecting the Official Conduct of the Secretary of Treasury" (1793) attacking the administration's fiscal policy and calling for a return to pure republican principles. Taylor published a similar pamphlet in 1794. See Anderson, *Giles*, p. 32; Henry H. Simms, *Life of John Taylor: The Story of a Brilliant Leader in the Early Virginia State Rights School* (Richmond, 1932), p. 51; William Nisbet Chambers, *Political Parties in a New Nation: The American Experience, 1776–1809* (New York, 1963), p. 65.

[35]*Annals*, 3d Cong., 2d sess., Nov. 19, 1794, pp. 787–88.

[36]Ibid., Nov. 24, 1794, pp. 899–900.

this reaction can be attributed to the partisan stand taken by members of the societies, whose resolutions and public statements were sympathetic to Republicans and highly critical of Federalist policies.[37] In the end, the motion condemning the societies was defeated, and the House response merely reiterated Washington's general description of the activities of the societies in western Pennsylvania.[38]

From his mountain retreat, Monticello, the retired Jefferson, pleased with the House action, wrote to Giles: "The attempt . . . to restrain the liberty of our citizens . . . has come upon us a full century earlier than I expected. To demand the censors of public measures to be given up for punishment is to renew the demand of the wolves in the fable that the sheep should give up their dogs as hostages of the pease and confidence established between them. The tide against our Constitution is unquestionably strong but it will turn."[39] Jefferson then implored Giles to "hold on then like a good and faithful seaman till our brother-sailors can rouse from their intoxication and right the vessel."[40]

Federalist and Republican conflict continued. Both parties supported the Naturalization Act of 1795; Federalists feared "disorganizers," and Jefferson Republicans were suspicious of aristocratic French immigrants. Giles proposed an amendment to the naturalization law to require titled foreigners to renounce their titles before being allowed the rights of citizenship. Giles added, "If we did anything to prevent an improper mixture of foreigners with Americans, this measure seemed to him one that might be useful." Following some debate Madison joined Giles in support of the amendment. The Federalists counterattacked Giles and Southern Republicans with an amendment proposing that "in case any such alien shall hold any person in slavery, he shall renounce it and declare that he holds all men free and equal."

[37]Eugene Perry Link, *Democratic-Republican Societies, 1790–1800* (Morningside Heights, N.Y., 1942). Link notes that forty groups were organized between March 1793 and 1800 (p. 13). The "Society for the Preservation of Liberty," founded in 1784, counted as members Madison, James Monroe, and Patrick Henry (p. 27).

[38]For Washington's statement, see *Annals,* 3d Cong., 2d sess., Nov. 19, 1794, pp. 787–88.

[39]Jefferson to Giles, Dec. 17, 1794, Jefferson Papers, Library of Congress, Washington, D.C.

[40]Ibid.

Giles's speech made in response to this amendment gave an indication of his own ambivalence on slavery:

> He [Giles] should begin to think of his motion of very peculiar importance, if such extraordinary resources were adopted to disappoint it. He was sorry to see slavery made a jest of in that House. He understood this to be intended as a hint against members from the Southern states. It had no proper connexion with the subject before the House. He had therefore no scruple about voting against it. It was calculated to injure the property of gentlemen. As to slavery, he lamented and detested it; but, from the existing state of the country, it was impossible at present to help it. He himself owned slaves. He regretted that he did so, and if any member could point out the way in which he could be properly freed from that situation, he should rejoice in it. The thing was reducing as fast as could prudently be done. He believed that slavery was infinitely more deprecated in countries, where it actually existed, and consequently where its evils were known, than in other countries where it was only an object of conversation.[41]

The following day Giles commented on Federalist accusations that his "anti-title" amendment was "calculated to hold up an idea to the world, that there was a party in that House in favor of Aristocracy. . . . In reality, there is no connexion. . . . The idea must have been in the head of the member himself."[42] After such political charges and countercharges, the Naturalization Act of 1795 passed. Giles's amendment was included, but the Federalist amendment on slavery was dropped.

The debate over the Naturalization Act provides a good example of Giles's floor style, something almost as important as winning elections, because the debates, which were published, helped pinpoint members' political tendencies. Those who voted with Giles on this measure could be approached for support on similar measures. This period, prior to the defining debates on the Jay Treaty, was one of political adjustment, and for Republicans it was a time devoted to "appealing, at all times, to that body of members who considered themselves inde-

---

[41]Edward C. Carter II, "A 'Wild Irishman' under Every Federalist's Bed: Naturalization in Philadelphia, 1789–1806," *Pennsylvania Magazine of History and Biography* 94 (1970):331–46, quotes from p. 336 and 336 n. *Annals,* 3d. Cong., 2d. sess., Dec. 31, 1794, pp. 1030, 1032; Jan. 1, 1795, pp. 1032, 1039–40.

[42]Ibid., Jan. 2, 1795, p. 1043.

pendent of parties and whose votes might decide a given issue."[43] On the basis of these early political skirmishes, both Federalists and Republicans were well prepared for the political machinations associated with the Jay Treaty.

The treaty, negotiated by Federalist John Jay, prevented war with Great Britain but moved the United States away from its position of neutrality vis-à-vis the Anglo-French conflict. The treaty clearly reflected the Federalists' pro-British policy. Republicans' pro-French attitude initially accounted for their negative response. However, when terms of the treaty reached the United States, Republicans were soon joined by nonaligned members in their opposition to its provisions. The treaty included the following: (1) western posts held by the British since the Revolutionary War were to be abandoned by June 1, 1796; (2) the Mississippi River was opened to British trade; (3) the United States was to compensate Great Britain for unpaid pre-Revolutionary debts owed to British citizens and for the captures made by Edmond Genêt's privateers in 1793; (4) trade with the British West Indies was granted only to American ships with a carrying capacity of seventy tons or more on the condition that the West Indian trade of the United States be free to British vessels and that American vessels should not carry to any port in the world, except their own, molasses, sugar, coffee, cocoa, and cotton;[44] (5) trade with the British East Indies was opened to the United States under the conditions that the United States open all her ports and give up the right to lay further restrictions on British commerce; (6) citizens of both Great Britain and the United States as well as Northwest frontier Indians were to be allowed to pass freely over the international boundary line and to carry on trade and commerce; (7) the list of contraband articles was to be extended to include tar, pitch, turpentine, and, in some cases, even provisions; (8) Great Britain was to pay for recent captures of vessels of the United States and to promise that compensation would be paid for provisions seized in the future as contraband of war; and (9) the United States was to receive the "peace and friendship" of Great Britain. No provisions were made to prohibit the impressment of seamen, to resolve the

---

[43]Cunningham, *Jeffersonian Republicans,* p. 77.
[44]This article was dropped by the Senate in its approved copy of the treaty.

Indian question, to reimburse Americans whose slaves had been carried off by the British during and at the end of the Revolutionary War, or to pay Loyalist claims.[45]

It appeared to Republicans and many nonaligned members, as well as some Federalists, that Jay had not uttered a word in favor of the American position at the treaty conferences. Republicans, joined now by nonparty men and Federalists alike, attempted to stop Washington from signing the treaty after the Senate ratified it on June 24, 1795, by the barest possible two-thirds majority of 20 to 10. Following the vote, Sen. Stevens Mason of Virginia gave a copy of the treaty to Benjamin Franklin Bache for publication in the *Aurora*.[46] Public displeasure with the treaty increased. Public acts of disobedience occurred in many cities; Jay was hanged in effigy in Philadelphia, New York, and Boston; Hamilton, whose plans Jay had carried out, was hit by a stone trying to speak in defense of the treaty. Amid the public outcry, Edmund Randolph, the Republican secretary of state, was accused of revealing information to the French minister in Philadelphia and welcoming French bribes. Washington, though claiming that this revelation did not affect his decision, signed the treaty.[47] Republicans now turned to preventing passage of the appropriations needed to carry out certain provisions of the treaty.

The first session of the Fourth Congress opened on December 7, 1795. Republican leaders faced a difficult dilemma, wishing to bring the treaty before the House for debate without appearing to do so for political reasons. Washington's opening address to Congress, couched in conciliatory terms, described the treaty but did not formally present it for consideration. The "manner in which the treaty . . . is mentioned . . . has embarrassed its opposers in deciding on the proper cause to be taken in the answer." Giles described the situation in a letter to Jefferson, noting that:

---

[45]Samuel Flagg Bemis, *Jay's Treaty: A Study in Commerce and Diplomacy* (New York, 1923), pp. 157–70. See also Jerald A. Combs, *The Jay Treaty: Political Battleground of the Founding Fathers* (Berkeley, 1970).

[46]Joseph Charles, *The Origins of the American Party System* (New York, 1961), p. 105. For the priority of Mason's revelation to Bache, see the footnote on p. 105.

[47]For Randolph's role in the Jay Treaty, see Daniel Moncure Conway, *Omitted Chapters of History Disclosed in the Life and Papers of Edmund Randolph* (New York, 1888).

You will observe that this speech wears conciliatory and not a dictatorial complexion; and in this respect, has not, I believe corresponded with the general expectation. The mild form of communication assumed by the President, clearly proves, that he is at length of opinion, that the public temper as well as that of the House of Representatives, requires perswasives, and will not tolerate threats, and that his personal influence would be more impressive, by presenting to them the amiable solicitude of his heart for the promotion of the general welfare; than by relying on the wisdom of his head in the means which have been pursued for its attainment.[48]

Giles believed an attempt should be made to show Republican disapproval of the president's speech, but only if the framers of the congressional response could put a "complimentary stricture . . . in the answer."[49]

Working in concert with Madison, Giles directed the drafting of a response. The result called the "attention" of the House to the president's speech, including the treaty, as opposed to the "assurances" of consideration as originally proposed.[50] The effect of the response was to serve notice that the House was not in total agreement with the state of affairs as presented by the president. This particularly applied to the treaty. Jefferson wrote that he was "well pleased with the manner in which your House have testified their sense of the treaty; while their refusal to pass the original clause of the reported answer proved their condemnation of it, the contrivance to let it disappear silently respected appearances in favor of the President, who errs as other men do, but errs with integrity."[51]

On February 29, 1796, the Jay Treaty was formally proclaimed, and on March 2 Rep. Edward Livingston of New York offered a resolution requesting that the president present "a copy of the instruction to the Minister of the United States, who negotiated the Treaty with the King

---

[48]For Washington's speech, see *Annals,* 4th Cong., 1st sess., Dec. 7, 1795, pp. 10–14; Giles to Thomas Jefferson, Dec. 9, 1795, Thomas Jefferson Papers, Library of Congress.

[49]Giles to Jefferson, Dec. 9, 1795, Jefferson Papers, Library of Congress.

[50]*Annals,* 4th Cong., 1st sess., Dec. 9, 1795, pp. 128–29; Dec. 10, 1795, pp. 131–32; Dec. 14, 1795, pp. 134–35; Dec. 15, 1795, pp. 144–48; Dec. 16, 1795, p. 148.

[51]Thomas Jefferson to Giles, Dec. 31, 1795, Jefferson Papers, Library of Congress.

of Great Britain."[52] This resolution gave rise to a debate on the constitutional right of the House of Representatives to share in the treaty-making process. Giles felt that the House had every right to be a part of this process as an expression of its proper role in the system of checks and balances. He claimed that the "right of annulling treaties is essential to national sovereignty" and that "checks over treaties" are provided by the Constitution including "the power to make appropriations." For this reason, Giles believed that the House must be consulted in treaty making and that its "deliberations should not be perfunctory."[53] The resolution stating the right of the House to participate in the treaty-making process passed by a vote of 62 to 37, but Washington refused to provide the requested information. He declared that jurisdiction over treaty making lay exclusively with the Senate. The House next passed resolutions disclaiming any part that it might have in treaty making but stipulating its right to ask for information on the passage of laws dealing with appropriations for the implementation of treaties. The passage of these resolutions by a clear majority showed that there was strong support for both an investigation of the treaty by the House and an assertion of its prerogatives.[54]

Deliberations on appropriations for carrying out the Jay Treaty began on April 14, as Madison, Albert Gallatin of Pennsylvania, and other leading Republicans addressed the House. Giles spoke on April 18, dividing his discussion in two parts: (1) an examination of the treaty article by article; and (2) a consideration of the probable consequences of refusing to accept it. He criticized the abandonment of the claim for compensation for property and slaves carried off by the British and the delay in the surrender of the western posts. In fact, he criticized every article and found "so much to condemn, and so little to applaud . . . that it was wonderful to him that the treaty should have found an advocate, upon its mere merits, in the United States." Giles concluded that the treaty restricted the national sovereignty of the United States, neglected its rights as a neutral nation, and allowed

---

[52]*Annals,* 4th Cong., 1st sess., Mar. 2, 1796, p. 401. The resolutions were amended to exclude "such of said papers as any existing negotiations may render improper to be disclosed" (p. 426), referring to ongoing negotiations on the treaty's twelfth article.

[53]Ibid., Mar. 11, 1796, pp. 500–514.

[54]Combs, *Jay Treaty,* pp. 172–77.

Britain to meddle in its internal affairs without providing for one guarantee of its rights.[55]

The efforts of Giles and other Republicans were of no avail. On April 29, 1796, the House voted 50 to 49 to appropriate funds to put the treaty into effect. The following day Madison presented a resolution that would have declared the treaty "highly objectionable," but it was defeated 51 to 48.[56] The defeat was due in part to a lack of party discipline and unity. Giles wrote Jefferson: "A great majority of the House is opposed to the treaty intrinsically; but some whose firmness has been counted upon, will not resist the weight of the President and the Senate." Giles had taken a commanding part in the debates, and, as evidenced in his letters to Jefferson, he had judged the possible actions of House members and had planned party strategy accordingly.[57] The loss of the treaty question, in part, was due more to the Republican party's inability to counteract the president's personal prestige than to the appeal of the treaty itself. There was another cause for the defeat. Funds were needed for public works at the new capital. Several Northern Federalists refused to support the necessary legislation unless Republicans voted for appropriations to support the Jay Treaty. New York Sen. Rufus King "deemed it foolish to adopt a bill which the South considered essential to the survival of the union [that of a permanent capital on the Potomac], while refusing appropriations for a treaty which the North believed equally vital to the same goal."[58]

During the 1796 presidential campaign, Republicans continued their attacks on Washington's and Hamilton's policies. Federalists, on the other hand, linked Republican policies with French influence and French attacks on American shipping. When the electoral votes were counted, John Adams won the presidency and Jefferson became vice president.[59] Although Republicans had preferred Jefferson for

[55]*Annals*, 4th Cong., 1st sess., Apr. 18, 1796, pp. 1025–53, quote on p. 1044.

[56]Ibid., Apr. 30, 1796, p. 1291.

[57]Giles to Jefferson, Dec. 9, 1796, Jefferson Papers, Library of Congress. See Giles-Jefferson correspondence of Oct. 29 and Dec. 9, 15, 20, 31, 1795. See also Mar. 19, 26, 31, and Apr. 6, 1796.

[58]Bowling, *Creation of Washington, D.C.*, p. 232.

[59]For an excellent account of the working of the party in this election, see Cunningham, *Jeffersonian Republicans*, pp. 89–115. Giles's correspondence for the period from May 1795 to March 1798 has not been located.

president, Adams's election caused Giles much less concern than campaign propaganda would have led one to believe.

Washington, however, was still president until March 1797 and subject to the slings and arrows of public debate. On December 5, 1796, Giles spoke against a flowery retirement resolution praising Washington's services to the country. "I wish him to retire. . . . the Government of the United States could go on very well without him," Giles said, adding, "[I hope] gentlemen would compliment the President privately, as individuals, at the same time, [I hope] such adulation would never pervade [the House of Representatives]."[60] Giles was capable of exhibiting great bitterness. His speech indicated his displeasure with Washington's administration, especially in the area of foreign policy. Giles also reminded his colleagues of the danger to Republican principle in glorifying any one public official. Even though Giles refused to vote for the resolution for the first "Federalist President," he did believe that John Adams "will make a good President. . . . But we shall have to check him a little now and then. That will be all."[61] Unfortunately for Giles, a check now and then would be of little consequence in the events that followed.

Although the Jay Treaty prevented war with Great Britain, it precipitated a belligerent French reaction. By 1796 French raids on American shipping matched or exceeded British hostile action in the years prior to the treaty's negotiation. The added insult of the XYZ Affair rallied public opinion in favor of war against France. The refusal of three unnamed French officials to negotiate with American representatives until a bribe had been paid was politically devastating to the Republicans. Attempts by Giles and other congressional Republicans could not reverse the effect of the French insult. However, in a three-hour speech in Congress, Giles attempted to show the reasons for France's aggressive actions against American shipping by pointing out that the Jay Treaty was an insult to France. Giles appealed for neutrality, but to no avail. The Republican party in Congress was defeated.

---

[60]*Annals,* 4th Cong., 2d sess., Dec. 14, 1796, p. 1616. Those voting with Giles against the resolution included Edward Livingston, his close friend Nathaniel Macon, and Abraham Venable, Giles's closest friend and confidant.

[61]Charles Francis Adams, ed., *The Works of John Adams,* 10 vols. (Boston, 1850–56), 1:495.

Giles, along with some other "staunch Republicans . . . with a broken heart and ruined constitution" returned to Virginia.[62]

The XYZ Affair provided Federalists with the opportunity to strike at their political opposition. Under the guise of "patriotic purpose and internal security, the Federalists enacted a program designed to cripple if not destroy the Jeffersonian Party." The Federalist position could not have been stronger. Within a few short months they controlled Congress, passed legislative measures which organized a provisional army, and established a Department of the Navy. In addition, Congress authorized the capture of French armed ships and suspended commercial intercourse.[63] The Federalists clearly meant to use repression as a means to retain political power, and in the second session of the Fifth Congress, they pushed through the passage of the Alien and Sedition Acts. Jefferson and some of his ardent followers, believing the very survival of republican liberties was at stake, developed a plan to counterattack the laws through state legislatures. Jefferson wrote resolutions for the Kentucky legislature that were passed by that body with some modifications, and Madison wrote resolutions for the Virginia legislature. These resolutions were part of the "opening guns of the campaign of 1800."[64] Republicans, including Giles, truly believed themselves to be fighting to preserve the rights gained in the American Revolution. The Virginia General Assembly now became Giles's stage.

In November 1798 Giles was elected to the General Assembly of Virginia. He brought with him not only his political skill but also "his familiar knowledge of life and manners in Virginia."[65] In an atmosphere of high partisan feeling—a Virginia Federalist who happened into a Republican boardinghouse during this time was hard pressed to leave without a fight—Giles eagerly assumed the challenge of promoting the Republican cause by presenting cogent arguments during the

---

[62]Robert Troup to Rufus King, June 10, 1798, quoted in Cunningham, *Jeffersonian Republicans*, p. 125.

[63]James Morton Smith, *Freedom's Fetters: The Alien and Sedition Laws and American Civil Liberties* (Ithaca, N.Y., 1966), p. 21. See also Manning J. Dauer, *The Adams Federalists* (Baltimore, 1953), and Alexander DeConde, *The Quasi-War* (New York, 1966).

[64]Cunningham, *Jeffersonian Republicans*, p. 129.

[65]Hugh Blair Grigsby, "The History of the Federal Convention of 1788," *Collections of Virginia Historical Society*, 10 (1891):226.

debates on the Virginia Resolutions.[66] Unfortunately, only an abstract of one of his speeches is available. Giles, who was "elegantly dressed in blue and buff, booted and spurred," praised the government of Virginia as being "the best and mildest; it had done little mischief and much good." According to Giles, "it possessed less energy than any other government. Energy was despotism, it had produced party distinctions, the bank, the sedition law; the object of the sedition law was the suppression of a certain party." It was the right of the legislators to speak "for the effects of the present government tended to monarchy." Giles declared that the aim of Adams's administration was to generate energy (despotism) and that the opposition to foreign powers "was always 'pretence' for the purpose of usurpation." Answering Federalist charges that the resolutions were strongly worded and prejudiced, Giles stated that "he doubted whether should even the Lord's prayer be introduced before them, and undergo a criticism, they could be brought to agree to it."[67]

With regard to the Alien Act, Giles argued that all people were entitled to trial by jury; there was "no cause for the law, either foreign or domestic." Consequently, if these laws were repealed, "the Government would be as firm as now. The Administration . . . was not the Government."[68] Giles further argued that the Constitution was "the source of the power of the government" and that the members of the legislature had taken "the same oath to support the Constitution as the members of the judiciary." Therefore, the members could declare a law unconstitutional; moreover, it was their sworn duty to do so.[69] Giles concluded his remarks by moving an amendment to Madison's draft. He wished to strike the word *alone* from the phrase: "states, which were parties to the compact, alone had power to interpose." Giles made his motion because he thought "it excluded the idea of intervention by the people as makers of the social compacts."[70] Madi-

---

[66]Ibid.
[67]Hugh Blair Grigsby, *The Virginia Report of 1799–1800: Touching the Alien and Sedition Laws* (1850; reprint ed., New York, 1970), pp. 143–47.
[68]Ibid.
[69]Ibid.
[70]Brant, *Madison*, pp. 462–63.

son believed that "the legislature declared the offending laws unconstitutional and asserted the power of the *states* (not its own power or
the power of one state) to take necessary and proper measures of
correction."[71] Thus the omission of the word *alone* changed his doctrine that only states, and not legislatures had the power of interposi-
tion. After several more days of debate, on December 21, 1798, the
Virginia Resolutions, including Giles's amendment, were adopted by a
vote of 100 to 63.[72]

The Virginia and Kentucky Resolutions attacked the constitutionality of the Alien and Sedition Acts.[73] Federalists countercharged that
Republicans supported disunion. For Giles the most important factor
was not disunion but the dangers of an oppressive federal government.
Giles saw oppression in Federalist efforts to increase the size and power
of the federal government through taxes, the army, and the navy.
These measures, when coupled with the Alien and Sedition Acts, were
evidence of "a government whose aim was to control its peoples."
Giles's position was clearly stated in a "public letter" of February 21,
1799: "As to the measures proposed [the Federalist program] . . . I
considered disunion as a deplorable event but less deplorable, than a
perpetuation of expensive armies, perpetuity of expensive navies, perpetuity of excessive taxes, and all the other oppressive consequences
resulting therefrom."[74] Later, at a dinner party, Giles stated that he was
"clearly for separation" if no other way could be found to save the
sovereignty of the people.[75]

In 1799 Giles was reelected to the General Assembly of Virginia. The
assembly passed resolutions proposed by Giles to instruct Virginia's
senators in Congress to (1) secure a repeal of the Alien and Sedition
Acts; (2) procure a reduction in the size of the army (Giles wanted a
military force based on the militia); (3) prevent any augmentation of

---

[71]Ibid.

[72]Grigsby, *Virginia Report*, pp. 236–37.

[73]Adrienne Koch and Harry Ammon, "The Virginia and Kentucky Resolutions: An
Episode in Jefferson's and Madison's Defense of Civil Liberties," *William and Mary
Quarterly*, 3d ser. 5 (1948):145–76. For a full explanation of Madison's role in the
writing of the Virginia Resolutions, see vol. 17 of the *Madison Papers*.

[74]Quoted in Anderson, *Giles*, p. 70.

[75]Ibid. (No date given.)

the navy; and (4) promote the possibility of reducing the navy.[76] These resolutions were clearly the immediate aims not only of Giles and other like-minded Virginians but also of the Republican party.

With the adoption of the Virginia and Kentucky Resolutions, the political fight for the election of 1800 had begun. Giles, as usual, continued his day-to-day political activity for the Republican cause. As one of Virginia's presidential electors, he played the role of a confident party member by casting his vote for Jefferson and Aaron Burr.

There can be little doubt that Giles's political career during the 1790s made him a leader of the opposition. Madison and Jefferson depended on him. Commenting on the debates in the House in February 1798, Jefferson, then serving as vice president, as if calling in reinforcements, wrote to Madison, "Giles is arrived."[77] With the Republican victory of 1800, Giles returned to the House of Representatives in the fall of 1801 as a recognized floor leader of the new administration. He would be Jefferson's leader in that body, and he would work with Secretary of State Madison in securing an approach to foreign policy more to their liking. It was ironic that, having fought against the Federalists' policies and having helped secure Republican victory, he before long would oppose some of President Jefferson's policies and those of President Madison. He would be "in opposition" once more.

---

[76]Ibid., pp. 73–74.
[77]Jefferson to Madison, Feb. 8, 1798, *Madison Papers,* 17:76.

William C. diGiacomantonio

A Congressional Wife at Home

The Case of Sarah Thatcher, 1787–1792

ETTERS TO AND FROM eighteenth-century congressmen and their wives at home hold up a mirror not only to the multidimensional life of the congressman, but to the partner with whom he was covenanted in the most important relationship of his life. Congressional wives at home performed, in varying degrees, three distinct roles: their husbands' emotional, intellectual, and spiritual companions; partners in domestic economy, including the parenting of future citizens; and helpmates in their husbands' political careers.

Unfortunately the mirrors reflecting the details of this type of partnership are few. To take the First Federal Congress as a sample: of its ninety-five members, twenty were not married. Five were widowers, and another four became widowers during the Congress. Making further exception for those who married women at the seat of government, who already resided in New York or Philadelphia, or who brought their wives and immediate families to live with them, the number of congressmen with wives at home falls to forty-nine, or slightly more than half of the total. Correspondence is known to exist between only fourteen of those couples. All but one were from states north of Virginia. Only three collections of correspondence exceed twenty letters. Of these, the largest is that between Rep. George Thatcher and his wife, Sarah Savage Thatcher. There are approximately fifty of his letters to her from the First Federal Congress, or roughly half of those known to have been written by him in that period. No letters from Sarah to George are known to exist.

The story of the partnership that emerges from this ample if one-sided correspondence tells about the joys and sorrows, the burdens and benefits, distributed between two parts of one legal, sacramental, and emotional entity separated for long stretches of time across hundreds of miles and quite different worlds. In this case the worlds were the cosmopolitan "public sphere" of the seat of government and the domestic "private sphere" of Biddeford, Maine, to which the thirty-year-old Thatcher brought his twenty-four-year-old bride shortly after their marriage on July 20, 1784.

Thatcher's initial move to the Massachusetts province of Maine four years earlier placed him well outside the orbit of influence of his fourth-generation Cape Cod family. His great-great-grandfather immigrated to Massachusetts from England in 1635 and nine times represented the town of Yarmouth in the colony's general court. Thatcher's great-grandfather also represented Yarmouth for fifteen years, additionally serving as town selectman, lieutenant of the local militia, and assistant to the governor for five terms. His grandfather's marriage to Thankfull Sturgis yielded one son, Peter, and two daughters, Thankfull and Temperance. Peter, George's father, married Anna Lewis, but the traditional names survived: George had older sisters Thankful and Temperance, whose names reflected qualities useful for surviving the desolate isolation of Cape Cod. Ralph Waldo Emerson, exploring the area in September 1853, fancied that "the people were only waiting for the railroad to reach them in order to evacuate the country."[1]

Like Yarmouth, the Biddeford in which the Harvard-educated Thatcher hung out his law sign in 1782, after two years' practice in nearby York, was one of the first permanent English towns to dot the New England coastline. Yet in both cases, he found himself on the edge of settlement. Yale President Timothy Dwight visited Biddeford in 1797, and what he found there anticipated Emerson's later verdict of the Cape Cod Thatcher had left behind. "The inhabitants," he wrote, seemed "to have planted themselves here because they could go no farther, or because they know not whither to go." The houses were

---

[1] Quoted in Robert D. Richardson, *Emerson: The Mind on Fire* (Berkeley, 1995), p. 515.

"dismal cottages placed on little tracts of cleared ground which can never repay the labor either of the scythe or the sickle." Understandably, "too many are still more fond of the axe than of the plough," as Rev. Jedidiah Morse noted in 1789. And the axe was busy. On the "cold, barren plains" of clay and sand soil north and south of town grew forests of pine and birch, which the sawmills lining the Saco River for seven navigable miles upstream from Biddeford converted into four million feet of board in the years before the Revolution.[2]

Knowing where George and Sarah Thatcher lived helps explain their expectations from life and how they helped each other meet those expectations. What drew Thatcher there? A population explosion along the northwestern frontier raised Maine's population from 56,000 at war's end to 96,000 at the first national census only six years later. Biddeford's own population in 1790 was 1,018; it was small and slowly growing. But Thatcher was its only lawyer. And in James Sullivan, his immediate predecessor, Thatcher had an example of the ascendancy to which he too might aspire. Sullivan's rise from a small-town attorney to governor of Massachusetts symbolized an upward mobility in the hinterland that characterized the unsettled aftermath of the Revolution.[3]

Over the first five years of their marriage, Thatcher's work following the judicial circuit court occasionally took him away from home. But it was his election to the Confederation Congress, then meeting at New York City, that set him on a wider stage farther away from home for longer periods. Between his election in June 1787 and the end of his second consecutive term in March 1789, Thatcher was away for several stretches lasting as much as three months at a time, without discontinuing his appearances before the state circuit courts when possible. Much of his personal perspective as a member of a distant Congress developed during these last days of the Confederation, of which, in this regard, the First Federal Congress was a mere extension.

---

[2]Timothy Dwight, *Travels in New-England and New-York,* 4 vols. (1821; reprint ed., Cambridge, Mass., 1969), 2:153, 155; Jedidiah Morse, *The American Geography* (1789; reprint ed., New York, 1970), pp. 195, 197.

[3]Laurel Thatcher Ulrich, *A Midwife's Tale: The Life of Martha Ballard, Based on Her Diary, 1785–1812* (New York, 1990), pp. 167, 232. For more on the post-Revolutionary settlement, see Alan Taylor, *Liberty Men and Great Proprietors: The Revolutionary Settlement on the Maine Frontier, 1760–1820* (Chapel Hill, 1990).

Thatcher's first letter to Sarah when he went off to Congress confided that, "tho I am in a World of Hurry and Bustle and Confusion—I am a great part of the time with you." The impression of homesickness prevails in the earliest years of George's correspondence. "I often think of Home & say to myself there only is true happiness." Service in Congress became a sort of Babylonian captivity. Thatcher certainly was not the only congressman to view his public service as banishment. Bad weather made him pine for the coziness of home; good weather made him regret not enjoying it with his family. Autumns in Maine he missed most of all. "Adieu my dearest creature," he signed with unusual feeling shortly after passing his first autumn outside of New England.[4]

His salutations and closings changed little over time. Letters from other members of the First Congress to their wives were commonly addressed to "My Dearest Love," or simply "Dear Wife." Only Connecticut's Benjamin Huntington—a generation older than Thatcher and the converted member of a revivalist Congregational church—refers to his wife, Anne, with Puritan prudery as "Dear Mrs. Huntington." William Few and Jeremiah Wadsworth addressed their wives, Catherine and Mehitable, respectively, as "Dear Friend"—a term better recognized from the famous correspondence between John and Abigail Adams. And yet it is a term that still sounds a little aloof in modern ears. In no case was the word *friend* used as casually as it is today. The recognition of a marital partner as a "friend" was a historically significant development in women's emerging autonomy in marriage choices, beginning around the time of the Revolution.[5] Nicknames playfully convey some of this new collegiality, such as "Affy" for William Paterson's wife, Euphemia, or the more obvious "Getty" for Gertrude Read. Well into middle age Elias and Hannah Boudinot still referred to each other by their courting names, "Narcissus" and "Eugenia." But for George Thatcher, Sarah was always "Sally," and his letters always began, simply, "Dear Wife" or "My Dear."

He wrote at least one letter a week during his first years at the

---

[4]George to Sarah Thatcher, Oct. 24, Dec. 16, 1787, Feb. 24, 1788, July 30, 1789, Thatcher Papers, Massachusetts Historical Society, Boston (hereafter TPMHS).

[5]See Nancy F. Cott, "Divorce and the Changing Status of Women in Eighteenth-Century Massachusetts," *William and Mary Quarterly*, 3d ser. 33 (1976):586–614.

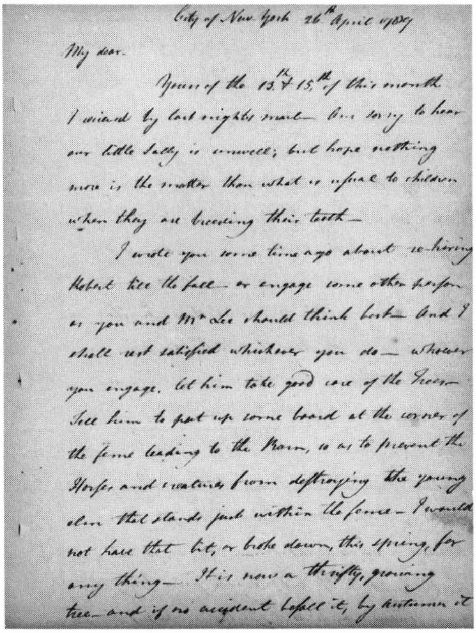

FIG. 1. George to Sarah Thatcher, April 26, 1789. This letter, written less than a month after the House of Representatives convened, demonstrated Thatcher's involvement in two important aspects of domestic life: his daughter's health and the hired hand's chores. The remainder of the nine-page letter included one of the most detailed firsthand accounts of the pomp and circumstance attending Washington's triumphal entry into New York City three days earlier, concluding with Thatcher's moralistic reminder, "But all these things are vanity!!!" *(Photo courtesy the author)*

Confederation Congress. It is clear from his acknowledgments that she wrote him almost as often, although at one point he complained of getting only one for every two or three he wrote. The balance was reversed during the First Federal Congress, when she began to write by almost every post, twice a week. Sunday was his preferred day for writing letters home. But even then conditions had to be perfect. "I cannot set down to write, unless all things around me are agreeable. I must feel at home, and then I can write home." Winter days huddled close to the fire tended to cut short his letter writing. Trouble breathing in spring (probably from allergies) prevented him from writing unless in a standing position. Other lapses in the receipt of letters were ascribed to theft by those "more curious than moral," as other congressmen discovered.[6]

Thatcher often complained, or responded to Sarah's complaints, about how long it would be before he could return home. When one

---

[6]George to Sarah Thatcher, Sept. 9, 1788, Dec. 26, Nov. 10, 1791, Thatcher Papers, Library of Congress, Washington, D.C. (hereafter TPLC); George to Sarah Thatcher, May 10, 14, 1789, TPMHS; Philip to Catherine Schuyler, Feb. 24, 1791, Allen K. Ford Autograph Collection, Minnesota Historical Society, St. Paul.

influential constituent expressed frustration that congressmen should sit so long — at the exorbitant cost to the public of six dollars per day per member — Thatcher reminded him that when the Constitution was ratified it was generally expected that the First Congress would be in session the entire time. Nevertheless, Thatcher consistently under-estimated the endurance necessary for his job. In a letter eventually published in Portland's *Cumberland Gazette* near the end of the second session, Thatcher predicted that if there was going to be a third session before Congress adjourned the following March, it would recess in early August; otherwise, they would persevere until September. In the event, they did both.

Thatcher might have alleviated some of his homesickness by resort-ing to periodic leaves of absence, as many of his colleagues did. Instead he continued a pattern of attendance begun during the Confedera-tion Congress, when he was one of the handful of delegates to appear in the last few months before it finally dissolved without ever having formed a quorum. Thatcher was present on the opening day of each session of the First Federal Congress — a distinction he shared with only three fellow representatives. He never requested a leave, although his letters repeated sincere but always broken promises to do so. No doubt recalling the disgraceful last few months of the Confederation Congress, Thatcher argued in his first recorded speech in the House that no member should be allowed to be seated who expected to be ab-sent for reasons other than illness or the death of a relation. Through-out the entire First Congress Thatcher missed only six roll call votes, three of them because he left Philadelphia early on the last day of the last session.[7]

Another antidote to Thatcher's homesickness would have been to bring Sarah and their children to live with him while Congress was in session. This was a recourse for eight of Thatcher's colleagues, not counting the five who already resided at New York City or Philadel-phia, or the four who were introduced (or reintroduced) to "Hyme-nial Joys" during the congressional term. But the proximity of New

---

[7]George Thatcher to Samuel Nason, July 18, 1790, TPMHS; *The Documentary History of the First Federal Congress, 1789–1791,* 14 vols. to date (Baltimore, 1972–), vol. 10 (Charlene Bickford, Kenneth R. Bowling, Helen Veit, and William C. diGiacoman-tonio, eds.), pp. 7–8.

England congressmen to the seat of government while it met in New York — so often cited as an unfair advantage by supporters of a more southern capital — did not redound to Thatcher's advantage. He never asked Sarah to come live with him; at best she would accompany him as far as her parents' home in Weston, Massachusetts, or meet him there on his way home. It is possible that Thatcher subscribed to the opinion of his famously frugal colleague, Benjamin Goodhue, who thought that members who brought their families to live with them only aggravated a popular impression of congressional wastefulness. It is at least as likely that Thatcher simply saw no way for it to happen, logistically. He would never consent, he said, for a woman to travel by stage without "her husband, brother, Sweet-heart or very particular friend." And more than once he projected onto her his terror of traveling by water — a strange mania, considering his maritime ancestry. Only once did Thatcher even consider returning from New York by ship to New Haven or Providence — and then it was purposely to get seasick in order to avoid having to take an emetic for some undisclosed illness.[8]

Congressmen by definition are social creatures. Long absences from home excluded them from the network of familiar relationships that gave life meaning and pleasure. Fisher Ames complained that his friends at home "needed by constant teazing to keep alive the recollection of my existence." But Ames was a bachelor. George Thatcher had Sarah, and one of her principal roles as congressional wife became maintaining his mental health by sustaining a lively connection with hearth and home.[9]

One obvious way of strengthening the Thatchers' ties to both the reality and the idea of home was to share every detail of their lives spent apart. First Congress Sen. Paine Wingate once wrote his daughter that "a letter is something like a short visit." Thatcher's letters to Sarah in fact read like one end of a very spontaneous, candid, and unmediated conversation, such as they might have had if they were

---

[8]Joshua to Frances Seney, Dec. 9, 1790, Gratz Collection, Pennsylvania Historical Society, Philadelphia; Benjamin Goodhue to Samuel Phillips, Jr., June 3, 1789, Phillips Family Papers, Massachusetts Historical Society, Boston; George to Sarah Thatcher, [Summer 1788], Oct. 28, Nov. 11, 1787, Oct. 14, 1788, TPMHS.

[9]Fisher Ames to [Samuel Hensaw?], Apr. 22, 1789, Miscellaneous Folder, Fisher Ames Account, Library of Congress.

sitting together in the kitchen at home. So he shares with her his awkward attempts to dress for his first diplomatic reception (Thatcher was color blind); he teases her with reports of the beauty of New York's fashionable women; he encourages her to indulge in a "bright and sprightly" robe, and not to buy a dark one — "suitable only for mourning" — just for the sake of not having to wash it so often; and he complains when someone else has to inform him that she had lost a tooth. He chides her, he says, not for losing the tooth, but for hiding it as would a "young flurt . . . fearful whether you should ever get an husband." Besides, he thought a gap was a beauty mark rather than a blemish, in that "it gave the appearance of good nature."[10]

Like other congressmen Thatcher provided his wife with detailed accounts of some social doings at the seat of government, such as the inauguration of the new federal government on March 4, 1789. But on the subject of parties he is relatively silent; perhaps he didn't attend many. In Maine he would dance two or three nights in succession, and in New York he was no stranger to the theater. But he was not enamored of New York, and — like most New Englanders — he liked Philadelphia even less. He was content to find in his chamber "a million of charms in comparason to the Meeting houses — play houses, or Assembly [dancing] Rooms," preferring, by his reclusiveness, "to lay up such improvements as will heighten the enjoyment of Domestic Life when I again return to my Sally." Swearing off the social scene served as an invitation to Sarah to entertain him instead. She was not much intellectual company for Thatcher; at least, he does not seem to expect much from her in this regard. Except for lecturing her on Enlightenment theories of children's education, the only apparent interest Thatcher showed in the cultivation of Sarah's mind was limited to sending her a small two-volume set of William Hill Brown's recently published novel *The Power of Sympathy: Or, The Triumph of Nature*. Not surprisingly, perhaps, it deals with women's corruption by too great a commerce with the world — through reading novels.[11]

---

[10]Paine Wingate to [Mary Wingate Higgins], Feb. 27, 1790, Wingate Papers, Harvard University, Cambridge, Mass.; George to Sarah Thatcher, Dec. 27, 29, 1787, Feb. 27, 1792, Aug. 30, 1788, TPMHS.

[11]George to Sarah Thatcher, Oct. 21, 30, 1791, TPLC; Feb. 24, 1788, May 10, 1789, TPMHS.

Thatcher's letters instead are filled with suggestions for overcoming the inherent loneliness of their situations by visiting friends. As Laurel Thatcher Ulrich points out in her Pulitzer Prize–winning biography of Maine midwife Martha Ballard, a person's movements and whereabouts are an important index of the vitality of eighteenth-century rural life, perhaps even more so in Maine. Quoting a nineteenth-century historian of a central Maine community, she writes that "the first settlers in a new country cultivate the social affections." In fact, continues Ulrich, "too great a concentration on one's own household was probably somewhat suspect" — even sociopathic. Thatcher obviously recognized the curative power of visiting and was effusive on the subject of maintaining close contact with their friends. During his first spring in New York City, when the weather reminded him of the Saco River Valley in May, he wrote Sarah that when he arrived home he would "act like a colt let out of his pen." Rather than hinting at his anticipation of some tender intimacies, the phrase describes his resolve to visit all their neighbors in the first forty-eight hours of his return![12]

Thatcher "always took delight in the company of young girls" and was gladdened by reports of young women visiting Sarah. His particular favorite was Betsy King, half sister of Thatcher's friend and colleague Rufus King. "I always love to hear she is with you — she is good company & I know, with her you . . . pass your time happily." According to the custom of the day and to justify a journey of several hours, perhaps, such visits might last for weeks. Sarah herself spent two weeks in February to March 1789 visiting friends in York, Maine. Making rounds as a member of the "Sweeter-water Club" provided other opportunities for visiting overnight. This would be an even greater comfort to George after June 1789, when their live-in helper and niece, Tempy, returned to Cape Cod for an extended visit.[13]

Maine communities of the early Federal period were the setting for a variety of social activities that Sarah might have attended and described for George's pleasure as well. "Frolics," of which barn raising is only the most familiar example, also took the form of apple parings,

---

[12]Ulrich, *Midwife's Tale,* pp. 91, 92; George to Sarah Thatcher, Mar. 16, 1788, TPMHS.

[13]George to Sarah Thatcher, Feb. 28, 1791, May 14, Mar. 1, July 12, 1789, TPMHS.

corn huskings, and spinning parties. Among women, quilting was even more widespread, and no doubt a fountain of endless gossip for the Thatchers. Sleighing and snowshoeing, besides means of transportation, were ends in themselves — except during the spring thaw, when people were caked in by mud. Militia training, elections, and, more solemnly, the Fourth of July, were all days for communal celebration. Ship launchings were also social occasions. It might have been news of an approaching launch that prompted George to advise Sarah against shipboard parties — citing, again, the dangers of being at sea, especially in winter.[14]

Sarah's participation in the civic life of her community was complementary but always subordinate to her role as her husband's partner in domestic economy. One constituent paid tribute to Thatcher's relatively diligent attendance at Congress by faulting other congressmen with being too concerned with "domestic concerns" to "conveniently adjust their private affairs." This male perspective predictably overlooked the fact that there was no "convenient" way to compensate for a husband's long-term absences from home. "In early America," quotes Ulrich, " 'men and women had to work in tandem in order to undertake any single life-sustaining chore.' " George's absences for as much as nine months at a time put Sarah on the same footing as the wife whose assumption of traditionally male roles in the wartime economy of the Revolution freed her husband to play the soldier, but left her, as Abigail Adams aptly described the condition, "doubled in wedlock."[15]

A frustratingly large part of Sarah's life at home can be recovered only inferentially from the diaries, journals, and letters between other mothers, daughters, and sisters. "Even today," as a recent Mary Todd Lincoln biographer has discovered, "when domesticity has emerged as a respectable historical topic, its allure is only collectively established, and a deep suspicion of home making as trivial and mundane remains."[16]

---

[14]George to Sarah Thatcher, Feb. 27, 1792, TPLC. For the social life in Maine communities, see Jane C. Nylander, *Our Own Snug Fireside: Images of the New England Home, 1760–1860* (New York, 1993), pp. 221–60.

[15]Daniel Cony to George Thatcher, May 16, 1789, Chamberlain Collection, Boston Public Library; Rosemary S. Keller, *Patriotism and the Female Sex: Abigail Adams and the American Revolution* (Brooklyn, N.Y., 1994), p. 105.

[16]Jean H. Baker, *Mary Todd Lincoln: A Biography* (New York, 1987), p. 105.

The Thatcher household, according to the 1790 census, comprised eight people: two free white males over age sixteen, two free white males under age sixteen, and four free white females. All eight cannot be positively identified. Along with George and Sarah, the three children (Sam, Sally, and George), and "Tempy," or Temperance Hedge, Thatcher's niece from Cape Cod, who had lived with them since mid-1784, also may have been Sam's nurse, Rachel, whom Thatcher calls "Holy Ratchel," possibly because of a conversion experience during Maine's late-eighteenth-century religious revival.

Two more female helpers, Jenny and Olly, apparently worked for Sarah on a part-time basis at various times during George's early congressional career. They would have been part of the "shuffling and reshuffling of workers [that] was part of the larger system of neighborly exchanges that sustained male as well as female economies in this period." The Thatchers' circumstances as a small and new family would have limited the labor that Sarah could provide in exchange. But for help combing wool or spinning yarn, she may have offered use of her oven for baking or their cow for milking.[17]

For heavier farmwork there were hired hands, although such labor was hard to attract on the edge of Maine's vast hinterland, where men were tempted to farm for themselves. In late 1791 Sarah failed to prevent Samuel, the hired hand, from leaving, even after a generous raise from forty-seven to fifty-four dollars per year. In 1790 the Thatchers' hired hands were Robert and Charles. They may have lived with the Thatchers, or either or both of them may have been among the six listed in Biddeford's census that year as free persons "not part of households" — probably free blacks. In May 1789 Thatcher wrote Sarah that "you have not, in any of yours, told me the name, colour or place of the abode of the man you have hired to live with us."[18]

Details of the farm were in any case scarce; Thatcher does not seem to have been particularly knowledgeable or even interested in the matter. We read a rare and uninspired instance of Thatcher's micromanagement when he asks Sarah to "tell Eben to be careful of the hay and not waste a single straw." Here was no George Washington

---

[17]Ulrich, *Midwife's Tale*, p. 82.
[18]George to Sarah Thatcher, Jan. 23, 1792, TPLC; May 14, 1788, TPMHS.

advising his estate's manager on the virtues of crop rotation or the latest importation of seeds from Europe. Fortunately Maine's press regularly carried husbandry tips to help wives like Sarah Thatcher — articles with tantalizing titles such as "The Cultivation of Mulberry Trees" and "On River Weeds as a Manure." Or she may simply have bought a copy of *The New England Primer,* sold by Titcomb of Portland for nine shillings ($1.50), equivalent to one-quarter of Thatcher's daily pay as a congressman.[19]

Along with government service, Thatcher derived income from his law practice, although his protégé Silas Lee took over the workload per an agreement of October 14, 1787, valid for the time Thatcher was away "for the confederation." Sarah helped little with this sector of their domestic economy, occasionally witnessing legal documents for Lee or relaying messages to his clerks. In June 1789 Sarah admonished Thatcher about the appearance of a second lawyer across the river in Saco. Far from apprehensive, Thatcher welcomed the company along with the competition and even asked Sarah to lend the as-yet-unknown newcomer whatever law books he might ask to borrow. On February 1790 Thatcher's professional credentials were rewarded with his selection as one of the first lawyers permitted to practice before the U.S. Supreme Court.[20]

Thatcher's income in specie offered a certain independence within the local economy and integration within a larger commercial realm. Sarah began to ask Thatcher to make purchases for their home from the moment he first departed for Congress. From Boston he tried to procure pickles and succeeded in procuring a bedstead. Four days before the First Congress adjourned, he bought a $115 chaise, which he then had shipped to Boston. He was content to let Sarah pay for other acquisitions with whatever cash he could furnish or whatever local merchants would supply on his account. From his constant promises to send cash as soon as he could, it seems fair to infer that Thatcher

---

[19]Daniel Cony to George Thatcher, May 30, 1789, Chamberlain Collection, Boston Public Library; George to Sarah Thatcher, Feb. 14, 1791, TPLC; *Gazette of Maine* (Portland), Nov. 4, 1790.

[20]Ephraim Pickard contract, Oct. 27, 1787; George to Sarah Thatcher, June 14, 1789, TPMHS.

did not deliberately hold Sarah to an allowance, although he told her that he expected one dollar a day would answer all her needs.[21]

On the other hand, it is not clear what considerations guided her in exercising autonomous financial decisions. When Sarah bought a cow, Thatcher told her after the fact that she had paid dearly for it. But he did not complain, admitting that "one good cow is worth three poor ones." Whatever else she did, Thatcher cautioned her, "don't run into debt for anything you buy if you can avoid it." On January 2, 1792, perhaps in the spirit of a New Year's resolution, he reminded her to keep a strict account of her expenditures.[22]

Domestic economy entailed more than just providing; it was policing, nursing, and educating. And in each of these functions Sarah played an exclusive role; George was relegated to an advisory capacity. The frustration that role might have caused may account for Thatcher's particularly strident tone on such matters. When he first went off to Congress he left behind a young and still relatively new wife. Fire was a threat that could strike even the most cautious and experienced matrons. Living in the compact, wooden cities of New York and (to a less extent) Philadelphia alerted Thatcher to the destructive effects of fire to which he in turn alerted Sarah in lengthy and detailed directions for its prevention in February 1790. This was followed by another letter the following January and a third in December of that year. Less than a month later a compounded nightmare occurred when their youngest child, George, burned himself by crowding too close to a fire in an unattended room.[23]

Treating such misfortunes typically fell to the female, even when the husband or father was home. With the help of midwives like Martha Ballard, who "mediated the mysteries of birth, procreation, illness and death" by serving simultaneously as physician, mortician, and pharmacist, late-eighteenth-century wives were expected to anticipate, prevent, and nurse a wide variety of ailments. Women in delivery ran

---

[21]George to Sarah Thatcher, Oct. 28, 1787, TPMHS; George to Sarah Thatcher, Dec. 27, 1790, Feb. 28, 1791, Jan. 23, 1792, TPLC.

[22]George to Sarah Thatcher, Jan. 2, 1792, Dec. 1, 1791, TPLC.

[23]George to Sarah Thatcher, Feb. 21, 1790, TPMHS; George to Sarah Thatcher, Jan. 31, Dec. 22, 1791, Jan. 23, 1792, TPLC.

the risk of succumbing to puerperal infection, while the bilious fever might strike entire families, usually toward summer's end, and was often accompanied by dysentery or the "bloody flux." Notwithstanding those and a host of other microbiological threats, in addition to whatever accidents providence delivered, the death rate for a Maine town on the edge of settlement was generally far less than that of a large city. Observers agreed that Maine was a healthy place overall, and newspapers tried to outdo each other in reporting local instances of exceptional longevity.[24]

Subscribing to the brand of homeopathic "social medicine" favored by unschooled female practitioners like Martha Ballard might have sent Sarah into Portland occasionally to purchase oil vitriol, verdigris, alum, and cochineal from S. Erving at the sign of the Golden Mortar. George — as a man and a member of the professional class — was more likely to credit the latest clinical insights offered by formal doctors like Biddeford's own Aaron Porter. When Sarah suffered from the influenza in March 1792, Thatcher had Dr. Porter send regular updates to him in Philadelphia. Only months earlier, perhaps in response to the outbreak of some related symptoms, Thatcher sent explicit directions for treating pimples with corrosive sublimate dissolved in rum or brandy, with minimal topical application.[25]

Probably the most dramatic demonstration of Thatcher's reliance on modern medicine, and Sarah's apparent reluctance to embrace it, was his secret decision to be inoculated for smallpox immediately upon his arrival in New York to begin his first term in the Confederation Congress. He temporarily suffered weak eyes and more than two thousand pockmarks on his body. For five weeks he did not write for fear of alarming Sarah about his condition. It is the longest gap in their correspondence.[26]

Despite Thatcher's solicitude for the physical well-being of the family he left behind, he frankly asserted about their eldest son, Samuel, that "I am more anxious about [his] Temper & Disposition, than his body." In this statement Thatcher was simply restating one of the Revo-

[24]Ulrich, *Midwife's Tale*, pp. 40, 47, 192, 68; Morse, *American Geography*, p. 127.
[25]George to Sarah Thatcher, Mar. 22, Jan. 2, 1792, TPLC.
[26]George to Sarah Thatcher, Dec. 16, 1787, TPMHS.

lution's supreme Republican truths: that public virtue was based on private virtue. This belief placed the highest emphasis on the education of future citizens. Implicit in Thatcher's "anxiety" over his son's upbringing is a tacit acknowledgment of his own failure to live up to the Puritan ideal, which demanded a "team relationship" between a husband and wife in the raising of a family more than in any other task.[27]

For George and Sarah this special team relationship began with the birth of their first child, named for Sarah's father — Samuel Phillips Savage. In keeping with the period's demographic average for intervals between births, by the time Congress moved to Philadelphia in 1790 Sarah and George had become parents to two more — also named Sarah and George.[28] They would have a total of ten, five sons and five daughters, exceeding the average by four. All the children but one daughter would outlive their father.

Nowhere was Thatcher's homesickness more apparent than in his constant inquiries about rambunctious George, fast-talking Sally, or "grave and sedate" Sam. Almost everyone who traveled by the Thatcher homestead felt obligated to furnish some report about how fast the children were growing, how well they spoke, how carefully they read, "and like other silly Fathers I believe every word." By his second week at the First Federal Congress, thinking about them only added to his unhappiness, so he endeavored to think about them as little as he could. But the thoughts always came back, triggered by sights as common as boys playing with a kite. At times his solicitude reached maniacal proportions; nothing else explains the letter to Sarah in January 1790, relaying in painful and maudlin detail the burial of a friend's ten-year-old daughter.[29]

He looked forward to hearing how his own little Sally "grows like a pig," but offered relatively little advice about her upbringing. He suggested when she ought to start wearing shoes, for example, "but as you

[27]George to Sarah Thatcher, Dec. 29, 1787, TPMHS; Keller, *Patriotism and the Female Sex*, p. 127.

[28]Mary Beth Norton, *Liberty's Daughters: The Revolutionary Experience of American Women, 1750–1800* (Boston, 1980), p. 72.

[29]George to Sarah Thatcher, Dec. 1, 1791, Feb. 24, 1788, Mar. 8, July 30, 1789, Jan. 24, 1790, TPMHS.

have been very good in permitting me to govern the son—I will give up the government of the daughter to you." Thatcher in time became obsessed with the education of his firstborn, whom he began calling by the nickname "Sambo," then "Sammy," and finally insisted on referring to as "Phillips" or "Savage." The successive sobriety of these names reflected the evolving seriousness with which Thatcher approached the task of his upbringing.[30]

As a father, Thatcher was remembered as a "kind and indulgent" man. But he was a virtual martinet in the regimen of training he framed for his son. In a thousand obscure ways he was to be taught self-reliance. While still less than three years old, he was not to wear any hat all winter, nor stockings, nor mittens. He was to spend as much time outside as he wanted, "but if he tarries so long as to be cold, take no notice of it; never tell him to go to the fire." Later he expected Sam to ride every day with their hired hand Charles and to help him water the horses. In fact Thatcher encouraged Sarah to let their son spend as much time as possible with Charles, that they might eat, drink, play, and even sleep together, so that "Sammy may never concieve of any difference between his & Charles situation." The goal was not Spartan deprivation, but stoic equanimity: "I had rather Phillips should kiss a negro or the devil than fight with an Angel or a prince." Sam's namesake once sent the boy a miniature coach as a toy, but Thatcher regretted the grandfather's indulgence, insisting that Sam "ought to be sensible to no pleasures but what are of his own procuring—and result from his activity."[31]

For his thoughts on education Thatcher drew heavily on the popular works of eighteenth-century Scottish thinker Henry Homes, Lord Karnes. Although he did not think Karnes the equal of Rousseau, he promised to mail home Karnes's *Loose Hints upon Education* (Edinburgh, 1781). In the meantime, beginning in February 1789, he contented himself with transcribing for Sarah long sections of the volume. *Loose Hints* as well as Karnes's earlier *Essays on the Principles of Morality and Natural Religion* (1751) were important influences in American

---

[30]George to Sarah Thatcher, Dec. 29, 1787, Mar. 16, Sept. 16, 1788, TPMHS.

[31]W. W. Clayton, *History of York County, Maine* (Philadelphia, 1880), p. 78; George to Sarah Thatcher, Oct. 28–Nov. 11, Dec. 16, 23, 1787, Mar. 16, 1788, June 9, 1789, Sept. 16, 1788, TPMHS.

education during the eighteenth century. What was unconventional was the way Thatcher thought of translating these conventional theories into practice. Sending three-year-olds into the snow without mittens or hats was probably unrealistic — if not to the kids, then for Sarah to enforce it. So Thatcher accepted the inevitable division of labor and deferred to Sarah to implement his Karnesian theories. "I know you will bring up him [Sambo/Sam/Phillips] & his Sister better than I could — I guess its best for me to talk about educating Children but never attempt to put my theories in practice — in this you are more skilled than I am — so we will divide the Subject — I will give the rules in Theory, & you shall put them in practice."[32]

The third important role of the congressional wife at home was as a partner in her husband's political career. Wives who lived with their husbands at the seat of government also contributed to their husbands' political careers. But as Mary Butler discovered to her regret, it was often as a slave to a "parade of ceremonious visiting." Other congressional wives may have enjoyed the rigorous schedule of New York City's reception circuit: Monday night at Abigail Adams's; Tuesday at Lady Temple's, wife of the British consul; Wednesday at Mrs. Lucy Flucker Knox's; and Thursday, Mrs. John Jay's, culminating Friday night with Martha Washington's famous levee. According to historians of the so-called Republican Court, "women and men actively engaged in political discussions in these venues; [where] women brokered and shaped information in a variety of ways."[33]

The congressional wife's opportunities to shine in a resplendent social scene were more limited in the home district, especially in Biddeford, Maine. But the opportunities to network — to broker and shape information — were correspondingly increased. Remaining at home offered more direct contact with those on whom her husband's political fate ultimately rested — the constituents. The congressional wife at home was well positioned to serve as her husband's principal liaison,

---

[32]George to Sarah Thatcher, Feb. 18, 22, May 24, 1789, TPMHS; Wilson Smith, ed., *Theories of Education in Early America, 1655–1819* (Indianapolis, 1973), pp. 127–29.

[33]Mrs. Pierce Butler to Rev. Weeden Butler, July 15, 1789, Butler Papers, Additional Manuscripts, British Museum, London; Abigail Adams to Mary Cranch, Jan. 24, 1789 [1790], Adams Letters, American Antiquarian Society, Worcester, Mass.; David S. Shields and Fredrika J. Teute, "The Republican Court and the Historiography of a Woman's Domain in the Public Sphere," unpublished manuscript, p. 4 n.

either as publicist, informant, or adviser. The documentary record clearly illustrates how Sarah Thatcher played the first of these roles very effectively.

No congressman needed the help more than George Thatcher. Ideologically he was a Federalist in a county that voted against the Constitution at the state's ratification convention. Before 1786 Thatcher himself had identified strongly with the decentralists and opponents of the great land proprietors versus the yeoman squatters whose claims to unsurveyed backlands were pressed in the spirit of the Revolution. Shays's Rebellion changed his outlook. Thereafter he was more afraid of mobocracy than of aristocracy.[34]

In the first federal election for the Maine district's sole representative to Congress, thirteen men stood as candidates in what today would be called a "negative campaign." Perhaps the negative tone of the campaign was responsible for the lowest proportional voter turnout of any congressional district in the state: Thatcher was elected with 60 percent of the mere 948 votes cast in a district with a population of 96,000.

Thatcher's tenuous mandate was further weakened by the limitations of communicating over time and space. On those grounds alone Antifederalist Thomas Tudor Tucker doubted that the House would be capable of anything but "a nominal Representation." In contrast to the delegates of the Confederation Congress, who were elected by their state legislatures, the members of the proposed House of Representatives, Tucker predicted, "must be totally unknown to nine tenths of their constituents."[35] This would have been especially true of the Maine district, which in population was the largest congressional district outside of North Carolina, and more than six times larger than the least populous district, located in Georgia.

Maine's peculiar political complexion was another potential handicap. It was a part of the country, warned one friend, in which "every one is in his own Ideas a Politician. There are two Letters in our Alpha-

---

[34]Taylor, *Liberty Men and Great Proprietors*, pp. 129–30.

[35]Thomas Tudor Tucker to St. George Tucker, Dec. 28, 1787, Paul Smith and Ronald Gephard, eds., *Letters of Delegates to Congress, 1774–1789*, 25 vols. (Washington, D.C., 1976–98), 24:600.

bet very easily learnt. . . . They are *great I* and *little u*." Dr. Daniel Cony, although a friend of Thatcher's, may serve as an example of the type of highly charged amateur politician who waited to battle candidates at every poll. A mutual friend wrote that after visiting with the man for less than half an hour, "my head turned round like a top with politics. I would not live in the same house with . . . Daniel Cony for ten thousand pounds per annum."[36]

Nor could Thatcher take for granted the traditional alliance between the Federalist politician and the merchant. Maine's merchant class, based in the principal port of Portland, appears to have been a particularly peevish lot. One constituent reminded Thatcher that he could expect to get along with them "as Cats & Dogs." When a committee of Portland merchants decided to register their complaint about the Coasting Act [HR-16] by petitioning Congress in January 1790, they registered their complaint with Thatcher as well by voting to ask Boston's representative, Fisher Ames, to present it to the House. Bypassing their own congressman in a matter of such basic constituent services was intended to signify their displeasure "that you had paid no attention to the traders of Portland — that you had heretofore neglected to answer their letters &c." Thatcher wrote a long letter apologizing and rededicating himself to their service, at which point they relented and asked Ames to let Thatcher take over.[37]

Despite the useful ability to humble himself occasionally, Thatcher's personality remained a political liability. Of all her husband's limitations, it was the one for which Sarah may have been the most effective in mediating and compensating. In the days before parties, political figures earned and retained the adherence of their followers in large part by the strength of their personal character, reputation, and honor. That is why political dialogue was so often fraught with shades of personal invective that in some cases led to the dueling

---

[36]Jeremiah Hill to George Thatcher, Mar. 24, 1789, Chamberlain Collection, Boston Public Library; Benjamin Wait to George Thatcher, Feb. 14, 1788, quoted in Ulrich, *Midwife's Tale*, p. 59.

[37]Jeremiah Hill to George Thatcher, Sept. 25, 1788, TPMHS; Thomas B. Wait to George Thatcher, Dec. 30, 1789, Thomas G. Thornton Papers, Maine Historical Society, Portland; George Thatcher to Thomas Robinson, Jan. 24, 1790, TPMHS.

ground.[38] While Thatcher does not seem to have had any permanent enemies, it is likely that his personality prevented him from accumulating too many friends either. Contemporaries record that he was eccentric and sarcastic.[39] During one congressional debate on the mint, when a colleague proposed striking a coin with an eagle, Thatcher — "by way of banter" — offered an amendment in favor of the goose instead, reserving goslings for the smaller denominations of coins. The bill's insulted mover challenged him to a duel. In reply, Thatcher told the messenger: "He had no right to hazard his life on such chances, but would write to his wife, and if she consented he would accept the challenge. But as a compromise, he proposed that his figure might be marked on a barn door, and if the challenger, standing at the proper distance, hit it, he would acknowledge himself shot."[40] The matter was dropped. Whether apocryphal or not, the story serves as a good illustration not only of the political culture of the time, but of the various ways in which a clever congressman like Thatcher could be expected to make good use of a distant wife.

In the First Congress Thatcher was seen as taking special pleasure in worrying his more sensitive colleague, Elbridge Gerry. Chroniclers recalled that later, as a judge, Thatcher's "manner on the bench was not always pleasant." Brusque and straightforward, he took express pride in acquitting himself of being "what is commonly called a *people pleaser*."[41]

Fortunately for Thatcher, Sarah seems to have been a people pleaser. He called her "the widow," but his frequent cautions against indulging in "Dull & gloomy feelings" seem at odds with other reports of Sarah's sociability. Emerson's step-grandfather, the Reverend Ezra Ripley, wrote that his daughter visited Sarah shortly after Thatcher's departure for the First Congress, and that "she cannot conceive, scarcely, of a more accomplished Lady, or one more capable of making every body

---

[38]For dueling's significance in the political culture of the Early Republic, see Joanne B. Freeman, "Dueling as Politics: Reinterpreting the Burr-Hamilton Duel," *William and Mary Quarterly,* 3d ser. 53 (1996):289–318.

[39]William A. Duer, *Reminiscences of an Old New Yorker* (New York, 1867), p. 72.

[40]Clayton, *History of York County, Maine,* p. 78.

[41]Duer, *Reminiscences,* p. 72; Clayton, *History of York County, Maine,* p. 78; George Thatcher to Robert Southgate, July 1, 1789, Scarborough Manuscripts, Maine Historical Society, Portland.

pleased and happy." Men as well as women sought out the pleasure of her company. Mocking the pretensions of the new Republican Court, the Thatchers' good friend Jeremiah Hill informed him "the other day I paid Miss Thatcher a visit *a la mode de New York.*"[42]

Everything that was said earlier about the social content of visiting in late-eighteenth-century rural Maine should be understood as having definite political overtones as well. Sarah became her husband's representative at social functions, where her success as hostess smoothed the way for pleasant and constructive political discussion. Jeremiah Hill described one such gathering: "I had the Honor & Pleasure of dining yesterday [Sept. 25, 1788] on Roast Beef with Mrs. Thatcher &c. in Company with Bro. [William?] Cobb & Dr. [Aaron] Porter & chatted over our old roast meat Stories, in turn brought in our friend George & other Acquaintances, talked over congressional Matters, rectified some Mistakes . . . and I believe in my Soul, if the roast beef had not been brought on in ten Minutes we should have compleately organised the new Congress but the roast Beef, a Glass of Grog & small Beer commanded our attention another way."[43]

Inquiries about Thatcher's reports from the seat of government were also made in the context of social visits with Sarah. Constituents were eager for news about the progress of the "ship of state," or in the more rustic Maine idiom, "the Continental Waggon." Congressmen often mailed newspapers home so that accounts of the debates could be circulated throughout their districts. But this did not obviate the prudence of maintaining an independent correspondence with strategically placed sources at home.[44]

Members of the First Congress employed several variations on this formula. Fisher Ames, whose fellow lodgers called him the "Secretary of State" for his incessant letter writing, provided political updates twice a week to a group of his Boston friends who formed the Wednesday Night Club just for that purpose. Benjamin Goodhue's stream of

---

[42]George to Sarah Thatcher, Feb. 14, 1791, TPMHS; Feb. 27, 1792, TPLC; Rev. Ezra Ripley to George Thatcher, Mar. 30, 1789, Jeremiah Hill to George Thatcher, June 14, 1789, Chamberlain Collection, Boston Public Library.

[43]Jeremiah Hill to George Thatcher, Sept. 25, 1788, TPMHS.

[44]Daniel Davis to George Thatcher, Oct. 9, 1788, Jeremiah Hill to George Thatcher, Oct. 2, 1788, TPMHS.

letters to the marine insurance offices of Massachusetts's North Shore filled the identical need. Some congressmen wrote circular letters addressed to the voters of their district. Thatcher wrote the equivalent of circular letters to his friend and confidant Thomas B. Wait, who regularly published them in his *Cumberland Gazette* as "Correspondence from New York" or "Philadelphia." Dr. Cony encouraged Thatcher to keep up his correspondence with other sources as well, "the utility of which (being dispersed in this Eastern Country) I need not mention." Within a month of the opening of the First Congress, a corresponding committee of eleven merchants was established in Portland, to whom Thatcher was requested to direct his letters—"or at least those of a publick nature, and which relates to the trade of this town."[45]

Thatcher did not include as much political information in his letters to Sarah as he did in his letters to Silas Lee, for example. But he wrote to Sarah much more often than to anyone else, and in the twilight of the Confederation Congress he made a conscious effort to include political information. Admittedly, wrote Thatcher, "I never discovered in you a disposition to meddle with politics, & if I had, I should not have cultivated it with any desire of making you a politician." He wrote, rather, in the conviction that "you ought to have now and then, for novelty sake, a little something about Congress and Congressional matters—that when your female friends enquire of you the state of politics, you may, if you do not choose to enter upon the subject in conversation, hand them the Letters for them to read for themselves." Two weeks later, he teased a friend that, in the interests of saving time and "to induce her Friends to visit her the oftener," he had resolved to gather all the news he could and write it to Sarah alone. The political content of the letters to Sarah dropped off during the federal Congresses, when alternate means of disseminating information were available. But the letters to Sarah indicate that Thatcher's friends never stopped plying her for news.[46]

It is less clear how much Thatcher relied on Sarah for political news.

---

[45]Dr. Daniel Cony to George Thatcher, May 16, 1789, Chamberlain Collection, Boston Public Library; Joseph McClellan to George Thatcher, May 5, 1789, Thatcher Papers, Essex Institute, Salem, Mass.

[46]George to Sarah Thatcher, Aug. 17, Sept. 16, 1788, Jeremiah Hill to George Thatcher, Oct. 8, 1788, TPMHS.

None of her letters survive to prove or disprove her role as a political informant or adviser. But Thatcher certainly never lacked for such assistance from other sources, including her father and brother. Marriage extended Thatcher's political network into central Massachusetts, where his father-in-law, Samuel Phillips Savage, sat as judge for the Middlesex County court. The letters between them are few and are mostly Savage's commentaries on congressional activities. Those between Thatcher and his brother-in-law, Joseph Savage, are more numerous but contain little politically useful information after Savage left Springfield, Massachusetts, to serve as captain of a federal artillery company stationed on the Georgia frontier in 1789. In addition, Thatcher regularly solicited and received information and advice from constituents — particularly the merchants. Philadelphia Rep. Thomas Fitzsimons, himself a merchant, grudgingly noted that the New Englanders were more successful in this than other congressmen.[47]

The only political advice Sarah is known to have given her husband was probably motivated more by a concern for his eternal than for his political life. The two had been linked since the first federal election, when his strongest challenge came from those who made an issue of his religious views, which were labeled unorthodox, antiestablishment, and, according to the usage of the time, deist. Even with the election secured, Massachusetts Federalist leader Christopher Gore hoped that "our friend Thatcher would talk with more discretion on some topics — they are important in the minds of many worthy men — and I should suppose such conduct might lessen his influence in the Government — at least I do not see any good consequence that can flow from running against the prejudices of any religious sect." William Widgery was more succinct: "Keep your Religion to your self."[48]

Thatcher's father had wanted him to be a preacher, and throughout his life he maintained a strong interest in theology. But his affinity for organized religion was ethical, not theological. He did not believe in

---

[47] *The Documentary History of the Ratification of the Constitution,* 14 vols. to date (Madison, Wis., 1976–), vol. 4 (John P. Kaminski, Gaspare J. Saladino, Richard Leffler, Charles Schoenleber, eds.), p. 291 n; Samuel P. Savage to George Thatcher, Jan. 28, 1791, Savage Papers, Massachusetts Historical Society, Boston; Thomas Fitzsimons to Tench Coxe, Apr. 25, 1789, Coxe Papers, Pennsylvania Historical Society, Philadelphia.

[48] Christopher Gore to Rufus King, Apr. 25, 1789, King Papers, New-York Historical Society, New York; William Widgery to George Thatcher, Jan. 5, 1791, TPMHS.

the existence of a soul outside of the body, although he did believe in the resurrection of the body. His instructions to Sarah on the education of their children were all rooted in the belief that we are what we make ourselves. The growing evangelical revival only reinforced the deception that "*God* or the *Holy Ghost* is able to produce the change in heart, that ought to be effected by discipline." The will to be happy was among those changes that "is more in our power . . . than most people are apt to believe." He hated the established, tax-supported church not because it was organized, but because it was corrupt, inculcating sentiments adverse to cheerfulness.[49]

In New York City he seemed to think that a minister preached well enough if he got it but half right. Once Congress moved to Philadelphia, the religiously diversified capital of Penn's "Holy Experiment," curiosity prompted him to try a different church every week. But at the first trial he "heard nothing to encourage me to repeat the experiment." A similar experiment during the Confederation Congress taught him that if he stood a reasonable chance of hearing good music he should not consider his time totally wasted.[50]

Travelers at the time observed that the people of Thatcher's district were "moderate Calvinists . . . candid, catholic and tolerant toward those of other persuasions." In 1790, only one-fifth of central Maine's towns had an organized (Congregational) church, and the ratio diminished in direct proportion to the distance from the coast. Even in those communities with a Congregational church — such as Biddeford's, established in 1730 — church members were only a tiny minority. Yet that theological latitudinarianism did not prevent Thatcher's opponents from making irreligion their principal charge against him in his first bid for reelection to Congress.[51]

Sarah seems to have done her best to make her husband a better, or at least a more visible, Christian. At home Thatcher devoted Sundays to rest, "except now & then you worry me to meeting." Once he went off to Congress, distance attenuated her means of persuasion. But still

---

[49]George Thatcher to Thomas B. Wait, Aug. 5, 1790, TPMHS; quoted in Taylor, *Liberty Men and Great Proprietors,* p. 131; George to Sarah Thatcher, Aug. 15, 1788, TPMHS.

[50]George to Sarah Thatcher, Dec. 27, 1789, Dec. 20, 1790, Aug. 16, 1788, TPMHS.

[51]Morse, *American Geography,* p. 198; Taylor, *Liberty Men and Great Proprietors,* p. 132.

she kept up her requests that he attend weekly worship. At some point they struck a bargain by which he promised to go to church every Sunday if she contented herself with only one letter from him every other week. Eventually she renewed her complaint that he did not write often enough. On the day after Christmas, 1791, he wrote back threatening to terminate their agreement altogether. The exchange is playful, but with an edge that reveals her influence at the same time he proclaims his independence of it.[52]

By that time Thatcher had survived the ordeal of several runoff elections — the most bitterly contested of any to the Second Congress. Supporters and detractors alike had flooded the pages of Maine's two weekly papers with editorials pseudonymously signed "A Real Republican," "A Countryman," "A Card," "Candidus," "Argumenticus," "Fair Play," "Plain Dealing," and, most creatively of all, "A Whip of Small Cords." Thatcher took a perverse pleasure in the public debate his religious views generated and warned his friends not to interfere when ministers railed from their pulpits against the "monster in wickedness." For, he believed, "the more they step out of their Line of duty the more will their influence fail them."[53]

At least one voter cast his ballot for Thatcher not because of the effectiveness of Sarah's home-front duties as a political operative, nor because of her checkered success rehabilitating his reputation as a Christian. A few days after the fourth runoff election, wrote Jeremiah Hill to Thatcher, "a Countryman came down to sell corn & called upon Miss Thatcher to see if she wanted to buy & very soon began upon Electioneering, said that he did not know Mr. Thatcher but that his wife was down last fall & that Mr. Thatcher *used her very well one night* therefore he gave Mr. Thatcher his vote, this is a manifestation of the Importance of keeping in with the women."[54]

Thatcher occupied Maine's sole seat in the U.S. House of Representatives until redistricting in 1793 gave it another two. Voters returned him for an additional three terms, making him the longest consecutively serving member of the original House of Representatives, and

---

[52]George to Sarah Thatcher, Aug. 10, Sept. 27, 1788, Dec. 26, 1791, TPMHS.

[53]George Thatcher to Thomas B. Wait, Aug. 5, 1790; to Samuel C. Johonnet, Dec. 12, 1790, TPMHS.

[54]Jeremiah Hill to George Thatcher, Jan. 16, 1791, TPMHS.

the only one to serve into the new century and see Congress installed in its permanent seat. Returning to Biddeford in 1801, Thatcher was appointed associate justice of the Massachusetts supreme court. When Maine separated from Massachusetts in 1820, he was forced to relocate to Boston in order to retain the position. Soon thereafter he resigned from the bench and moved back to Biddeford, where he died in 1824. Sarah Savage Thatcher followed him in 1843.

Only five years into the Thatchers' marriage, George's older bachelor friend William Frost wrote to thank him for his advice to "go & take a wife . . . [and] answer the end of my creation."[55] Another thirty-five years of life together stretched out before George and Sarah. Whether or not the experience of those years confirmed Thatcher in the belief that Sarah answered the end of his creation is buried in the pages of a two-hundred-year-old correspondence, half of which has never been recovered. Yet as a political creature in the first years of his long political existence, Thatcher benefited by Sarah's performance of domestic roles that had public significance. Whether as comforter, provider, co-parent, or political supporter, Sarah was a congressional partner in every sense worthy of the term.

––––––––––

[55]William Frost to George Thatcher, June 9, 1789, Chamberlain Collection, Boston Public Library.

III. Congress and the Executive and Judicial Branches in the 1790s

Wythe Holt

Separation of Powers?

Relations between the Judiciary and the Other Branches of the Federal Government before 1803

> Something there is that doesn't love a wall.
>
> ROBERT FROST

Introduction

O N FEBRUARY 15, 1800, the Philadelphia *Aurora,* the most important Jeffersonian newspaper in the city that was still the nation's capital, reported that Federalist congressmen had been holding a series of "secret meetings . . . a few evenings past in the Senate chamber." Fearful that a Jeffersonian majority would capture the presidency and both houses of Congress in the upcoming November 1800 elections, the Federalists were putting together a plan, the *Aurora* "shrewdly suspect[ed]," that would result "in a consolidation of the states into a *republic one and indivisible.*" Central to their plan were "alterations to be made in the judiciary." The meeting of the previous Wednesday

Research for this paper, and for the project of which it forms a part, has been generously supported by the University of Alabama School of Law and my deans, particularly Charles Gamble and Ken Randall. Thanks are owed to many friends and colleagues in the field of early American federal judicial history, some of whom are mentioned in the text; I wish I could name them all here. And thanks are owed to many librarians and many repositories of papers, newspapers, and other material useful for my research. I have greatly benefited from the suggestions of those who have read earlier versions of the chapter, especially Bill Casto and my colleagues Forrest McDonald, Ken and Susan Randall, Martha Morgan, Norman Stein, and Susan Pace Hamill.

evening had been devoted to that task, and, the *Aurora* reported, "the federal judges being now in town [the Supreme Court justices, meeting for their February 1800 term], they of course are consulted."[1]

This report of Supreme Court justices secretly joining ("of course") with members of Congress to draft a revision of the national judiciary system designed to entrench and consolidate Federalist power seems strange to modern eyes. It might be thought the paranoid raving of partisans deluded by the heat of the intense political battles that characterized John Adams's single term as president. That it was not, however, is demonstrated by a letter written ten days later by Samuel Sewall, Federalist congressman from Massachusetts and member of the House committee to produce judiciary reform legislation. Sewall reported to William Cushing, a Supreme Court justice, that two other Supreme Court justices, William Paterson and Bushrod Washington, had met "with the Committee according to appointment and favoured us with the details of a bill calculated upon the plan which had been suggested, and which in the principal points will be adopted by the Committee."[2] Note that Sewall says that Paterson and Washington actually drafted the bill—which, after many significant alterations, became the Judiciary Act of 1801, the infamous "midnight judges bill."

Most modern lawyers and historians of the federal judiciary assume that only one notion of separation of powers is consistent with the Constitution: a wall of separation between the judiciary and the other branches.[3] According to this view, the justices supposedly erected the

---

[1]*Aurora* (Philadelphia), Feb. 15, 1800 (emphasis in original).

[2]Samuel Sewall to William Cushing, Feb. 25, 1800, *The Documentary History of the Supreme Court, 1789–1800,* 5 vols. to date (New York, 1985–), vol. 4 (Maeva Marcus, James C. Brandon, Robert P. Frankel, Jr., Stephen L. Tull, and Natalie Wexler, eds.), p. 628, hereafter *DHSC.* After the bill failed in the spring of 1800, the committee asked Justice Paterson to give his attention to formulating "an uniform system of Practice and pleadings for the Courts of the United States" to accompany the bill "which will probably be taken up early in the next Session" (Robert Goodloe Harper to William Paterson, May 10, 1800, ibid., 4:650). While another version of the judiciary bill was introduced in the next session of Congress in the fall, no accompanying process and pleadings bill was introduced, and we do not know what further aid Paterson may have given.

[3]For expositions of this view by modern legal historians, see, e.g., Russell Wheeler, "Extrajudicial Activities of the Early Supreme Court," *Supreme Court Review* (1973):124, 152; Maeva Marcus and Emily Field van Tassel, "Judges and Legislators in the New Federal System, 1789–1800," in *Judges and Legislators: Toward Institutional Comity,* ed. Robert A. Katzmann (Washington, D.C., 1988), p. 35.

For lawyers, my claim is more tendentious. Recent Supreme Court decisions such as *Morrison* v. *Olson,* 487 U.S. 654 (1988), and *Mistretta* v. *United States,* 488 U.S. 361

wall in 1792 in *Hayburn's Case* when they refused on constitutional grounds to accept the revision of their judicial opinions by members of the other branches, and in 1793 when they refused to answer President Washington's request for advisory judicial opinions.[4] One mainstream commentator who noticed the 1800 aid to Congress by the justices has been content with stating astonishment at this breach in the wall, while others just fail to notice.[5] Maeva Marcus adheres to the notion of a rule of strict separation, when, in order to excuse the 1800 instance and other 1790s interbranch collaborations by the justices, she asserts that the justices contrived and adhered to a distinction between official advice from the whole Court, which they understood to be banned by the separation of powers doctrine, and informal advice from individual justices, which was not so banned.[6] The evidence to be recounted here shows, however, that advisory opinions both from individual justices and from the Court as a whole, as well as other interbranch collaborations, were commonplace in the 1790s. A new interpretation, advanced independently in recent work by William R. Casto

---

(1989), according to the succinct summary by two of the most perceptive and widely quoted lawyer observers of the Court, "may be said to have given two sets of answers. One approach[, which] may be called . . . formalist[,] . . . puts great weight on the text of the Constitution and on formal observance of a strict separation of powers. The Court's other approach is a functional one [in] which . . . the constitutional text and the lines between the Branches must on occasion be subordinated to flexibility and function" (Jerome A. Barron and C. Thomas Dienes, *Constitutional Law in a Nutshell* [St. Paul, Minn., 1995], pp. 118–19). Whether the Court's view of separation of powers can be so neatly categorized is doubtful, as "most commentators have correctly criticized those opinions as being hopelessly inconsistent" (Kenneth C. Randall, "The Treaty Power," *Ohio State Law Journal* 51 [1990]:1113). In any case, the remarks quoted from professors Barron and Dienes demonstrate that the ideal held by modern scholars is a strict separation, which functionalists allow to be "subordinated . . . *on occasion*" to more important needs (emphasis added). The putative functional approach has almost nothing of the openness of the view the judges took in the 1790s, where separation was never thought of rigidly and was invoked only when some interaction demanded by a nonjudicial branch threatened the independence either of the judiciary or of the other branch.

[4]See, e.g., Charles Alan Wright, *Law of Federal Courts,* 5th ed. (St. Paul, Minn., 1994), p. 65; Erwin Chemerinsky, *Federal Jurisdiction,* 2d ed. (Boston, 1994), pp. 48–49, 50–51; Marcus and van Tassel, "Judges and Legislators," pp. 37–43.

[5]Kathryn Conway Turner [Preyer], "The Judiciary Act of 1801," Ph.D. diss., University of Wisconsin, 1959, pp. 86–87 (astonishment); George L. Haskins and Herbert A. Johnson, *History of the Supreme Court of the United States,* vol. 2, *Foundations of Power: John Marshall, 1801–15* (New York, 1981), pp. 122–25 (failure to notice).

[6]Maeva Marcus, "Separation of Powers in the Early National Period," *William and Mary Law Review* 30 (1989):274. See also Marcus and van Tassel, "Judges and Legislators," p. 43.

and Stewart Jay and joined by me in this article,[7] uses this evidence to question the very existence of the supposed wall of separation.

The justices of the Supreme Court in the 1790s understood "separation of powers" in terms of the relations of power. They saw it as a matter of balancing power against power, not as a matter of strict separation. In order to protect the rights of the people, the enhanced power of a reorganized national government had been institutionally divided into three parts by creating three branches. Each branch was supposed to maintain its "independence," and thus to protect against tyranny, by carefully guarding against encroachment by either or both of the other branches. As a result, separation of powers worked in two ways utterly at odds with a wall of separation. First, it required interaction between branches when circumstances made interaction necessary in order to prevent encroachment. Second, when there was no danger of encroachment, nothing prevented members of the branches from acting together, and such might even be necessary in order to engage in an equally important endeavor: protecting the government against its enemies. It would be up to the judgment of the members of any branch as to which circumstances constituted encroachment and which circumstances provoked a need to work together.

Our new interpretation discards another myth about the federal judiciary in the 1790s: that the justices were outside of politics, or at least that they thought of themselves as apolitical. On the contrary the justices of that time knew they were political actors; saw themselves as political actors; did not imagine this to be odd or wrong, or only occasional or temporary; and openly acted as members of the Washington and Adams Federalist administrations to protect the government and to further Federalist goals. They were primarily motivated to keep the Constitution and the new government running smoothly rather than to concoct abstract theories of how the government ought to work.[8]

---

[7]See William R. Casto, *The Supreme Court in the Early Republic: The Chief Justiceships of John Jay and Oliver Ellsworth* (Columbia, S.C., 1995); Stewart Jay, *Most Humble Servants: The Advisory Role of Early Federal Judges* (New Haven, 1997). In this article I cite, with permission, from Professor Jay's draft manuscript dated May 1995.

[8]"The fact that [the justices] were willing, as individuals, to perform tasks in circumstances in which they might later individually or collectively be called upon to issue judicial opinions demonstrates that their theory of separation of powers was neither very elaborate nor presented remotely as rigid a dividing line between the branches as

Thus, what justices Paterson and Washington did in February 1800 was absolutely typical and normal for them in their times.

The others who advance the new interpretation of separation of powers in the 1790s would agree with me thus far, I think, but I want to go even further. While it would be very rare for justices today secretly to draft legislation or meet with a congressional committee for a partisan purpose, advisory opinions have been usual since 1803, and indeed are normal for us in our times. The justices are and always have been just as political as they were in the 1790s. The wall of separation is a modern, positivist invention; moreover, it is a myth, and never has existed.

The judges of the 1790s neither understood nor desired a strict divide either between themselves and the other branches or between law and politics — one of the positivist assumptions underlying modern separation-of-powers theory. They did not believe that their pronouncements were "the law" either — the other positivist foundation for modern separation-of-powers theory. They did not adhere to the tenets of positivism because positivism was just emerging, and they had all been reared in a natural law tradition. That tradition said that law was searched for by judges, not made by them; and it understood judges to be a part of the political world.

Let us now take a look at the other evidence for my position. Much of this evidence has been produced by the tireless researchers who put together the collections of documents at the documentary histories of the First Federal Congress, 1789–91, and of the Supreme Court, 1789–1800, and by the assiduous research of professors Jay and Casto.[9] Where I suggest an interpretation different from those they have advanced, I want it understood that I could not have done so without their fine work, that I am standing on their shoulders, as it were.

---

modern theorists would contend to be the sine qua non of any separation of powers doctrine. They were practical politicians and judges attempting to get a new system started, not isolated jurisprudential thinkers elaborating an ideal scheme" (Wythe Holt, " 'The Federal Courts Have Enemies in All Who Fear Their Influence on State Objects': The Failure to Abolish Supreme Court Circuit Riding in the Judiciary Acts of 1792 and 1793," *Buffalo Law Review* 36 [1987]:332 n. 127).

[9]Moreover, I must pay homage to the excellent work done by such researchers as Charles Warren, Mary K. Tachau, Wilfred J. Ritz, Kathryn Preyer, my Alabama colleague Forrest McDonald, and H. Jefferson Powell. The work of Maeva Marcus and her coworkers also has been important.

Formal Interbranch Interaction

First, the Constitution nowhere establishes a wall of separation between each pair of the three branches of the federal government; rather, it joins them together in many ways. Thinking only of the judicial branch, the chief justice presides over any impeachment of the president, and impeachments are tried in the Senate, thus uniting all three branches.[10] No president was impeached during the 1790s, but in another fashion the three branches were (and are) regularly and routinely joined: the president must nominate members of the federal judiciary and the Senate must confirm them.[11] One presidential nomination of a Supreme Court justice did meet rejection in the Senate in the 1790s, an instance that demonstrates vividly the political nature of the judicial office.

Upon the resignation of John Jay as chief justice in 1795, President Washington immediately turned to his old friend John Rutledge, then serving as chief justice of South Carolina. Rutledge had been a distinguished patriot and lawyer, wartime governor of South Carolina, important member of the Constitutional Convention and of its committee on detail, and one of the first appointees to the new Supreme Court in 1789. Disgusted by the time spent and the hardships the new justices encountered in circuit court travel, and upset that he was passed over for chief justice in 1789, Rutledge soon resigned his first Court appointment, but accepted Washington's new offer without hesitation. It was a recess appointment, since the Senate was not in session, and was subject to Senate vote at the next sitting of Congress.[12] Unfortunately, he had just given a characteristically fiery speech against the Jay Treaty, which was very important to the Northern Federalists who predominated in Rutledge's party. Though Rutledge did a creditable job in presiding over the Supreme Court's most case-filled August term up to that time, and in holding circuit court in South Carolina thereafter, the Senate in December quickly rejected his nomination on the political ground that he had given a speech against the views of the Federalists. Discouraged over his bodily infirmities, ashamed of the criticism and

---

[10]U.S. Constitution, Art. I, sec. 3, para. 6.

[11]U.S. Constitution, Art. II, sec. 2, para. 2.

[12]U.S. Constitution, Art. II, sec. 2, para. 3.

calumny heaped upon him, hopelessly in debt, and recently having lost his mother and his wife, Rutledge twice attempted suicide by drowning, on the way home from his circuit riding and again at home in late December.[13]

The federal courts, and particularly the Supreme Court, were expected to entertain cases "arising under this Constitution, the Laws of the United States, and treaties made . . . under their authority."[14] The opposite of a wall of separation but the very embodiment of checks and balances, one branch would construe and apply statutes made by another branch, and the judiciary, it was widely expected, would reject those it found void for unconstitutionality. Largely because all the justices saw their primary duty as political — namely, to ensure that the new Constitution and government, and the Federalist policies of the group who wrote the one and established the other, were firmly implanted and just as firmly defended against the attacks of dissenters or disputers[15] — statutes and Federalist policies for the most part received warm endorsement.

Two important cases demonstrate that the Court was willing to go to extremes to uphold the government in a crisis. In *Hylton* v. *United States*[16] it unanimously rejected a constitutional challenge to an excise tax on carriages Congress had passed in 1794 to help fund the army and navy during the nation's first grave international crisis, a war scare with Great Britain. The delinquent "defendant," Richmond, Virginia,

---

[13]See Wythe Holt, "How a Founder Becomes Forgotten: Chief Justice John Rutledge, Slavery, and the Jay Treaty," *Journal of Southern Legal History* 5 (1999):5–36. For Rutledge's life and contributions, see James Haw, "John Rutledge: Distinction and Declension," in *Seriatim: The Supreme Court before John Marshall,* ed. Scott Douglas Gerber (New York, 1998).

[14]U.S. Constitution, Art. III, sec. 2.

[15]"The federal judiciary figured prominently in the political struggles of the 1790s. Its courtrooms promoted national economic policies by serving as forums for debt collection, . . . [by providing] the underpinning for the revenue laws, by prosecuting tax evaders and by uncompromising punishment of the Whiskey rebels. . . . When the Washington administration decided in 1793 on a policy of strict neutrality in the ongoing war among the European powers, the federal courts were the first line in the enforcement effort. . . . [At] circuit [court] sessions, . . . they used grand jury charges — reprinted widely in newspapers — to explain and defend national policies" (Jay, "Most Humble Servants," pp. 93–94).

[16]3 U.S. (3 Dall.) 171 (1796), ably discussed in Casto, *Supreme Court in the Early Republic,* pp. 101–5, where the anomalies discussed in this and the next paragraph of the text are documented.

Federalist Daniel Hylton, owned only one carriage, but he was willing to stipulate that he owned 125. This "fiction," really a blatant falsehood crafted by Federalist leader and Secretary of the Treasury Alexander Hamilton and other high officers of the other "party" to the "case," made the amount in controversy equal to the two-thousand-dollar minimum amount necessary to appeal the case to the Supreme Court.[17] Moreover, in the Supreme Court, the United States paid the lawyers' fees on both sides. The case was thus "feigned," or phony.[18]

However, in Casto's words, "the Court winked at all these problems and gave the government the functional equivalent of an advisory opinion" in a headlong rush to uphold the government's power to levy direct taxes without regard to population. Antifederalists had all along been opposed to the new national taxation powers, and the Court's decision attempted to legitimate all exercises of such powers, both the carriage tax (which disproportionately burdened Southerners) and the hotly disputed excise tax on whiskey that was at the same time causing unrest in the back country from the western Piedmont to the Ohio and Kentucky settlements. In their *Hylton* opinions justices Samuel Chase and William Paterson frankly admitted that the government needed broad powers to levy taxes. Atty. Gen.William Bradford had written to Hamilton that "the [tax] act should be supported . . . by the unanimous opinions of the Judges," and, while there is no record that Hamilton passed the word along, the justices quickly did exactly that.[19]

---

[17]The Judiciary Act of 1789 did not allow the United States to lay its suit for collection of the delinquent taxes (eight dollars per carriage) plus penalties (another eight dollars per carriage) as an original action in the Supreme Court, so that suit had to be brought in the Virginia circuit court and then, to get an authoritative publicized result, hastily decided and appealed. The statute actually allowed appeals only "where the matter in dispute *exceeds* the sum or value of two thousand dollars," so Hamilton's fiction did not quite qualify, but neither the Court nor the litigants noticed in their hurry to reach a decision. "An Act to establish the Judicial Courts of the United States," *Statutes at Large* (Boston, 1848), chap. 20, sec. 11, 13, 22, 1:78, 80–81, 84 (emphasis added). Another stipulation, not challenged by the United States but equally indicative that the "case" was bogus, was that Hylton would owe only sixteen dollars if he lost.

[18]"Feigned and contrived suits were reasonably common in this period, and appear to have raised no red flags" (Susan Low Bloch, "The Early Role of the Attorney General in our Constitutional Scheme: In the Beginning There Was Pragmatism," *Duke Law Journal* [1989]:612).

[19]Casto, *Supreme Court in the Early Republic*, p. 103; William Bradford to Alexander Hamilton, July 2, 1795, Harold C. Syrett and Jacob Cooke, eds., *The Papers of Alexander Hamilton*, 27 vols. (New York, 1961–87), 18:393. For greater detail, see *The Law Practice*

Federalist judges did not wish the government and the Constitution to seem weak in this time of crisis.

The second case arose out of the early stages of the same crisis. War between Britain and France had pulled most European powers into the fray. The new French ambassador to the United States, Edmond Genêt, began in 1793 to use French consuls in American ports as prize courts, condemning British (and other enemy) merchant vessels his privateers captured. The anomaly of French courts sitting upon American soil greatly upset not only the British minister, but also the whole American government because it seemed to indicate both national weakness and a partiality toward the French. Since in the 1790s the United States was in fact weak, it had declared neutrality in the war between the European giants, and it would have been unable to withstand any British military pressure provoked by Genêt's actions.[20]

The owners of the captured ships went for help to the federal district courts sitting in admiralty, claiming that the French prize courts were illegal. To the consternation and embarrassment of the Washington administration, which had confidently told the British minister that American courts would make matters right, five (out of six) district judges ruled that international law gave prize jurisdiction only to the courts of the captor nation, so that courts of a neutral nation (like the United States) had no jurisdiction to consider even the legality of foreign prize courts established in its midst.[21] One of the cases made its way to the Supreme Court very quickly.

In *Glass* v. *The Sloop Betsy* the Court, without giving any reason or citation for its ruling, and without adhering to its usual practice in the 1790s whereby each justice gave his opinion in important cases, decreed that American district courts "clearly" had jurisdiction in such instances. The justices were obviously more worried about ruling the way the administration desired "in an important case that directly implicated the nation's ability to avoid being drawn into the European

---

of Alexander Hamilton, 5 vols. (New York, 1964–81), vol. 4 (Julius Goebel, Jr., and Joseph H. Smith, eds.), pp. 297–355.

[20] For the Genêt crisis, see generally Casto, *Supreme Court in the Early Republic,* pp. 82–87.

[21] Five of the cases are discussed in ibid., pp. 82–84 and n. 31; Professor Casto has since the publication of his book discovered the sixth, from North Carolina. See *Daily Advertiser* (New York), July 29, 1793.

war" than they were about the law.[22] From both *Hylton* and *Glass* the two lessons were that politics was more important than law, and that advisory opinions to the other branches, and to the world, would be forthcoming when necessary.

The two most important decisions handed down by the Court in the 1790s were similarly advisory opinions (based upon today's positivist standards), and the judges and their contemporaries all understood that their importance was more political than legal. In opinions (which we know collectively as *Hayburn's Case*) issued in spring and fall 1792 by the justices at four circuit courts — the Supreme Court justices were also traveling circuit judges then, and circuit courts were primarily trial courts — the Invalid Pension Act passed by Congress the previous winter was ruled unconstitutional. Since the act allowed judicial opinions about the fitness of Revolutionary War veterans appearing to apply for pensions to be revised by the secretary of war or by Congress itself, the judges believed their branch of the government to be threatened by encroachment.[23]

Although this was the first exercise of judicial review to overturn an act of Congress, the upset created by the rulings concerned the independence the judges exhibited and the fear many Federalists had that open disagreement between different branches of the shaky new government might promote fatally disruptive public dissent, not the power the judges asserted to nullify a statute duly passed by Congress. Chief Justice Jay and Justice Cushing demonstrated their understanding of "separation of powers" as dealing with branch interaction to promote branch independence, rather than some abstract wall of division, when they remarked that the federal government "is divided into *three* distinct and independent branches; and it is the duty of each to abstain from and to oppose encroachments on either."[24]

---

[22]3 U.S. (3 Dall.) 6, 16 (1794); Casto, *Supreme Court in the Early Republic*, p. 86. "The major recurring theme of the decade was the Justices' ongoing efforts to assist the Washington and Adams Administrations in evolving a stable relationship with the European powers — especially France and Great Britain" (ibid., p. 71).

[23]This episode is well analyzed in Maeva Marcus and Robert Teir, "*Hayburn's Case:* A Misinterpretation of Precedent," *Wisconsin Law Review* (1988):527–46. See also Casto, *Supreme Court in the Early Republic*, pp. 175–78.

[24]*Hayburn's Case,* 2 U.S. (2 Dall.) 410–11 n. (1793), opinion of Jay, Cushing, and District Judge William Duane, Apr. 5, 1792, issued at C.C.N.Y. (emphasis in original).

Moreover, three of the four circuit opinions in *Hayburn's Case* were advisory, as only in the Pennsylvania circuit court did the judges wait for an actual veteran to appear before they pronounced the act unconstitutional. In an action likely concerted by the justices (without adversarial argument or even a controversy before them) when they met in Philadelphia for their Supreme Court session in February,[25] they were so angry at Congress for failing to terminate their burdensome circuit riding while adding lengthy administrative hearings to the regular judicial duties they must perform on circuit, that they agreed to declare the act unconstitutional rather than finding some less confrontational method of action. Although Justice James Iredell's letter announcing his views openly admits that his "opinion" was given when no case had "yet come regularly and judicially" to him, the advisory ruling of John Jay and William Cushing was entered into the New York circuit court records as an "Opinion." As Professor Jay sums it up, "plainly their doubts on the wisdom of volunteering an extrajudicial opinion did not rise to the level of a constitutional obstacle."[26]

In the most important construction of statute and Constitution made in the 1790s, the judges in *Chisholm* v. *Georgia* created a furor in February 1793 by finding unconsenting states subject to suit by individuals in federal court.[27] Congress soon proposed what was to become the Eleventh Amendment, which reversed *Chisholm* (another type of interaction between judiciary and legislature entirely within the contemplation of the system). For these purposes, the important fact about *Chisholm* was that nobody argued Georgia's side. Modern "case or controversy" theory requires adversity. Just as in perhaps the most important ruling in our constitutional history, *Marbury* v. *Madison*,[28] in which only one side was argued, the kind of sharpening of the issues in the crucible of expert professional legal disputation was absent and the opinion was advisory in the sense of being uninformed.

---

[25]Jay, "Most Humble Servants," p. 101.

[26]Ibid., pp. 100–106, quote on p. 103; *Hayburn's Case*, 2 U.S. (2 Dall.) 414 n. (circuit opinion of Iredell and District Judge John Sitgreaves, JJ.), 410 n. (circuit opinion of Jay, Cushing, and Duane, JJ.).

[27]2 U.S. (2 Dall.) 419 (1793).

[28]5 U.S. (1 Cranch) 137 (1803).

Informal Interbranch Interaction

In their informal dealings with the executive and with Congress, the justices demonstrated even more resoundingly that they knew of no absolute division between them. Interaction occurred all the time, indeed some of it was mandated. Not only did the judges repeatedly give openly advisory opinions, they gave much extrajudicial advice and commentary, all in instances that might have come before them officially in a litigated case, and almost all without a recorded qualm about impropriety.

Justices were appointed to executive positions both by Presidents Washington and Adams and by Congress. John Jay served Washington both as chief justice and as acting secretary of state from the fall of 1789 through March 1790, when Thomas Jefferson finally arrived to take the job.[29] While some inclined to the mainstream concept of a wall of separation might excuse this as an emergency occurring before any decision of the secretary of state might come before the chief justice, it is difficult to ignore the simultaneous service of John Marshall as secretary of state and chief justice by Adams's appointment in the winter of 1801. Marshall, probably Adams's most trusted adviser during this twilight of his term, was instrumental in aiding the president in selecting the nineteen new circuit court appointments he made in the last two weeks before March 3 (dubbed by the Jeffersonian newspaper *Aurora* the "midnight judges"), all Federalists, fostering the continued partisan control of that branch with watchdog oversight over the whole.[30]

In addition, Washington named Jay to be special ambassador to England in 1794 to negotiate a new treaty, while Adams named Jay's successor, Oliver Ellsworth, as special commissioner to France in 1799 to negotiate a peace treaty. Both appointments came during warlike crises with the two European powers that, if escalated, could have been very dangerous for the weak new United States. Both treaties were

---

[29]Jay, "Most Humble Servants," pp. 80–81.

[30]See, e.g., Albert J. Beveridge, *The Life of John Marshall*, 4 vols. (Boston, 1916, 1919), 2:494–514, 522–23, 530–31, 553–60; Turner, "Judiciary Act," pp. 213–18, 268, 276–79, 282–84. For the source of the phrase "midnight judges," see *Aurora* (Philadelphia), Sept. 29, 1801.

highly controversial and could easily have been foreseen to provoke legal issues that might have been presented to their drafters as judges. Jeffersonian senators raised pertinent questions, during the fight over Jay's confirmation, about the judiciary becoming beholden to the executive and about judges making laws they would later construe and expound, but such partisan qualms did not deter either confirmation.[31]

Congress also appointed federal judges to executive positions. At the behest of Alexander Hamilton, Chief Justice Jay was appointed to the commission to inspect the mint and, more important, as one of the commissioners of the sinking fund, to help establish public credit by retiring the government's obligations. The investment decisions Jay participated in as a manager of the fund could have been subject to litigation. They quickly became controversial as part of a broader attack on Hamilton's economic plans.[32]

As Casto notes, "the first few Congresses assigned an astonishing number of nonjudicial administrative duties to the federal judges." The judges were given assignments that were quasi-judicial in nature, being most often asked to certify documents, determine and certify the existence of facts, or administer oaths. When they had to form an opinion, as in ascertaining the good character of an applicant for naturalization or in notifying the president when opposition to federal law existed "by combinations too powerful to be suppressed by the ordinary course of judicial proceedings," in most cases the opinion was not subject to alteration by another executive officer or by Congress.[33]

In the single instance in which Congress specified that judicial opinion could be revised by executive or congressional action — the duties assigned under the Invalid Pension Act of 1792 — the judges, as has been seen,[34] ruled the statute unconstitutional. They believed that

---

[31]Casto, *Supreme Court in the Early Republic,* pp. 87–90, 118–19, 181; *DHSC,* 4:243–47.

[32]Jay, "Most Humble Servants," pp. 78–80; Wheeler, "Extrajudicial Activities," pp. 139–42; Casto, *Supreme Court in the Early Republic,* p. 174.

[33]Casto, *Supreme Court in the Early Republic,* p. 181; "An Act to provide for calling forth the Militia to execute the laws of the Union, suppress insurrections and repel invasions," *Statutes at Large,* chap. 28, sec. 2, 1:264. See generally Wheeler, "Extrajudicial Activities," pp. 132–36; *DHSC,* 4:723–29. Justice James Wilson made a certification to the president under the Militia Act concerning the Whiskey Rebellion in 1794. See Jay, "Most Humble Servants," pp. 99–100.

[34]See text accompanying note 24.

such supervision by members of the other branches constituted encroachment upon the judiciary and therefore found it a breach of "separation of powers."[35] Even so, there was no mention of an absolute wall of separation. In order to avoid the embarrassment and the possibly disruptive effects of an overt disagreement between two branches of a new government that Federalists knew to have less than majority support and to be liable to break up from internal upheaval — a political decision trumping their legal one — most of the justices decided to perform the tasks voluntarily. They tortured a reading of the statute that allowed them to act as "commissioners"[36] and to hear the veterans' applications — a reading that they themselves later overturned in *United States* v. *Todd*.[37]

The justices also actively engaged in lobbying Congress for changes in legislation. Indeed, James Madison expressed a sentiment common in the 1790s that the defects in the Judiciary Act of 1789 "may speedily undergo a reconsideration under the auspices of the Judges who alone will be able to set it to rights." That this view of interbranch interaction was the norm in the 1790s is given additional cachet from the fact that the president sent the justices on their first circuit ride in April 1790 with explicit instructions that "it will be agreeable to me to receive such Information and Remarks on [the revision of the judiciary system], as you shall from time to time Judge expedient to communicate." Probably thanks to Washington's letter, all formal requests from the justices for changes in the laws went to Congress through the president; and probably thanks to the imperious attitude of their chief as well as the need to present a unified front, all letters about change save one came from the whole Court.[38]

---

[35]An excellent treatment of this meaning of "separation of powers" may be found in Jay, "Most Humble Servants," pp. 11–14, 24–25, 29–34, where it is explained that the word *power* in the late eighteenth century invariably meant "the ability to coerce," "the ability to bind others." Encroachment upon the judiciary power, the evil to be guarded against, thus meant, to these judges, the ability of another branch to control the judiciary. A proper balancing of powers, their "separation," if you will, then meant denying the authority of the other branch(es) to interfere.

[36]Casto calls it "a wildly implausible construction of the Act's language" (*Supreme Court in the Early Republic,* p. 176).

[37]See Wythe Holt, "John Blair: A Safe and Conscientious Judge," in Gerber, *Seriatim.*

[38]James Madison to Edmund Pendleton, Sept. 14, 1789, George Washington to the Justices of the Supreme Court, Apr. 3, 1790, *DHSC,* 4:511, 2:21.

The prime concern of the Court was to eliminate their long, tiring, and arduous circuit riding.[39] Their August 1790 session was largely taken up with discussion toward drafting a letter, which was apparently never sent, perhaps because Jay's draft presented constitutional objections in strong tones, perhaps because they learned that Attorney General Randolph would ask for a termination of circuit riding in the report on the judiciary that the House of Representatives had asked him to draft.[40] The Randolph initiative had no effect, as did later pleas on the same subject the judges actually sent in August 1792 and February 1794. Justice James Iredell took it upon himself to report what he considered to be two serious defects in the Judiciary Act in February 1792.[41] And, as Professor Jay astutely notes, the letters the justices sent to Washington protesting the unconstitutionality of the Invalid Pension Act were no different in effect, as they pushed for legislative change.[42]

Not only is there no evidence that anyone thought such interbranch contact wrong, the justices also engaged in much informal lobbying to achieve desired changes in the judiciary laws. Iredell, for example, frequently dealt with his brother-in-law, Sen. Samuel Johnston of North Carolina, while Jay persistently exploited his close friendship with Sen. Rufus King of New York. While in New York for the August 1790 term

[39]The story is told at length in Holt, " 'The Federal Courts Have Enemies,' " pp. 301–40. The letters discussed in the text are: Justices of the Supreme Court to George Washington, ca. Sept. 13, 1790; Justices of the Supreme Court to the Congress of the United States [enclosed in a letter to Washington], Aug. 9, 1792; Justices of the Supreme Court to the Congress of the United States [enclosed in a letter to Washington], Feb. 18, 1794, *DHSC,* vol. 2 (Maeva Marcus, James M. Buchanan, Christine R. Jordan, and Natalie Wexler, eds.), pp. 89–92, 289–92, 443–44.

[40]See generally Wythe Holt, " 'Federal Courts as the Asylum to Federal Interests': Randolph's Report, The Benson Amendment, and the 'Original Understanding' of the Federal Judiciary," *Buffalo Law Review* 37 (1987):341–72. In yet another indication of the absence of sentiment that "separation of powers" meant a wall of division, Randolph wrote Justice Wilson for help in this project (Edmund Randolph to James Wilson, Aug. 5, 1790, *DHSC,* 2:535). There is no indication that Wilson gave the requested aid.

[41]James Iredell to George Washington, Feb. 23, 1792, *DHSC,* 2:239–43. Iredell clearly indicated the lack of any thought that volunteering this sort of advisory opinion to the other branches was an unconstitutional breach of separation of powers when he said that he understood his action to be "not only proper for a single Judge, but his express duty when he deems it of importance to the public service" (ibid., p. 239).

[42]Jay, "Most Humble Servants," p. 102.

of the Supreme Court, Iredell provided a sort of precedent for the actions taken by justices Washington and Paterson in 1800 when he drafted the act by which Congress altered the times of meeting of the circuit courts in South Carolina and Georgia. The frequency and apparent propriety of interbranch contact of this sort is indicated by Chief Justice Jay's letter to Justice William Cushing while Congress was sitting in January 1793: "I have heard that some members of Congress doubt the Expediency of adopting our Plan — You will have many opportunities of conversing with them on the Subject." Professor Jay sums it up: "The judges were well-connected with the political elite, and they frequently exchanged correspondence with political figures on a variety of topics, . . . including passing on political intelligence gained during circuit rides or at home . . . [appointments to office, and] lobbying for reforms in the [judiciary system]."[43]

The regularity of informal contact with and opinion-giving by the judges to members of the executive branch completes this picture of separation of powers in the 1790s. Washington treated Chief Justice Jay, and Adams treated chief justices Ellsworth and Marshall, as trusted and intimate advisers. Until the capital was moved away from Jay's hometown of New York in the summer of 1790, Washington considered Jay as a member of his cabinet, openly noting his happiness with such arrangements.[44] And there is every indication that the first chief justices accepted these ties with full approval and collaboration.

Washington frequently sought Jay's legal opinion as well as his political judgment. Washington asked his advice, for example, on the tense

---

[43]Marcus and van Tassel, "Judges and Legislators," pp. 44–46; Circuit Courts Act of Aug. 11, 1790, in *Documentary History of the First Federal Congress,* 14 vols. to date (Baltimore, 1972–), vol. 4 (Charlene Bangs Bickford and Helen Veit, eds.), pp. 216–19, esp. p. 217 n. 3 (brought to my attention by Kenneth R. Bowling); John Jay to William Cushing, Jan. 9, 1793, *DHSC,* 2:343; Jay, "Most Humble Servants," p. 95. Justice Thomas Johnson, so deeply concerned over circuit riding that he soon was to resign his seat because of it, noted to Iredell that "some time agoe I took the Liberty of communicating to a Gent in Congress my Wish" on the subject, "but from his Answer I do not think that or either of several other Hints will gain Attention" (Thomas Johnson to James Iredell, Mar. 31, 1792, *DHSC,* 2:251).

[44]"By having Mr. Jefferson at the Head of the Department of State, Mr. Jay of the judiciary, Hamilton of the Treasury and Knox that of War, I feel myself supported by able Co-adjutors" (George Washington to the Marquis de Lafayette, June 3, 1790, *DHSC,* vol. 1 [Maeva Marcus, James R. Perry, James M. Buchanan, and Christine R. Jordan, eds.], pp. 711–12).

Nootka Sound crisis between Spain and Great Britain in 1790 and on the composition of his state of the union messages in 1790 and 1791. Jay soon came to offer advice unasked. Although the frequency of contacts dropped when Washington went with the government to Philadelphia and much of Jay's time was taken up by circuit riding, Jay remained a close adviser to the president and always closeted with him when visiting Philadelphia. Ellsworth felt himself so close to President Adams that, at a key point in the tense dealings between Adams and Congress over the Quasi-War with France in 1799, he sought out and convinced the president to accept a solution to the problem that he had previously rejected. Marshall did not sever himself from the office of adviser to Adams when he accepted the chief justiceship in January 1801, but on the contrary worked closely with him in the selection of the "midnight judges," as we have seen.[45]

Alexander Hamilton similarly considered his friend and political cohort Jay to be freely available for advice, whether political or legal. Moreover, Hamilton had no compunctions against asking Jay to use his judicial office for partisan purposes. When in November 1790 the Virginia House of Delegates passed strong resolutions against his funding system, Hamilton queried Jay: "Ought not the collective weight of the different parts of the Government to be employed in exploding the principles they contain?" When in September 1792 the Whiskey Rebels began to tar and feather federal agents, and to threaten arson, Hamilton concluded that "a high misdemeanor has been committed." He asked Jay whether the Pennsylvania federal circuit court, to meet in October, should be "noticing the state of things," and whether the president should not publicly proclaim the criminality of this conduct and warn of its prosecution. Both times Jay counseled caution, the second time after taking Hamilton's advice to bring a representative of the third branch (Sen. Rufus King of New York) into the consultation, but in neither instance did he scruple about separation of powers. In fact in his second response he indicated his "view that there was no contradiction between separation of powers and cooperation between

---

[45]On Jay's advice to Washington, see generally Jay, "Most Humble Servants," pp. 77–88. On Ellsworth and Marshall, see Wheeler, "Extrajudicial Activities," pp. 145–47; Casto, *Supreme Court in the Early Republic,* pp. 118–19. See also text accompanying note 29.

the branches in achieving national objectives": "Let all the branches of Gov.t move together, and let the chiefs be committed publickly on one or the other Side of the Question."[46] Moreover, Chief Justice Jay's correspondence with Hamilton reveals many comments about politics, policy, and his unswervingly fierce partisanship; for example, "the unceasing Industry and arts of the Anti's, render Perseverance, union, and constant Efforts necessary."[47]

Throughout the 1790s, individual members of the Supreme Court had no compunction about issuing written advisory opinions. Jay's written opinion to the president on the Nootka Sound crisis in August 1790 dwelt mostly on applicable principles of international law; in March 1792 he wrote a legal opinion to the sinking fund commissioners construing a pertinent statute; and in April 1793 at Hamilton's request he was happy to draft a neutrality proclamation, during the Genêt crisis, which in strong terms urged the president to call for criminal prosecution of those who violated American neutrality, thereby "prejudg[ing] the propriety of common-law prosecutions."[48] In March 1796, shortly after Ellsworth became chief justice, he wrote a nine-page advisory opinion counseling the president on a constitutional dispute Washington was having with the House of Representatives concerning its power over treaties; in June of the same year, Secretary of State

[46]Alexander Hamilton to John Jay, Nov. 13, 1790, and Jay to Hamilton, Nov. 28, 1790, in Syrett and Cooke, *Papers of Alexander Hamilton,* 7:149–50, 167 (discussed in *Documentary History of the First Federal Congress,* vol. 8 [Kenneth R. Bowling, William C. diGiacomantonio, and Charlene Bangs Bickford, eds.], pp. 270–71); Alexander Hamilton to John Jay, Sept. 3, 1792, Jay to Hamilton, Sept. 8, 1792 ("neither a Proclamation nor a *particular* Charge by the Court to the G. Jury would be adviseable at present" [emphasis in original]), *DHSC,* 2:292–95; Jay, "Most Humble Servants," pp. 88–92, quote on p. 91.

[47]John Jay to Alexander Hamilton, Dec. 29, 1792, Syrett and Cooke, *Papers of Alexander Hamilton,* 13:384–85.

[48]On Nootka Sound, see John Jay to George Washington, Aug. 28, 1790, *The Papers of Thomas Jefferson,* 27 vols. to date (Princeton, 1950–), vol. 17 (Julian P. Boyd, ed.), pp. 134–37; Casto, *Supreme Court in the Early Republic,* pp. 71–72; Jay, "Most Humble Servants," p. 83. On the sinking fund opinion, see John Jay to Edmund Randolph [and the other sinking fund commissioners], Mar. 31, 1792, Walter Lowrie et al., eds., *American State Papers,* 38 vols. (Washington, D.C., 1834–61), *Finance,* 1:236; Casto, *Supreme Court in the Early Republic,* p. 174; Jay, "Most Humble Servants," pp. 78–80. On the neutrality proclamation draft, see John Jay to Alexander Hamilton, Apr. 11, 1793, Syrett and Cooke, *Papers of Alexander Hamilton,* 14:307–10; Casto, *Supreme Court in the Early Republic,* pp. 74, 178–79, quote on p. 179; Jay, "Most Humble Servants," pp. 115–20.

Timothy Pickering requested an advisory opinion from Ellsworth on the detailed handling of some prize cases in Boston, upon the obvious assumption that Ellsworth would give the advice (though we do not know whether he did); and in December 1798, "notwithstanding the fact that Ellsworth expected to preside over criminal prosecutions under the [Sedition] Act [passed earlier that year]," the chief justice wrote Pickering a firm advisory opinion that there was no doubt the act was constitutional.[49]

Justice William Paterson in October 1797 wrote an advisory opinion to Commissioner of Revenue Tench Coxe that Robert Worrall, who had tried to bribe Coxe, could only be guilty of a common law offense since no federal statute forbade Worrall's alleged act. Justice Samuel Chase in May 1800 wrote Secretary of War James McHenry an advisory opinion about whether President Adams could appoint a public printer without confirmation by the Senate.[50] "Arguably," as Professor Jay notes, "the letter [of the Justices in 1793 refusing the administration's request for an advisory opinion] itself was an advisory opinion . . . as to the President's authority involved, . . . affirm[ing Hamilton's] assertion that the president was assigned full authority under the Constitution to interpret the treaties and the related questions concerning the law of nations."[51]

Advisory opinions were given by the justices in other ways too. The charges that the Supreme Court justices gave to circuit court grand juries were, according to Anglo-American custom, political speeches urging political virtue and support for the government and Federalist

---

[49]On the treaty opinion, now resting in the Washington papers, see Oliver Ellsworth to Jonathan Trumbull, Mar. 13, 1796, George Washington Papers, Library of Congress; Casto, *Supreme Court in the Early Republic,* p. 98; Jay, "Most Humble Servants," p. 170. On the Pickering request, see Timothy Pickering to Oliver Ellsworth, June 30, 1796, Timothy Pickering Papers, Massachusetts Historical Society; Casto, *Supreme Court in the Early Republic,* pp. 116–17. On the Sedition Act opinion, see Oliver Ellsworth to Timothy Pickering, Dec. 12, 1798, Pickering Papers; Casto, *Supreme Court in the Early Republic,* p. 149 (source of the quote).

[50]On the Worrall opinion, see William Paterson to Tench Coxe, Oct. 16, 1797, excerpted in *DHSC,* vol. 3 (Maeva Marcus, Mark G. Hirsch, Christine R. Jordan, Stephen L. Tull, and Natalie Wexler, eds.), p. 322 n. 29; Casto, *Supreme Court in the Early Republic,* p. 141. For the public printer episode, see Samuel Chase to James McHenry, [May 1800], McHenry Papers, American Philosophical Society; Jay, "Most Humble Servants," p. 170; Casto, *Supreme Court in the Early Republic,* p. 178.

[51]Jay, "Most Humble Servants," p. 181.

policies, delivered with the expectation that they would be published in many newspapers. In addition, justices frequently spoke about politically sensitive legal issues in their charges. For example, Jay's May 22, 1793, Virginia circuit grand jury charge gave his justification for the neutrality proclamation he had recommended to the president. Justice John Blair's April 27, 1795, Georgia circuit grand jury charge condemned the Whiskey Rebels as "licentious abusers, of liberty," and Samuel Chase's April 12, 1800, Pennsylvania grand jury charge praised President Adams as "the determined foe of Vice, the uniform friend of Religion and piety, morality and Virtue." The charges were thus advisory opinions, and often they adhered to "private executive branch advice."[52]

Moreover, justices like William Paterson, who published a series of essays of a political nature in the newspapers during his tenure, used yet another form of the advisory opinion.[53] The most bizarre instance of this was a publication by Jay and Senator King, under their signatures, on August 14, 1793. French Ambassador Genêt had been endangering the safety of the United States through his arming of privateers and his establishment of French prize courts on supposedly neutral American soil. This threatened to cause the British to declare war, and the weak United States could not defend itself. As public support for the French and for the Francophile Jeffersonian party appeared to be strong and growing, Jay and King, in a blatant, almost desperate attempt to discredit Genêt, averred that the French ambassador had vowed he would appeal adverse rulings by President Washington over his head to the American people. Although this was precisely his strategy, Genêt angrily denied the allegation and tried to have a criminal libel suit instituted against the chief justice in his own

---

[52]See Casto, *Supreme Court in the Early Republic,* pp. 75–76, 126–28, 164, 166. For Jay's charge, see *DHSC,* 2:380–91; for Blair's, see ibid., 3:35; for Chase's, see ibid., 3:416. "At first these charges were mild civic lessons. . . . As the 1790s unfolded, however, and the Federalists increasingly were the subject of harsh attacks from opposition groups, the charges became more specifically political rather than general, more emphatic in their warnings of danger to the new republic from abroad and from enemies within" (Jay, "Most Humble Servants," p. 94, quoting Kathryn Preyer, "*United States v. Callender:* Judge and Jury in a Republican Society," in *Origins of the Federal Judiciary: Essays on the Judiciary Act of 1789,* ed. Maeva Marcus [New York, 1992], p. 178).

[53]Paterson published at least forty-six essays while he was on the Court. See Casto, *Supreme Court in the Early Republic,* p. 179.

Court. The suit came to nothing and Genêt was soon recalled, but this extraordinary extrajudicial political activity by the chief justice, in open conjunction with a member of Congress, dealt with matters that might have come before him in judicial form.[54]

In this context the refusal of the justices to give an advisory opinion in response to the request of President Washington and the cabinet in August 1793 — just two weeks before the letter of Jay and King just mentioned — seems strange and discordant. Professor Jay has recently argued convincingly, however, that the refusal concerned only the particular instance and was not intended to establish a general rule, much less an absolute wall of separation,[55] as modern commentators have supposed. The request dealt with international law and with the politics of the Genêt controversy, and the primary reason the Court demurred was the strong conviction of its leader, Jay (as well as of Hamilton and other Federalists), that the country could not survive and prosper unless the executive took firm charge in matters of foreign affairs, and especially in desperate crises like the one presented in the summer of 1793.[56] They thought the denial would be a put-down to Jefferson, who had pushed the cabinet to make the request consistent with the longstanding position of the secretary of state, now the center of a growing and determined opposition, that as a republican democracy, all the branches of government in the United States should collaborate both in foreign affairs and in all crises. Secondary reasons for the refusal included the power of the judges to give rulings on the legal questions in other ways (in grand jury charges and in litigated cases); a suspicion that the request contained overtones of demand, and the judges wanted to retain their independence against any possible

---

[54]The story is well told in Jay, "Most Humble Servants," pp. 158–64.

[55]The letter of the justices "specifically declined to answer 'the questions alluded to,'" as opposed to rejecting advisory opinions in a more general way" (Jay, "Most Humble Servants," p. 168).

[56]The judges' letter of refusal noted that the only power given in the Constitution to the president to require answers was "*purposely* as well as expressly limited to the *executive* Departments," and spent one of its three paragraphs praising the discernment and firmness of the president "in surmount[ing] every obstacle to the Preservation of the Rights, Peace and Dignity of the united States" (John Jay, James Wilson, John Blair, James Iredell, and William Paterson to George Washington, Aug. 8, 1793, Henry Johnston, ed., *Correspondence and Public Papers of John Jay,* 4 vols. [New York, 1891], 3:488 [emphasis in original]).

encroachment;[57] and a hesitation to accept continued involvement of the Court in foreign affairs crises on a public, corporate, and wholly advisory basis.[58]

Moreover, Jay and the Court were well aware that much opposition to the Supreme Court existed in Congress and elsewhere, which could have coagulated into dissent and rebellion — or fueled the taxpayers' rebellion then rumbling along the western frontier — if the justices acted too forcefully to aggrandize the new government and Federalist policy. In their other rulings in the early and mid-1790s, they were quite cautious not to move too far or too fast in elaborating and underscoring the power given in the Constitution to a new national government supported by less than a majority of the citizens, and it is not unlikely that a similar caution also played a part in their surprising 1793 refusal to the president and the cabinet.[59]

Conclusion

Historians have treated the justices' refusals in *Hayburn's Case* to accept executive supervision of judicial opinion, and in the Genêt controversy to give an advisory opinion, as though they represented a rule, when it is clear from the evidence I have presented that they were

---

[57]In addition to the language quoted in the beginning of the previous note, the letter also noted that "the Three Departments of Government" were "in certain Respects checks on each other" and that the writers were "Judges of a court in the last Resort."

[58]Jay, "Most Humble Servants," pp. 171–82, 190–96.

[59]I have elaborated this theme elsewhere, primarily in "John Blair." Jay, "Most Humble Servants," pp. 183–90, attributes their caution primarily to a strong desire not to upset Congress so much that their circuit-riding duties would not be eliminated. I do not doubt that the justices dearly wanted to end their circuits and did not wish to provoke Congress, but Chief Justice Jay and the others were well aware of widespread if often latent opposition to federal judicial aggrandizement. See John Jay to Rufus King, Dec. 22, 1793, *DHSC*, 2:434 ("The federal Courts have Enemies in all who fear their Influence on State objects"); Wythe Holt and James R. Perry, "Writs and Rights, 'Clashings and Animosities': The First Confrontation between Federal and State Courts," *Law and History Review* 7 (1989):89–120. The Court in the early and mid-1790s acted boldly in any sphere of law and politics *only* when it judged it had to, and this caution, I think, also played into the August 1793 refusal, especially after the public uproar against the Court's decision in *Chisholm* v. *Georgia* the previous February.

the exceptional instances in a decade in which the justices had very few qualms about collaborating with members of the other branches. Moreover, it is clear that the judges viewed themselves as political actors, indeed as part of the Federalist governments of Washington and Adams. Their view of separation of powers was neither as a rule nor as a wall of separation.[60]

The justices in the 1790s viewed separation of powers as a principle. Each member of each branch, and each judge in particular, must avoid those interactions which, by subordinating his judgment to those made in another branch, allowed that other branch to encroach upon the independence of their branch and thus disturb the balance of power among them which the Constitution established by dividing them. Each instance of interbranch contact must then be scrutinized for the dangers of encroachment, but only those in which encroachment loomed were forbidden.[61] Other interactions were proper and indeed necessary to defend the new nation against its enemies, domestic

---

[60]The contrary view is expressed in Wheeler, "Extrajudicial Activities," and in Marcus and van Tassel, "Judges and Legislators." According to the latter, for example, the justices during the 1790s took actions that began development of "the rigid formal institutional separation that exists today," and "Congress often required the judges to act in ways not wholly consistent with a strictly independent judiciary performing only judicial tasks." Moreover, this view continues, it was circuit riding that "gave the justices both a semipolitical assignment and a vehicle for their continued politicization. . . . Instructed to explicate the . . . structure of the new government . . . an essentially political task, the justices could hardly avoid thinking of themselves in political terms" (ibid., pp. 33, 35, 32). These phrases assume that a wall of separation became and remains the norm, and that the judges were essentially apolitical and were forced into the political arena. Both assumptions are erroneous.

[61]John Jay cast the notion of separation of powers in precisely this way. He was "far from thinking it illegal or unconstitutional, however it may be inexpedient[,] to employ [federal judges] for other Purposes, provided the latter Purposes be consistent and compatible with [their judicial position]" (John Jay [draft of a letter to be sent by the whole Court] to George Washington, ca. Sept. 13, 1790, *DHSC*, 2:90). In his first grand jury charge, in New York on April 12, 1790, he said: "Men have . . . very unanimously agreed . . . That [Government's] powers should be divided into three, distinct, independent Departments. . . . The Constitution . . . has accordingly instituted these three Departments, and much Pains have been taken so to form and define them, as that they may operate as Checks one on the other, and keep each within its proper Limits; it being universally agreed to be of the last Importance to a free People, that they who are vested with executive legislative and judicial Powers, should rest satisfied with their respective Portions of Power, and neither encroach on the Provinces of each other" (ibid., 2:26–27).

and foreign — proper for the judges even though in most instances the subject that brought about their interaction with another branch might come before them judicially.[62]

Not only was there no wall of separation in the 1790s, there never has been one. Justice William Johnson gave a written advisory opinion to President Monroe in 1822, Chief Justice Roger B. Taney gave a written advisory opinion to Senator (soon to be Chief Justice) Salmon P. Chase in 1862, and Chief Justice Charles Evans Hughes gave a written advisory opinion to Sen. Burton K. Wheeler in 1937; the first of these purported to be from the whole Court, while each was approved by other members of the Court. Justices have regularly served as presidential advisors, including Taney, Felix Frankfurter, William O. Douglas, and Abe Fortas among the most blatant examples. Five justices served on the commission (with ten members of Congress) to decide which candidate won the 1876 presidential election — and the eight-to-seven vote in favor of Republican Rutherford B. Hayes was strictly by party. At Congress's request, members of the Supreme Court drafted the Judiciary Act of 1925, known as the "Judges' Bill." Justice Robert Jackson served as a Nuremberg prosecutor. Chief Justice Earl Warren chaired the commission inquiring into President Kennedy's assassination, even though he suspected that in doing so he was violating the principle of separation of powers. In every one of these instances the judges could anticipate the possibility of their work or advice coming before them in a litigated case, but a supposed wall of separation did not deter them from accepting their extrajudicial activities.[63]

---

[62]Marcus recognizes that the advice the judges gave in these interbranch interactions "could later come before the courts" in cases, but she creates out of whole cloth a distinction or rule, that all of the advice by judges was given *as individuals* rather than *as an institution* ("Separation of Powers," p. 273). This distinction makes very little sense, since conscientious believers in judicial independence behind a wall of separation would commit breaches of that wall whether the advice that came back before them was given collectively or individually. In any case, none of the 1790s judges is on record as adopting or even discussing such a rule, and the letters written to request alteration of their circuit-riding duties came from the Court, not from individual judges. Grand jury charges were also official pronouncements of the judges as members of a court.

[63]For the advisory opinions by Johnson, Taney, and Hughes, and for the 1925 Judiciary Act, see Richard H. Fallon, Jr., Daniel J. Meltzer, and David L. Shapiro, *Hart and Wechsler's The Federal Courts and the Federal System,* 4th ed. (Westbury, N.Y., 1996), pp. 38, 96. For Taney, see Bernard C. Steiner, *Life of Roger Brooke Taney* (1922; reprint

What remains to be answered is why we have this historical myth that members of the federal judiciary, and in particular justices of the Supreme Court, do not interact with members of the other two branches. There are two parts to the answer, one historical, the other philosophical. I will tell the story of the first and assert the second.

Historically, the answer is that the Federalists lost the election of 1800, and their bitter enemies, the Jeffersonian Republicans, took over the executive branch and the Congress and declared war on the Federalists still entrenched in the judiciary. As their first important action, the Jeffersonians repealed the "midnight judges act," the Judiciary Act of 1801, thereby eliminating what the Constitution denominated as lifetime offices for fifteen federal circuit court judges, all Federalists.[64] There were thus many fewer opportunities for the judges to plot and confer with members of the other two branches. Also, the judges, fully understanding their political nature, had every reason to think of themselves and their institution as embattled.

This moved members of the Court in two opposite directions. One direction was open hostility to the new regime, and Justice Samuel Chase castigated the Jeffersonian repeal in a grand jury charge. For his efforts he was impeached, and on March 1, 1805, a majority of senators voted to convict him on three of eight articles of impeachment. He fell only four votes short of the constitutional requirement of two-thirds for conviction on Article VIII, dealing with the grand jury attack on the Jeffersonians — but he was acquitted. Had he been convicted, the impeachments of Justice Paterson and Chief Justice Marshall — universally seen as the Federalist leaders on the Court — would likely

---

ed., Westport, Conn., 1970), pp. 232–66; for Douglas, see William O. Douglas, *The Court Years, 1937–1975* (New York, 1980), pp. 267–354; for Fortas, see Laura Kalman, *Abe Fortas: A Biography* (New Haven, Conn., 1990), pp. 193–227, 293–318. Frankfurter's constant contact with the executive branch while on the Court is a matter of legend, but his biographers are remarkably unforthcoming about it. For the rest of the activity cited here and much more, see John R. Schmidhauser, "Extrajudicial Activities," in Kermit L. Hall et al., eds., *The Oxford Companion to the Supreme Court of the United States* (New York, 1992), pp. 270–73.

[64]See Turner, "Judiciary Act of 1801"; Richard E. Ellis, *The Jeffersonian Crisis: Courts and Politics in the Young Republic* (New York, 1971), pp. 60–68; Wythe Holt, " 'If the Courts Have Firmness Enough to Render the Decision': Egbert Benson and the Protest of the 'Midnight Judges' against Repeal of the Judiciary Act of 1801," in *Egbert Benson: First Chief Judge of the Second Circuit (1801–1802)*, ed. John D. Gordan III (New York, 1987), pp. 9–24.

have ensued.[65] The Jeffersonians were playing hardball too, and the independence of the judiciary was directly threatened.

The second direction, at the insistence of Chief Justice Marshall, was to retreat into an artificially created apolitical stance. This tack was taken in the two major decisions made by the Court in February 1803, both cases in which Federalists advanced claims of unconstitutional action by the new administration. In *Marbury* v. *Madison,* where four Federalist justices of the peace appointed by Adams in the waning moments of his presidency claimed that Jefferson was unconstitutionally withholding their undelivered commissions, the Court, in one of the more political decisions in our history, repeatedly asserted that the judiciary is not a part of the political process, and, while rhetorically claiming the power to issue judicial orders to the president, refused on technical grounds to award the claimants their commissions. In *Stuart* v. *Laird,* the Court completely ducked the issue of the constitutionality of the Jeffersonian elimination of the tenure of the Federalist circuit judges. Newspapers noted, with satisfaction, how the chief justice (and Justice Chase) made no political statements in grand jury charges. Marshall hushed up all dissent on the Court and began delivering most of its opinions himself, as though they were unanimous — even reading opinions he did not personally agree with. For a decade after 1803 the Court remained quiet, essentially a nonplayer in political history. The Court desperately wished to make it appear that it was not political, since both being political and the appearance of being political would probably snuff it out.[66]

---

[65]Robert Goodloe Harper to James A. Bayard, Jan. 22, 1804, Etting Collection, Historical Society of Pennsylvania; James Haw et al., *Stormy Patriot: The Life of Samuel Chase* (Baltimore, 1980), pp. 191–241, esp. p. 220 and sources cited at note 24; Dumas Malone, *Jefferson the President: First Term, 1801–1805* (Boston, 1970), p. 469.

[66]*Marbury* v. *Madison,* 5 U.S. (1 Cranch) 136 (1803); *Stuart* v. *Laird,* 5 U.S. (1 Cranch) 299 (1803); *Raleigh Register; and North Carolina Weekly Advertiser,* June 20, 1803 ("Chief Justice Marshall delivered a very neat and appropriate charge to the Grand Jury, unaccompanied, as heretofore, with any political matters"); *National Intelligencer* (Washington, D.C.), May 5, 1805 ("Judge Chase delivered a short and pertinent charge to the grand jury — his remarks were pointed, modest and well applied"); Susan Low Bloch and Maeva Marcus, "John Marshall's Selective Use of History in *Marbury* v. *Madison,*" *Wisconsin Law Review* (1986):302 and n. 3; William Johnson to Thomas Jefferson, Dec. 22, 1822, Thomas Jefferson Papers, Library of Congress ("Soon [after Johnson's appointment] I disagreed with my brethren and thought it a thing of course to deliver my opinion. But, during the rest of the session I heard nothing but lectures

The political reason, then, for the myth that the federal judiciary does not interact with members of the other two branches is the strategic if uncourageous conclusion of Chief Justice Marshall (backed by his associates on the Court) that to do so, or to appear to do so, would be greatly injurious to the independence of the third branch in a time of the ascendancy of a Jeffersonian party deeply suspicious of that branch's Federalist leanings and partisan political activity both in grand jury charges and in their conduct of their judicial office. But why would a temporary historical strategy become a permanent ideology — the wall of separation?

While history played a part here too — in the appointment after 1820 of several persons to the Court who were much more states' rights oriented than Marshall and most of his pre-1820 colleagues, climaxed perhaps by President Jackson's elevation of Roger Taney to the chief justiceship upon Marshall's death — the primary answer is philosophical. During the nineteenth century the legal philosophy of positivism (the legal concomitant of liberal capitalism) replaced the natural-law philosophy that predominated in the eighteenth century. Among its many dangerous and harmful notions, legal positivism separates law from politics. Its rhetorical ground for doing so is in order that courts will obtain answers to legal questions that seem to be derived solely from legal rules, eliminating the obvious favoritism of class that permeated prior legal systems. The goal of positivism, in this regard, is to have a government of laws, not of men. The underlying political effect of positivism's separation of law from politics is to protect behind a veil of ignorance the influence which property and capital exert over the law, so that most people have great difficulty fathoming the manipulations which the power of capital performs upon law.[67]

---

on the indecency of judges cutting at each other, and the loss of reputation. . . . At length . . . I bent to the current.") The standard view of such matters is taken by G. Edward White, *The Marshall Court and Cultural Change, 1815–1835* (New York, 1991), pp. 190–200; a slightly more nuanced view may be found in a careful reading of Herbert A. Johnson, *The Chief Justiceship of John Marshall, 1801–1835* (Columbia, S.C., 1997), pp. 54–58, 62, 87, 90, 100, 102–3 n. 42.

[67]For example, see Wythe Holt, "Recovery by the Worker Who Quits: A Comparison of the Mainstream, Legal Realist, and Critical Legal Studies Approaches to a Problem of Nineteenth Century Contract Law," *Wisconsin Law Review* (1986):677–732; idem, "Labour Conspiracy Cases in the United States, 1805–1842: Bias and Legitimation in Common Law Adjudication," *Osgoode Hall Law Journal* 22 (1984):591–663.

Positivism swept up Marshall's pragmatic political defense of being apolitical and made it into a fundamental political tenet of the legal philosophy we are all supposed to believe. And so, today, many people are astounded at the story I have told here, that in the 1790s the justices not only were political but understood themselves to be political actors, and that there was no wall of separation between them and the other branches of our government, either in theory or in practice.

William R. Casto

French Cruisers, British Prizes, and American Sailors

Coordinating American Foreign Policy
in the Age of Fighting Sails

IN THE LATE TWENTIETH CENTURY, separation of powers played a prominent role in the resolution of controversial foreign affairs issues—especially issues related to war. In terms of the structural separation of powers written into the Constitution, the major players are Congress and the president, and the perennial problem is to coordinate these two institutions' independent views of foreign policy. Today the third branch of government—the federal judiciary—plays a minor role in resolving foreign affairs issues. The courts operate as comparatively disinterested arbiters of the Constitution. Even when the courts are called upon to apply legal principles to foreign policy disputes, federal judges usually try their best to avoid rendering a decision on the merits. In addition to this structural separation of powers, we have come to have a more informal—but probably more significant—separation of powers between the two major political parties. Today all significant foreign affairs controversies involve a blending of the formal separation between the president and Congress and the informal separation between the Republican and Democratic parties. Virtually all contemporary foreign affairs controversies are between the president and members of Congress who are not of the president's party.

The interplay between separation of powers and the coordination of foreign policy was different in the first decade of the federal government's operation under the Constitution. The nation's first major foreign affairs crisis took place in 1793 when the French Revolution had begun, France was at war with Great Britain, and George Washington was president. Today Congress would play a significant role in developing the government's position on a major war, but in 1793 Congress played no significant role. In contrast, today's federal courts are not generally seen as an organ of foreign policy, but in 1793 Supreme Court justices acted as virtually an arm of the executive branch.

America's position on this European war was not merely an abstract policy issue. Every American remembered the vital assistance that France had provided us just a few years earlier in our war for independence. French financial support had provided funding for our revolutionary armies, and a French army and French fleet had secured the war-ending victory at Yorktown. Chief Justice John Marshall later remembered that the new war between France and Great Britain "restored full vivacity to a flame, which a peace of ten years had not been able to extinguish. A great majority of the American people deemed it criminal to remain unconcerned spectators of a conflict between their ancient enemy and republican France." Moreover, the European conflict quickly expanded to North America. Up and down the Eastern seaboard, France waged a maritime war against British shipping. The question was whether we should support our ally from the Revolutionary War or our "ancient enemy."[1]

The immediacy of the problem is illustrated by a fascinating incident in the summer of 1793. In June *L'Embuscade*, a French frigate commanded by Jean Baptiste François Bompard (a good revolutionary who refused to sport the title of captain, simply calling himself Citizen Bompard), was using New York Harbor as a base for preying on British shipping (fig. 1). Bompard's escapades infuriated the British, who dispatched one of their own frigates from Nova Scotia, the *Boston* commanded by George William Augustus Courtenay, to deal with him. In early July the ladies of Halifax "gave a splendid ball to Captain Courtenay and his officers," and he sailed south to drub the "frogs."

---

[1]John Marshall, *The Life of George Washington*, 5 vols. (1832; reprint ed., Fredericksburg, Va., 1926), 5:8.

FIG. 1. Citizen Bompard in a romanticized contemporary engraving. *(Courtesy Musée de la Marine, Paris)*

On the way Captain Courtenay told every ship he met that he had "positive orders" to take or destroy *L'Embuscade*.[2]

When Captain Courtenay arrived off New York, he was flying French colors, and members of his crew were wearing the French national cockade in their hats. Using this stratagem he tricked and captured *L'Embuscade*'s first lieutenant and a boat's crew on a reconnaissance mission. On July 28, a Sunday, he fell in with an American revenue cutter commanded by Patrick Dennis. He took Captain Dennis on board and personally told Dennis to "tell Capt. Bompard that I have come all the way from Halifax, on purpose to take the Ambuscade, and I shall be very happy to see her out this way." Captain Dennis immediately sailed back to New York and relayed the challenge to Citizen Bompard that same night.[3]

---

[2]*New-York Journal*, Aug. 10, 1793; *Diary; or, Loudon's Register* (New York), Aug. 8, 1793, hereafter *Diary*.

[3]*Daily Advertiser* (New York), July 30, 1793; *Diary*, Aug. 6, 1793. For the capture of *L'Embuscade*'s reconnaissance boat, see *Diary*, July 31, 1793; *Weekly Museum* (New York), Aug. 3, 1793; Henry Remsen to Thomas Jefferson, Aug. 1, 1793, *The Papers of Thomas*

When the challenge was received, the crew of *L'Embuscade* was on holiday, but they immediately began preparing the frigate for action. At the same time Citizen Bompard had the challenge posted on the books of the Tontine Coffee House — which at times served as an unofficial headquarters for the city's pro-French citizenry. He added his reply to Captain Courtenay's challenge: "Citizen Bompard will wait on Capt. Courtenay tomorrow, agreeable to invitation; he hopes to find him at the Hook." In addition to being posted at the coffeehouse, the challenge and reply were immediately reported in the city's newspapers.[4]

New York was agog. Everyone who could afford it arranged charters to view the impending battle. Nine or more vessels were chartered, and one enterprising shipowner even placed an ad in the paper. "The beautiful and fast sailing Schooner EXPERIMENT," relates the ad, "Will sail as soon as the French frigate Ambuscade gets under way." Although some New Yorkers were pro-British, the *New-York Journal* reported that "the great majority [support] our gallant *Gallic* friends [and] many bets are laid on the subject." So many vessels were chartered that *L'Embuscade* was unable to hire a pilot boat to guide her out to sea. Finally, she left without a pilot, but contrary winds forced her back to port.[5]

While this was going on, the *Boston* was not idle. Continuing the ruse of flying false colors, Captain Courtenay captured the *Republican*, an eight-gun French privateer, and sent her into New York as a prize. These successful masquerades enraged Citizen Bompard, who sent a sarcastic letter out to Captain Courtenay. In the letter, which of course was published in the New York newspapers, Bompard explained, "I would not employ an artifice or stratagem unbecoming the character of a brave and candid soldier [but] you have conducted yourself in different manner." If Bompard was actually angry about Courtenay's masquerade, there is some irony in the fact that earlier that summer

Jefferson, 27 vols. to date (1950–), vol. 26 (John Catanzariti, Eugene R. Sheridan, and J. Jefferson Looney, eds.), pp. 599–600, hereafter cited as *PTJ*; William Laird Clowes, *The Royal Navy*, 7 vols. (London, 1897–1903), 4:478.

    [4]*Daily Advertiser*, July 30, 1793; *New-York Journal*, July 31, 1793; *Diary*, July 29, 30, 1793.

    [5]*Daily Advertiser*, July 30, Aug. 1, 1793. For "the great majority," see *New-York Journal*, July 31, 1793. *Accord,* Henry Remsen to Thomas Jefferson, July 29, 1793 ("A great majority of us . . . wish and expect the Ambuscade success"), *PTJ*, 26:582.

FIG. 2. *L'Embuscade* sails past the Battery of New York in a contemporary engraving. *(Courtesy New York Public Library)*

Bompard himself had used a British ensign to take unsuspecting British merchantmen.[6]

The next day *L'Embuscade* was finally able to leave the harbor (fig. 2), and on the morning of August 1 the two frigates met before a fleet of sightseers. Citizen Bompard, sporting a red knit liberty cap, as was his want, called three times to Captain Courtenay by name, and the *Boston* responded with a broadside. The ensuing battle lasted about two hours, with the French maintaining the weather gauge. At various times each ship's colors were shot away, and the French tried twice without success to board the *Boston*. In the words of a witness on the *Boston*, "the engagement was very smart." The British paid particular attention to *L'Embuscade*'s sails and rigging and charged their cannon with "a quantity of old iron, nails, broken knives, broken pots, and

<hr />

[6]*New-York Journal*, July 31, Aug. 3; *Diary*, Aug. 6, 1793; *Weekly Museum* Aug. 3, 1793. For Bompard's letter, see *New-York Journal*, Aug. 3, 1793; *Daily Advertiser* Aug. 1, 1793; *Diary*. For Bompard's use of British colors, see Memorial from George Hammond, May 2, 1793, *PTJ*, vol. 25 (John Catanzariti, Eugene R. Sheridan, and J. Jefferson Looney, eds.), pp. 637–40.

broken bottles." For their part, the French apparently responded in kind. After the battle, a "crow bar was found sticking in the Boston's side from the Ambuscade."[7]

Something had to give. Citizen Bompard was a fearless commander who had been in "five successful actions." He was a hands-on officer who believed that a captain's presence on the quarterdeck during battle had "more of a ceremonious parade in it, than real utility." Instead he "was busily employed in directing the management of his main deck great guns during the greater part of the engagement." As for Captain Courtenay, in view of his challenge and Bompard's sarcastic reply, he could not break off. A prisoner on board the *Boston* gave "it as his opinion that [Courtenay] would have sunk with his frigate rather than have surrendered, or fled from Ambuscade." Finally the *Boston's* main topmost was shot away, and at about the same time Captain Courtenay was struck by a cannon ball "the whole back part of his head being carried away."[8]

At this point, the *Boston's* captain and lieutenant of marines were dead and all the lieutenants were severely wounded. John Edwards, the first lieutenant, had "a long splinter [of wood] which being driven in horizontal direction thro' the fleshy part of his nose, there lodged, remaining fixed something in the manner of a ship spint[le] sail yard." Sporting this gruesome decoration, he took command and decided to retire before the wind. Bompard tried to pursue, but his frigate's masts, sails, and rigging had taken so much damage that he was unable to overtake the *Boston*. Finally, spying a rich Portuguese (some say Spanish) brig laden with indigo, coffee, and sugar, Bompard broke off the chase, took the brig as a prize, and sailed back to New York.[9]

When the victorious *L'Embuscade* sailed back into New York, the people of the city thronged to the waterfront and "stood upon the piers, shouting and cheering and waving their hats." As the frigate

---

[7]The quotations are from *Diary,* Aug. 6, 9, 1793; and *New-York Journal,* Aug. 7, 1793. For accounts of the battle, see *Daily Advertiser,* Aug. 2, 19, 1793; *Diary,* Aug. 5, 6, 7, 9, 12, 1793; *New-York Journal,* Aug. 3, 7, 1793; Henry Remsen to Thomas Jefferson, Aug. 1, 1793, *PTJ,* 26:599–600.

[8]*New-York Journal,* Aug. 7, 1793; *Daily Advertiser,* Aug. 19, 1793; *Diary,* Aug. 12, 1793.

[9]Clowes, *Royal Navy,* 4:478; *Diary,* Aug. 12, 1793. For the prize, see *Weekly Museum,* Aug. 3, 1793; Charles S. Hyneman, *The First American Neutrality* (Urbana, Ill., 1934), p. 108.

slowly sailed the East River, "continued shouts and huzzas were vociferated, which were returned from on board." The "ship's colours, torn as they were at the close of the action [were] presented to the Tammany Society." Bompard was subsequently presented with a gold medal, and Captain Courtenay's widow and children were given a pension.[10]

News of the battle quickly spread throughout the nation. Supporters of the new French Republic were jubilant. Poems were published, ballads were sung, and toasts were given. For example, at a celebration in Philadelphia, Americans drank to the toast: "May British bombast ever meet the fate of Capt. Courtenay, when opposed to the sons of freedom." Needless to say, those who favored the British were angry. Secretary of State Thomas Jefferson received a private account of the battle just before a cabinet meeting on August 3 and gleefully reported the news to his fellow members. In his notes he recorded with satisfaction that "Knox [secretary of war] broke out into the most unqualified abuse of Capt. Courtnay. Hamilton [secretary of Treasury], with less fury, but with the deepest vexation, loaded him with censures. Both shewed the most unequivocable mortification at the event."[11]

As this now-forgotten incident illustrates, the war in Europe was not a distant affair that could be ignored. Moreover, many Americans — probably most — were pro-French. The day before the battle, Jefferson's former clerk reported to him from New York that "a great majority of us here, wish and expect the Ambuscade success in the event of an engagement." Americans were delighted by the French success — they cheered and waved their hats. At the same time, however, most of the merchant class was pro-British. This split of public opinion and the immediacy of the war presented immense problems to the new federal government.[12]

This essay recounts some of the efforts of the executive, judicial, and

---

[10]John B. McMaster, *A History of the People of the United States from the Revolution to the Civil War,* 8 vols. (New York, 1883–1913), 2:123; *Diary,* Aug. 3, 6, 1793; *Weekly Museum,* Aug. 3, 1793; *New-York Journal,* Aug. 7, 1793; Clowes, *Royal Navy,* 4:478.

[11]For poems, see *Daily Advertiser,* Aug. 19, 1793; *New-York Journal,* Aug. 10, 1793. For ballads, see Poor Jack, "An excellent new patriotic song," 1793 (broadside), Brown University; McMaster, *History of the People of the United States,* 2:124. For toasts, see *New-York Journal,* Aug. 10, 1793. For the cabinet meeting, see Thomas Jefferson, Notes of Cabinet Meeting on Neutrality, Aug. 3, 1793, *PTJ,* 26:607–8.

[12]Henry Remsen to Thomas Jefferson, July 29, 1793, *PTJ,* 26:582.

legislative branches to deal with the problems caused by the war between France and Great Britain. The Neutrality Crisis of 1793 exposed some of the strengths and weaknesses of each branch of government in dealing with foreign affairs. In addition, the crisis revealed an approach to the separation of powers that is radically different from today's generally accepted theory and practice.

The Neutrality Proclamation

The European war that caused the Neutrality Crisis began when France declared war on Great Britain on February 1, 1793, but two months passed before firm news of the war reached America. President Washington was home at Mount Vernon when Secretary of State Thomas Jefferson wrote him on April 7 that it was "extremely probable that [France and Britain] are at actual war." The next day Secretary of the Treasury Alexander Hamilton wrote the president a similar letter. Almost immediately, President Washington resolved to return to Philadelphia, the nation's capital during the 1790s, and at the same time he wrote both secretaries that he was determined "to maintain a strict neutrality." He asked them to consider how best to implement this neutrality and noted in particular that he was already hearing of privateers being fitted out in American ports.[13]

President Washington's determination to maintain a strict neutrality was complicated by the fact that the United States had a treaty of alliance with France that had been entered into during the Revolutionary War. Among other things, the United States "forever" guaranteed French possessions in the West Indies from attack by all other powers. Although the French decided not to invoke this guarantee, other portions of the 1778 treaty granted French naval vessels and privateers special rights during wars between France and other countries. These special rights were to create serious problems. Moreover, neutrality is a fairly flexible concept, and as the crisis developed, different members

---

[13]Thomas Jefferson to George Washington, Apr. 7, 1793, *PTJ*, 25:518; Alexander Hamilton to George Washington, Apr. 8, 1793, and George Washington to Alexander Hamilton, Apr. 12, 1793, in Harold C. Syrett and Jacob E. Cooke, eds., *The Papers of Alexander Hamilton*, 27 vols. (New York, 1961–87), 14:295–96, 314–15, hereafter *PAH*; George Washington to Thomas Jefferson, Apr. 12, 1793, *PTJ*, 25:541.

of Washington's cabinet had conflicting ideas concerning what neutrality entailed. The group led by Hamilton favored a strict and impartial neutrality that would emasculate the Treaty of Alliance and, in effect, favor Britain. Conversely, Jefferson wanted to give fuller scope to the treaty and adopt a course of neutrality more favorable to France.[14]

Even before Washington asked Hamilton for his opinion, Hamilton had written Chief Justice John Jay. In addition to asking the chief justice for advice regarding the recognition of the new French government, Hamilton was thinking about a formal presidential proclamation of neutrality and asked Jay, "If you think the measure prudent could you draft such a thing as you would deem proper?" Jay had no qualms about rendering the requested assistance. The day he received Hamilton's letter, he immediately turned his full attention to the problem and among other things prepared a draft presidential proclamation of neutrality that he sent to Hamilton. Jay recommended that the president "require that the Citizens of the U.S. do abstain from acting hostilely against any of the belligerent powers [and further that the president] cause all offenders to be prosecuted & punished in an Exemplary manner."[15]

The notion of the chief justice giving advice to the executive branch was by no means extraordinary. Chief Justice Jay routinely provided extrajudicial legal and policy advice on a wide range of issues including, among others, issues of international law during the Nootka Sound Crisis, the Sinking Fund Commission's statutory authority to repurchase specific government debt, the president's unilateral authority to appoint an agent to the Creek Nation without Senate approval, and the president's unilateral authority to determine the rank of diplomatic officers. Nor was his conduct a historical anomaly. In the later half of the 1790s, Oliver Ellsworth, who served as chief justice after Jay, was equally willing to provide advisory opinions. From Jay's tenure as the first chief justice to the present, more than seventy obscure and not so

---

[14]Treaty of Amity and Commerce, Feb. 6, 1778, Hunter Miller, ed., *Treaties and Other International Acts of the United States of America*, 8 vols. (Washington, D.C., 1931–48), 2:3–29; Charles Marion Thomas, *American Neutrality in 1793: A Study in Cabinet Government* (1931, reprint ed., New York, 1967), chap. 1; Albert Hall Bowman, *The Struggle for Neutrality* (Knoxville, 1974), chap. 2.

[15]Alexander Hamilton to John Jay, Apr. 9, 1793 (two letters), and John Jay to Alexander Hamilton, Apr. 11, 1793, *PAH*, 14:297–300, 307–10.

obscure Supreme Court justices have served as informal advisers to presidents and members of Congress. The main difference between the 1790s and today's practice is that in the 1790s rendering advisory opinions seemed to be the rule, while today it is more of an exception.[16]

To modern eyes the most unusual and troubling aspect of Jay's draft proclamation is the fact that the chief justice called for "offenders [against neutrality] to be prosecuted & punished in an Exemplary manner." These are strong words, indeed, from a judge who would preside over the criminal trial of the offenders. To further complicate the matter, at the time that Jay penned his advice there was no act of Congress making a violation of neutrality a crime. Therefore his draft proclamation can be read as implicitly advising that the existing criminal code enacted by Congress could be supplemented by an unwritten federal criminal law.[17]

In addition to providing Secretary Hamilton with private advice, Jay almost immediately resolved to address the legal issues implicated by the Neutrality Crisis in a formal public opinion that would be published to the nation in the form of a grand jury charge. In the late eighteenth century, judges frequently used grand jury charges as a vehicle for addressing important political issues of the day. Moreover, there was a well-established tradition of publishing these charges in leading newspapers. In writing this grand jury charge, Jay probably was motivated in part by a widespread condemnation of the president's proclamation in the pro-French press. As a leading editor put it, "The course of France is the course of man, and neutrality is desertion." Jay's charge, when published, would serve as a rebuttal to the opposition press's objections.[18]

---

[16]William Cibes, "Extra-Judicial Activities of Justices of the United States Supreme Court, 1790–1960," Ph.D. diss., Princeton University, 1975; Russell Wheeler, "Extra-judicial Activities of the Early Supreme Court," *Supreme Court Review* (1973):123–58. For a comprehensive and marvelous treatment of Chief Justice Jay's activities through the Neutrality Crisis of 1793, see Stewart Jay, *Most Humble Servants: The Advisory Rule of Early Judges* (New Haven, 1997). For Chief Justice Ellsworth, see William R. Casto, "I Have Sought the Felicity and Glory of Your Administration," in *Seriatim: The Supreme Court before John Marshall*, ed. Scott Douglas Gerber (New York, 1998).

[17]William R. Casto, *The Supreme Court in the Early Republic: The Chief Justiceships of John Jay and Oliver Ellsworth* (Columbia, S.C., 1995), pp. 129–63.

[18]Donald A. Stewart, *The Opposition Press of the Federalist Period* (Albany, N.Y., 1969), pp. 146–51; Casto, *Supreme Court in the Early Republic*, pp. 126–29.

Although there is no surviving evidence, Jay undoubtedly conferred with fellow New Yorkers Hamilton and Sen. Rufus King while he was drafting his charge. Seven months earlier these three New Yorkers had worked together on the desirability of using a grand jury charge by Jay to focus attention on the problem of tax protesters in western Pennsylvania, and about four months later the three again acted in concert to discredit the French ambassador. Jay's guiding principle in the matter of tax protesters was "let all the Branches of Govt. move together, and let the chiefs be committed publickly on one or the other Side of the Question." In any event, less than two weeks after giving a private advisory opinion to Hamilton, the chief justice had a fully developed draft of a public advisory opinion that he then reworked and delivered the next month as a charge to a grand jury in Virginia. This charge was immediately published in full by leading newspapers, and Jay personally directed that two copies be sent to Secretary Hamilton.[19]

At the time, this coordination between the executive and the judicial branches was not viewed as suspect or improper. Obviously the chief justice saw no problem. Nor did Secretary of State Jefferson. While Jay was working on his charge, Jefferson wrote Atty. Gen. Edmund Randolph: "The Judges generally, by a charge, instruct the Grand jurors in the infractions of law which are to be noticed by them; and our judges are in the habit of printing their charges in the newspapers. . . . It will be easy to suggest this matter [i.e., enforcing American neutrality] to the attention of the judges."[20]

Jay's charge was an admirable general treatment of American neutrality, and the government sent copies of the charge to Europe as a formal explanation of its position. The course of events, however, rapidly overtook the chief justice's efforts. When Jay began drafting the charge in mid-April, Washington and his cabinet were concentrating

---

[19]For the earlier concerted action by Hamilton, Jay, and King, see Alexander Hamilton to John Jay, Sept. 3, 1792, and John Jay to Alexander Hamilton, Sept. 8, 1792, *PAH,* 17:316–17, 334–35. For Jay's initial draft and final grand jury charge, see John Jay, "Draft Grand Jury Charge," and John Jay, "Charge to the Virginia Grand Jury," in *The Documentary History of the Supreme Court of the United States, 1789–1800,* 5 vols. to date (New York, 1985–), vol. 2 (Maeva Marcus, James M. Buchanan, Christine R. Jordan, and Natalie Wexler, eds.), pp. 334–35, 380–91. John Jay to Alexander Hamilton, June 24, 1793, *PAH,* 15:20.

[20]Thomas Jefferson to Edmund Randolph, May 8, 1793, *PTJ,* 25:691–92.

upon general principles. By the middle of May, the administration was up to its neck in a serious foreign policy crisis implicating a staggering array of specific and very important questions.

The French Maritime Campaign Commences

In early April, Citizen Bompard sailed into Charleston, South Carolina, with Edmond Genêt, the new French ambassador. Being a representative of a revolutionary republican government, Genêt eschewed titles. Like Bompard, he simply called himself Citizen Genêt. After dropping off Ambassador Genêt, Bompard put to sea and sailed up the East Coast, taking British ships willy-nilly. The appearance of these prizes streaming into American ports electrified the nation. In late April, Bompard took two merchantmen, the *Grange* and the *Little Sarah,* and sent them into Philadelphia. Jefferson reported that when these two prizes arrived, "thousands and thousands of the . . . *yeomanry* of the city (not the fashionable people nor paper men) shewed prodigious joy when, flocking to the wharves, they saw the British colours reversed and the French flying above them. . . . [T]hey burst into peals of exultation."[21]

Although *L'Embuscade*'s exploits put a strain on Anglo-American relations, the depredations of French privateers created far more serious problems. When Genêt arrived in Charleston, he had more than the frigate *L'Embuscade* at his disposal. He also had numerous blank privateer commissions. The practice of privateering fell into disuse more than a hundred years ago, but in the eighteenth century it was used by all the European powers. Simply put, privateering was a capitalist supplement to a regular navy. Merchant venturers would receive a formal commission from one country to rove the seas and attack another country's shipping for profit. It was legalized piracy.[22]

Citizen Genêt put his blank commissions to good use, and within a

---

[21]Thomas Jefferson to James Monroe, May 5, 1793, and Thomas Jefferson to Thomas Randolph, Jr., May 6, 1793, *PTJ,* 26:661, 668–69. For the identity of the prizes, see *The Counter Case of Great Britain as Laid before the Tribunal of Arbitration, Convened at Geneva* (Washington, D.C., 1872), p. 610.

[22]William R. Casto, "The Origins of Federal Admiralty Jurisdiction in an Age of Privateers, Smugglers, and Pirates," *American Journal of Legal History* 37 (1993):117–57.

few weeks of his arrival in Charleston four privateers, including the *Citoyen Genêt,* set sail. The *Citoyen Genêt* was a schooner that mounted either four or six quite small cannon and carried a crew of about fifty men. Her captain and most of her crew were French, but she also had many Americans in her crew. In the latter part of April, she set sail from Charleston, and by May 3 she was close to Delaware Bay, where she captured a British merchantman, *The William,* and sent her into Philadelphia to be sold.[23] *The William* was brought into Philadelphia by a small prize crew under the command of Gideon Henfield, a forty-year-old American from Salem, Massachusetts. Henfield had been in Charleston when Citizen Genêt arrived and was trying to obtain a berth on a northbound ship. He joined the *Citoyen Genêt* on condition that he would be made prize master of the first prize that it took.[24]

The William's arrival in Philadelphia presented serious diplomatic problems, and the federal courts were quickly called upon to play a direct role in the enforcement of neutrality. The privateer, *Citoyen Genêt,* had been fitted out in an American port in violation of American neutrality, and *The William*'s capture was a direct fruit of this violation. Two separate legal proceedings were commenced almost immediately to remedy the violation. A suit was commenced on behalf of *The William*'s owners in the local federal district court to reclaim the vessel on the theory that her capture was tainted by the unlawful fitting out of the *Citoyen Genêt* in an American port. At this time, the federal district courts were essentially admiralty courts presided over by a single local federal judge. At the same time, a separate criminal prosecution was commenced by the federal government against Henfield in the federal circuit court. In contrast to the district courts, the circuit courts were staffed by the local federal judge and one or two circuit riding justices of the Supreme Court. The circuit courts were the primary federal trial courts.[25]

---

[23]Memorial from George Hammond, May 8, 1793; Memorial from George Hammond, June 21, 1793, *PTJ,* 26:686–87, 335–36. For the French maritime campaign, see generally Melvin H. Jackson, *Privateers in Charleston, 1793–1796* (Washington, D.C., 1969); Hyneman, *The First American Neutrality;* Charles M. Thomas, *American Neutrality in 1793* (1931; reprint ed., New York, 1967).

[24]See *United States* v. *Henfield,* Wharton at 77–78 (C.C.D. Pa. 1793).

[25]*Findlay* v. *The William,* 9 F. Cas. 57 (D. Pa. 1793) (No. 4790); *United States* v. *Henfield,* 11 F. Cas. 1099 (C.C.D. Pa. 1793) (No. 6360). For the two kinds of federal trial courts, see Casto, *Supreme Court in the Early Republic,* pp. 41–47.

The criminal prosecution against Henfield was somewhat complicated by the fact that there was no statute making his activities a crime.
This lack of statutory authority could have been an embarrassment to
Chief Justice Jay, who had in effect assured the Washington administration that violations of American neutrality were subject to criminal punishment. There was, however, a neat solution to this problem. Virtually
all American lawyers of the Founding Era were natural-law lawyers who
believed that laws — including criminal laws — existed in nature independent of governments. To them, laws regulating human society were
like the law of gravity: both had a natural existence based upon divine
wisdom and the perfection of human reason. They existed independent from human government. In England and the United States, this
body of natural legal principles was called the common law.[26]

Using this natural law philosophy, Jay and his fellow justices delivered grand jury charges declaring that violations of American neutrality were obviously contrary to the law of nature and therefore were indictable offenses punishable by criminal sanctions. This analysis was
not innovative. Secretary Jefferson noted privately that the "Atty. Gen.
gave an official opinion that [Henfield's] act was [an indictable of-
fense], it coincided with all our private opinions, and the lawyers of this
state [Pennsylvania], New York, and Maryland who were applied to,
were unanimously of the same opinion." Accordingly, Henfield was in-
dicted and tried for his alleged crimes. Although virtually all American
lawyers agreed that this natural or common-law approach was sound —
at least where violations of treaties were involved — a funny thing happened on the way to the conviction. The jury acquitted Henfield.[27]

This acquittal sparked many public celebrations, and various reasons for the acquittal were advanced. Attorney General Randolph told
the president that "the leading man" on the jury had stated that Hen-

---

[26]Casto, *Supreme Court in the Early Republic,* pp. 129–63.

[27]For representative grand jury changes, see John Jay, Charge to the Virginia Grand
Jury, May 22, 1793; James Wilson, Charge to the Pennsylvania Grand Jury (July 22,
1793); and James Iredell, Charge to the South Carolina Grand Jury, May 12, 1794, in
Documentary History of the Supreme Court, 2:380–91, 414–23, 454–70. For Thomas Jeffer-
son's approval, see Thomas Jefferson to James Monroe, July 14, 1793, *PTJ,* 26:501–3.
See also, Opinion of Attorney General Edmund Randolph, May 30, 1793, *American
State Papers: Documents, Legislative and Executive of the Congress of the United States,* 38 vols.
(Washington, D.C., 1832–61) Foreign Relations Series, 1:152.

field was acquitted because he had enlisted without knowledge of the president's neutrality proclamation and that the jury believed Henfield's "declaration that he would never have enlisted, had he known it to be against General Washington's opinion." Jefferson advanced the same theory in a letter to the American ambassador in France. Like many criminal defendants, Henfield was somewhat of a con artist. Notwithstanding his impassioned plea that he would never go against "General Washington's opinion," following his acquittal, Henfield "sailed forth in a new [privateering] excursion, which resulted in his capture by a British cruiser."[28]

Another possible reason for Henfield's acquittal is that American jurors unschooled in the metaphysical niceties of the common law just did not believe in it. The next year Justice James Iredell, one of Jay's brethren on the Supreme Court, wrote Attorney General Randolph that he was concerned about the efficacy of common-law prosecutions as a means of enforcing American neutrality. Iredell believed that "an explicit Act of Congress on the subject [was needed because] it is scarcely possible to explain to a Jury's satisfaction the obligations arising from Common law."[29]

In addition to being asked to impose criminal sanctions upon Henfield, the federal courts were asked to return Henfield's prize, *The William,* to its British owners. At first glance this requested restitution seems entirely reasonable. If the privateer *Citoyen Genêt* was outfitted in violation of American neutrality, why shouldn't American courts return the privateer's prizes to their original owners? This straightforward analysis was quite consistent with American neutrality, and Jefferson officially urged the British ambassador to petition the federal courts for restitution.[30] But as in the case of the Henfield prosecution,

---

[28]For a good description of *Henfield's Case* including the subsequent celebration and possible reasons for the verdict, see Stephen B. Presser, *The Original Misunderstanding: The English, the Americans, and the Dialectic of Federalist Jurisprudence* (Durham, N.C., 1991). Edmund Randolph to George Washington, Aug. 21, 1793, and Thomas Jefferson to Gouverneur Morris, Aug. 16, 1793, *PTJ,* 26:713, 702. For Henfield's subsequent fate, see Francis Wharton, *State Trials of the United States during the Administrations of Washington and Adams* (1899; reprint ed., New York, 1970), p. 89 n.

[29]James Iredell to Edmund Randolph, May 2, 1794, *Documentary History of the Supreme Court,* 2:451–52.

[30]Thomas Jefferson to George Hammond, June 13, 1793, and George Hammond to Thomas Jefferson, June 14, 1793, *PTJ,* 26:270–71, 284–85.

a funny thing happened on the way to judgment. The federal district judges refused to order restitution.

Although the Supreme Court justices were actively involved in the trial of criminal cases, suits for restitution of a prize were considered civil admiralty proceedings that had to be filed in a federal admiralty court presided over by a federal district judge rather than in a circuit court staffed in part by Supreme Court justices. When the federal district judges turned to the law of prizes, they encountered a clear and widely accepted rule that only the courts of a capturing nation could rule on the legality of a particular capture or prize. In comparatively short order five different federal district judges in Pennsylvania, New York, Maryland, North Carolina, and South Carolina recognized the existence of this doctrine and ruled that they could not grant restitution of a French prize. Only the federal district judge in Massachusetts held that restitution was available, and his opinion was limited to suits in which American property happened to have been seized.[31]

These district court decisions facilitated the French maritime campaign and were an embarrassment to the president's policy of neutrality. Nevertheless, the law of prize jurisdiction was clear, and the conservative district judges were reluctant to be innovative. In the leading case of *The William,* Pennsylvania District Judge Richard Peters noted that if the losing ship owners were dissatisfied, "there is an appeal, from any determination I may give, to a superior tribunal." Despite this express invitation, the plaintiffs in that case elected to forgo a judicial appeal and instead sought a remedy from the executive branch.[32]

In fall 1793 the district judge in Maryland ruled the same as Judge Peters, and the owners elected to pursue a judicial appeal. As soon as possible Justice William Paterson, who was riding circuit, summarily affirmed the district court, and an appeal to the Supreme Court was immediately filed. When the Supreme Court finally got the case in 1794, it quickly announced judgment that the federal trial courts had juris-

---

[31]Casto, *Supreme Court in the Early Republic,* pp. 82–84. For reports of the North Carolina and Massachusetts cases, see *Daily Advertiser,* July 29, 1793; *Columbian Centinel* (Boston), Jan. 4, 1794.

[32]*Findlay* v. *The William,* 9 F. Cas. 57, 61 (D. Pa. 1793); Memorial from George Hammond, June 21, 1793, *PTJ,* 26:335–36.

diction to grant the restitution of prizes taken in violation of American neutrality. In issuing this judgment the court made no effort whatsoever to deal with the rationale of the lower court's opinion. Instead the new rule of jurisdiction was an act of raw political power.[33]

President Washington Requests an Advisory Opinion

While these civil and criminal proceedings were being unsuccessfully prosecuted in the federal courts, a staggering array of major and minor legal issues were raised regarding the extent to which our treaty with France gave the French a right to use American ports to mount and maintain their privateering campaign. When these issues arose in the context of litigation, they could be resolved by the federal judges. But the issues frequently arose in nonjudicial contexts like advising federal and state officers or presenting the government's views to French and British diplomats. The French ambassador vehemently asserted the broadest possible interpretation of his country's rights, while President Washington, upon advice from his cabinet, took a far more narrow view. At about the same time that the criminal prosecution against Henfield and the admiralty suit for restitution of *The William* were going on, the dispute with the French ambassador over the meaning of the Treaty of Alliance coalesced around the fitting out of yet another French privateer.

In April *L'Embuscade* had captured the *Little Sarah,* an armed British merchant vessel, and sent her into Philadelphia as a prize. As Jefferson reported, the appearance of this prize was met with "peals of exultation." But instead of selling the *Little Sarah,* the French renamed her the *Little Democrat* and increased her armament from four to fourteen cannon. In other words, she was outfitted as a privateer. The French ambassador was pressed to stop the *Little Democrat,* and in a conversation with Pennsylvania Secretary of State Alexander Dallas, Genêt expressed his immense dissatisfaction with President Washington's narrow construction of the Treaty of Alliance. He then stated that if this

---

[33] *Glass* v. *The Sloop Betsy,* 3 U.S. (3 Dall.) 6 (1794); Casto, *Supreme Court in the Early Republic,* pp. 83–87.

narrow construction was not changed, he, Genêt, "would appeal from the President to the people."[34]

The *Little Sarah/ Little Democrat* problem was quite upsetting to President Washington. On July 11, he wrote Secretary Jefferson, "What is to be done in the case of the *Little Sarah* now at Chester? Is the Minister of the French Republic to set the Acts of this Government at defiance — *with impunity*? and then threaten the executive with an appeal to the people?" The next day the cabinet resolved to ask the Supreme Court for a written opinion on a wide array of issues related to the Treaty of Alliance and on July 18 submitted a long list of twenty-nine detailed questions to the justices.[35]

These questions were so complex that only a lawyer working on an hourly basis could love them. Those justices then in Philadelphia initially delayed their response until their absent brethren had arrived for the Court's August session. Finally, on August 8, the justices replied that they would not answer the president's questions. They explained that "the Lines of Separation drawn by the Constitution between the three Departments of Government — their being in certain respects checks on each other — and our being Judges of a court in the last Resort — are considerations which afford strong Arguments against the Propriety of our extrajudicially deciding — the questions alluded to; especially as the Power given by the Constitution to the President of calling on the Heads of Departments for opinions, seems to have been *purposely* as well as expressly limited to *executive* Departments."[36]

The justices obviously believed that they were not obliged to answer the president's twenty-nine questions. One of the reasons they suggested was the "separation of powers" concept that "the three departments of government [are] in certain respects checks upon each other." This argument is superficially relevant but ultimately not com-

---

[34]See generally Alexander DeConde, *Entangling Alliance* (Durham, N.C., 1958), pp. 217–23; Thomas Jefferson, Memorandum of a Conversation with Edmond Charles Genêt, July 10, 1793, *PTJ*, 26:463–67.

[35]George Washington to Thomas Jefferson, July 11, 1793, and Cabinet Opinion on Consulting the Supreme Court, July 12, 1793, *PTJ*, 26:481–82, 484–85. On this episode, see generally the editorial note "The Referral of Neutrality Questions to the Supreme Court," ibid., 26:524–37.

[36]The Justices of the Supreme Court to Thomas Jefferson, Aug. 8, 1793 (emphasis in original), *PAH*, 15:111 n. 1.

pelling because the request for an opinion presented the Court with a clear opportunity to provide a prior check upon the executive branch. Courts typically review government actions by adjudicating lawsuits filed after the fact of executive action. In contrast, Washington's request allowed the Court to counterbalance executive action at the planning stage.

The justices also stated that "our being judges of a court in the last resort [is one of the] considerations which afford strong arguments against the propriety of our extrajudicially deciding the questions alluded to." Exactly what they meant is unclear because they did not elaborate. Perhaps they were concerned that their answers might improperly bias their participation in future litigation involving the same questions. If so, their concern was more of a consideration than a firm rule. Individual justices frequently gave advisory opinions before and after their joint correspondence with Secretary Jefferson in 1793.[37]

The superficial plausibility of the justices' reasons for not answering the president's questions is at odds with the then well established practice of giving advisory opinions. We know that the justices were not operating in a vacuum. Jay talked with the president in private before and after the questions were submitted. Moreover, given Jay's close relationship with Hamilton, the two men almost certainly discussed the questions. Hamilton had objected to the president in private that because many of the issues embodied in the questions should be "settled by reasons of state, not rules of law," the courts were not "competent" to decide the issues. He publicly reiterated this position less than two weeks before the questions were referred to the Court. Hamilton probably lobbied the Court not to answer the questions.[38]

If circling the wagons to defend the president against Genêt's threats played a significant role in asking for an advisory opinion from the Supreme Court, the Court's refusal — at least Jay's refusal — was probably made easier by a raw and powerful political development. Genêt's threat in July during the *Little Sarah / Little Democrat* incident to appeal

---

[37]Casto, *Supreme Court in the Early Republic*, pp. 178–83.

[38]Alexander Hamilton to George Washington, May 15, 1793, *PAH*, 14:454–60; Alexander Hamilton, "Pacificus No. I," June 29, 1793, ibid., 15:33–43. For a reference to Jay's private conversations with the president, see George Washington to Thomas Jefferson, July 18, 1793, *PTJ*, 26:537–38.

the president's decision to the people was passed by word of mouth among the political elite. The chief justice and Sen. Rufus King — acting in concert as was their wont — decided to make a public issue of Genêt's threat. A few days after the justices declined to answer the president's twenty-nine questions, Jay and King published a notice in a New York City newspaper formally stating that the "French Minister, had said he would appeal to the People from certain decisions of the President."[39] This notice, which was reprinted in newspapers throughout the nation, created a sensation. The chief justice and Senator King were, in effect, telling the country that Citizen Genêt was demanding that Americans choose between the French cause and George Washington. Given the president's political and social stature, the choice was obvious. Needless to say, Hamilton was in on this scheme from almost the beginning and subsequently published his own affirmation of Genêt's threat against the president. Throughout the rest of 1793, charges and countercharges were made as the French minister and his supporters tried unsuccessfully to refute the allegations. Genêt became so upset that he formally asked the federal government to indict Jay and King for spreading lies. When this request was refused, Genêt decided that he personally would prosecute the chief justice and the senator. The notion of a private criminal prosecution seems strange today, but at that time there was a well-established common-law mode of prosecution called an appeal that authorized private persons to commence and prosecute criminal actions.[40]

Although Genêt retained counsel to prosecute the case, the prosecution never came to pass. In February 1794, a new French ambassador arrived with orders to replace Genêt and ship him home to be guillotined. When President Washington magnanimously refused to permit this deadly repatriation, the new ambassador reminded Genêt that under French law Genêt's mother and sisters were subject to execution if he persisted in embarrassing the French government with his planned prosecution.[41] And so the matter was concluded.

---

[39]*Diary*, Aug. 14, 1793. For this episode, see editorial note, *PAH,* 15:233–39.

[40]Casto, *Supreme Court in the Early Republic,* pp. 137–39. For Hamilton's involvement, see introductory note, *PAH,* 15:233–39.

[41]Frederick J. Turner, ed., "Correspondence of the French Ministers to the United States, 1791–1797," *Annual Report of the American Historical Association for the Year 1903* (Washington, D.C., 1904), 2:279 n.

Congress

Today Congress would be a major player while these events were unfolding, but in 1793 Congress did nothing because it was not in session. The Second Congress adjourned on March 2, 1793, about a month before America learned of the European war, and the Third Congress was not scheduled to meet until nine months later, in December. When news of the war arrived in April, President Washington specifically asked his cabinet whether "it is necessary or advisable to call . . . Congress with a view to the present posture of European Affairs?" Jefferson was probably inclined to believe that an early emergency session should be convened, but after the cabinet decided that the president had full authority to proclaim the nation's neutrality, Jefferson and the other cabinet officers agreed unanimously that Congress would not be convened. A knowledgeable insider later commented that a decision to convene Congress early would have cast doubt upon the president's authority to issue the Neutrality Proclamation.[42]

Four months later, in early August, President Washington again asked his cabinet whether a special early session of Congress should be convened. He was especially concerned about the jury's failure to convict Henfield, the decision to request France to recall Citizen Genêt, and what he called "the *general* complexion of matters." Jefferson favored an early session, but Hamilton, Secretary of War Henry Knox, and Attorney General Randolph were in opposition. Although President Washington personally was in favor of calling Congress, he acquiesced to the opinion of his cabinet.[43]

When Congress was finally convened on schedule in early December, President Washington formally asked the members to clarify the jurisdiction of the federal courts to regulate the activities of foreign privateers and grant restitution of prizes in appropriate cases. He also

---

[42]Thomas Jefferson to James Madison, Mar. 24, 1793; George Washington to the Cabinet, Apr. 18, 1793; Thomas Jefferson to George Washington, Apr. 28, 1793; and Thomas Jefferson's Notes on Washington's Questions on Neutrality and the Alliance with France, May 6, 1793, in *PTJ*, 25:442–43, 568–70, 607–8, 665–67; Theodore Sedgwick to Alexander Hamilton, Aug. 26, 1793, *PAH*, 15:285–86.

[43]George Washington to the Cabinet, Aug. 3, 1793, *PTJ*, 26:611; Alexander Hamilton to George Washington, Aug. 5, 1793, *PAH*, 15:194–96; Thomas Jefferson, "Opinion on Convening Congress," and Thomas Jefferson, "Notes of Cabinet Decisions," *PTJ*, 26:615, 627.

was worried about the failure to obtain a conviction in *Henfield's Case.* He asked Congress to enact criminal sanctions for violations of American neutrality and specifically noted "these offenses [against neutrality] can not receive too early and close an attention, and require prompt and decisive remedies."[44]

Although Congress almost immediately took up the president's request, the pro-French congressmen staged a long delaying action against the measure's passage. Chief Justice Marshall later related: "Necessary as this measure was, the whole strength of the opposition in the senate was exerted to defeat it. Motions to strike out the most essential clause were successively repeated, and each motion was negatived by the casting vote of the vice president. It was only by his voice that the bill finally passed. In the house of representatives also, this bill encountered a serious opposition." Finally, a somewhat watered down version was passed some six months later in June, on almost the last day of the session. After this statute was enacted, federal prosecutors were able to obtain convictions for violations of American neutrality.[45]

Concluding Thoughts

These events from two hundred years ago teach valuable lessons that have held true to the present. As early as the Neutrality Crisis of 1793 many of the strengths and weaknesses of the three branches of government in dealing with foreign affairs issues were readily apparent. Moreover, the Supreme Court justices—especially Jay—obviously viewed the idea of separation of powers as significantly less limiting than we do today.

During the Neutrality Crisis, the Supreme Court operated as virtually an arm of the executive branch. When Secretary Hamilton asked Jay to lend a hand in drafting a neutrality proclamation, the chief justice immediately dropped everything and promptly penned a draft

---

[44]George Washington, Fifth Annual Address, Dec. 3, 1793, *Annals of the Congress of the United States,* 42 vols. (Washington, D.C., 1834–56), 4:10–13. For a discussion of this message, see introductory note, *PAH,* 15:425–28.

[45]Marshall, *Life of George Washington,* 5:146; An act in addition to the act for the punishment of certain crimes against the United States, 3d Cong., 1st sess., ch. L, 1 stat. 381–84; *United States* v. *Guinet,* Wharton 93 (C.C.D. Pa. 1795).

proclamation. Jay did not limit himself to this informal private advice. He also wrote a long and detailed legal analysis to justify the United States' position of strict neutrality and had the opinion published to the nation in the form of a grand jury charge. Associate Justice James Wilson did the same thing, and Jefferson sent these two formal advisory opinions to Europe as justification for American neutrality. At least these advisory opinions involved legal issues in which the justices had special expertise. Jay's most astonishing service to the executive branch was his public attack upon Ambassador Genêt. Jay and Senator King's certification that Genêt had threatened an appeal to the people did not involve any legal issues. Nor did the two men even have direct knowledge of the threat. They were simply publishing hearsay. The chief justice and the senator, as respected public figures, were clearly using the prestige of their offices to destroy Genêt's political credibility with the American people.

Today, some two hundred years after these events, Jay's enthusiastic support of the administration is almost entirely forgotten. The incident that we remember is the Court's refusal to answer President Washington's formal request for advice. The lesson that we draw is that under the Constitution the judiciary should restrict itself to the resolution of strictly judicial cases and should not participate in the activities of the political branches.[46] In stark contrast, the early justices of the Supreme Court clearly had a significantly less restrictive view of separation of powers.

So how do we explain the justices' refusal to provide the president with the requested advisory opinion? I believe that two significant factors influenced the justices. Alexander Hamilton had stated and restated that he doubted the political wisdom of requesting the justices' opinion. I believe that Hamilton successfully lobbied the justices in private not to give an opinion. In addition, I believe that Hamilton was equally successful in lobbying the president to acquiesce in the justices' refusal. In other words, the justices were not confronted with an insistent request from President Washington.

The Neutrality Crisis also revealed some of the strengths and weak-

---

[46]See, e.g., Laurence H. Tribe, *American Constitutional Law,* 2d ed. (Mineola, N.Y., 1988), p. 73.

nesses of the three branches of government in dealing with foreign affairs. Under the Constitution, Congress is clearly intended to be a major player in this area. For example, Congress is given express constitutional authority "to regulate Commerce with foreign Nations [and] to declare War." One of the most salient features of the government's attempts to grapple with the Neutrality Crisis was that Congress was never in session during it. To invoke the wisdom of Sherlock Holmes, Congress was the dog that didn't bark in the middle of the night.[47] That is one of the major structural weaknesses of the institution. It is not always in session. If a crisis arises when Congress is not in session, immediate action must be taken by some other branch of government. Moreover, even if Congress is in session, its multifarious nature may prevent swift and resolute action. For example, when Congress was finally convened in December 1793, bills were immediately proposed to outlaw violations of American neutrality, but pro-French members stalled enactment until the summer of the next year.

In other words the composition of Congress can make it indecisive and slow to act when there are significant disagreements among the people whom Congress represents. At the same time, when Congress does act — as it did when it finally outlawed violations of American neutrality — the government may proceed with far more certainty. Justice Iredell believed that criminal convictions for violation of American neutrality would have been easier to obtain if he could have pointed to an act of Congress. President Washington evidently believed the same thing when he urged "prompt" enactment of a criminal statute. Moreover, in the event, juries actually were willing to convict individuals after the statute was finally enacted.

As for the executive, the Neutrality Crisis clearly illustrates the immense structural power of the president in the area of foreign affairs. We like to think of the imperial presidency as a phenomenon of the middle and late twentieth century, but its embryo was completely developed in 1793. Unlike Congress, the president is always in session. Moreover, the president has the capability to act swiftly and decisively. There were clear disagreements within Washington's cabinet on how

---

[47]Arthur Conan Doyle, "Silver Blaze," in *The Annotated Sherlock Holmes,* ed. William S. Baring-Gould, 2 vols. (New York, 1967), 2:261–81.

to deal with the crisis, but the president could listen to the opposing views and make a decision within a matter of days — even hours.

In addition, foreign affairs frequently present issues that must be resolved fairly quickly. Because Congress was not in session, the president had to act immediately without its aid. Any government — no matter what its form — has to have power to act immediately in an emergency situation. Under our Constitution, that power to deal with emergencies clearly rests with the president. It always has and always will.

The lessons that the Neutrality Crisis teaches about the strengths and weaknesses of the legislative and executive branches are as familiar and cogent today as they were two hundred years ago. But some aspects of the role played by the judiciary during the crisis — at least the actions of Chief Justice Jay — seem foreign. When the crisis began, Jay wholeheartedly supported the pro-British, Hamilton faction of President Washington's administration by writing private and public advisory opinions fully supporting the policy of strict neutrality. He continued this firm support throughout the crisis. When the French ambassador threatened to appeal the president's policy of strict neutrality to the people, Jay gave the prestige of his name and office to a blatantly political (albeit truthful) public attack upon the ambassador.

I do not mean to suggest that modern justices have been cloistered saints aloof from the political processes. For example, Chief Justice Earl Warren was quite willing to lend the prestige of his name and office to the commission investigating the Kennedy assassination.[48] Indeed, the commission was commonly called the Warren Commission. Nevertheless, I see significant differences between the justices' nonjudicial activities during the Neutrality Crisis and today's understanding of nonjudicial activities. Chief Justice Jay's provision of advisory opinions was not an ad hoc reaction to a particularized situation. His practice of giving advisory opinions formed a pattern that began in the earliest days of the Washington administration and carried through into the Adams administration, when Chief Justice Ellsworth was equally willing to serve in an advisory capacity. I am not

---

[48]President's Commission on the Assassination of President Kennedy, *Report of the President's Commission on the Assassination of John F. Kennedy* (Washington, D.C., 1964).

certain that a modern justice would give even a single, isolated advisory opinion. I am certain, however, that no modern justice would provide the executive branch with advisory opinions as a matter of course.

The second major difference between then and now is epitomized by the difference between Chief Justice Jay lending his name and office to public attacks upon Ambassador Genêt, and Chief Justice Warren lending his name and office to the Warren Commission. Both were public extrajudicial acts, but in an important sense Warren's service on the commission was apolitical. To be sure, his service was politically motivated in that he probably saw the Kennedy assassination as posing some threat to the existing political order, and he probably saw his service as a political device to reassure the public that all was in order. But I am not referring to the kind of politics that is implicated in the basic defense of the standing political order. Rather, I am referring to what today we call partisan politics.

Within the standing political order in 1793 there was a disagreement over whether the United States should tilt toward France or Great Britain. Chief Justice Jay was clearly in the latter camp, and his attack upon Ambassador Genêt was clearly intended to affect this much mooted national issue. I cannot conceive of a modern chief justice participating in partisan politics in such a blatant and public manner.

How does what I have said fit into the justices' refusal to answer the president's twenty-nine questions? I see their refusal as part of the overall pattern of trying to support the administration. They refused to answer because Alexander Hamilton convinced them that an answer would be politically inexpedient and he probably convinced President Washington that an answer was not crucial.

Although the justices of 1793 had a very expansive understanding of the propriety of extrajudicial service, the cases that they adjudicated illustrate some of the enduring strengths and weaknesses of the judicial branch. One of the Supreme Court's greatest strengths is illustrated by the technical issue of whether the federal courts could order the restitution of prizes taken by the French. There were persuasive arguments denying that the federal courts had this power. But when the Court finally got to this issue and rejected the arguments without explanation, the issue was at an end. The Court had spoken. This ability to have the final word and conclusively decide issues is a source of major strength for the Court.

On the other hand, the restriction of judicial power to the adjudication of actual cases and controversies makes the Supreme Court an inherently unreliable source for legal advice. The problem is that the special circumstances of particular cases frequently prevent courts from providing unambiguous and timely advice. For example, the government needed a decision on the courts' power to restore prizes to British owners in the summer of 1793. District Judge Peters's refusal to order restitution of *The William* should have provided the Supreme Court with an early opportunity to pronounce a definitive judgment, but no appeal was taken. Instead, a Supreme Court decision had to be delayed until a second case worked its way up from the federal district courts.

Another example of the way that the facts of a particular case can forestall an unambiguous judicial opinion is found in *Henfield's Case*. All the justices believed that common-law prosecutions were legitimate, but coincidentally Henfield apparently enlisted with the French without knowledge of the president's proclamation. As a result he was acquitted, and the legitimacy of common-law prosecutions was obscured.

Of course the Neutrality Crisis suggests that the ambiguities and problems posed by the facts of particular cases can be avoided by the use of advisory opinions. To a significant degree, however, the justices' willingness to provide advisory opinions was a function of unique circumstances that can never again be repeated. The justices were uniquely in agreement with each other. Every justice was appointed by the same president and fully supported him. Moreover, the president was George Washington, who had a unique claim upon the justices' loyalty. Beginning with Thomas Jefferson's election to the presidency in 1800, the unique solidarity between the executive and judicial branches was terminated, never to be replicated.

Jack D. Warren, Jr.

"The Line of My Official Conduct"

George Washington and Congress, 1789–1797

G EORGE WASHINGTON ASSUMED the presidency in 1789 enjoying greater advantages than any of his successors. His election was
almost universally praised, even by the recent opponents of the Federal Constitution. He was widely celebrated as the incarnation of a
classical hero, and he possessed a popular mandate that was confirmed
by the unanimous vote of the presidential electors. The First Congress
consisted overwhelmingly of his political allies, who could be expected
to join him in seeking to endow the new federal government with the
energy and vigor so lacking in the government of the Confederation.

Yet Washington also faced difficulties and challenges unknown to
his successors. His office was entirely untried, its authority untested.
The Federal Constitution invested the presidency with sweeping powers, but these powers were almost completely undefined. Many would
require congressional legislation to be made effective in practice. Others would be defined only through a process of trial and experimenta-

The author thanks Kenneth Bowling, Charlene Bickford, Dorothy Twohig, and Mark
Mastromarino for comments and suggestions on the manuscript. Aspects of the argu-
ment in this article were presented to the first Mount Vernon Symposium on George
Washington in November 1996, sponsored by the Barra Foundation. The author
thanks Richard Norton Smith, Peter Henriques, Richard Brookhiser, and Roger Brown
for useful ideas, challenges, and cautionary advice offered on that occasion, as well as
James Rees, resident director of the Mount Vernon Ladies Association, and Mount
Vernon historian John Riley, who organized the event.

tion between the president and Congress. The Federal Constitution delegated to the president primary responsibility for the military, the conduct of foreign affairs, the nomination of most federal officers, and the faithful execution of federal laws, but gave him no authority to initiate legislation. He was authorized only to recommend to the consideration of Congress "such Measures as he shall judge necessary and expedient." Congress was at liberty to ignore any or all such recommendations. The president's only formal recourse against congressional action was the veto, which the Framers of the Constitution seem to have fashioned as a shield for the presidency against legislative encroachment, but this authority was qualified and limited by the power of Congress to override.[1] Antifederalist critics complained that the Constitution invested the president with almost monarchical powers, but from Washington's viewpoint, as he contrasted the responsibilities and functional authority of his office in the spring of 1789, the powers at his disposal must have seemed inadequate to the responsibilities delegated to him.[2]

Washington was nevertheless determined to establish the presidency as an energetic and effective institution — a determination that placed him in a predicament peculiar to the revolutionary generation. Americans of that generation were especially suspicious of executive power. The revolutionary movement had been fueled by real and perceived abuses of executive authority — by customs officials, tax

---

[1]Some of Washington's political confidants, including James Madison and Alexander Hamilton, as well as James Wilson, George Read, and others, had argued in the Philadelphia Convention in favor of an absolute veto for the president; some Federalists regarded this as vital for the office's effectiveness. Madison would even have extended the veto power to the states; see Charles F. Hobson, "The Negative on State Laws: James Madison and the Crisis of Republican Government," *William and Mary Quarterly*, 3d ser. 36 (1979):215–35. On the veto power as a tool for defending executive authority against legislative encroachment, see Hamilton's argument in *Federalist* No. 73 and Gordon S. Wood, *The Creation of the American Republic, 1776–1787* (Chapel Hill, 1969), pp. 552–53.

[2]One of the many Antifederalist critics of the presidency, "Philadelphiensis," predicted that the president would dominate Congress, which would be composed of "his sycophants and flatterers" who would not dare to mention any law "contrary to his sentiment." See Philadelphiensis IX, *Freeman's Journal* (Philadelphia), Feb. 6, 1788, in *The Documentary History of the Ratification of the Constitution*, 13 vols. to date (Madison, Wis., 1976–97), vol. 16 (John P. Kaminski, Gaspare Saladino, and Richard Leffler, eds.), pp. 57–60.

collectors, colonial governors, and the distant colonial bureaucracy in London. In creating their own governments the revolutionaries had gone to great lengths to prevent the abuse of executive power by vesting executive authority in committees rather than individuals, limiting the time individuals could hold executive offices, banning individuals from holding more than one office at a time, stripping governors of power over appointments, and shifting executive authority to local governments, where alert citizens could keep watch over officials for signs of corruption. The government established by the Articles of Confederation had no independent executive branch at all.[3]

The Federal Convention agreed that the establishment of a more effective executive branch was essential for the preservation of the union, but its members were not immune to ideological anxiety about the abuse of executive power. They were also aware of popular concerns about strong executives. The convention considered vesting executive authority in a committee and, once the decision was made to have a single executive, debated the powers of the office before agreeing to invest a single president with the entire executive authority of the federal government. The convention only took this step because, as one of the delegates wrote, "many of the members cast their eyes towards General Washington as President; and shaped their Ideas of the Powers to be given to a President, by their opinions of his Virtue." Federalists, indeed, relied on the influence of Washington's name to persuade reluctant congressmen to vest the president with broad authority. "The extent of our Country and the deliberative freedom of its legislative authority," Gouverneur Morris wrote, "requires the Compensation of an active and vigorous Execution. Every subordinate Power should be tied to the Chief." Washington's "virtues and abilities," Rep. John Steele wrote in 1790, led Congress to invest him "with powers not delegated by the Constitution, which I suppose they would have invested to no other man."[4] Despite the faith that Americans had

---

[3]On the emasculation of executive power in the revolutionary state constitutions, see Wood, *Creation of the American Republic*, pp. 132–50.

[4]Pierce Butler to Weedon Butler, May 5, 1788, Max Farrand, ed., *The Records of the Federal Convention of 1787*, 3 vols. (New Haven, Conn., 1911–37), 3:301–4; Gouverneur Morris to William Carmichael, July [4–11], 1789, Gouverneur Morris Papers, Library of Congress (DLC); John Steele to Joseph Winston, May 22, 1790, H. M. Wagstaff, ed.,

in Washington, however, hostility to the energetic use of executive authority persisted under the new government. "The doctrine of energy in government," John Page declared on the floor of First Congress, "is the true doctrine of tyrants."[5]

Washington did not share this ideological preoccupation with the corrupting influence of executive power. He believed that executive authority, properly checked but concentrated in the hands of a relatively few leaders, was essential to effective government. Yet Washington was always conscious of the popular belief that power was an almost inevitable source of corruption. His own unprecedented personal prestige — his reputation for selfless devotion to the public good — rested on his repeated refusal to grasp at power. During the Revolutionary War he had been studiously deferential to the Continental Congress. He had refused to reach for dictatorial authority, and when the war ended, he had resigned his commission and returned to his home at the first opportunity. This act had secured his public reputation as a living embodiment of the ideal republican hero. He was reluctant to reenter the public arena, largely because he was concerned that critics would charge that he had finally succumbed to the irresistible allure of power. It required considerable effort to persuade him to serve as a delegate to the Federal Convention in 1787. As president, Washington understood that asserting and wielding the powers of his office would probably call into question the reputation for disinterested public virtue that he had cultivated so long and so carefully. This is why he looked on his inauguration with such dread and compared himself to "a culprit who is going to the place of his execution."[6]

Washington was willing to risk his reputation because he believed

———————

The Papers of John Steele, 2 vols. (Raleigh, N.C., 1924), 1:61. I owe these last two citations to Kenneth Bowling. See his *Politics in the First Congress* (New York, 1990), esp. chap. 4, " 'Every Subordinate Power should be Tied to the Chief': Congress and the Executive and Judicial Branches."

[5]*Documentary History of the First Federal Congress,* 14 vols. to date (Baltimore, 1972–), vol. 11 (Charlene Bangs Bickford, Kenneth R. Bowling, and Helen E. Veit, eds.), pp. 990–91, hereafter cited as *DHFFC.*

[6]George Washington [hereafter GW] to Henry Knox, Apr. 1, 1789, *The Papers of George Washington,* Presidential Series, 7 vols. to date (Charlottesville, 1987), vol. 2 (Dorothy Twohig, ed.), pp. 2–3, hereafter cited as *PGWPS.*

that the fate of republican government depended on the success of the federal government. While Washington did not assume the presidency with a legislative agenda like a modern president, he did have a series of goals for the new government — all of which he believed were essential to his broader purpose of securing the Union — and all of which assumed a prominent place in his correspondence during the last years of the Confederation. "If I can form a plan for my own conduct," Washington wrote to Lafayette in January 1789, "my endeavours shall be unremittingly exerted (even at the hazard of former fame or present popularity) to extricate my country from the embarassments in which it is entangled, through want of credit; and to establish, a general system of policy, which, if pursued, will insure permanent felicity to the Commonwealth. I think, I see a *path*, as clear and as direct as a ray of light, which leads to the attainment of that object."[7]

The first goal, the one upon which all others depended, was the establishment of a government endowed with enough energy to respond effectively to the domestic problems and foreign crises that threatened the new nation — a government led by men of unimpeachable character, whose honesty, integrity, and devotion to the republic would command the respect of the American people. The great challenge to this government was the just settlement of the outstanding Revolutionary War debts of the Confederation government and the establishment of the credit of the new federal government on a sound basis — Washington's second goal. Washington knew little about the principles of large-scale debt finance, but he understood that unless the outstanding debts of the Confederation were resolved, the nation's credit would be ruined. His third goal was the final implementation of the treaty of peace with Great Britain, most importantly securing control of the posts in the Northwest Territory still held by the British army. Intertwined with this were the goals of pacifying the western frontier of the new nation and opening it up to American settlement, and opening the Mississippi River to American commerce. Washington was also deeply interested in the long-debated federal capital, which he hoped Congress would locate on the Potomac River, as a center for the political, economic, and cultural life of the new re-

---

[7]GW to Lafayette, Jan. 29, 1789, *PGWPS*, vol. 1 (Dorothy Twohig, ed.), pp. 262–64.

public. Finally, and perhaps most important for Washington, was the maintenance of peace. Washington, as Edmund Morgan has pointed out, "had ample experience that war was the way to poverty, and poverty meant impotence." Peace would give the new nation time to grow in population, economic power, and geographic extent—all of which would ultimately secure the strength and respectability of the United States and establish its place among nations.[8]

To achieve these goals Washington had to act with energy and determination, wielding the powers of his office with vigor. But to preserve the popular reputation for disinterested public virtue that was the foundation of his moral authority and the basis of his leadership, he had to avoid the appearance of grasping at power and disavow any interest in increasing it. Ideological hostility to executive power, Washington understood, was based largely on the fear that a strong executive would corrupt and overawe the legislature and usurp its authority. Many of the powers of the presidency, including the direction of military and foreign affairs, had been carved out of the authority possessed by Congress under the Articles of Confederation. The Federal Convention had augmented these powers by granting the president exclusive authority to nominate federal officials. Legislation enacted by the First Congress granted the president extensive power over the executive departments, but many members of Congress, jealous of their own prerogatives, remained skeptical about the energetic use of presidential power.

Washington sought to overcome such anxieties by scrupulously avoiding encroaching on congressional prerogatives. Washington's principal task, he insisted, was to execute the laws passed by Congress, not to devise a legislative program or interfere in the legislative process. The "Constitution of the United States, & the Laws made under it," Washington explained to Edmund Randolph in February 1790, "must mark the line of my official conduct."[9] But in practice the boundaries of presidential authority were not so clear, and the line between presidential and congressional prerogatives was often contested. Though

---

[8]Edmund S. Morgan, *The Genius of George Washington* (Washington, D.C., 1980), p. 22.

[9]GW to Edmund Randolph, Feb. 11, 1790, *PGWPS*, vol. 5 (Dorothy Twohig, Mark A. Mastromarino, and Jack D. Warren, Jr., eds.), pp. 131–32.

he deferred to Congress in many areas, Washington was determined to establish the authority of his office, defend the prerogatives of the presidency, as he understood them, against legislative encroachment, and provide effective executive leadership. Doing so without compromising his reputation for virtuous public service presented Washington with one of the greatest challenges of his public career, and made his relationship with Congress — despite the cordial tone that prevailed between the president and the legislative branch through most of his presidency — a tense and uneasy one.

Washington's personal experience as a legislator was confined to an uneventful and undistinguished tenure in the Virginia House of Burgesses before the Revolutionary War and brief service as a delegate to the Continental Congress prior to his selection as commander in chief of the Continental Army. Washington's formative experience with legislative bodies had been chiefly as commander of the army, and this experience did not give him much confidence in the capacity of deliberative bodies to act effectively or expeditiously in the public interest. He conducted himself throughout the war with deliberate deference to civilian authorities, but he believed that the war was needlessly protracted by congressional inaction. After returning to private life Washington continued to be appalled by the lethargy of Congress, and when he assumed the presidency, one of his greatest concerns was "the stupor, or listlessness with which our public measures seem to be pervaded."[10]

In the first stages of his presidency, Washington sought to secure energy in government while protecting his own reputation for disinterested patriotism by drawing the other branches of government into a close, consultative relationship under his leadership. Washington had little appreciation for the celebrated separation of powers doctrine. An impractical division of authority and purpose among the contending states, he believed, had doomed the Confederation government to impotence; the Constitution offered the possibility of forging a new unity of purpose, but only if the officers of the federal

---

[10]GW to Henry Knox, Apr. 10, 1789, *PGWPS*, 2:45–46; GW used this phrase in criticizing the slowness of Congress to make a quorum, but it expressed his anxiety about the state of public affairs generally.

government acted in concert. He was determined to exploit the talents of every available man, and he saw no reason why he should be denied the counsel of able men simply because they were serving in another branch of the government. "No man is a warmer advocate for proper restraints and wholesome checks in every department than I am," he wrote to his nephew Bushrod Washington, "but I have never yet been able to discover the propriety of placing it absolutely out of the power of men to render essential services, because a possibility remains of their doing ill."[11]

James Madison and John Jay were among Washington's most important advisors before he assumed office, and he continued to appeal to them for counsel during his presidency, without regard for their positions in the new government. During the first months of the Washington presidency, Madison acted much like a prime minister, pushing legislation through the House of Representatives while conferring constantly with Washington. Jay continued to render policy advice after becoming chief justice, although he surprised and disappointed Washington in 1793 by refusing, along with the other members of the Supreme Court, to render an official opinion on the application of the Treaty of Alliance with France. Washington's request that the chief justice travel to London to negotiate the treaty that bears Jay's name is the most dramatic example of Washington's disregard for the principle of separation of powers.[12]

Washington's efforts to break down the separation of powers between the executive branch and Congress were not particularly successful, despite the fact that the Constitution provided him with an

---

[11]GW to Bushrod Washington, Nov. 10, 1787, W.W. Abbot, ed., *The Papers of George Washington*, Confederation Series, 6 vols. (Charlottesville, 1992–97), 5:420–25.

[12]GW's reliance on Madison during the early months of his presidency is reflected in his correspondence. Unfortunately, GW's diary is not available to document their interaction. GW apparently kept a diary during the spring and summer of 1789 — two entries were published by Jared Sparks and Washington Irving in the nineteenth century — but the manuscript of the diary is now lost. Since it survived into the nineteenth century it is possible that this manuscript still exists. If recovered it would probably constitute an invaluable source for documenting the interaction between the president and members of the First Congress during the early months of the new government (Donald Jackson and Dorothy Twohig, eds., *The Diaries of George Washington*, 6 vols. [Charlottesville, 1976–79], 5:445). On the extrajudicial activities of judges in the 1790s, see Gordon S. Wood, *The Radicalism of the American Revolution* (New York, 1992), pp. 323–24, and the essay by Wythe Holt in this volume.

opportunity to draw the Senate into a close consultative relationship by requiring him to seek the advice and consent of that body to treaties and appointments. From the start, the Senate was jealous of its prerogatives, and senators proved unwilling to act as formal counselors to the president, establishing a pattern of suspicion and contention between the Senate and the president that lasted throughout Washington's administration.

Presidential authority over appointments (checked only by the process of Senate confirmation) constituted one of the most important — and the most politically explosive — grants of power to the executive made by the Federal Constitution. The British patronage system, dominated by the prime minister, epitomized executive corruption for the revolutionary generation. The political significance of the appointment power was magnified during the Washington administration by the size of the task. During his eight years in office, Washington was called upon to make nearly four hundred nominations to appointive office requiring Senate confirmation.[13] Nearly the whole federal service owed its place to him — heads of departments, territorial governors and officials, ministers and consuls at foreign posts, Indian commissioners and superintendents, treasury officials, loan commissioners, revenue officers, marshals, district attorneys, and federal court judges. The process dictated by the Constitution almost guaranteed contention between the president and the Senate over many of these appointments.

Even before taking office, Washington foresaw that filling appointive offices would be one of the most politically sensitive jobs of his presidency. "I have no conception of a more delicate task than that which is imposed by the Constitution on the Executive," he wrote to a friend in March 1789. "It is the nature of Republicans, who are nearly in a state of equality, to be extremely jealous as to the disposal of all honorary or lucrative appointments." A mistake in this regard, Washington worried, would put the new government "in the utmost danger of being utterly subverted." Because the appointments were so nu-

---

[13]The pioneering study of appointments during GW's presidency, Gallaird Hunt, "Office-Seeking during Washington's Administration," *American Historical Review* 1 (1896):272, slightly underestimates the total.

merous and varied, and would reach into nearly every community in the nation, Washington recognized that the manner in which they were filled would be widely perceived as a test of his reputation for disinterested statesmanship. "My political conduct in nominations," Washington confided to his nephew Bushrod, "even if I was uninfluenced by principle, must be exceedingly circumspect and proof against just criticism, for the eyes of Argus are upon me, and no slip will pass unnoticed."[14]

Washington responded to this challenge by committing himself to a high and seemingly impartial standard for nominees, and by persuading members of Congress — in most cases — to accept that standard as well. To all of the importunings for office, Washington responded in the same way: that he would go into the presidency "without being under any possible engagements of any nature whatsoever," and "would not be in the remotest degree influenced, in making nominations, by motives arising from ties of amity or blood." Pursuing any other course, Washington felt certain, would expose the administration to "endless jealousies" and possibly "fatal consequences." A "single disgust excited in a particular State . . . might, perhaps, raise a flame of opposition that could not easily, if ever, be extinguished." To avoid this outcome, Washington wrote, "three things ought to be regarded . . . the fitness of characters to fill offices, the comparative claims from the former merits & sufferings in service of the different Candidates, and the distribution of appointments in as equal a proportion as might be to persons belonging to the different States in the Union."[15] The first of these — "fitness of character" — became Washington's most important criterion for appointive office.

Washington's standard of fitness was not the impersonal standard of technical ability generally applied to civil servants in our century, although ability to perform the duties of the office was an important consideration.[16] Fitness was mainly a judgment of character. A fit candidate

---

[14]GW to Samuel Vaughan, Mar. 21, 1789, GW to Bushrod Washington, July 27, 1789, *PGWPS*, 1:424–30, 3:334.

[15]GW to Samuel Vaughan, Mar. 21, 1789, *PGWPS*, 1:424–30.

[16]Leonard White argues that GW considered technical competence mainly in filling legal and scientific posts, but this assertion is not supported by the evidence (*The Federalists: A Study in Administrative History, 1789–1801* [New York, 1948], p. 259). GW

for office was a man of unimpeachable personal integrity and bearing — sober, discreet, and reliable — and one well regarded in his community or state.[17] It was the standard of a premodern, face-to-face
society. It was implicitly elitist, since only gentlemen, in the premodern
sense of that term, could possibly possess the kind of public reputation
for integrity and public virtue that Washington demanded.[18]

It would be easy today to overlook the extraordinary importance —

<hr />

also inquired into the technical competence of potential nominees for foreign service
and treasury posts, although command of foreign languages or proven mercantile
ability were not absolute prerequisites to these appointments. It goes without saying
that GW was concerned with the technical ability of nominees for senior military
appointments.

[17]GW's concern about exciting local, state, and sectional jealousies also led him to
adopt an inflexible rule of residence as a characteristic of fitness. He insisted that
nominees be residents of the locales for which they were appointed. This was hardly the
practice in contemporary European bureaucracies, and its importance should not be
overlooked. The integration of the American economy after the Revolution was leading
to the development of a cosmopolitan commercial class, particularly in the Middle
Atlantic states, consisting of men without unalterably fixed homes or state and local
allegiances. Gouverneur Morris, one of the best exemplars of this group, was a New
Yorker, but he represented Pennsylvania in the Constitutional Convention in 1787.
Timothy Pickering, a New Englander, held appointive office for several years in Pennsylvania before being appointed postmaster general in 1791. GW's decision not to appoint men to posts outside their home states may have discouraged the development of
this cosmopolitan class among federal officeholders. Although the policy avoided exciting state and local tensions in the 1790s, in the long run it reinforced state and local
jealousies and may have undermined the growth of American nationalism.

[18]Note the injunction that candidates, at least for important appointments, should
be men of age and experience, "tried and proved" by public service, in GW's letter to
James McHenry of Nov. 30, 1789 (*PGWPS*, vol. 4 [Dorothy Twohig, ed.], pp. 342–45).
This standard sometimes led GW to offer appointments to men who were not technically qualified. In his desperate search for a fit secretary of state after the resignation
of Edmund Randolph in 1795, GW sounded out or actually offered the post to a series
of men — William Paterson, Thomas Johnson, Charles Cotesworth Pinckney, Patrick
Henry, and Rufus King — only two of whom (Pinckney and King) had any significant
knowledge of foreign affairs. All, however, were men GW believed to be of unimpeachable integrity and public virtue. Throughout his administration, GW sought to secure
the services of what he called "the first characters" for the federal government. His
standards were extraordinarily high, and he experienced considerable difficulty in
finding men who met them and in persuading those who did to accept public office.
For a different interpretation of GW's standards for presidential appointees, see Gordon S. Wood, "Launching the 'Extended Republic': The Federalist Era," in Ronald
Hoffman and Peter J. Albert, eds., *Launching the "Extended Republic": The Federalist Era*
(Charlottesville, Va., 1996), pp. 14–16. Wood argues that GW conceived of fitness
for public office in classically republican terms, expecting to fill appointments with
members of a leisured patriciate free from the corrupting influence of direct market
interests.

indeed the revolutionary implications — of this commitment on Washington's part to what seems to us to be the self-evident proposition that appointed officials should be qualified in some meaningful sense for the offices they hold. Yet throughout contemporary Europe appointive offices were generally and frankly regarded as personal patronage to be dispensed at the pleasure of the appointing official. Many offices in the British and French administrative systems, particularly in the revenue services, were regarded as aristocratic sinecures, with office-holders enjoying the fees and emoluments of their positions while leaving the actual work to hired subordinates. Administrative reformers began to remedy this situation in Great Britain and France during the 1780s, but their halting efforts had made only marginal inroads against the entrenched system of patronage.

In the United States the situation was significantly different in ways that made Washington's decision seem natural. The Revolution had thrown the whole British aristocratic patronage system into disrepute and overturned the entire network of colonial patronage. Neither the Confederation government nor the states had established substantial administrative bureaucracies in its place (with the exception of the temporary military command and supply apparatus created during the Revolutionary War). Many of the offices that were retained or created by the states were filled by legislative action rather than the appointive power of a single executive, thereby weakening the patron-client relationship inherent in the traditional patronage system. There was also the completely practical consideration that few appointments in the new government offered sufficient salary or fees to support the titular officeholder and a paid hireling, so most appointees would actually have to perform the work for themselves. This made it essential that appointees be at least marginally qualified for their posts.

None of these facts can diminish the importance of what Washington did. Some of his closest supporters and advisers — Alexander Hamilton first among them — expected Washington to use the patronage at his disposal to build a reliable group of administration allies in Congress. They believed that members of Congress could be tied to the president by lines of dependence and patronage by dispensing offices to the relatives of members and to their political allies at home in the states. Many members of Congress shared this expectation and were among the first to importune Washington for patronage. Washington resisted this temptation, looking beyond the immediate problem of building support in Congress to the greater problem of establishing the new government's reputation for rectitude as well as defending his own reputation for nonpartisan leadership.

Washington's public commitment to fitness as a standard for appointment never wavered, but it would be absurd to contend that political considerations did not play a role in his appointments. In the first years of his administration, Washington generally bestowed appointments only on avowed Federalists, or at least upon men who, upon inquiry, were found not to have taken a partisan stand against the ratification of the Constitution. To James McHenry, he noted in 1789 that William Paca might be a suitable candidate for district judge in Maryland, but that Paca's "sentiments have not been altogether in favor of the general Government."[19] McHenry discussed the appointment with Paca and subsequently assured Washington of his competence and loyalty; despite Washington's initial reluctance, Paca received the appointment. Washington's closest advisers were less guarded in commenting on a potential nominee's political loyalties; Hamilton could normally be counted on to find out whether an unfamiliar candidate was known as a friend to the national government and advise the president accordingly.[20] The intense partisanship that marred Wash-

---

[19]GW to James McHenry, Nov. 30, 1789, *PGWPS*, 4:342–45.

[20]The argument of Carl Prince, in his book *The Federalists and the Origins of the U.S. Civil Service* (New York, 1977), that political allegiance was the preeminent consideration in GW's appointments is badly overdrawn. See also the more subtle argument of Gordon Wood that "Hamilton deliberately set out to 'corrupt' American society" by exploiting "the patronage of the Treasury Department with its 800 or more customs officials, revenue agents, and postmasters" (*Radicalism of the American Revolution*, p. 263). This argument is also overdrawn (postmasters, at least, were not Treasury officials), although Hamilton was not particularly circumspect in recommending Federalist partisans for Treasury appointments. On the idea that Hamilton was intent on marshaling a "phalanx" of Treasury placemen, see the essay by Joanne Freeman in the present volume. Even after the new government seemed safely launched, GW continued to withhold appointments from avowed Antifederalists. Never was this more pointedly (or amusingly) plain than in May and June 1790, following Rhode Island's long-delayed ratification of the Constitution. During these weeks GW lay seriously ill with a case of influenza that developed into pneumonia. For a few desperate days in May his doctors actually expected him to die, but he managed to recover and return to business by the end of the month. All the while he was receiving letters from Rhode Island state officeholders — nearly all of them Antifederalists — desperate to hang onto their offices as authority was transferred to the federal government. But even in his weakened state,

ington's second term forced Washington to begin applying a stricter standard of political loyalty in making appointments late in his presidency. "I shall not, whilst I have the honor to Administer the government," he explained in September 1795, "bring a man into any office of consequence knowingly whose political tenets are adverse to the measures which the *general* government are pursuing; for this, in my opinion, would be a sort of political Suicide."[21]

From the beginning of his administration, Washington also relied on members of Congress — usually but not exclusively members of the House of Representatives — to provide him with lists of potential candidates for office and to advise him on the fitness of potential nominees.[22] After the first rush of appointments in 1789–90, Washington shifted responsibility for screening applicants and collecting recommendations to his department heads. After taking up his responsibilities as secretary of state in March 1790, Thomas Jefferson assumed responsibility for collecting information about candidates for offices in his department, as well as for district judge, U.S. marshal, and U.S. attorney — offices related to the domestic functions of the State Department. Hamilton assumed the same responsibility with regard to treasury appointments. After 1790 memoranda and letters from congressmen advising the president about potential nominees sometimes came addressed to Tobias Lear or one of Washington's other secretaries. There are also memoranda on candidates in Lear's hand that demonstrate that the young secretary sometimes conducted interviews with congressmen who came to discuss appointments with Washington.[23]

GW knew the difference between a Federalist and an Antifederalist, and most of the state officeholders were turned out in favor of friends of the Federal Constitution. These applications and related correspondence in May and June 1790 are in *PGWPS*, 5:passim.

[21]GW to Timothy Pickering, Sept. 27, 1795, John C. Fitzpatrick, ed., *The Writings of George Washington*, 39 vols. (Washington, D.C., 1931–44), 33:314–16.

[22]In his diary for Feb. 5, 1790, for example, GW noted that he had received a memorandum from Rep. Hugh Williamson of North Carolina, listing potential candidates for customs appointments in the state, and added that he had submitted the list to the North Carolina senators for their consideration and alteration. GW's deference to senators in such cases did not extend to a veto of potential nominees (Jackson and Twohig, *Diaries of George Washington*, 6:28; see also Williamson to GW, Feb. 5, 1790, *PGWPS*, 5:98–99).

[23]For an example of Jefferson's involvement in screening candidates, see his memorandum on Vermont candidates in Nathaniel Chipman to GW, Feb. 22, 1791, n. 1, *PGWPS*, vol. 7 (Jack D. Warren, Jr., ed.), pp. 399–401; for Hamilton's involvement in

During most of the First Congress, however, members enjoyed fairly open access to the president. Yet this access did not assure them of success when recommending potential nominees. No one, said Thomas Jefferson, was ever more determined than Washington to keep "motives of interest or consanguinity, of friendship or hatred" from influencing his decisions. "No man," John Adams wrote in the summer of 1789, "I believe, has influence with the President. He seeks information from all quarters, and judges more independently than any man I ever knew."[24]

In practice, this meant that Washington reserved judgment about a potential candidate's fitness for himself. But the Senate demonstrated that it was not always willing to allow the president to impose his standard of fitness — regardless of its outward impartiality — on their deliberations. On August 5, 1789, the Senate rejected the appointment of Benjamin Fishbourn as revenue officer of Savannah at the insistence of Georgia Sen. James Gunn, who was unrelenting in his attack on Fishbourn's character. According to an account by the son of Washington's secretary Tobias Lear, "The President immediately repaired to the Senate Chambers & entered, to the astonishment of every one. The Vice-President left his chair & offered it to the President, who accepted it & then told the Senate that he had come to ask their reasons for rejecting his nomination of Collector &c. After many minutes of embarrassing silence, Genl. Gunn rose and said, that as he had been the person who had first objected to the nomination, & had probably been the cause of its rejection, it was perhaps his office to speak on this occasion. That his personal respect for the personal character of Genl. Washington was such that he would inform him of his grounds for recommending this rejection, (and he did so,) but that he would have it distinctly understood to be the sense of the Senate, that no explanation of their motives or proceedings was ever due or

---

selecting candidates for Treasury appointments, see Hamilton to GW, Sept. 29, 1790, *PGWPS*, vol. 6 (Mark A. Mastromarino, ed.), pp. 518–20; for Lear's involvement in the appointment process, see Tobias Lear's Notes on a Conversation with Jonathan Trumbull, Jr., Feb. 18, 1791, Washington Papers, DLC, and William Loughton Smith to Tobias Lear, Feb. 19, 1791, *PGWPS*, 7:389–90.

[24]Thomas Jefferson to Walter Jones, Jan. 2, 1814, Paul Leicester Ford, ed., *Writings of Thomas Jefferson*, 10 vols. (New York, 1892–99), 9:448; John Adams to Silvanus Bourne, Aug. 30, 1789, Adams Family Manuscript Trust, Massachusetts Historical Society.

would ever be given to any President of the United States. Upon which the President withdrew." The next day Washington addressed a letter to the Senate defending the nomination and insisting on Fishbourn's eminent fitness for office.[25]

Fishbourn was only the first of Washington's appointments to be challenged or rejected by the Senate. In the Second Congress senators began to challenge far more important appointments, including those of Anthony Wayne to serve as commander of the American army on the northwest frontier and Gouverneur Morris as minister to France. Later, in the intensely partisan atmosphere of the Jay Treaty debate, the Senate rejected Washington's nomination of John Rutledge as chief justice. Washington's unwavering appeal to an impartial standard of fitness for appointive office was nonetheless one of the most astute policies of his presidency, lifting the most potentially controversial power delegated to the president above partisanship and insulating him from the charge that he was using presidential patronage to dominate the government.

Washington's conduct on appointments nevertheless had critics in Congress, some of whom did not hesitate to present the president with applications and recommendations, even for relatives and friends. In June 1789, William Maclay went personally to Washington's secretary, David Humphreys, to present an application from David Harris, Maclay's brother-in-law. "I cannot say what will come of it," Maclay wrote in his diary, "but my hopes are not high," adding that "the part I have taken in the Senate, has marked me as no Courtier, and I fear will mark poor Davy as a man not to be brought forward." When Washington nominated another man, Maclay attributed it to the fact "that I have never been at the Table of the President or Vice President . . . but I care not a fig for it."[26]

---

[25]This event probably took place on August 5, 1789, when William Maclay was absent from the Senate. The account was recorded by Benjamin Lincoln Lear, only son of GW's secretary Tobias Lear, in a letter to Washington publishers Gales and Seaton, dated March 12, 1818, two years after the suicide of his father. Stephen Decatur, Jr., quotes the letter at length in his *Private Affairs of George Washington, from the Records and Accounts of Tobias Lear, Esquire, His Secretary* (Boston, 1933), pp. 58–59; GW to the U.S. Senate, Aug. 6, 1789, *PGWPS*, vol. 3 (Dorothy Twohig, ed.), pp. 391–93.

[26]Kenneth Bowling and Helen Veit, eds., *The Diary of William Maclay and Other Notes on Senate Debates* (Baltimore, 1988), vol. 9 of *DHFFC*, pp. 90, 127.

The next year Maclay was railing against the tendency in Congress "to make offices for Men, to provide for Individuals without regarding the public or Sparing Expense," and "to create & multiply Offices and Appointments Under the General Government by every possible Means." This, he reported, "is called Giving the President a respectable *Patronage* . . . Which I take to Mean neither more or less, That the President should Always have A number of Lucrative Places in his Gift, to reward those Members of Congress Who may promote his Views or Support his Measures, More especially if by such Conduct they Should forfeit the Esteem of their Constituents," and (he added darkly), "We talk of Corruption in Brittain. I pray We may not have Occasion for complaints of a Similar Nature here." Yet four days later Maclay was back in Washington's office, presenting an application from a friend, never seeming to sense the incongruity of charging Washington with corruption while pursuing offices for relatives and friends of his own.[27]

Maclay seems to have been unusual only in leaving us a diary recording his actions and impressions of this process.[28] Other members were equally assiduous in pursuing federal offices for friends and relations, and some of them were later critical of Washington's dispensation of federal patronage. Maclay charged in his diary that Washington was using his extensive patronage to buy votes in Congress.[29] Yet the surviving evidence does not support the charge. Washington did not use presidential patronage to build either a court party in Congress or support for specific legislation. By scrupulous devotion to the principles about appointments that he had laid down at the beginning of the administration — of not making prior commitments, of accepting

---

[27]Ibid., pp. 172, 352–53, 355.

[28]Maclay was not the only Senate diarist. Benjamin Hawkins kept a diary from 1790 through at least 1793, but it was burned along with other records in a Creek raid in the early nineteenth century.

[29]Maclay charged that GW bought Sen. John Langdon's vote on the supplemental seat of government bill, which passed the Senate on Feb. 25, 1791, by appointing the senator's brother Woodbury as one of the commissioners for settling accounts between the United States and New Hampshire (Bowling and Veit, *Maclay Diary*, p. 390). The appointment had been made on December 23, 1790, and was indeed probably motivated, at least in part, by a desire to cultivate what Alexander Hamilton described as the "Langdon & Gilman party in New Hampshire." The sequence of events makes it impossible for this to have been a political payoff, though it is possible that Langdon was reminded of GW's favor in order to induce him to change his vote on the federal district legislation (Hamilton to GW, Dec. 2, 1790, GW to the U.S. Senate, Dec. 23, 1790, *PGWPS*, 7:19–21, 115).

applications but not making personal replies, of accepting recommendations but insisting on his ultimate independence in making nominations—Washington avoided the appearance of using his appointive power as a partisan tool, securing the authority of the president without arousing popular anxieties about executive usurpation and ministerial corruption—at least until alarmed Republicans began to charge that Alexander Hamilton was employing his influence over Treasury appointments to create a mercenary phalanx to support his designs.

Washington's efforts to secure presidential authority over treaties and foreign relations by persuading the Senate to assume the role of an executive council was, by contrast, one of the most dramatic failures of his presidency. At the end of August 1789, Washington appeared personally before the Senate to seek its advice on impending treaty negotiations with the Creek Indians. The outcome of this venture was one of the most important of Washington's presidency. Arriving with Secretary of War Henry Knox, Washington presented the Senate with a series of propositions to which they were asked to give their "advice and consent." The members turned out to be entirely unprepared for this procedure, and after an embarrassing scene, the senators insisted on being given time to consider the matter on their own. Washington then withdrew from the Senate chamber in frustration. Two days later he presented himself again, and this time received the assent of the Senate to the treaty proposal. This was the last time Washington appeared personally before the Senate to solicit its advice.[30]

Stanley Elkins and Eric McKitrick have perceptively interpreted this familiar drama not as bringing Washington's treaty-making authority into question, but as affirming and reinforcing Washington's powers. The episode, they argue, demonstrated conclusively that it was impractical for the president to consult formally with the Senate prior to entering into treaty negotiations, and that it was unnecessary. Washington had come before them like a prime minister to argue his case, and the embarrassed reaction of the Senate demonstrated that Washington was more than a prime minister and did not need to risk his prestige by coming before them in this way.[31]

This interpretation has considerable merit, but it overlooks the fact

---

[30]The scene is most vividly described in Bowling and Veit, *Maclay Diary,* pp. 128–32.
[31]Stanley Elkins and Eric McKitrick, *The Age of Federalism* (New York, 1993), p. 58.

that the Senate had refused to accept the role that Washington had expected and wanted it to assume: that of an executive council to the president, analogous to a colonial governor's council or a military council of war, prepared to advise him, but moreover to defer to his authority and judgment in so doing. Two weeks before this dramatic scene, Washington had met with a committee of senators to discuss the best mode of communication between the president and the Senate and had expressed to the committee his belief that the time, place, and most of all the manner of consultation was entirely at the discretion of the president.[32]

In refusing to respond to his queries as he expected, the Senate had rejected these assumptions and demonstrated its determination to act on foreign affairs as a deliberative body independent of the president. Although there is no credible documentary evidence to support the tradition that Washington announced to those within earshot as he walked out of the Senate chamber that he would be damned if he ever came there again, the tale amply illustrates Washington's frustration with the Senate's conduct and underscores the uneasy connection between Washington and the upper house that continued through the remainder of his presidency. By declining to take an active, practical role in advising Washington, the Senate may have been affirming the president's prerogative to act independently of their counsel, as Elkins and McKitrick contend, but it was also asserting its own independence and putting the president on notice that in considering treaties it would not accord him the deference and, most importantly, the cooperation he expected.[33]

Washington's efforts to establish a strong cooperative relationship with the Senate were based on the belief—evident in nearly every act

---

[32]Conference with a Committee of the U.S. Senate, Aug. 8, 1789, *PGWPS*, 3:400–403.

[33]The story that GW swore on leaving the Senate chamber that he "would be damned" before he ever came there again is not credible. It appears in the diary of John Quincy Adams for Nov. 10, 1824; Adams heard the story from William H. Crawford. Crawford seems to have had it from James Monroe, but Monroe can have heard of the event only at second hand, since he did not take his seat in the Senate until December 1790. The later antipathy between GW and Monroe makes the latter an unreliable source. If GW had made such a statement, Maclay (if not some other member) would have made a note of it.

of his public life — that effective government was founded on building consensus rather than on brokering between conflicting interests. The emerging liberal politics, with its frank promotion of self-interest and its view that government was primarily an instrument to resolve conflicts between interested parties, was repulsive to him. It was just this sort of petty, parochial, self-oriented conception of public life, Washington argued in his private correspondence, that had rendered the Confederation government so ineffective. His hopes for the new federal government rested on the belief that it offered a more unified mechanism for pursuing public ends. The reluctance of the Senate to act in concert with him was thus a source of considerable frustration to Washington, and remained so throughout his presidency.

The failure of Washington and the Senate to establish an effective formal mechanism for consultation in foreign affairs had far-reaching consequences for the Washington administration — and for American history more generally. Elkins and McKitrick suggest that the advice provision was worked out in informal discussion and accommodation between the administration and individual members of the Senate. Yet this was precisely the kind of cloakroom arrangement that Washington, in most of his dealings with Congress, sought to avoid. Ever conscious of protecting his reputation for disinterested public service, Washington preferred whenever possible to insulate himself from behind-the-scenes negotiation with members of Congress, rather than expose himself to charges that he was bargaining for congressional support. In foreign policy, Washington soon concluded that to act effectively he would have to act independently of Congress, and he turned increasingly to the use of personal agents and secret missions to secure his ends, beginning with the secret missions of Marinus Willett to the Creek Indians and of Gouverneur Morris to London, initiated in the summer and fall of 1789.

As Washington's efforts at establishing a close consultative relationship with Congress met resistance, he seems to have concluded that the needs of an energetic, effective government required him to take a more active role in leading Congress, particularly in regard to foreign affairs and the military — areas over which the Constitution had granted the president broad authority. The means Washington employed were sometimes so subtle that modern historians overlook them, or attribute them to one or another of his advisers working through the president.

The third and final session of the First Congress seems to have been a turning point in Washington's relationship with Congress, and one in which he began to assume a more active, and more discernibly modern, executive role in shaping the public policy debate. He began to pay much closer attention to the course of legislation. He directed his secretary to obtain copies of pending bills from both houses as soon as they were printed, and he sought and received more detailed information about congressional proceedings than he had during the first two sessions. Washington quickly learned to use the powers at his disposal to prompt congressional action and to move legislation through Congress that he regarded as particularly important.

When Washington arrived in Philadelphia at the beginning of December 1790, three interrelated matters seem to have been foremost in his mind. The first was the fate of Brig. Gen. Josiah Harmar's punitive expedition against the northwestern Indian tribes. This expedition — the largest military venture yet undertaken by the new government — had been dispatched after the recess of Congress on the exclusive authority of the president. Washington had not asked for the consent of Congress for the expedition, considering it what we would call a military police action and not an act of war. The army had marched north from Fort Washington on the Ohio River at the end of September, and for several anxious weeks Washington had waited at Mount Vernon for news of the expedition. Harmar and the governor of the Northwest Territory, Arthur St. Clair, did not report to Washington until late in November, and even then the report was partial and unrevealing. Washington concluded that the army had met an ugly fate, as indeed it had. Although not slaughtered wholesale, the expedition had lost an appalling number of men while failing to force the Indians into a decisive engagement that would put an end to depredations on the northwestern frontier.[34]

By the time Washington reached Philadelphia, rumors of Harmar's defeat were beginning to spread, and Washington had received enough

---

[34]GW to Henry Knox, Nov. 2, 1790, *PGWPS*, 6:615–16.

unofficial but reliable reports from the frontier to know what had happened to Harmar, and what it would mean. In the spring of 1791, Washington knew, Indian attacks on the frontiers of Kentucky, western Virginia, and western Pennsylvania would increase. If not put down immediately, the northwestern tribes might be joined by the Seneca to the north and the Creeks to the south, embroiling the new nation in an expensive and bloody Indian war extending from the Great Lakes to Florida — a war that would strain the resources of the federal treasury and undermine the stability of the union.

The second matter that weighed upon Washington's mind as he made his way to Philadelphia was the failure of Gouverneur Morris's secret mission to England. In October 1789 Washington had empowered Morris to visit England to sound out the British ministry on executing the still-unfulfilled provisions of the treaty of peace — most importantly the evacuation of the western posts — and to determine whether the British government had any disposition to conclude a commercial treaty with the United States. Morris also was to sound out the ministry on the possibility of a regular exchange of ambassadors. The duke of Leeds had engaged in desultory conversations with Morris during the late spring and summer of 1790 but had broken them off in September. Washington received Morris's final, disheartening dispatch from London, dated September 18, while still at Mount Vernon. He read it with the full knowledge that the ineffectiveness of the American army on the northwestern frontier would certainly not incline the British to evacuate the western posts.[35]

The third matter on Washington's mind, and a more pleasant one, was the establishment of the new federal city on the Potomac. Under the terms of the Residence Act, passed the preceding summer, Washington had been authorized to select a site for the federal district anywhere on the Potomac River between the mouth of Conococheague Creek (just west of Hagerstown, Maryland) and the mouth of the Eastern Branch, or Anacostia River. There were probably few men alive who were more familiar with this stretch of the Potomac River than

[35]GW to Gouverneur Morris, Oct. 13, 1789 (second letter), *PGWPS*, 4:179–83, and Morris to GW, Sept. 18, 1790, *PGWPS*, 6:470–77; see also Samuel Flagg Bemis, *Jay's Treaty: A Study in Commerce and Diplomacy* (rev. ed., New Haven, 1962), pp. 66–85.

FIG. 1. *The Washington Family,* by Edward Savage, 1789–96. With the Potomac River in the background, George Washington reviews a survey of the federal city site with his wife, Martha, and her grandchildren. *(Courtesy Andrew W. Mellon Collection, National Gallery of Art)*

Washington, and he knew almost immediately where he would prefer to locate the district (fig. 1). The propriety of giving at least token consideration to other sites as well as the need to gain a certain bargaining leverage with the landowners of the chosen Georgetown–Eastern Branch site led Washington to tour the possible alternatives in October, but his mind was made up well before he departed for Philadelphia at the end of November. There was a general expectation that the site would be announced in Washington's address to the opening of Congress.[36]

These three concerns were subtly interwoven. The rationale for the creation of a great republican city on the Potomac was not so much

[36]Memorandum from Thomas Jefferson, Aug. 29, 1790, Memorandum from James Madison, ca. Aug. 29, 1790, Agreement of Georgetown, Md., Property Owners, Oct. 13, 1790, GW to Elizabethtown, Md., Citizens, ca. Oct. 20, 1790, Otho H. Williams to GW, Nov. 1, 1790, William Deakins, Jr., to GW, Nov. 3, 1790, *PGWPS,* 7:368–70, 371–72, 554–57, 571–72, 608–14, 616.

that the river was at the geographical center of the nation but because the Potomac seemed to provide the most readily developed access to the Ohio Valley, which ambitious and farsighted men like Washington expected to become the agricultural heartland of an expanding republican empire. The project would become an absurdity if the Washington administration proved unable to assert the authority of the federal government over the Northwest Territory by suppressing the Indians and wresting control of the frontier posts from the British.

These three matters — the pacification of the frontier, the settlement of Anglo-American relations, and the establishment of the federal city on the Potomac — were among the most important goals of Washington's administration. During the short twelve weeks of the last session of the First Congress, the administration sought congressional actions of various sorts on each one. By the time he presented his annual message to Congress on December 8, Washington was aware that the defeat of Harmar would require the federal government to mount a larger and more expensive campaign in the ensuing year, and that this would require potentially controversial legislation expanding the army. He was also aware that fixing the federal district on the site he had selected — a part of which was below the mouth of the Eastern Branch — would require a potentially controversial bill to amend the Residence Act of the preceding summer.

Though he would have to present each of these matters to Congress during the course of the session, Washington barely raised them at all in his annual message to Congress. In regard to the Indian war, he reminded Congress briefly of the string of depredations committed during the previous year by "certain banditti of Indians" and reported that "these aggravated provocations" had prompted him to call out the militia for the defense of the frontiers and to "authorize an expedition" consisting of militia and regular army troops under General Harmar, but he concluded that "the event of the measure is yet unknown to me." This was true only in an official sense; Washington was already well aware that the expedition had not achieved its goals. Washington made no reference at all in the address to the secret Morris mission, nor, to the surprise of many, did he announce the location of the federal district.[37]

---

[37]GW to the U.S. Senate and House of Representatives, Dec. 8, 1790, *PGWPS*, 7:45–49.

Washington's silence on these matters might be explained by reference to the particular circumstances governing each case. Washington had not yet received definitive reports from Harmar or St. Clair; he felt under no obligation at all to report the details of the Morris mission, even to the Senate; and to announce the location he had selected for the federal district at this time would have exposed Washington to the charge that he had not given the competing upriver sites sufficient opportunity to present their offers.[38] But considered together, Washington's silence on these crucial matters suggests an inclination to influence the course of congressional action, not merely by suggesting matters for congressional consideration, but by presenting them at times and under conditions that would prompt Congress to act in accordance with his designs. This inclination was amply verified in the course of the ensuing twelve weeks as the administration's plans for a new campaign against the northwestern Indians, the selected location for the federal district, and the details of the Morris mission were revealed to Congress at propitious moments.

Of these three, Washington's calculated disclosure of the fate of the Morris mission provides a striking example of his increasingly active style of leadership. Shortly after arriving in Philadelphia, Washington turned over the entire record of the Morris mission to Jefferson and asked the secretary for his opinion as to what steps ought to be taken. Washington did not then indicate any need or intention to turn the matter over to the Senate, nor did Jefferson in his report to Washington dated December 15, 1790. The entire matter was allowed to lie dormant for two months, until February 14, 1791, when Washington informed both houses of Congress that Great Britain had rebuffed his unofficial emissary. Washington simultaneously laid the record of the Morris mission — including Morris's instructions and selections from his correspondence — before the Senate.[39]

The timing of this disclosure, and the fact that it was made to both

---

[38]Joseph Chapline and William Good, representing landowners in the vicinity of Sharpsburg, Maryland, enclosed a plat of their area in a letter to GW dated Dec. 4, 1790 (*PGWPS*, 7:25–27).

[39]GW to Thomas Jefferson, Dec. 11, 1790, GW to James Madison, ca. Dec. 12, 1790, Jefferson to GW, Dec. 15, 1790, GW to Thomas Jefferson, Feb. 9, 1791, and GW to the U.S. Senate and House of Representatives, Feb. 14, 1791, *PGWPS*, 7:58, 59, 84–86, 325, 346–47.

houses of Congress, is indicative of Washington's true purpose in making it. He and Jefferson had agreed in December that no further overtures should be made to Great Britain in the immediate future, and nothing had changed during the ensuing two months to alter that judgment. However, a particular piece of legislation favored by Jefferson and supported by the president had stalled in the House of Representatives. In his annual message to Congress on December 8 Washington had recommended the consideration of measures to protect and develop American shipping—which meant restrictions on the access of British ships to the lucrative carrying trade. This proposal had been referred to a committee of the House of Representatives, where it had languished for two months. Washington had watched with increasing impatience as his recommendation went unattended. Finally on February 12, the committee was discharged without having reported a navigation bill.

Two days later, in a move calculated to prompt Congress to action, Washington laid the record of the Morris mission before the House and the Senate.[40] The effect of this disclosure was immediate. Just as Washington must have expected, an outraged House recommitted the matter of navigation legislation, and the new committee soon reported a bill that directly imitated the British navigation laws, prohibiting the importation into the United States of goods not of the growth or manufacture of the nation under whose flag they were shipped when that nation refused to allow American vessels to carry American goods into its ports, as Great Britain refused to do in the case of the West Indies. This bill was aimed directly at the British carrying trade and threatened British access to their best foreign market.[41]

The timing of the disclosure had other implications. Both Washington and Jefferson were aware that Congress might not have sufficient time to pass a navigation bill before adjourning, pressed at it was with other business. They were also aware that the bill would meet the continued opposition of the mercantile interests in Congress, including the close allies of the secretary of the treasury. But whether or not a

---

[40]This report, in the estimation of Julian Boyd, was "an instrument carefully designed and deliberately chosen at this particular moment to meet an exigent legislative situation" (*The Papers of Thomas Jefferson,* 27 vols. to date [Princeton, 1950–], 18:233).

[41]Bemis, *Jay's Treaty,* pp. 112–13.

bill was enacted or the matter was delayed until the Second Congress convened in the fall, the disclosure of the British rebuff of Morris's overtures and the immediate response of Congress in bringing out a navigation bill would send the British ministry an unmistakable message that the American government was not prepared to accept the status quo in Anglo-American relations indefinitely. Alexander Hamilton assured British agent George Beckwith that Washington's actions had not been timed to benefit the French party in the United States, but British consul Phineas Bond certainly believed that Washington's intention was to send a warning to the British without causing a commercial rupture between the two nations. Bond wrote to the duke of Leeds after adjournment that the timing of Washington's disclosure had been calculated "to prevent any hasty measures which might interrupt the commercial intercourse with Great Britain and to give the members of the legislature during the recess an opportunity to consider and digest plans the most expedient for the encouragement of . . . the general navigation of the United States."[42]

The House committee to which Washington's message was referred acted quickly, reporting a bill discriminating against British commerce on February 21; but by that time it was too late to get such a bill through Congress. The threat that the matter would be taken up by the Second Congress when it convened in the fall, however, was probably one of the factors that prompted the British to dispatch George Hammond to serve as first minister to the United States. This outcome was probably less than Jefferson—a persistent advocate of commercial discrimination—wished. But it was probably as much as Washington hoped to achieve.

Before Congress adjourned at the beginning of March, the administration achieved similar successes in securing legislation increasing the size of the army for a new expedition in the Northwest—the ill-fated expedition that would meet disaster later that year under Arthur St. Clair—as well as amendatory legislation authorizing the president to locate some of the federal district partly below the mouth of the Eastern Branch, taking in Alexandria, Virginia. The passage of the latter, in particular, called upon nearly all of Washington's political resources and skills. Passage of the bill, which was certainly as impor-

---

[42]Bond to Leeds, Mar. 14, 1791, quoted in Boyd, *Papers of Thomas Jefferson,* 18:238 n.

tant to the president as any legislation considered by Congress during the session, was ultimately secured by a barely disguised threat to veto the bill creating the Bank of the United States if reluctant northern representatives, mostly friends of the bank, refused to fall into line.[43]

This more assertive style of presidential leadership came to characterize Washington's approach to Congress, particularly with regard to foreign affairs and the military. Although his most attentive critics, such as William Maclay, might contend that the president encroached on the authority of the legislative branch and attempted to dictate congressional action, this charge had little meaning for people outside the immediate sphere of the government, who could hardly be expected to perceive how the content and timing of the president's reports to Congress constituted an executive invasion of legislative authority.

For much of his presidency, in fact, Washington was publicly applauded for deferring to Congress. In December 1790, for example, Washington received a packet from France addressed to the "President & Members of the American Congress." Believing that the ambiguously addressed packet came from the French National Assembly, Washington referred it, unopened, to the Senate. Vice President Adams promptly returned it, along with the opinion of the Senate that the president should open the packet and "communicate to Congress such parts . . . as in his opinion might be proper to be laid before the Legislature." This incident has been cited by generations of historians as an illustration of Washington's deference toward Congress.[44] "An

---

[43]GW's political role in securing the supplemental seat of government act is detailed in Kenneth Bowling, "The Bank Bill, the Capital City, and President Washington," *Capitol Studies* 1 (1972):59–72, and summarized in the same author's *The Creation of Washington, D.C.: The Idea and Location of the American Capital* (Fairfax, Va., 1991), pp. 212–19. Bowling argues that the Senate held the supplementary federal district legislation hostage to compel GW to sign the bank bill, while I contend that GW used the threat of vetoing the bank bill to compel reluctant senators to vote for the supplementary federal district legislation. It remains unclear how far GW was prepared to take this exercise in political brinkmanship. It seems unlikely that Hamilton's famous written opinion on the constitutionality of the bank bill, which runs some thirteen thousand words, influenced GW much, since it was presented to the president just two days before he signed the bill into law (see Hamilton to GW, Feb. 23, 1791, editorial note, *PGWPS,* 7:422–52). Forrest McDonald suggests that GW capitulated first, signing the bank bill on February 25 before the supplemental seat of government bill was reconsidered by the Senate, but it seems likely that pledges had already been extracted from Morris, Schuyler, Read, and Langdon to support the federal district legislation (*Alexander Hamilton: A Biography* [New York, 1979], pp. 209–10).

[44]Thomas Jefferson to GW, Dec. 9, 1790, and notes, *PGWPS,* 7:51–54.

executive who took pains of this sort to respect the authority of the legislative branch," wrote Douglas Southall Freeman, Washington's most comprehensive biographer, "is not likely to have a clash."[45] In fact, the incident illustrates something far more complicated. European correspondents, unfamiliar with the constitutional changes in the United States, sometimes addressed him as the "President of Congress." Washington had received and opened such letters from abroad without scruple in the past and would do so in the future. The difference in this case was that he had recently received a letter from the French National Assembly addressed to him as president of the United States, so he knew that the French National Assembly knew how to address a letter to him. Washington apparently believed this packet was intended for Congress alone. He was praised by contemporaries for the "delicacy" with which he treated the prerogatives of Congress, but in fact he seems to have simply sent over a packet he thought had been delivered improperly.[46] He turned out to be wrong. The packet—which Washington referred to Thomas Jefferson after Adams returned it unopened—was not from the National Assembly at all. It was from the president of the Commune of Paris and was apparently intended jointly for Washington and Congress. The significance of this incident is not that it illustrates Washington's deference to Congress, but the disposition of contemporaries to credit Washington with greater deference to Congress than he actually demonstrated. Similar episodes—often no more substantive than this one—built on the public trust that Washington had cultivated for years and deflected criticism when he used the powers of his office more assertively.

George Washington's repeated insistence that his primary role as president was to carry out the will of Congress has persuaded many

---

[45]Douglas Southall Freeman, *George Washington: Patriot and President* (New York, 1954), pp. 302–3. For a contrasting reading of this event, see Boyd, *Papers of Thomas Jefferson,* 19:78–106. Boyd hypothesizes that GW was attempting to determine the temper of the Senate in regard to French tributes to Benjamin Franklin before transmitting the letter he had received from the French National Assembly on that subject. Boyd's argument depends on GW having known the true identity of the writer of the unopened letter, which he did not.

[46]"Delicacy" was the motive attributed by William Maclay; see Bowling and Veit, *Maclay Diary,* p. 341.

historians to attribute to him a degree of deference for Congress and an aversion to involving himself in the legislative process, that are not borne out by a close reading of the evidence.[47] Washington was clearly averse to interfering with Congress in those areas—the most important being public finance—that were clearly and unequivocally delegated to Congress by the Federal Constitution. But he was prepared to assert himself in matters he believed were within the sphere of the president—to lead Congress, as he did by revealing the Morris mission, and to act independently of Congress, as he did when he issued his Neutrality Proclamation in 1793 without prior consultation with the Senate.

Washington was determined to defend the prerogatives of the presidency because he knew that precedents were being set that would shape the course of the American republic for generations. "Many things which appear of little importance of themselves and at the beginning," he wrote in May 1789, "may have great and durable consequences from their having been established at the commencement of a new general Government." He added wisely that it would be easier to begin with "a well adjusted system . . . than to correct errors or alter inconveniences after they shall have been confirmed by habit."[48]

Washington's conduct nonetheless reassured Americans that a strong executive was not a threat to legislative independence. Considering the materials with which he had to work—the vague outline of his office provided by the Constitution and the extraordinary limits put on his political role by the ideals of disinterested public service he tried so hard to uphold—Washington's achievement in establishing the authority of the presidency and in working out an effective, if not always an easy, relationship with Congress ranks among his most important accomplishments.

---

[47]According to Douglas Southall Freeman, GW's conduct in regard to Congress was marked by caution, deference, and most of all a conviction that "the initiative, the choice, the form, the scope and the prompt enactment or deliberate postponement of legislation were for the determination of Congress, unhindered by the Executive" (*George Washington: Patriot and President,* p. 221). More recently, political scientist Glenn Phelps has argued that GW did not engage in "politicking" for policies he preferred [Glenn A. Phelps, *George Washington and American Constitutionalism* [Lawrence, Kans., 1993], p. 140).

[48]GW to John Adams, May 10, 1789, *PGWPS,* 2:245–50.

Shortly after assuming the presidency, Washington wrote to his friend David Stuart that "the eyes of America — perhaps of the world — are turned to this Government; and many are watching the movements of all those who are concerned in its administration." Toward the end of his administration, Washington could write truthfully that the "powers of the Executive of the U. States are more definite, and better understood perhaps than those of almost any other Country; and my aim has been, and will continue to be, neither to stretch, nor relax from them in any instance whatever, unless imperious circumstances should render the measure indispensible." By working constantly to define the boundaries of presidential power, and scrupulously remaining within those boundaries, Washington succeeded in pursuing a wide range of policy goals while demonstrating to his countrymen that an energetic executive was compatible with republican liberty.[49]

---

[49]GW to David Stuart, July 26, 1789, *PGWPS*, 3:321–27; GW to Alexander Hamilton, July 2, 1794, Fitzpatrick, *Writings of Washington*, 33:420–22.

Joanne B. Freeman

"The Art and Address of Ministerial Management"

Secretary of the Treasury Alexander Hamilton and Congress

Iɴ 1818, ᴀᴛ ᴛʜᴇ ᴀɢᴇ of seventy-five, Thomas Jefferson (fig. 1) wrote an autobiographical statement about his service as secretary of state. Trying to make sense of the period's politics from the distance of time, he attributed its evils to one source: Alexander Hamilton (fig. 2). To prove his point, he related an anecdote. In April of 1791, Secretary of State Jefferson, Secretary of the Treasury Hamilton, Secretary of War Henry Knox, and Vice President John Adams were dining together at Jefferson's home. When dinner was over and the cloth was removed, the conversation turned to the subject of the British constitution. As Jefferson recalled it, Adams said, "Purge that constitution of its corruption, and give to its popular branch equality of representation, and it would be the most perfect constitution ever devised by the wit of man." At this point, "Hamilton paused," Jefferson wrote dramatically, and said, "Purge it of its corruption, and give to its popular branch equality of representation, and it would become an impracticable government: as it stands at present, with all its supposed defects, it is the most perfect government which ever existed."[1]

To Jefferson, this story held the key to Hamilton's politics. "Hamilton was not only a monarchist," he wrote, "but for a monarchy

---

[1]Thomas Jefferson, Feb. 4, 1818, introduction, Franklin B. Sawvel, ed., *The Complete Anas of Thomas Jefferson* (New York, 1903), p. 37.

FIG. 1. *Thomas Jefferson,* by
Charles Willson Peale, 1791.
*(Courtesy Independence National
Historical Park)*

FIG. 2. *Alexander Hamilton,* by
Charles Willson Peale, 1791.
*(Courtesy Independence National
Historical Park)*

bottomed on corruption." It was Hamilton's corruption—defined by Jefferson as his ability to sway Congress to his will—that most disturbed the elder statesman.[2] As he explained to Washington in 1792, Hamilton had at his disposal a "squadron devoted to the nod of the treasury."[3] Out of the public eye and able to serve their own interests, such men would "form the most corrupt government on earth."[4]

Jefferson's image of Hamilton remains powerful even today: the corrupt and manipulative schemer plotting behind closed doors.[5] Hamilton did much to live up to this image, for he was indeed superb at marshaling and organizing a political fighting force, and his web of influence was wide reaching. But to stop at this point—to condemn Hamilton without studying his politics in an eighteenth-century context—is to limit ourselves to a conventional narrative of the Federalist era, a tale of virtuous Jeffersonians and corrupt Hamiltonians, complete with a hero, a villain, and a happy ending—Jefferson's election as president in 1801. Hamilton forged his unique relationship with Congress in the national government's formative years, when the process of national politics was yet undetermined. His "corruption" was, in

[2]Ibid., p. 36. See also Jefferson, [Memorandum], Dec. 25, 1791, and Mar. 23, 1793, ibid., pp. 45, 114–15; Jefferson to James Monroe, Apr. 24, 1794, *The Papers of Thomas Jefferson,* 27 vols. to date (Princeton, 1950–), vol. 16 (Julian P. Boyd, Alfred L. Bush, and Lucius Wilmerding, Jr., eds.), p. 264 head note, hereafter cited as *PTJ.* In his political history of the early republic, Charles Carter Lee (son of Henry Lee) pokes fun at Jefferson's account of Hamilton's dramatic pause. Noting Jefferson's claim that Hamilton made another such pause after stating that Julius Caesar was the greatest man who ever lived, Lee writes that "at whatever time the pause of this pregnant anecdote was made, either over the corruption of the British constitution, or in front of 'the world's great master and his own [Caesar],' it shews that when Hamilton was about to talk treason he was apt to make a significant stop, in order to rivet the attention of his auditors" (*Observations on the Writings of Thomas Jefferson, with Particular Reference to the Attack They Contain on the Memory of the Late Gen. Henry Lee* [Philadelphia, 1839], pp. 199–200).

[3]Jefferson, [Notes of a Conversation with George Washington], Oct. 1, 1792, *PTJ,* vol. 24 (John Catanzariti, Eugene R. Sheridan, George H. Hoemann, Ruth W. Lester, and J. Jefferson Looney, eds.), p. 435. See also Jefferson to Washington, May 23, 1792, ibid., vol. 23 (Charles T. Cullen, Eugene R. Sheridan, George H. Hoemann, Ruth W. Lester, and J. Jefferson Looney, eds.), pp. 536–38.

[4]Thomas Jefferson to George Washington, May 23, 1792, ibid., 23:537.

[5]The best biographical studies of Hamilton include Broadus Mitchell, *Alexander Hamilton,* 2 vols. (New York, 1957–62); Forrest McDonald, *Alexander Hamilton* (New York, 1979); John C. Miller, *Alexander Hamilton: Portrait in Paradox* (New York, 1959); and Gerald Stourzh, *Alexander Hamilton and the Idea of Republican Government* (Stanford, Cal., 1970).

part, a pragmatic attempt to forge a mechanism of government within a new and undefined political realm. To understand his motives and logic, we must move beyond name-calling and try to see his world through his eyes.

As a starting point, we must understand corruption in an early national context. To Hamilton and his contemporaries, corruption encompassed not simple financial malfeasance, but rather the personal influence and private agreements that bound together the king or executive branch with the Commons or Congress. As David Hume wrote in reference to the British government, "We may . . . give to this influence what name we please; we may call it by the invidious appellations of corruption and dependence; but some degree and some kind of it are inseparable from the very nature of the constitution and necessary to the preservation of our mixed government." It was Hume that Hamilton paraphrased at Jefferson's dinner table, as he had once before at the Federal Convention.[6] To a population that was hypersensitive to abuses of power and political accountability, such backroom bargains reduced the process of republican governance to a series of personal deals grounded on the ambitions and desires of individual politicians. To Hamilton, this was precisely the point. In a sense, Jefferson was correct in selecting this anecdote as a window into Hamilton's style of leadership. For in praising the efficiency of corruption, Hamilton said much about his view of the practical business of politics.

Corruption, in Hamilton's sense of the word, signified the very basis of efficient governance. Without the ability to bargain behind closed doors, the government would come to a grinding halt, its constitutional checks and balances producing a state of perpetual stalemate. In his eyes, private agreements and political logrolling were the very stuff of politics, and a politician was both foolish and impractical to think otherwise. It was this assumption that led foreign diplomats to

---

[6]Hume, "Of the Independency of Parliament," in *Essays Moral, Political, and Literary,* ed. Eugene F. Miller (Indianapolis, 1985), p. 45. On Hamilton and Hume, see Stourzh, *Alexander Hamilton,* pp. 83–85. On Hamilton's administrative methods, see Lynton K. Caldwell, *The Administrative Theories of Hamilton and Jefferson: Their Contribution to Thought on Public Administration* (2d ed., New York, 1988); Leonard D. White, *The Federalists: A Study in Administrative History* (New York, 1948), passim; Mitchell, *Alexander Hamilton,* 2:24–31. On Hamilton's views of the business of politicking, see Clinton Rossiter, *Alexander Hamilton and the Constitution* (New York, 1964), and Stourzh, *Alexander Hamilton.*

single out Hamilton as the most cosmopolitan member of the new national government. Other politicians seemed overly conscious of their every action; as French minister Comte de Moustier said to Jefferson in 1789, American politicians seemed always as tense as "a tight rope," engaged in a "type of play" that seemed "neither agreeable nor useful."[7] In such a strained, self-conscious atmosphere, any political business conducted out of the public eye was highly suspect. Hamilton, however, was willing and eager to meet with diplomats and other public men informally, for it was at the dinner table or in private conversation that alliances were forged and understandings were reached. As British minister George Hammond said of him, "The S.[ecretary] of the T.[reasury] is more a man of the world than J.[efferson] and I like his manners better, and can speak more freely to him. J.[efferson] . . . prefers writing to conversing and thus it is that we are apart."[8]

Hamilton's assumptions about politics and his understanding of his public office went hand in hand. He assumed that the American secretary of the treasury would resemble the minister of finance as defined in France and England: a first minister whose agenda set the terms of debate in the legislature. Based on this assumption, he entered office in 1789 with a national economic system in mind, composed of a multitude of individual proposals, each requiring enactment by Congress. Congressional support was vital to Hamilton's success — indeed, important enough that without it, he would have refused the office from the start.[9] And the best and most efficient way to elicit congressional support was through the informal politicking and bargaining that many termed *corruption* of the legislature.

---

[7]Eleanor Francois Elie, Comte de Moustier to Thomas Jefferson, June 24, 1789, *PTJ*, 15:210–12 (translation by author). The original phrase reads: "Passe encore pour la dignité des premiers personages dans les occasions, mais voir toujour la corde tendue[,] c'est bien serieux et c'est un genre de jouissance dont je ne conçois ni l'agrement ni l'utilité."

[8]Jefferson, [Memorandum of Conversation between Sen. Philemon Dickinson and George Hammond], Mar. 26, 1792, ibid., 23:344–45. See also Louis Guillaume Otto to Montmorin, Dec. 13, 1790, ibid., vol. 18 (Julian P. Boyd, Ruth W. Lester, and Lucius Wilmerding, Jr., eds.), p. 539 head note.

[9]Hamilton (hereafter AH) to Edward Carrington, May 26, 1792, Harold C. Syrett and Jacob E. Cooke, eds., *The Papers of Alexander Hamilton*, 27 vols. (New York, 1961–87), 11:427, hereafter cited as *PAH*. See also AH to Marquis de Lafayette, Oct. 6, 1789, ibid., 5:425–27.

The statutory description of his office confirmed him in his opinions. According to the act that established the Treasury Department, the secretary was "to make report, and give information to either branch of the legislature, in person or in writing . . . respecting all matters referred to him by the Senate or House of Representatives." He was also to "digest and prepare" plans for the administration of the revenue and the management of public credit.[10] Out of the three executive departments, only the Treasury Department had this explicit link with Congress, a seemingly official sanction of Hamilton's impulse to influence the legislature. It was this very implication that had produced an uproar during the initial debate over the creation of the Treasury Department. Concerned that the secretary of the treasury might have undue influence over Congress, representatives closely monitored the phrasing of the Treasury Bill, voting, for example, that the secretary should "digest and prepare" plans rather than "digest and report" them, the latter suggesting that he would defend his measures on the floor, in person.[11]

Hamilton used his department's ambiguous connection with both the executive and legislative branches to full advantage. His ability to report to Congress gave him a voice and presence in the House and Senate, enabling him to propose policy and further his agenda. His status as an executive officer enabled him to fend off congressional investigation by claiming executive privilege. As Hamilton expressed it during a 1792 cabinet meeting, "as to his department the act constituting it had made it subject to Congress in some points; but he thought himself not so far subject as to be obliged to produce all papers they might call for. They might demand secrets of a very mischeivous nature." Needless to say, Jefferson saw things differently, charging that Hamilton "endeavored to place himself subject to the house when the Executive should propose what he did not like, and subject to the

[10]Signed Sept. 2, 1789 (*U.S. Statutes at Large,* 1:65–67). On the act itself, see Mitchell, *Alexander Hamilton,* 2:14–21.

[11]On the revision of the Treasury Bill, see *Documentary History of the First Federal Congress, 1789–1791,* 14 vols. to date (Baltimore, 1972–), vol. 6 (Charlene Bangs Bickford and Helen E. Veit, eds.), pp. 1975–91; vol. 11 (Bickford, Kenneth R. Bowling, and Veit, eds.), pp. 1045–76, hereafter cited as *DHFFC.* See also White, *The Federalists,* pp. 67–76.

Executive when the house shd. propose any thing disagreeable."[12] Hamilton's connection with Congress was so clearly his primary source of power that, beginning in 1791, his enemies tried repeatedly to cut it off.[13] When, in 1794, the House for the first time declined to ask Hamilton for his recommendation on additional revenue — appointing a committee instead — he could barely suppress his outrage. As one committee member put it after Hamilton attended one of their meetings, the secretary of the treasury "appeared cursedly mortifyed."[14] Joined with his seemingly boundless energy, his brash self-confidence, and his unrivaled administrative skills, this ambiguity about his position kept him mired in controversy throughout his term of office.

Hamilton missed no opportunity to advance his agenda. Whether asked for a simple yes-or-no response to a petition or for straightforward information about federal expenditures, he often managed to interweave policy proposals into his response.[15] Indeed, on at least one occasion he drafted actual legislation. In 1790, dissatisfied with the House revision of the first revenue bill, he provided a Senate committee with a bill that he preferred; the committee submitted Hamilton's version to the full Senate as its final report.[16] Each such intrusion raised increasingly urgent questions about the role of the secretary of the treasury in proposing legislation. He seemed to fuel the government in and of himself. As Pennsylvania Rep. William Findley complained in 1793, Hamilton "seemed to take the whole Government upon his shoulders. . . . His reports spoke the language of a Frederick

---

[12]Jefferson, [Memorandum], Apr. 2, 1792, *PTJ*, 23:262. See also Report to the Select Committee Appointed to Examine the Treasury Department, Mar. 24, 1794, Syrett and Cooke, *PAH*, 16:193–95.

[13]For an excellent summary of the attack on references to heads of departments, see White, *The Federalists*, pp. 68–74.

[14]William B. Grove to John Steele, Apr. 2, 1794, in ibid., p. 73.

[15]See, for example, Report on the Petition of Christopher Sadler, Jan. 19, 1790; Report on Supplementary Appropriations for the Civil List for 1790, Mar. 1, 1790; Report on Additional Sums Necessary for the Support of the Government, Aug. 1790; Report on Distilleries, Mar. 1792; Report on the Holland Loan of Three Million Florins, Feb. 24, 1791; Report on the Petition of Comfort Sands and Others, Feb. 24, 1791, in Syrett and Cooke, *PAH*, 6:191–92, 280–82, 633–44; 11:85–86; 8:136–38, 138–41. For Hamilton's influential petition reports to the precedent-setting First Federal Congress, see *DHFFC*, vols. 7–8 (Kenneth R. Bowling and William C. diGiacomantonio, eds.).

[16]*DHFFC*, 6:2043–52.

of Prussia, or some other despotic Prince . . . not the language of a dependent Secretary, under a free and well-ordered Government."[17] Pennsylvania Sen. William Maclay was more concise. "Congress may go home," he fumed in 1791. "Mr. Hamilton is all powerful and fails in nothing which he attempts."[18]

By using his connection with Congress to full advantage, Hamilton went far toward suiting his office to his ideals and expectations, but creating a public forum was only half the battle. To effect change, he needed reliable supporters—men who could speak for him on the floor, recognize and refute opposing arguments, and, if nothing else, provide consistently favorable votes in numbers large enough to defeat the opposition. Some congressmen had strong reasons to support Hamilton, either ideological—such as Massachusetts Rep. Fisher Ames and New York Sen. Rufus King—or personal—such as his father-in-law, New York Sen. Philip Schuyler, or his friend John Laurance. Others were less committed. Such men needed tending; they had to be persuaded to support Hamilton's program in principle and vote for it in practice. A politics without a permanent two-party system was like a war without uniforms: without the identifying label of membership in a particular party, friends and enemies were indistinguishable and ever shifting, and loyalties were trustworthy only after close scrutiny and continual testing—and even then, the most diligent efforts to monitor one's congressional friends sometimes failed.[19]

---

[17]*Annals of Congress*, Mar. 1, 1793, 3:922–23, cited in White, *The Federalists*, p. 70 n. 15.

[18]Feb. 9, 1791, Kenneth R. Bowling and Helen E. Veit, eds., *The Diary of William Maclay and Other Notes on Senate Debates*, vol. 9 of *DHFFC*, p. 377.

[19]On the personal nature of early national politics, see Joanne B. Freeman, "Slander, Poison, Whispers, and Fame: Jefferson's 'Anas' and Political Gossip in the Early Republic," *Journal of the Early Republic* 15 (1995):25–57; idem, "Dueling as Politics: Reinterpreting the Burr-Hamilton Duel," *William and Mary Quarterly*, 3d ser. 53 (1996): 289–318; idem, "Affairs of Honor: Political Combat and Character in the Early Republic," Ph.D. diss., University of Virginia, 1998; Jan Lewis, "The Blessings of Domestic Society: Thomas Jefferson's Family and the Transformation of American Politics," *Jeffersonian Legacies*, ed. Peter S. Onuf (Charlottesville, Va., 1993), pp. 109–46, esp. 116–23; Alan Taylor, " 'The Art of Hook and Snivey': Political Culture in Upstate New York during the 1790s," *Journal of American History* 79 (1993):1371–96; idem, *William Cooper's Town: Power and Persuasion on the Frontier of the Early American Republic* (New York, 1995), pp. 170–98, 229–55; Robert H. Wiebe, *The Opening of American Society: From the Adoption of the Constitution to the Eve of Disunion* (New York, 1984), pp. 98–104. On methods of politicking in the early republic, see Noble Cunningham, Jr., *The Jeffersonian*

To avoid just such an unexpected congressional loss, Hamilton focused much of his time and energy on courting and counseling potential supporters. Aware that an executive officer was not supposed to interfere with congressional deliberations, Hamilton rarely took part in such political bargaining himself, instead dispatching agents to make his thoughts known. A congressman approached by any of Hamilton's "particular friends" knew that he represented Hamilton's interests and acted under his direction. Thus, when Assistant Secretary of the Treasury Tench Coxe proposed a bargain over the location of the national capital, Maclay knew that Hamilton was "the Principal in this Business." Robert Morris assumed the same thing during a conversation with Coxe on another occasion.[20] And Coxe himself, so often Hamilton's agent, immediately recognized the meaning of an unexpected visit by Connecticut Sen. William Samuel Johnson. Coxe had declared that the secretary of state should succeed the president in case of emergency; Johnson's visit was, in fact, a reprimand from Hamilton, who considered such a proposal "a preference of a person whom he called his Enemy."[21]

Sometimes indirect politicking was not enough. Sometimes a controversial proposal required a sophisticated defense strategy or an organized attack. In such cases Hamilton typically held an after- hours meeting behind closed doors to formulate plans, inviting only his most trusted supporters. These strategy sessions outraged Senator Maclay, who took careful note of Hamilton's "ministerial management" throughout the pages of his diary.[22] Dubbing Hamilton's devoted followers his "gladiators," Maclay raged at their coordinated campaigns and marveled at their willingness to let Hamilton propose and implement legislation. A meeting of Hamilton and his gladiators was a sure

---

Republicans: The Formation of Party Organization, 1789–1801 (Chapel Hill, 1957); idem, "John Beckley: An Early American Party Manager," *William and Mary Quarterly*, 3d ser. 13 (1956):40–52; David Hackett Fischer, *The Revolution of American Conservatism: The Federalist Party in the Era of Jeffersonian Democracy* (New York, 1965); James Sterling Young, *The Washington Community, 1800–1828* (New York, 1966).

[20]June 14, 1790, Bowling and Veit, *Maclay's Diary*, pp. 291–92. On Tench Coxe, see Jacob Cooke, *Tench Coxe and the Early Republic* (Chapel Hill, 1978).

[21]Tench Coxe to Jefferson, n.d. [between Dec. 1801 and May 1802], in Cooke, *Tench Coxe*, p. 249 n. 30.

[22]Apr. 16, 1790, Bowling and Veit, *Maclay's Diary*, p. 247.

sign that something significant would be attempted that day in the House or Senate. "This the important Week & perhaps the important day, When the question will be put on the Assumption of the State debts," Maclay wrote on March 8, 1790. "I suspect this from the rendevouzing of the Crew of the Hamilton Galley. [I]t seems all hands are piped to Quarters."[23]

Maclay's choice of metaphor strikes at one of the most distinctive — and most threatening — characteristics of Hamilton's style of leadership. Bold, energetic, and organized, with a passion for military command, Hamilton led his supporters like a general at the head of an army. He sized up the enemy, devised campaign strategies, marshaled his troops, issued orders, and spurred them into battle. It was this hierarchical, organized, quasi-military style of leadership that most disturbed Hamilton's opponents. Jefferson frequently resorted to military terminology when complaining about Hamilton's methods: he headed a "squadron," a "corps," a "campaign."[24] To Jefferson, such control over the legislature destroyed the government's intricate system of checks and balances, enabling the executive branch to swallow up the legislative branch.[25] It was Hamilton and his self-interested friends — not the people — who reigned supreme.

Jefferson, of course, denied any such interference on his part. Unlike Hamilton, he had determined "to intermeddle not at all with the legislature. . . . If it has been supposed that I ever intrigued among the members of the legislature to defeat the plans of the Secretary of the Treasury, it is contrary to all truth." As he explained it, he was guilty only of enunciating his "sentiments in conversation, and chiefly among those who, expressing the same sentiments, drew mine from

---

[23]Mar. 8, 1790, ibid., p. 214.

[24]Jefferson to Washington, May 23, Sept. 9, 1792, Feb. 7, 1793, and [Notes of a Conversation with George Washington], Oct. 1, 1792, *PTJ*, 23:537, 24:353, 435, 25:155; Jefferson to Thomas Mann Randolph, Jr., Nov. 2, 1792, ibid., 24:556–57. Given the prevailing fears of military despotism arising from government control of a standing army, Jefferson's military metaphor had particular power. See Gordon Wood, *The Creation of the American Republic, 1776–1787* (Chapel Hill, 1969), pp. 32–34; Lawrence Delbert Cress, *Citizens in Arms: The Army and Militia in American Society to the War of 1812* (Chapel Hill, 1982).

[25]Jefferson, [Notes of a Conversation with George Washington], Oct. 1, 1792, *PTJ*, 24:435.

me."[26] In Jefferson's mind, such innocent dinner conversations could scarcely be considered congressional intrigue.[27]

Jefferson's protestations might be convincing until we look more closely at the unfolding of some of his innocent dinner parties. The most famous one affected the location of the national capital. As Jefferson later recalled, it was born of Hamilton's despair over the impending failure of his plan for the assumption of state debts:

> Going to the President's one day I met Hamilton as I approached the door. His look was sombre, haggard, and dejected beyond description. Even his dress uncouth and neglected. He asked to speak with me. We stood in the street near the door. He opened the subject of the assumption of the state debts, the necessity of it in the general fiscal arrangement and it's indispensible necessity towards a preservation of the union: and particularly of the New England states, who had made great expenditures during the war. . . . . He observed at the same time, that tho' our particular business laid in separate departments, yet the administration and it's success was a common concern, and that we should make common cause in supporting one another. He added his wish that I would interest my friends from the South, who were those most opposed to it.

True to character, Hamilton issued instructions, asking Jefferson to speak with his Southern friends. Jefferson was equally true to form.

> I answered that I had been so long absent from my country that I had lost a familiarity with it's affairs, and being but lately returned had not yet got into the train of them. . . . On considering the situation of things I thought the first step towards some conciliation of views would be to bring Mr. Madison and Colo. Hamilton to a friendly discussion of the subject. I immediately wrote to each to come and dine with me the next

---

[26]Jefferson to Washington, Sept. 9, 1792, ibid., 24:352. See also Jefferson, [Memorandum], Aug. 6, 1793, ibid., 26:628.

[27]On Jefferson's political method, see Caldwell, *The Administrative Theories of Hamilton and Jefferson;* Cunningham, *The Jeffersonian Republicans in Power*, chaps. 1–4, 9–10, 12, passim; idem, *The Process of Government under Jefferson* (Princeton, 1978); Freeman, "Slander, Poison, Whispers, and Fame"; Dumas Malone, *Thomas Jefferson as a Political Leader* (Los Angeles, 1963); Leonard D. White, *The Jeffersonians: A Study in Administrative History, 1801–1829* (New York, 1951), pp. 29–88; Young, *Washington Community*, pp. 128–31, 163–78.

day, mentioning that we should be alone, that the object was to find some temperament for the present fever, and that I was persuaded that men of sound heads and honest views needed nothing more than explanation and mutual understanding to enable them to unite in some measures which might enable us to get along.[28]

The solution to a political stalemate, Jefferson suggested, was the social informality of a dinner party.

At the ensuing dinner, Madison and Hamilton did indeed forge a compromise, Madison agreeing to tone down his opposition to assumption and secure votes for it, and Hamilton agreeing to support the relocation of the capital to the banks of the Potomac. Looking back on this dinner in later years, Jefferson declared it the single greatest regret of his life, ultimately denying all responsibility. He had taken "no part in it but an exhortatory one," he explained, claiming the deniability of a mere host. But given that such dinner parties were Jefferson's political modus operandi, such protestations become suspect, at best. Indeed, Jefferson was so self-consciously aware of the political implications of such private encounters that he kept a careful log of their proceedings, recording dinner conversations throughout his public life; in 1818, binding them together with his public papers, he presented them to posterity as a history of Washington's first term. Featured prominently in Jefferson's introductory essay were Hamilton's dinner party musings about corruption, to Jefferson, a vital insight into Hamilton's corrupt ways.[29]

Intended to incriminate his enemies, Jefferson's memoranda expose his masterful dinner table politicking as well. For example, on Janu-

---

[28]Jefferson, [Memorandum], 1792, *PTJ*, vol. 17 (Julian P. Boyd and Lucius Wilmerding, eds.), pp. 205–7. This account differs from Jefferson's later account of the dinner, in which he protected his friend James Madison's reputation by eliminating his role in the negotiation entirely, describing a dinner between Jefferson, Hamilton, and "a friend or two" (Jefferson, Feb. 4, 1818, introduction, *Anas*, p. 33). On the complexities of the Compromise of 1790, see Kenneth R. Bowling, *The Creation of Washington, D.C.* (Fairfax, Va., 1991), chap. 7; idem, "Dinner at Jefferson's: A Note on Jacob E. Cooke's 'The Compromise of 1790,'" *William and Mary Quarterly*, 3d ser. 28 (1971): 629–48; Jacob E. Cooke, "The Compromise of 1790," *William and Mary Quarterly*, 3d ser. 27 (1970):523–45; Norman K. Risjord, "Compromise of 1790: New Evidence on the Dinner Table Bargain," *William and Mary Quarterly*, 3d ser. 33 (1976):309–14.

[29]The quote is from Jefferson, Feb. 4, 1818, introduction, *Anas*, p. 34. On Jefferson's "Anas," see Freeman, "Slander, Poison, Whispers, and Fame"; *PTJ*, vol. 22 (Charles T. Cullen, Eugene R. Sheridan, Ruth W. Lester, eds.), pp. 33–38.

ary 2, 1792, he invited representatives Thomas Fitzsimons of Pennsylvania, Amassa Learned of Connecticut, and Elbridge Gerry of Massachusetts to dinner, along with several other guests. After everyone but the three congressmen had left, the conversation "turned" to "the subject of References by the legislature to the heads of departments," as Jefferson phrased it in a strategically indirect manner. The four men discussed the "mischief" inherent in Congress's ability to request reports from executive officers, leading Jefferson to note in a memorandum at evening's end that Gerry and Fitzsimons were "clearly opposed" to such references. Two days later, when the House referred a question to the secretary of the treasury, Jefferson noted on the same memorandum with some satisfaction, "Gerry and FitzSimmons opposed it." Two weeks later, Fitzsimons again opposed a reference to Hamilton, and Jefferson again took careful note of it on that same page. Finally, six weeks later, on March 7, Republicans in Congress broached the issue in earnest, arguing that the House was capable of doing its own business. After an animated debate, Hamilton's supporters prevailed. "Gerry changed sides" in favor of Hamilton, Jefferson observed, concluding, "On the whole it shewed that treasury influence was tottering."[30] His innocent dinner party was in truth a deliberate attempt to test and reinforce the sympathies of potential supporters in the House, the start of a campaign against Hamilton's congressional influence, documented in Jefferson's detailed memorandum.[31]

Jefferson was, indeed, simply talking with friends. Yet he was also engaged in a political discussion criticizing Hamilton's influence over the legislature — a discussion aimed at encouraging three representatives to vote along properly Republican lines. Thus, in the same way

---

[30]Jefferson, [Memorandum on References by Congress to Heads of Departments], [Mar. 10, 1792], *PTJ,* 23:246–48.

[31]John Trumbull describes another strategic Jeffersonian dinner party in 1793, during which Virginia Rep. William Branch Giles was given the opportunity to humiliate Trumbull as revenge for Trumbull's recent humiliation of Giles; at a tea party Trumbull had caught Giles pontificating to an unnamed woman about John Adams's "Defence of the Constitutions" and had tricked him into revealing that he had never read it. At Jefferson's "pay-back" dinner party, he supposedly smiled benignly as Giles attacked Trumbull, turning a deaf ear to Trumbull's appeal to his host for rescue (*The Autobiography of Colonel John Trumbull, Patriot-Artist, 1756–1843,* Theodore Sizer, ed. [1841; reprint ed., New Haven, 1953], pp. 173–75; Rufus Wilmot Griswold, *The Republican Court* [1867; reprint ed., New York, 1971], p. 396 n).

that Jefferson was justified in attacking Hamilton's command of a squadron of supporters, Hamilton had every right to accuse Jefferson of guiding a "formed party in the Legislature . . . bent upon my subversion."[32] To Hamilton, Jefferson's clandestine whisper campaign was dishonest, self-serving, and opposed to the principles of honest government. It was Jefferson's denial of his active politicking that so enraged Hamilton, leading him to brand Jefferson a hypocrite. As Hamilton wrote in the *Gazette of the United States* in September 1792, accusing Jefferson of attacking him indirectly through *National Gazette* editor Philip Freneau, "Mr. Jefferson has hitherto been distinguished as the quiet modest, retiring philosopher — as the plain simple unambitious republican. He shall not now for the first time be regarded as the intriguing incendiary — the aspiring turbulent competitor."[33]

In the same way that Jefferson could boast of his unwillingness to influence congressmen, Hamilton could pride himself on his candor and honesty in acknowledging that his political strategy sessions were, indeed, just that. Unlike Jefferson, when Hamilton wished to engage in a political discussion, he said so, explicitly. Compare Jefferson's masterfully indirect dinner with a similar dinner orchestrated by Hamilton. "I wish to have the advantage of a conversation with you," he wrote to Robert Morris in November 1790. "If you will name a day for taking a family dinner with me, I shall think it the best arrangement. . . . The chief subjects will be additional funds for public Debt and the Bank. Would you have any objection that Mr. Fitsimmons should be of the party?"[34]

Each man was most discomfited by the other's distinctive style of leadership: Hamilton distrusted Jefferson's indirection and secrecy, and Jefferson despised Hamilton's open command. Yet both were effecting the same purpose. Both were executive officers who wanted to advance a political agenda within Congress. And the practice was by no means limited to Jefferson and Hamilton. On several occasions even

---

[32]AH to Washington, Sept. 9, 1792, *PAH*, 12:348.

[33][AH], "Catullus III," *Gazette of the United States* (Philadephia), Sept. 29, 1792, ibid., 12:504.

[34]AH to Morris, Nov. 9, 1790, ibid., 7:146. Fitzsimons's presence is significant as well; a mere three days earlier he had offered his services to Hamilton. See Thomas Fitzsimons to AH, Nov. 6, 1790, ibid., 7:141; and Cooke, *Tench Coxe,* p. 171.

President Washington attempted to influence congressional votes through the persuasive efforts of his presidential staff. His use of Virginia Rep. James Madison as a wedge into Congress was so customary as to be considered routine.[35] Indeed, the entire cabinet sometimes engaged in such persuasion. For example, on April 2, 1792, disturbed at the implications inherent in a request by the House for executive department documents, the cabinet as a whole determined to "speak separately to the members of the [congressional] committee, and bring them by persuasion into the right channel." The cabinet decided to influence a congressional committee — a decision that Jefferson considered routine enough to merit only the briefest of mentions in one of his memoranda.[36] Clearly it was Hamilton's manner, not his methods, that so bothered his contemporaries. He issued commands — he had a congressional "system."

Jefferson's more indirect style of politicking enabled him to deny his influence in Congress even to himself. By drawing a distinction in his mind between private social functions and public business, he could host strategic dinner parties while upholding his stance of political detachment. Such intellectual line-drawing enabled him to denounce Hamilton for the very sins of which he himself was guilty. For example, in 1793 Jefferson drafted and revised a series of resolutions for Virginia Rep. William Branch Giles to present in the House — resolutions demanding a congressional investigation of Hamilton and his subsequent removal from office; though Jefferson envisioned himself as a passive observer of such partisan violence, his initial draft was venomous enough to require toning down by Giles.[37] Yet Jefferson was

---

[35]On the political activities of Washington's secretaries, see the entries for Apr. 4, 10, May 20, and June 14, 1790, in Bowling and Veit, *Maclay's Diary*, pp. 235–36, 240, 272–73, 291–93. On Madison's function as a congressional conduit, see, for example, AH to Washington, Apr. 8, 1794, *PAH*, 16:251; Washington to Madison, Apr. 30, May 5, 12, 17, 1789, Apr. 27, Dec. 2, 11, 12, 1790, *The Papers of George Washington*, Presidential Series, 6 vols. to date (Charlottesville, 1987–), vol. 2 (Dorothy Twohig, ed.), pp. 152–58, 216–17, 282, 314–15; vol. 5 (Dorothy Twohig, Mark A. Mastromarino, Jack D. Warren, Jr., eds.), pp. 349, 7:21, 59, 395–97. See also Kenneth R. Bowling, *Politics in the First Congress, 1789–1791* (New York, 1990), p. 245.

[36]Jefferson, [Memorandum], Apr. 2, 1792, *PTJ*, 23:262.

[37]Eugene R. Sheridan, "Thomas Jefferson and the Giles Resolutions," *William and Mary Quarterly*, 3d ser. 49 (1992):589–608; Thomas Jefferson, [Memorandum], Mar. 2, 1793, *Anas*, pp. 113–14; Mitchell, *Alexander Hamilton*, 2:306.

quick to attack such ghostwriting efforts among his Federalist foes. That same year, Jefferson denounced Hamilton for drafting a speech to be delivered in the House by South Carolina Rep. William Loughton Smith. "I am at no loss to ascribe Smith's speech to its true father," he wrote to Madison. "Every tittle of it is Hamilton's."[38]

Jefferson's indirection might have afforded him some peace of mind, but it could scarcely compete with Hamilton's energetic congressional campaigning. It was Hamilton's ability to marshal his forces quickly and quietly that enabled him to defeat the 1792 proposal to ban congressional references to executive officers—an idea championed by Madison and deliberately aimed at subverting Hamilton's power and influence. Informed of the threat the night before the final vote, Hamilton used "much industry" to influence key congressmen, as Jefferson phrased it, and won the field. In Hamilton's more colorful words:

> My overthrow was anticipated as certain and Mr. Madison, laying aside his wonted caution, boldly led his troops as he imagined to a certain victory. He was disappointed. Though, *late* I became apprized of the danger. Measures of counteraction were adopted, & when the Question was called, Mr. Madison was confounded to find characters voting against him, whom he had counted upon as certain.[39]

Hamilton's pride in his accomplishment almost leaps from the page.

Despite his most diligent efforts, however, Hamilton sometimes lost a congressional battle. Even the most ardent supporters could stray from the path, given reason. Men's loyalties shifted, their interest flagged, their friendships and enmities clouded their judgment. In 1795, for example, the House defeated parts of Hamilton's final plan for public credit, a failure he attributed to false friends who had abandoned the cause. Urging Rufus King to press the bill's adoption in its entirety in the Senate, he explained that it was his "wish [that] the true friends of public credit may be distinguished from its enemies" in a public forum. He voiced similar sentiments to Massachusetts Rep. The-

---

[38] Jefferson to Madison, Apr. 3, 1794, *The Papers of James Madison*, 17 vols. to date (Charlottesville, 1962–), vol. 15 (Thomas A. Mason, Robert A. Rutland, and Jeanne K. Sisson, eds.), pp. 301–2. For discussion of Hamilton's authorship of Smith's speech, see *PAH*, 13:407; Mitchell, *Alexander Hamilton*, 2:502–3.

[39] AH to Edward Carrington, May 26, 1792, *PAH*, 11:433.

odore Sedgwick. "Let the yeas and nays separate the wheat from the chaff," he exclaimed. "I may otherwise have to feel the distress of wounding a friend by a shaft levelled at an enemy."[40] As Hamilton's comments make clear, roll call votes were clarifying moments that differentiated friends from enemies by forcing politicians to declare their loyalties.

Congressional elections served the same purpose; they separated the wheat from the chaff, friends from enemies, and forged new political friendships in the process. For this reason, the 1792 elections were particularly important. Convinced by early spring that there was a "formed party in the Legislature . . . bent upon my subversion," Hamilton well recognized that his success in office, as well as his reputation and career, rested on his ability to preserve his influence in Congress.[41] He thus initiated a nationwide campaign in support of Federalist candidates, justifying his actions by the urgency of the crisis at hand. As he explained to North Carolina Rep. John Steele, the results of these elections would "either anchor the Government in safety or set it afloat."[42] In letter after letter he apologized for intervening in congressional elections. "Let me not be thought to travel out of my sphere," he wrote to South Carolinian Charles C. Pinckney as he did just that.[43]

To effect his purpose, Hamilton made use of his national prestige and influence, publicly sanctioning his preferred candidates by word-of-mouth endorsements and in letters written explicitly for circulation.[44] Focused most intently on electoral contests in Maryland, North Carolina, and South Carolina — states with equivocal political leanings — he asked for "means to be used" to secure the candidacy and election of specific supporters, or solicited support for them himself. In New York, Pennsylvania, and Virginia, where Hamilton had friends and allies, he made his preferences known by declaring them.[45] He also

---

[40]AH to Rufus King, Feb. 21, 1795, ibid., 17:278–81; AH to Theodore Sedgwick, Feb. 18, 1795, ibid., 17:277–78.

[41]AH to Washington, Sept. 9, 1792, ibid., 12:348.

[42]AH to John Steele, Oct. 15, 1792, ibid., 12:569.

[43]AH to Charles Cotesworth Pinckney, Oct. 10, 1792, ibid., 12:544.

[44]See, for example, AH to David Ross, Sept. 26, 1792, ibid., 12:490–92.

[45]See, for example, AH to Charles Cotesworth Pinckney, Oct. 10, 1792, ibid., 12:543–44; AH to John Steele, Oct. 15, 1792, ibid., 12:567–69; AH to David Ross, Sept. 26, 1792, ibid., 12:490–92; James McHenry to AH, Sept. 20, 1792, ibid., 12:406–

asked friends to transmit campaign promises to more distant reaches of the union, for example, asking Gen. William Irvine to tell his friends in the Northwest Territory that Hamilton favored the taking of the Mississippi from Spain by force. According to Clerk of the House and ardent Republican John Beckley, Hamilton had spoken with Irvine "in seeming confidence," assuming a guise of secrecy with full knowledge that Irvine would be sure to spread such confidential and thus important information.[46] Hamilton was especially active in Virginia, in his mind the fount of Republican sentiment: he made known his support of Federalist Richard Henry Lee, spent much time "closetted" with Virginians Arthur Lee, Francis Corbin, and William Heth, and even contemplated a trip to Virginia himself. According to Beckley, "thro' the agency of one or more of those closetted friends," Hamilton's "secret workings" could be felt "*even in the Virga. Legislature.*"[47]

It is difficult to determine the precise influence of Hamilton's electioneering efforts. As important as immediate electoral results, however, were the organizational implications of Hamilton's nationwide campaign. By suggesting that his correspondents were part of a nationwide effort to defeat the enemies of good government, he galvanized his supporters and transformed his informal network of friends into a national political alliance. As Beckley explained to Madison, far more effective than Hamilton's newspaper forays were his efforts to urge "a private and united influence of his friends thro' the States."[48]

The harvesting of supporters was a difficult and time-consuming activity, complicated by the intricacies of local politics and the ability

---

7. On New York, Pennsylvania, and Virginia, see AH to Rufus King, Sept. 23, 1792, ibid., 12:415–16; AH to unknown correspondent, Sept. 21, 1792, ibid., 12:408; AH to Washington, Sept. 23, 1792, ibid., 12:418–19; AH to unknown correspondent, Sept. 26, 1792, ibid., 12:480–81; John Beckley to Madison, Sept. 2 and Oct. 17, 1792, *Madison Papers,* vol. 14 (Robert A. Rutland, Thomas A. Mason, Robert J. Brugger, Jeanne K. Sisson, and Fredrika J. Teute, eds.), pp. 354–58, 383–86.

[46]John Beckley to Madison, Sept. 10, 1792, *Madison Papers,* 14:361–63. For an account of Republican Clerk of the House John Beckley's friendship with Irvine, see Edmund Berkeley and Dorothy Smith Berkeley, *John Beckley: Zealous Partisan in a Nation Divided* (Philadelphia, 1973), pp. 67–68.

[47]Beckley to Madison, Sept. 2 and Oct. 17, 1792, *Madison Papers,* 14:354–58, 383–86. On Hamilton's plans to visit Virginia, see AH to Washington, Sept. 9, 1792, Syrett and Cooke, *PAH,* 12:347–50.

[48]Beckley to Madison, Sept. 10, 1792, *Madison Papers,* 14:361–63. See also Sept. 2, 1792, ibid., 14: 354–58.

to act only through agents. Travel was slow and the mails were unreliable, making communication with state organizers difficult. Yet such support was vital for Hamilton, as for any national politician with an agenda. The appearance of local support for a proposal had great influence on legislators both local and national who looked to the body politic to determine public opinion, and on a more personal level, to return them to office. With the support and guidance of the local political elite, a national politician could shape the course of local debate, influence local electoral contests, and in so doing affect the membership of both the state and national legislatures.

Like other national politicians, Hamilton relied on a nationwide network of friends, their support secured by the unspoken assumption that it earned them the reciprocal support and influence of their high-placed political chief.[49] Typically, he had one or two "particular friends" in a state whose job it was to marshal support, disseminate favorable newspaper essays and pamphlets, convert the unconverted, and prevent supporters from straying from the path. In Maryland, James McHenry was one of Hamilton's agents, a close friend from their days together in the army as Washington's aides.[50] Maryland Rep. Samuel Smith, South Carolina Rep. William Loughton Smith, and New York Sen. Philip Schuyler served a similar purpose in their respective states. As these last three examples suggest, Hamilton's agents were sometimes congressmen who could cross the bounds between state and national politics with ease.

William Loughton Smith was particularly active on Hamilton's behalf. Not only did he influence the local political elite, but he also had great interest in the political leanings of the southern backcountry. On at least one occasion he toured the far reaches of South Carolina and Georgia to determine and sway local political sentiment, reporting his findings to Hamilton in detail. Smith chatted with people he met on the street or in taverns, offering Federalist pamphlets, news-

---

[49]See, for example, William Heth to AH, Feb. 29, 1792, Syrett and Cooke, *PAH*, 11:62–63; AH to William Heth, ibid., Jan. 25, 1791, 7:452–54; John Lamb to AH, Jan. 1791, ibid., 7:613–14.

[50]See, for example, James McHenry to AH, Aug. 16 and Sept. 20, 1792, Syrett and Cooke, *PAH*, 11:212–14, 12:406–7. On James McHenry, see Bernard C. Steiner, *The Life and Correspondence of James McHenry* (Cleveland, 1907).

papers, and conversation wherever he went. Because he was a congressman — a rare sight on the frontier — his opinions were invariably respected. To identify those who had strayed from the Federalist path, he looked for men reading the Republican *National Gazette.* In one case, spying the paper on a farmer's mantel, he expressed shock at discovering something so reprehensibly partisan in a seemingly decent household. He left behind a copy of the "liberal" national newspaper, the Federalist *Gazette of the United States,* confident, he later explained to Hamilton, that his "stay . . . will have not been without some benefit." Spotting a man on the street reading the "wrong" newspaper, Smith likewise offered him the Federalist *Gazette,* later assuring Hamilton that "before I left him, he was quite one of us."[51] In the early republic's small-scale, localized political realm, such individual conversions might mean the difference between victory and defeat.

Though Hamilton had regular correspondents throughout the states, any like-minded man of influence was a potential agent. For example, in 1795 he asked Christopher Gore, federal attorney in Massachusetts, to influence the votes of Massachusetts Rep. Benjamin Goodhue and Sen. Caleb Strong.[52] Other friends were quick to inform him about hostile whisper campaigns and political attacks, keeping a particularly close eye on congressmen.[53] When someone of unknown loyalties won a seat in Congress, friends offered detailed descriptions of his character, politics, and interests. For example, Sedgwick expressed concern about the political loyalties of newly elected Massachusetts Rep. William Lyman. Lyman was a Federalist at present, Sedgwick warned, but "I hope Neglect will not make him otherwise" — thereby alerting Hamilton to take special care to secure his support.[54] Similarly, in 1793, Rep. John Steele reported on North Carolina's

---

[51]William Loughton Smith to AH, Apr. 24, 1793, Syrett and Cooke, *PAH,* 14:338–41.

[52]Christopher Gore to AH, Apr. 20, 1795, ibid., 17:331–32. For similar state interference on Hamilton's part, see also AH to Henry Lee, Sept. 2, 1794, ibid., 17:173–74.

[53]John Page to AH, Mar. 22, 1792, ibid., 11:169–70. See also William Heth to AH, Nov. 11, 1791, ibid., 9:511–13; James Watson to AH, Aug. 30, 1793, ibid., 15:311–12; David Ross to AH, [Aug. 30, 1793], ibid., 15:309–10; Rufus King's comments about Charles Carroll and Robert Barnwell's comments about Virginia Rep. William Branch Giles, as detailed in AH to Edward Carrington, May 26, 1792, ibid., 11:436; Uriah Forrest to AH, Nov. 7, 1792, ibid., 13:23–24. On Hamilton's network of Virginia informants and friends, see also John Jay to AH, June 24, 1793, ibid., 15:20.

[54]Theodore Sedgwick to AH, Aug. 26, 1793, ibid., 15:285–86.

newly elected congressmen, "as it is certainly important that a man in your situation should know what sort of Materials he has the misfortune to work with."[55]

In his strategic use of political friends, Hamilton differed from his peers in manner more than method; he was bold and direct when others were hesitant. Far different—and thus more threatening—was his use of Treasury Department subordinates. The department was the largest in the government by far; by 1801, it employed over half of the total civilian government personnel.[56] Supported by a staff of hundreds of customs officials and revenue officers, it had influence in every city and section of the country, touching on commerce, land ownership, finance, and the mails. Secretary Hamilton thus had at his disposal an organized network of political friends incorporated into the government's very infrastructure, a cadre of public men commissioned to report on state affairs. Their names appear throughout Hamilton's correspondence, the sources of local news and gossip, an advance warning system about hidden enemies and brewing plots. This national web of influence enabled Hamilton to wage a coordinated national campaign against his foes: to transmit and collect information, to monitor and influence electoral campaigns, and, ultimately, to fill the House and Senate with loyal supporters who owed him allegiance for helping them obtain office. An ingeniously indirect means of furthering his goals, Hamilton's organized network of agents raised troubling questions about the nation's federal system of government— about the ability of the states to preserve their autonomy and the ability of Congress to resist the directive force of the national executive.

The efficiency and impact of Hamilton's network are evident in his response to two 1790 resolutions and the memorial based on it from the General Assembly of Virginia. Denouncing the assumption of state debts as "repugnant to the Constitution of the United States," the resolutions lashed out against the concept of implied powers and suggested that states had the right to declare acts of Congress unconstitutional. With the assistance of an unnamed Virginian—probably John

---

[55]John Steele to AH, Apr. 30, 1793, ibid., 14:358–60. See also James Tillery to AH, Jan. 1791, ibid., 7:614–16; William Heth to AH, June 14, 1793, ibid., 14:544–45.

[56]White, *The Federalists*, p. 123. See also table 4 in Carl E. Prince, *The Federalists and the Origins of the U.S. Civil Service* (New York, 1977), p. 278.

Hopkins, Virginia's commissioner of loans — Hamilton had the resolutions in his hands within a week of their passage, enabling him to plan a hasty counterattack.[57] He first sent copies to Chief Justice John Jay; declaring them "the first symptom of a spirit which must either be killed or will kill the constitution of the United States," Hamilton suggested that the "collective weight of the different parts of the [national] Government . . . be employed in exploding the principles they contain." Jay responded to Hamilton's "sudden & indigested thought" with caution.[58] Hoping to set a precedent, Hamilton probably also helped secure a quick response to a Pennsylvania memorial petitioning Congress to amend the Funding Act; in the course of the ensuing debate, Hamilton's father-in-law, Philip Schuyler, played a key role in passing a Senate resolution against changing the funding system. Such efforts proved successful: both houses of Congress tabled the Virginia memorial.[59]

As the national center of this political force, Hamilton consulted primarily with his chief officers — collectors of customs in major cities and high-ranking revenue officials. These men, in turn, had their own networks of influence, peopled by local merchants, political elites, and their own subordinate treasury officials. Thus in 1793, eager to counter the influence of the Virginia campaign to remove him from office, Hamilton turned to Virginia's supervisor of the revenue, Edward Carrington, among others, aware that Carrington could influence his merchant friends and the local gentry.[60] Coxe, friend to Philadelphia's

---

[57]The editors of the First Federal Congress papers suggest Hopkins as Hamilton's source, based on the fact that he later sent the Treasury Department a copy of Virginia's Dec. 16, 1790, draft memorial on the same topic (*DHFFC*, 8:270). On the Virginia resolutions and memorial in general, see ibid., 8:270–71, 298–301.

[58]AH to John Jay, Dec. 13, 1790; Jay to AH, Nov. 28, 1790, Syrett and Cooke, *PAH*, 7:149–50, 166–67. As an additional response to the threatening Virginia resolutions, Hamilton's suggestions for Washington's second annual message to Congress are worth noting; among other things, he suggested that Washington note the growing public approbation for the national government and the obviation of any "symptom of discontent which may have appeared in particular places respecting particular measures" ([Notes of Objects for Consideration of the President,] [Dec. 1, 1790], ibid., 7:172–73).

[59]The editors of the First Federal Congress papers suggest that Hamilton and friends, anxious about the looming threat of Virginia's resolutions, urged a quick Senate response to Pennsylvania's complaint about the funding system (*DHFFC*, 8:271).

[60]Edward Carrington to AH, Feb. 14, Mar. 26, Apr. 26, July 2, 1793, Syrett and Cooke, *PAH*, 14:80–81, 247–48, 346–52, 15:50–52.

wealthy and powerful, also proved helpful, as in July 1790 when he identified Charles Pettit as Pennsylvania's foremost opponent to Hamilton's funding plan and suggested a means of converting him.[61] Hamilton used the officers of the Bank of the United States to similar purpose, asking them to urge their friends to support Federalist candidates for Congress.[62] Other Treasury Department informants included Massachusetts customs collector Benjamin Lincoln, Rhode Island customs collector Jeremiah Olney, and Virginia customs collector William Heth. The ever-vigilant John Beckley had good reason to brand Hamilton's staff "an Organized System of Espionage thro' the medium of Revenue Officers."[63]

Ever eager to strike a blow at his Virginian adversaries, Hamilton was particularly interested in Heth's observations and activities. In August of 1792 the Virginia customs collector visited Philadelphia and, as he noted in his diary, had "several private interviews" with Hamilton during which they "spoke confidentially on several . . . subjects."[64] Beckley took careful note of these meetings, warning Madison that Heth had "been a good deal closetted with" Hamilton. A chat with Heth revealed at least one of their topics of conversation. Heth informs me, Beckley told Madison, "that Mr: H.[amilton] unequivocally declares, that yo. are his personal and political enemy" — a declaration of open warfare that Hamilton had deliberately asked Heth to transmit to Madison.[65] It was Heth who informed Hamilton about the ill will harbored by Baltimore customs collector Otho Holland Williams, the political temper in Virginia after the defeat of Giles's accusatory resolutions, Coxe's questionable loyalty, and a suspected leak in the Treasury Department.[66]

---

[61]Tench Coxe to AH, July 10, 1790, ibid., 6:490–91. See also Tench Coxe to AH, July 9, 1790, ibid., 6:486–88.

[62]William Seton to AH, Feb. 3, 1791, ibid., 8:4–5.

[63]Beckley to Tench Coxe, Jan. 24, 1800, in *Justifying Jefferson: The Political Writings of John James Beckley,* ed. Gerard W. Gawalt (Washington, D.C., 1995), pp. 164–65; also Cooke, *Tench Coxe,* p. 372 n. 3.

[64]William Heth, diary, Aug. 31, 1792, William Heth Papers, Library of Congress.

[65]Beckley to Madison, Sept. 2, 1792, *Madison Papers,* 14:354–58; AH to Edward Carrington, May 26, 1792, Syrett and Cooke, *PAH,* 11:444–45.

[66]Heth to AH, Nov. 20, 1791, ibid., 9:511–13; Heth to AH, July 6, 1794, ibid., 16:570–72. See also Heth, diary, Aug. 31, 1792, June 14, 1793, William Heth Papers, Library of Congress.

Perhaps Hamilton's most active state agent was Virginian Edward Carrington, a loyal political lieutenant with important friends such as Washington, Madison, and Jefferson. Messages passed through Carrington reached some of Madison's and Jefferson's most powerful supporters, and some of Washington's most trusted advisers. Well aware of the significance of his actions, Carrington was tireless in his campaigning. He was particularly active in 1793 after the House found Hamilton innocent of misconduct. Virginians had conceived, drafted, and delivered the accusatory Giles resolutions; their defeat provided Hamilton with a golden opportunity to reveal the corruption of his foes to their own constituents. He asked Carrington to publish news of his clearance in "the most public and generally circulating paper" in several cities in Virginia, and to circulate copies of his statement of self-defense; Carrington likewise mentioned his private knowledge of Hamilton's innocence whenever possible.[67] To Carrington, such campaigning did more than salvage Hamilton's reputation, for by circulating among the state's political elite as Hamilton's "particular friend," he won himself influence and acclaim. As Heth reported to Hamilton in 1794, Carrington was now lauded with toasts at public events while Giles was all but ignored.[68]

Republican John Beckley both admired and feared Hamilton's coordinated campaigning; as he wrote to Madison in September 1792, "with . . . a subtle and contriving mind, and a soul devoted to his object, all his measures are promptly and aptly designed, and like the links of a chain, dependent on each other, acquire additional strength by their union and concord."[69] But Beckley's observations did not go unheeded. For even as he noted the effectiveness of Hamilton's network of friends, he helped to create a Republican equivalent. That same month, he traveled to New York to meet with the state's leading

---

[67]For example, see Edward Carrington to AH, Feb. 15, Mar. 26, and July 2, 1793, Syrett and Cooke, *PAH,* 14:80–81, 247–48, 15:50–52.

[68]Heth to AH, July 6, 1794, ibid., 16:570–72.

[69]Beckley to Madison, Oct. 17, 1792, *Madison Papers,* 14:383–86. On John Beckley, see Jeffrey L. Pasley, " 'A Journeyman, Either in Law or Politics': John Beckley and the Social Origins of Political Campaigning," *Journal of the Early Republic* 16 (1996):531–69; idem, " 'Artful and Designing Men': Political Professionalism in the Early American Republic, 1775–1820," Ph.D. diss., Harvard University, 1993, 2:164; Berkeley and Berkeley, *John Beckley;* Gawalt, *Justifying Jefferson.*

Republicans and encourage a joint campaign. He made similar efforts in Pennsylvania. Jefferson's and Madison's famed 1791 "botanical" trip to northern climes was born of similar motives. Although they protested that the trip was purely for pleasure and innocent of political purpose, their dinners with New Yorkers Aaron Burr and the powerful George Clinton suggest otherwise. Indeed, as revealed in Jefferson's memoranda, beginning in 1792, a continual stream of incriminations against Hamilton flowed from New York to Philadelphia, the national political center. Such organized personal coalition building proved highly effective, for the Republicans made great gains nationwide in the congressional elections held two months later.

Hamilton's mistake was thus not in his instinctive efforts at organization, nor in his ability to influence politicians on local and national levels. Indeed, Republicans eventually surpassed Federalists on both counts; Jefferson, in particular, gave full scope to his masterfully subtle influence over Congress as president when his innocent dinner parties became a means to instruct and direct a cadre of congressional agents.[70] Rather, Hamilton's crucial error was one of principle, not practice — an error that he himself recognized after Jefferson's presidential victory. In forging his network of agents and "particular friends," Hamilton made manifest in American public life what he had only suggested at Jefferson's dinner table in 1791; he demonstrated the efficiency and practicality of what Jefferson termed government by corruption. But he had corrupted the wrong people. The Federalists "have neglected the cultivation of popular favour," he ruefully admitted in 1802. To win political victories, they would have to learn from their opponents; as he put it, they would have to "unite in corrupting public opinion."[71]

---

[70]Young, *Washington Community,* pp. 167–70; Noble Cunningham, *The Jeffersonian Republicans in Power* (Chapel Hill, 1963).

[71]AH to James A. Bayard, Apr. 16–21, 1802, Syrett and Cooke, *PAH,* 25:605–10.

John Ferling

"Father and Protector"

*President John Adams and Congress
in the Quasi-War Crisis*

JOHN ADAMS (fig. 1) was nervous and expectant on the morning of his inauguration, March 4, 1797. He received the Massachusetts congressional delegation at his lodging, and just before noon he entered his handsome new carriage — the first he had ever owned, and his initial purchase with the twenty-five-thousand-dollar annual salary provided the president of the United States. He rode to Congress Hall, a two-story structure on Chestnut Street, just west of the Pennsylvania State House, where Congress had met during much of the Revolutionary War. Adams wore a pearl gray broadcloth suit, a matching cockade, and a sword strapped to his side. Servants dressed in livery accompanied him.

The president-elect was escorted into the House chamber on the lower floor of Congress Hall just before noon. Thomas Jefferson, who had already been sworn in as the new vice president of the United States and president of the Senate, was present and presiding. Moments later President George Washington, dressed solemnly in black, entered the hall. After the congressmen and spectators cheered loudly for the outgoing president, a hush fell over the assemblage and every eye turned toward the dais, occupied only by Washington, Adams, and Jefferson. Jefferson, attired in a long blue frock coat, his hair powdered in a queue and tied with a black ribbon, rose and introduced Adams.

FIG. 1. *John Adams,* by Gilbert
Stuart, 1815. *(Courtesy National
Gallery of Art, gift of Mrs. Robert
Homans)*

So unnerved was the incoming president that he felt faint and feared
he might not be able to read his speech.[1]

However, Adams overcame his anxiety and delivered the inaugural
address. It was brief and devoid of rhythmic rhetoric or rhapsodic
phrases, but he enunciated a clear theme. He warned that the greatest
threat to the union came from the possibility that European courts
might influence public opinion, fostering a "spirit of intrigue" and
malevolent party divisions that could destroy the new nation. Above all
else, Adams added, he would seek to preserve the neutrality of the
United States and keep it out of the widening European war, a con-
flagration that had been touched off five years before by the French
Revolution.[2]

[1]John Adams to Abigail Adams, Mar. 17, 1797, Adams Family Papers, Massachusetts
Historical Society, microfilm edition, reel 383; John Ferling, *The First of Men: A Life of
George Washington* (Knoxville, 1988), p. 484; Dumas Malone, *Thomas Jefferson,* 6 vols.
(New York, 1948–81), 3:297; Richard S. Miller, "The Federal City: 1783–1808," in
Philadelphia: A 300-Year History, ed. Russell F. Weigley (New York, 1982), pp. 172–74.

[2]John Adams, Inaugural Address, Mar. 4, 1797, James D. Richardson, ed., *A Compila-
tion of the Messages and Papers of the Presidents,* 20 vols. (New York, 1897–1917), 1:218–22.

Curiously, Adams took the oath of office after he completed his speech. Thereafter, Washington congratulated him, his visage as bright and sunny, Adams thought, as was this mild, cheerful winter day. Adams also thought the retiring president's manner appeared to say: "Ah! I am fairly out and you fairly in! See which of us will be the happiest." Adams knew the answer to Washington's imaginary query. He knew, as he soon remarked, that he had assumed "an office of hard labor and Severe duty."[3]

Indeed, Adams would face a difficult presidency. It was his misfortune to be president during an era of bitter contention and anxiety, what historians now agree was an "Age of Passion." Like the 1850s or the 1960s, the 1790s was a time of ferocious intensity and emotion, of conspiratorial ravings, apocalyptic visions, and threatened and actual political violence. Jefferson said the period was "afflicting to peaceable minds." President Adams thought it a time when emotions reached a "bitter, nauseous, and unwholesome" level. It was a feverish decade when Americans grappled with the legacy of their recent Revolution, including how best to define the character of their newly embraced republicanism. Moreover, all knew that the choices they made would be difficult to alter in the future, for as George Washington had warned at the outset of the decade, policies and institutions tend to become inviolable when "confirmed by habit."[4]

In addition, Adams's party, the Federalist party, was deeply divided even before he took office. Some within the party had not wanted Adams to succeed President Washington. A faction led by Alexander Hamilton, formerly the secretary of the treasury in Washington's ad-

[3]Adams to Abigail Adams, Mar. 5, 1797, Charles Francis Adams, ed., *Letters of John Adams Addressed to His Wife*, 2 vols. (Boston, 1841), 2:244; Adams to Abigail Adams, Mar. 17, 1797, Adams Family Papers, reel 383; Adams to Richard Cranch, Mar. 25, 1797, ibid., reel 117.

[4]Thomas Jefferson to Edward Rutledge, June 24, 1797, Paul Leicester Ford, ed., *Writings of Thomas Jefferson*, 10 vols. (New York, 1892–99), 7:155; Adams to Abigail Adams, Jan. 20, 1796, Adams, *Letters of John Adams Addressed to His Wife*, 2:191; George Washington to Adams, May 10, 1789, *Papers of George Washington: Presidential Series*, 7 vols. to date (Charlottesville, 1987–), vol. 2 (Dorothy Twohig, ed.), p. 247. On the fervor and turbulence of the 1790s, see Marshall Smelser, "The Federalist Period as an Age of Passion," *American Quarterly* 10 (1958):391–419; and John R. Howe, Jr., "Republican Thought and the Political Violence of the 1790s," *American Quarterly* 19 (1967):148–65.

FIG. 2. *Abigail Adams,* by
Gilbert Stuart, 1800. *(Courtesy
Massachusetts Historical Society)*

ministration, had conspired in 1796 to elect Thomas Pinckney of
South Carolina, who together with Adams was the party nominee selected by the Federalist caucus. Fearing Adams's independence, Hamilton and his followers preferred Pinckney, whom they believed could
be easily manipulated. The conspirators not only failed but were also
unable to keep their machinations secret. In the course of the campaign Adams told his wife, Abigail (fig. 2), that Hamilton was responsible for "maneuvers and combinations" against him. When he took
the oath of office, Adams knew that he was more popular with many
members of the Republican party than he was with one wing of his own
party. In fact, in the same letter in which he informed his wife of
Hamilton's plotting, Adams reported that the opposition was un-
dismayed by his election and informed her of a Virginia Republican
who had observed that "the old man [Adams] will make a good
President."[5]

---

[5]Adams to Abigail Adams, Charles Francis Adams, ed., *The Works of John Adams,
Second President of the United States: With a Life of the Author,* 10 vols. (Boston, 1850–56),
1:455–56, hereafter *Works;* John Ferling, *John Adams: A Life* (Knoxville, 1992), p. 330;
James Roger Sharp, *American Politics in the Early Republic: The New Nation in Crisis* (New

The optimism concerning Adams's prospects stemmed from a widely shared belief among contemporaries that he was a man of extraordinary learning as well as an experienced politician who had been an especially effective member of the Continental Congress between 1774 and 1777. However, many viewed him as a vain and irascible individual who sometimes acted impulsively, even imprudently. Almost everyone viewed him as resolute and independent, and before he took office some in both parties remarked on his "headstrong" character.[6]

Adams came to the presidency without prior executive experience, but he had been in public life for twenty-five years. He had served one term in the Massachusetts legislature and four years in the Continental Congress, where he quickly emerged as a leading figure. After one year in the Continental Congress, Adams had become the "first man in the house," according to one observer. He served on more than sixty committees; chaired the board of war, perhaps Congress's most important panel during the War of Independence; and led the forces fighting for independence. His colleague Jefferson called him a legislative "Colossus" and Congressman Richard Stockton of New Jersey referred to Adams as "the Atlas of Independence." Adams served abroad as a diplomat during the ten years that followed his resignation from Congress in late 1777. He returned home to serve two terms as vice president under Washington. As a congressman, Adams had to work in concert with others; but as an isolated diplomat in faraway Europe, he had been compelled to make heavy and lonely decisions without consultation. Adams had grown accustomed to working by himself.[7]

It was perhaps Adams's lack of executive experience that led him into an immediate and remarkable blunder that would dramatically

---

Haven, 1993), pp. 147–49; Page Smith, "Election of 1796," in *History of American Presidential Elections, 1789–1968,* ed. Arthur M. Schlesinger, Jr., 4 vols. (New York, 1971), 1:57–98.

    [6]On Adams's character, see Peter Shaw, *The Character of John Adams* (Chapel Hill, 1976) and Joseph J. Ellis, *Passionate Sage: The Character and Legacy of John Adams* (New York, 1993). On the "headstrong" characterization, see Ralph Adams Brown, *The Presidency of John Adams* (Lawrence, Kans., 1975), p. 18; and Ellis, *Passionate Sage,* p. 28.

    [7]Shaw, Character of John Adams, p. 95; George W. Conner, ed., *The Autobiography of Benjamin Rush: His "Travels Through Life" together with his Commonplace Book for 1789–1813* (Philadelphia, 1948), p. 140; John Hazelton, *The Declaration of Independence: Its History* (New York, 1906), pp. 161–62.

haunt his presidency. In what he later acknowledged to have been his greatest mistake as president, Adams asked the members of Washington's cabinet to remain in office. Adams subsequently claimed that he had shrunk from removing these individuals from fear of splitting the Federalist party, but the contemporary evidence suggests that he was unaware of the peril to which he was opening himself. Others understood what Adams failed to grasp. Several of the cabinet officers were more loyal to Hamilton than to the chief executive. Jefferson intuitively saw what Adams had brought on himself. The "Hamiltonians who surround him are only a little less hostile to him than to me," the vice president remarked soon after Adams took office.[8]

Three of his four cabinet officers would add to Adams's woes. Timothy Pickering, the secretary of state, was rigid, humorless, austere, and a Francophobe who imagined that Jacobins lurked everywhere. If Pickering was sour and almost universally disliked, even hated, James McHenry, the secretary of war, was amicable and companionable. Born in Ireland and raised in Baltimore, McHenry had fought in the Continental Army, briefly practiced medicine, and served for several years in the Maryland legislature. The secretary of the treasury, Oliver Wolcott, Jr., was twenty-five years younger than Adams. He had practiced law in Connecticut before becoming auditor and later comptroller under Washington's first treasury secretary, Hamilton. These three exhibited very different temperaments and capabilities but shared one common attribute. Each admired Hamilton virtually to the point of subservience. Each was willing to share administration secrets with Hamilton, each solicited his advice, each was swayed by his counsel, and each eagerly sought to persuade Adams to embrace their — which is to say, Hamilton's — program.[9]

Adams may have lacked executive experience, but he had devoted

---

[8]Adams to Benjamin Rush, Aug. 23, 1804, Jan. 6, 1806, Apr. 22, 1812, John A. Schutz and Douglass Adair, eds., *The Spur of Fame: Dialogues of John Adams and Benjamin Rush, 1805–1813* (San Marino, Calif., 1966), pp. 36, 46, 214; Jefferson to Elbridge Gerry, May 13, 1797, Ford, *Writings of Jefferson*, 7:120.

[9]For excellent brief descriptions of Pickering, McHenry, and Wolcott, as well as Adams's more loyal attorney general, Charles Lee, and Benjamin Stoddert, who headed the newly created Department of the Navy midway through Adams's presidency, see Stanley Elkins and Eric McKitrick, *The Age of Federalism: The Early American Republic, 1788–1800* (New York, 1993), pp. 623–31, 634–35.

considerable thought to issues of governance. Among subsequent presidents, perhaps only Jefferson and James Madison had given as much thought to political theory before entering the presidency, and no other president's conduct in office was shaped to a greater degree by his philosophy of government. Adams had long been esteemed for his expertise in the science of politics. His colleagues in Congress had thought him the most knowledgeable member in that regard and turned to him for guidance as the states drafted their first constitutions in 1776.[10] In 1779 the Massachusetts Constitutional Convention availed itself of Adams's talents; he was the principal author of the state's initial constitution. During the next dozen years he wrote two tracts on political science: *A Defence of the Constitutions of the United States of America,* a three-volume tome, and "Discourses on Davila," a series of newspaper essays.[11]

The core of his outlook remained unaltered over the years. Adams never wavered from the view that ultimate power resided with the people and that internal governmental powers must be divided between a bicameral legislature and a chief executive. The "mystery" of government, he once remarked, could be solved by the simple realization that power "must be opposed to power, force to force, strength to strength, interest to interest."[12]

---

[10]Adams to John Penn, [ante Mar. 27, 1776], *Papers of John Adams*, 10 vols. to date (Cambridge, Mass., 1977), vol. 4 (Robert J. Taylor, ed.), pp. 78–84, hereafter *PJA*; [John Adams], *Thoughts on Government*, ibid., 4:86–93; "The Massachusetts Constitution," Oct. 28–31, 1779, ibid., 8:228–71.

[11]The *Defence of the Constitutions of Government of the United States of America* can be found in Adams, *Works*, 4:271, 6:220. All but the final essay in Adams's "Discourses on Davila" were reprinted in ibid., 6:227–403; for the final essay see the original source, *Gazette of the United States* (Philadelphia), Apr. 27, 1791.

[12]John Howe, *The Changing Political Thought of John Adams* (Princeton, 1966), pp. 84–94, 165–92; Adrienne Koch, *Power, Morals, and the Founding Fathers* (Ithaca, 1961), p. 82; Adams, *Thoughts on Government*, *PJA*, 4:87; Adams, *Works*, 4:290; Adams, "Davila," ibid., 6:257. On Adams's political philosophy, also see Edward Handler, *America and Europe in the Political Thought of John Adams* (Cambridge, Mass., 1964); Zoltan Haraszti, *John Adams and the Prophets of Progress* (Cambridge, Mass., 1952); Stephen G. Kurtz, "The Political Science of John Adams: A Guide to His Statecraft," *William and Mary Quarterly*, 3d ser. 25 (1968):605–13; Bruce Miroff, "John Adams: Merit, Fame, and Political Leadership," *Journal of Politics* 48 (1986):116–32; George A. Peek, "John Adams and the Nature of Men and Government," *Michigan Alumnus Quarterly Review* 58 (1951):70–76; Randall B. Ripley, "Adams, Burke and Eighteenth Century Conservatism," *Political Science Quarterly* 80 (1965):216–35; Clinton Rossiter, "Homage to John

However, Adams's views concerning the role of the executive changed dramatically after 1776 and would have profound ramifications for his presidency, eventually even shaping his conduct in that office. While Adams in 1776 had favored a stronger executive than had most of his contemporaries, he assumed the legislature would be the dominant branch in government. This was especially true in America, which had a long history of popularly elected assemblies that made the laws and controlled the public finances. Nevertheless, at the time of independence, Adams had urged the presence of a strong executive in every polity, an official who might be permitted "a free and independent Exercise of his Judgment" as a balance against the legislative branch.[13]

Adams never wavered in his commitment to balanced government, but the self-serving behavior of his countrymen during the War of Independence, as well as Shays's Rebellion in Massachusetts in 1786 and the trauma of the French Revolution, which turned dark and bloody in the early 1790s, led him to rethink some earlier ideas. In 1776, naively believing in the homogeneity of American society, he had written that it was possible for a legislative body to be "an exact portrait of the people at large." By the 1790s he had come to believe that his country was dividing, as the nations in Europe long ago had done, into two classes: "the rich, the well-born and the able" and the remainder of the citizenry. Furthermore, he now believed that at the national level the Senate was, or soon would be, the bastion of what he called the aristocracy, and the House of Representatives was, and was likely to remain, the voice of democracy.[14]

Adams was hardly the only American in the 1790s to take note of this development. Most articulate Americans feared the licentiousness of the "lower sorts," as the common people often were called, and believed that, if unchecked, a government of the people would

---

Adams," *Michigan Alumnus Quarterly Review* 64 (1958):228–38; Edward Ryerson, "On John Adams," *American Quarterly* 6 (1954):253–58; Francis N. Thorpe, "The Political Ideas of John Adams," *Pennsylvania Magazine of History and Biography* 44 (1920):1–46; Correa Moylan Walsh, *The Political Science of John Adams* (New York, 1915).

[13]Adams to Penn, [before Mar. 27, 1776], *PJA*, 4:80; L. H. Butterfield, ed., *Diary and Autobiography of John Adams*, 4 vols. (Cambridge, Mass., 1961), 3:294–95.

[14]Adams, *Thoughts on Government*, *PJA*, 4:87; Adams, *Defence*, Adams, *Works*, 4:290; Adams, "Davila," ibid., 6:257.

carry liberty to such excess that tumultuous anarchy would be the inevitable result. Others feared unbridled executive hegemony, which would result inevitably in cruel despotism.[15] Adams was not insensitive to either of these dangers, but he perceived a different and more likely threat to good government and public happiness. What distinguished his thought from that of most of his contemporaries was his belief that the wealthy, not the people and not strong executives, posed the greatest threat to the public weal.

"You are Apprehensive of Monarchy; I of Aristocracy," Adams remarked to Jefferson in 1787. Adams's study of history convinced him that the wealthiest class had ultimately secured power in every society and that, when unchecked, the elite had utilized its authority to suppress the citizenry. He did not romanticize commoners; in fact, he thought the common people were cut from the "same clay" as the wealthy, equally passionate and almost always more ignorant. He simply thought it unlikely that the common people could secure sufficient power to do much harm. Throughout history, he believed, power had been most often possessed by the monied class and government had been exercised chiefly for the benefit of those who possessed the greatest wealth and power. Thus, Adams feared that oligarchical rule was a distinct likelihood, and in his tracts of political theory in the 1780s and early 1790s he especially advised that precautions must be taken to prevent such an occurrence.[16]

By the 1790s Adams's fear of class divisions and oligarchy prompted him to argue for a much stronger executive than he had initially desired. It was a reassessment that would have profound ramifications for his presidency. In 1776 Adams had looked upon the executive as merely one of the three counterweights in a system of balances; at that time, Adams would have given the executive sufficient power to maintain its independence, but too little power to do anything more. By the 1790s Adams had concluded that the executive must be the very "essence of government." He had come to see the executive as the bul-

---

[15]Gordon S. Wood, *The Creation of the American Republic, 1776–1787* (Chapel Hill, 1969), pp. 18–28, 36–43, 235–36, 404, 432, 442, 474, 484, 519.

[16]Adams to Jefferson, Dec. 6, 1787, Lester J. Cappon, ed., *The Adams-Jefferson Letters: The Complete Correspondence between Thomas Jefferson and Abigail and John Adams,* 2 vols. (Chapel Hill, 1959), 1:213; Adams, *Defence,* Adams, *Works,* 4:289–91; 6:73, 97–99.

wark that would protect the common people from the rich. In fact, he argued that the common people inevitably looked upon the executive as their "father and protector," for that official offered them the best hope of defense against the elite. Commoners, he said, knew they could expect little from the judiciary, press, or upper legislative chamber, and too often they were betrayed even by the popularly elected lower house.

A good executive, Adams said, must be "always ready, always able, and always interested to assist the weakest," but that was only one of his responsibilities. He must also provide firm moral leadership in the interest of the general well-being. Adams believed the executive alone would be in a position to achieve the greatest happiness for the greatest number, although to achieve this end he knew that the executive must be fully independent and possessed of authority equal to that exercised by the legislators. Adams additionally stressed that the executive must embody two virtues. He must be sagacious, the very "Reservoir of Wisdom." Secondly, the executive must be nonpartisan. The battle between the "gentlemen" and the "simplemen," as he put it, would inevitably produce "parties, divisions, tumults, and war." The executive must stand above this factionalism. He must be the "antidote against rivalries." He must compel every citizen to submit to the laws. He must be the watchman on guard against humankind's "natural passions and habits," its vanity, avarice, ambition, passion, ignorance, and insatiable love of glory. It was the moral responsibility of the executive to resist selfish interests and malevolent parties, even if such actions carried the risk of personal loss. To accomplish the end of government this official must be — and here Adams quoted poet Alexander Pope — "more wise, more learn'd, more just, more every thing."[17]

Adams had reached this point in his thinking before he returned to America in 1788, but the emergence of political parties during Washington's administration reinforced his views on executive authority.

---

[17]Adams, *Defence*, Adams, *Works,* 4:585; 5:473; 6:186–87; Adams, "Davila," ibid., 6:241–48, 252, 254, 256, 323; Adams to Thomas Hollis, June 11, 1790, ibid., 9:570; Adams, *Thoughts on Government, PJA,* 4:86; Howe, *Changing Political Thought of John Adams,* p. 96; Wood, *Creation of the American Republic,* pp. 578–80; Ralph Ketcham, *Presidents above Party: The First American Presidency, 1789–1829* (Chapel Hill, 1984), pp. 57–68, 93–99.

Fearful that political parties would be the death knell of the infant republic, Adams recoiled at the factionalism he observed in the 1790s. He characterized parties as monstrous and declared that contested elections would lead inevitably to corruption, sedition, and civil war. He exhibited his principles in 1796, refusing to campaign during the presidential election. It was Adams's view that the qualified voters and electors were capable of selecting the best man for the presidency on the basis of "pure Principles of Merit, Virtue, and public Spirit." Adams embraced what was rapidly becoming the old-fashioned view that a man should not pursue an office, the office should search out the man, and while the Federalist party and its Jeffersonian Republican adversary churned out partisan handbills and newspaper essays brimming with invective, Adams remained at home in Quincy, Massachusetts, making no speeches, issuing no statements. It had to be this way, he believed, or the candidate would compromise himself and be unable to provide disinterested leadership.[18]

The level of party rancor that existed in the 1790s, coupled with Adams's views on factional strife, made it a certainty that he was sailing into troubled waters the moment he took the oath of office. However, Adams might have enjoyed a relatively tranquil relationship with Congress had relations with the major powers in Europe been good. Instead, throughout his term he faced a foreign policy crisis that devoured all other matters and shaped his presidency. Moreover, Adams's behavior as president in part resulted from his belief that as a veteran diplomat he had a feel for the art of diplomacy, a prowess that no congressman could claim.

When Congress had first turned its attention to diplomatic concerns in 1776, Adams was acknowledged by his colleagues as the member who had most "fully considered and better digested the subject of foreign" relations.[19] He was selected to draft the Model Treaty, a guide

---

[18]Page Smith, "Election of 1796," in Schlesinger, *History of American Presidential Elections,* 1:65; Adams to Adrian Vanderkemp, Feb. 27, 1780, Vanderkemp Papers, Historical Society of Pennsylvania; Adams to Abigail Adams, Feb. 20, 1796, Adams, *Letters of John Adams Addressed to His Wife,* 2:203; Manning J. Dauer, *The Adams Federalists* (Baltimore, 1953), pp. 92–111; Brown, *Presidency of John Adams,* pp. 15–21; Elkins and McKitrick, *Age of Federalism,* p. 535.

[19]James H. Hutson, *John Adams and the Diplomacy of the American Revolution* (Lexington, Ky., 1980), p. 28.

for America's first foreign envoys to France, and in 1778 he was sent to France by Congress. He served out the American Revolution as a diplomat in Paris, The Hague, and Amsterdam. He learned three great lessons in the course of this service.

First, when Adams arrived in France in 1778, he had been certain that Great Britain was doomed and that the War of Independence soon would end in an American victory. France, he thought, would send a fleet to America that would quickly compel the British to make peace. The French disappointed him. For years he hectored French officials to send a larger fleet, then to dispatch an army, and finally to order the navy and army to act in concert with the Continental Army in America, precisely the strategy that eventually paid dividends at Yorktown in 1781. Thereafter, Adams knew from his frustrating firsthand experience that France, when imperiled at home, was unlikely to engage in unfettered adventurism abroad.[20]

Second, Adams emerged from the American Revolution convinced that Congress was not the proper body to engage in diplomacy. Faced in 1779 with the necessity of determining the conditions upon which the United States would agree to peace, Congress had promptly divided into ugly factions. Eight months of wrangling had been required for Congress to decide the issue—nor was that all: Congress subsequently buckled under French pressure and instructed the American peace commissioners in Europe to act according to the "advice and opinion" of France.[21] This dubious record convinced Adams that Congress could not manage the nation's diplomacy.

Third, Adams came home from Europe with the unmistakable conviction that the United States must remain independent of the major European powers. He had come to understand that when a weak nation tied itself to a great power, the alliance could not exist on equal terms. The great power would inevitably predominate, nudging its partner along whatever path it chose. During the War of Independence

---

[20]On Adams's Revolutionary diplomacy, see ibid., pp. 33–141; John Ferling, "John Adams, Diplomat," *William and Mary Quarterly*, 3d ser. 51 (1994):227–52; Page Smith, *John Adams*, 2 vols. (New York, 1962), pp. 356–599; Shaw, *Character of John Adams*, pp. 105–91.

[21]Ferling, "John Adams, Diplomat," pp. 245–46; William Stinchcombe, *The American Revolution and the French Alliance* (Syracuse, 1969), pp. 62–90, 153–69; Butterfield, *Diary and Autobiography of John Adams*, 3:39 n.

Adams had been the first to warn that France would attempt to shape American behavior "by Attaching themselves to Reasons, Parties, or Measures in America." By 1781 he saw better than any other American envoy that a war-weary France might push the United States into an unfavorable peace. After Yorktown, he displayed no hesitancy in ignoring Congress's order to be bound by France during the peace negotiations.[22] As Adams entered the presidency he believed that a "French party" and a "British party" existed within Congress, and more than ever he was convinced that if the national interest was to be served, the president, the "essence of government," must control American foreign policy, at least in part to prevent the United States from becoming the client state of a European superpower.

Adams's administration was dominated by a foreign policy crisis, as was true of Washington's second term. Faced with the outbreak of war in Europe during his third year in office, President Washington had immediately proclaimed American neutrality. Nevertheless, war fever gripped the land. Numerous Democratic-Republican societies blossomed and hailed French victories, sponsored banquets at which French anthems were sung, and scorned American neutrality. Their numbers grew when London blockaded French trade and seized American vessels attempting to conduct commerce in French ports. However, Washington quieted the hysteria when he dispatched John Jay to London to negotiate the differences between the two countries. Jay ultimately brought home a treaty that the Senate ratified, but the rapprochement with Great Britain provoked a deterioration in relations with Paris, signaled by a French decree on July 4, 1796, which stated that henceforth it would seize American vessels attempting to trade with the British in the Caribbean. Anti-French fervor immediately bubbled. As the date of Adams's inauguration neared, the nation waited expectantly for word from America's new minister

---

[22]Adams to Samuel Adams, Nov. 27, 1778, Feb. 14, 1779, *PJA*, vol.7 (Gred L. Lint, Robert J. Taylor, Richard Alan Ryerson, Celeste Walker, and Joanna M. Revelas, eds.), p. 234; vol. 8 (Lint, Taylor, Ryerson, Walker, and Revelas, eds.), p. 413; Adams to Elbridge Gerry, Dec. 5, 1778, ibid., 7:248; Adams to Roger Sherman, Aug. 6, 1778, ibid., 7:254; Adams to Thomas Cushing, Dec. 8, 1778, ibid., 7:263; Adams to James Warren, Feb. 25, 1778, ibid., 7:429.

to France, Charles Cotesworth Pinckney, whom Washington had appointed a few months earlier.[23]

Word arrived sometime during the first ten days of Adams's term. It was not what the new president had hoped to hear. The French government had refused to accept Pinckney and ordered him from the country; within the next few weeks the United States also learned that France had seized numerous American vessels, launching an undeclared war that historians have labeled the Quasi-War.[24] Adams's first response was to summon Congress to a special session in mid-May.

Even before taking office Adams had decided that he would notify Congress of his intention of sending a special commission to France to pursue reconciliation, but in selecting the envoys the president demonstrated a penchant for doing things his way. He consulted with no one about his plans until forty-eight hours prior to his inauguration, then he sought counsel from vice president–elect Jefferson, a Republican. When he got around to informing his cabinet that he wished to name a commission that would include one or two Republicans, he encountered a firestorm. Adams's plan made perfect sense diplomatically; he wished to send at least one representative of America's pro-French party to Paris, an envoy whom the French could trust. But party passions intruded. Some in the cabinet wished to reappoint Pinckney as the envoy extraordinary and others insisted that the commission consist only of Federalists. Faced with threats of resignation by the most strident members of his cabinet, the president agreed to name two Federalists, Pinckney and John Marshall, and Elbridge Gerry, an old friend from Massachusetts who was an antiparty man.[25]

---

[23]Eugene Perry Link, *The Democratic Republican Societies, 1790–1800* (New York, 1942), pp. 125–55; Anna C. Clauder, *American Commerce Affected by the Wars of the French Revolution and Napoleon, 1793–1812* (Philadelphia, 1932), pp. 36–37; James Thomas Flexner, *George Washington: Anguish and Farewell (1793–1799)* (Boston, 1969), pp. 202–20, 226–32, 245–49, 264–76, 285–91, 318–27; Elkins and McKitrick, *Age of Federalism*, pp. 375–449; Ferling, *First of Men*, pp. 429–39, 454–61.

[24]Marvin R. Zahoisher, "The First Pinckney Mission to France," *South Carolina History Magazine* 56 (1965):205–17; Alexander DeConde, *The Quasi-War: The Politics and Diplomacy of the Undeclared War with France, 1797–1801* (New York, 1966), pp. 3–24; Albert Hall Bowman, *The Struggle for Neutrality: Franco-American Diplomacy during the Federalist Era* (Knoxville, 1974), pp. 228–61.

[25][Thomas Jefferson], *Anas*, Mar. 2–6, 1797, Ford, *Writings of Jefferson*, 1:272–73; Adams to Henry Knox, Mar. 30, 1797, Adams Family Papers, reel 117; Adams to

The Congress that gathered in May for the special session was deeply divided. The Republicans controlled the House, while the Federalists possessed nearly a two-to-one majority in the Senate. In addition, by May, Adams had sensed that the citizenry, which remembered the long, difficult War of Independence only too well, favored a cautious response to France, lest the nation blunder into another war. The prospect of hostilities, the president told one of his cabinet officers, had, "according to an Indian expression[,] . . . 'put petticoats on them.' " Nevertheless, the nation faced a crisis and Adams saw it as his responsibility to reshape public opinion and prepare for the possibility of war. Thus, Adams informed Congress that France had subjected Minister Pinckney to "indignities" and treated the United States as if it were not a sovereign nation. The nation must not cower under a "spirit of fear and sense of inferiority," he thundered, and proposed a series of defensive measures. He asked Congress to strengthen the navy so that it might better protect American commerce. Although he told Congress that he believed a French invasion was unlikely, Adams proposed an increase in coastal fortifications, an augmentation of the artillery and cavalry in the U.S. Army, and the reorganization of the militia. However, he did not urge any expansion in the nation's tiny army. Finally, he informed Congress of the three-member commission he planned to dispatch to Paris.[26]

The Republicans in Congress, who had supported Adams as reasonable and moderate, turned on him. They regarded his address as tantamount to a declaration of war; Jefferson, in fact, termed the speech an "insane message." Many of the vice president's fellow Re-

---

Benjamin Rush, Aug. 23, 1805, Alexander Biddle, ed., *Old Family Letters, Copied from the Original for Alexander Biddle*, 2 vols. (Philadelphia, 1892), 1:76–77; Oliver Wolcott to Alexander Hamilton, Mar. 31, 1797, Harold C. Syrett and Jacob S. Cooke, eds., *The Papers of Alexander Hamilton*, 27 vols. (New York, 1961–79), 20:571, hereafter *PAH;* Elkins and McKitrick, *Age of Federalism*, p. 555.

[26]John Adams, "Correspondence Originally Published in *The Boston Patriot,* " Adams, *Works*, 9:243–44, 301; Adams to Oliver Wolcott, Oct. 27, 1797, ibid., 8:559; Adams, Message to the Special Session, May 16, 1797, Richardson, *Messages and Papers of the Presidents*, 1:233–39. On Adams's affinity for a strong navy, see William G. Anderson, "John Adams, the Navy, and the Quasi-War with France," *American Neptune* 30 (1970):117–32, and Frederick H. Hayes, "John Adams and American Sea Power," *American Neptune* 25 (1965):35–45.

publicans were convinced that Adams's object was to lead the United States into war with France as soon as the military preparations were complete; some of the Republican press portrayed Adams as the puppet of an anti-French faction within the cabinet and the Federalist congressional delegation, an element that allegedly sought war with France in order to create the necessity for an Anglo-American alliance.[27]

President Adams did not desire war. He confided to his son that he would resort to war only if the French "push us beyond our bearing" and "too much humiliation is demanded." Adams told his cabinet that he was not afraid to go to war, but he did not seek hostilities; he desired peace on terms consistent with national honor, he insisted. To the president, the linkage between defense measures and diplomacy was conventional practice in Europe and the best means of inducing France to enter into productive negotiations.[28]

Nor was Adams anyone's dupe. What he requested of Congress was modest compared with that desired by the extremists in his party. Secretary of State Pickering and Treasury Secretary Wolcott advised more extensive preparations for war, a program that included proposals for the creation of a provisional army of 25,000 men, new taxes, an embargo of France, and legislation that would permit the expulsion of aliens. President Adams requested none of these things and attempted to build bipartisan support for his policy, consulting with Jefferson and, through him, James Madison, the leading Republican in the House. Nevertheless, while the president believed that he had adopted a reasoned tone, he succeeded only in angering both parties. The more truculent wing of his own party, the High Federalists, believed he had not gone far enough. The Republicans believed that Adams's proposed defensive preparations were the first step on the road to war. As a result, the deeply divided Congress did almost

---

[27]Jefferson to Peregrine Fitzhugh, June 4, 1797, Ford, *Writings of Jefferson*, 7:136; Jefferson to Madison, Mar. 21, 1798, ibid., 7:218–22; Elkins and McKitrick, *Age of Federalism*, p. 552.

[28]Adams to John Quincy Adams, Mar. 31, July 15, 1797, Adams Family Papers, reels 385, 117; Adams to Henry Knox, Mar. 30, 1797, ibid., reel 117; Adams to Elbridge Gerry, Feb. 13, 1797, ibid., reel 117; Adams to Richard Cranch, Mar. 25, 1797, ibid., reel 117.

nothing. It voted only to complete three frigates already under construction, thus denying Adams the strong fleet he had sought.[29]

The moment the special session ended, President Adams and his wife sped home to Quincy. It was a practice that he would repeat annually, and it eventually caused him considerable difficulty. Washington had established the precedent by returning to Mount Vernon each year, but he had never remained away from the capital for more than three months in any year. In contrast, President Adams generally resided in Philadelphia or Washington, which became the new national capital in 1800, only from late in November until sometime in March or early April. In fact, the First Lady once characterized her husband's life in the presidency as six months of ease and tranquility followed by six months of stress and hard labor. Adams's habits eventually provoked criticism. His cabinet grew exasperated at serving under an executive who was often unavailable for consultation and guidance. During his second year in office Adams learned of whispers that he had abrogated his responsibilities and that his behavior was a "kind of abdication." During his third year in office a loyal supporter from Baltimore bluntly told Adams that the public was outraged by his continuous absence. "The people elected you to administer the government," he wrote. "They did not elect your officers . . . to govern, without your presence and control." Even that did not budge Adams. Only in 1800, when he was warned by the secretary of the navy that his conduct was likely to cost him reelection in 1800, did Adams cut short a vacation that had already exceeded six months.[30]

What prompted Adams to act in such a manner? His working vacation in Quincy in 1798 was lengthened because the First Lady fell

---

[29]James McHenry to Hamilton, Apr. 14, 1797, *PAH,* 21:48; Hamilton to McHenry, Apr. [?], 1797, ibid., 21:72–75; Hamilton to Timothy Pickering, May 11, 1797, ibid., 21:81–84; Pickering to Adams, May 1, 1797, in Octavius Pickering and Charles W. Upham, *The Life of Timothy Pickering,* 4 vols. (Boston, 1867–73), 3:369; Dauer, *Adams Federalists,* pp. 135, 303; Elkins and McKitrick, *Age of Federalism,* pp. 553, 555; Sharp, *American Politics in the Early Republic,* p. 167.

[30]Abigail Adams to John Quincy Adams, Dec. 30, 1799, Adams Family Papers, reel 396; Uriah Forest to Adams, Apr. 28, 1799, Adams, *Works,* 8:637–38; Benjamin Stoddert to Adams, Aug. 29, Sept. 13, 1799, ibid., 9:18–19, 26–29.

seriously ill that autumn and was thought by her physician to be near death. President Adams refused to leave her side until she improved.[31] In addition, Adams and many others fled Philadelphia before the annual onslaught of summer fevers. Yellow fever had struck the city on several occasions since 1793, usually commencing its assault in July and running its course by early autumn; in the worst episode nearly 15 percent of the population had perished. This was a danger that "obliged us to fly for our lives," Adams once remarked.[32] However, these circumstances cannot explain why he routinely spent only about four months of each year in the capital.

To some degree, Adams's behavior appears to have stemmed from a radical transformation that he experienced in his relationship with his wife. Before the American Revolution Adams's duties as a lawyer usually kept him on the legal circuit and away from home for about three months annually; when he served in Congress between 1774 and 1777, it was not uncommon for him to be separated from Abigail for nine or ten months each year. His service as a diplomat resulted in even longer separations. On one occasion Adams and his wife never saw one another for almost five years. But Adams changed in midlife. After his return to the United States at age fifty-three, he appeared to grow more passive and dependent on Abigail. His correspondence with her took on uncharacteristic sensuous qualities, and he seemed as never before to require the nurture that only she could provide. Because of her physical ills—Abigail suffered from rheumatoid arthritis—she seldom accompanied her husband to the capital during his vice presidency or presidency. In those years when she was unable to leave Quincy, he came home to her at the first opportunity. When Abigail did come to the capital, she was unhappy with the tense

---

[31]Adams to Benjamin Stoddert, Aug. 31, 1798, Adams Family Papers, reel 119; Adams to Pickering, Sept. 10, 1798, ibid., reel 119; Adams to Wolcott, Sept. 24, 1798, ibid., reel 391; Adams to McHenry, Oct. 22, 1798, ibid., reel 391; Abigail Adams 2d to John Quincy Adams, Sept. 28, 1798, ibid., reel 391.

[32]Adams to John Quincy Adams, Oct. 16, 1798, ibid., reel 119; Adams to McHenry, Aug. 29, 1798, Adams, *Works*, 8:589; Adams, "Correspondence Originally Published in *The Boston Patriot*," ibid., 9:251. On disease in early Philadelphia, see J. H. Powell, *Bring Out Your Dead: The Yellow Fever in Philadelphia in 1793* (Philadelphia, 1949) and John Duffy, *The Healers: A History of American Medicine* (Urbana, Ill., 1979), pp. 195–96.

political environment and Philadelphia's miasmal climate (she referred to the city as a "baking oven" during the summer months) and refused to stay for more than a few weeks. When she departed, the president left with her.[33]

His actions may have been compensatory, a restitution for the terribly long separations he had imposed upon her during the Revolutionary War. But Adams's behavior was consistent with that of many men in their later adult years. He exhibited a sense of urgency about the time that was left to him. In an age when few males lived past their mid-sixties, Adams—who was sixty-two at the time of his inauguration—realized that he might not survive his presidency. Like many men at this stage of life, Adams wished to build a new life structure, one which would enable him to relish those things that were most important in his life, including an intensely intimate relationship with his spouse. "I want my Horse my farm my long walks and more than all the Bosom of my [wife]," he once cried in despair to Abigail.[34]

In addition, Adams's seemingly bizarre behavior was influenced by health considerations. Adams had suffered four episodes of grave illness between 1771 and 1783, three of which were so serious that he collapsed and was believed by his physicians to be in a life-threatening emergency. There is a strong likelihood that Adams suffered from hyperthyroidism, or overactivity of the thyroid, a disease that may go into remission and ultimately resurface. In each medical emergency Adams was afflicted with emotional lability, acute anxiety, weakness, insomnia, heat insensitivity, eye symptoms, dermatological disorders, irritability, and tremors, all common symptoms of thyrotoxicosis. Although neither Adams nor his doctors understood the etiology of his

---

[33]Shaw, *Character of John Adams*, p. 244; Phyllis Lee Levin, *Abigail Adams: A Biography* (New York, 1987), pp. 309–10, 319, 341, 354; Lynne Withey, *Dearest Friend: A Life of Abigail Adams* (New York, 1981), pp. 221–67.

[34]Roger L. Gould, "Transformation during Early and Middle Adult Years," in *Themes of Work and Love in Adulthood*, ed. Neil J. Smelser and Erik H. Erikson (Cambridge, Mass., 1980), pp. 235–36; Daniel J. Levinson, "Toward a Conception of the Adult Life Course," ibid., pp. 284, 286–87; Roger L. Gould, *Transformation: Growth and Change in Adult Life* (New York, 1978), pp. 309–19; Daniel Gutman, "An Exploration of Ego Configurations in Middle and Late Life," in *Personality in Middle and Later Life: Empirical Studies*, ed. Bernice L. Neugarten (New York, 1964), pp. 119–30; Adams to Abigail Adams, Apr. 1, 1796, Adams Family Papers, reel 381.

illnesses, he believed his recurring condition was at least exacerbated by stress, and he sought to preserve his health through diet, exercise, and a diminution of tension and adversity in his life.[35]

From the outset of his presidency, Adams worried about the toll that the office would take on his health. Halfway through his term he confided that "I am old — very old very Old and shall never be very well — certainly while in this office." He added that he felt as if he had aged forty years during the past two years. After he had been only a few months on the job, Abigail wrung her hands over his thin, pale, and tired appearance and advised that staying away from the capital might be an antidote to physical and mental exhaustion.[36] He agreed that a protracted annual residence in Quincy would diminish the tension in his life. Perhaps his regimen succeeded. At any rate, Adams, who had last fallen seriously ill in 1783, did not suffer a medical emergency during his presidency.

Finally, Adams genuinely believed that he could tend to his duties in Quincy as well as he could in Philadelphia. "Nothing suffers or is lost," he exclaimed, and in reality he kept atop the paperwork and reports that crossed his desk. What Adams failed to understand was that his protracted absences not only prevented him from consulting with other high officials, but also may have encouraged them to plot to achieve their contrary objectives. Adams once remarked that he was "unpractised in intrigues for power." His naïveté was never more in evidence.[37]

When Adams finally returned to dark, cold, rainy Philadelphia in late November 1797 he confronted a Congress that was still inclined to block his program. In his State of the Union address Adams once again urged Congress to strengthen the nation's defenses. Nothing else, he said, would convince France of the United States' "energy and unanimity" in this crisis. However, Congress, which was inclined to do nothing

---

[35]On Adams's health problems, see John Ferling and Lewis E. Braverman, "John Adams's Health Reconsidered," *William and Mary Quarterly*, 3d ser. 55 (1998):83–104.

[36]Adams to Abigail Adams, Jan. 7, 1796, Adams, *Letters of John Adams Addressed to His Wife*, 2:188–89; Adams to Abigail Adams, Dec. 25, 1798, Feb. 4, 1799, Adams Family Papers, reels 392, 393; Abigail Adams to Cotton Tufts, June 8, 29, 1798, ibid., reel 389.

[37]Adams to Benjamin Rush, Aug. 23, 1805, Jan. 6, 1806, Apr. 22, 1812, Schutz and Adair, *The Spur of Fame*, pp. 36, 46, 214.

until it learned of the reception of the commissioners in Paris, enacted even less of Adams's program than it had the preceding summer.[38]

On March 4, the first anniversary of his inauguration, Adams at last heard from Pinckney, Marshall, and Gerry, the commissioners who had reached Paris in October. Their dispatch was not what he had hoped for. Not only had the French foreign ministry refused to receive the diplomats, it had demanded bribe payments, a United States loan as a precondition for negotiations, and an apology for President Adams's request that the American navy be strengthened. Adams immediately sought advice from his cabinet. Since his return the previous autumn Adams's advisers had urged a truculent policy, including requests that he ask Congress to authorize a provisional army of twenty thousand men. Half the cabinet now recommended that he also ask Congress for a declaration of war; one member wished to use the army to seize Louisiana, a French possession, and another urged a treaty of alliance with Great Britain.[39]

Two weeks later Adams addressed Congress. Once again, he ignored the bellicosity within his cabinet and delivered a restrained speech that he hoped would appeal to the moderate elements in both parties. He merely said that he saw "no ground of expectation" that his commissioners' mission could be accomplished. He reiterated his call for the enactment of the defensive measures that he had urged in May and November. Moreover, he did not divulge the combustible materials that he had received regarding the shameful treatment of the three envoys, probably because he feared for the safety of his diplomats.[40]

Many Federalists were dismayed that Adams had not revealed the dispatches from Paris, as they believed that these damning accounts would compel Congress to enact tough defensive measures. Likewise, many Republicans wanted the dispatches made public. They suspected that Adams, eager to force Congress into a more belligerent posture,

---

[38]Adams, First Annual Address, Nov. 22, 1797, Richardson, *Messages and Papers of the Presidents*, 1:250–54.

[39]McHenry to Adams, Feb. 15, 1798, Adams Family Papers, reel 387; Hamilton to Pickering, Mar. 17, 1798, *PAH*, 21:364–66; Smith, *John Adams*, 2:953–54; DeConde, *Quasi-War*, p. 65.

[40]Adams, Address to Congress, Mar. 19, 1798, Richardson, *Messages and Papers of the Presidents*, 1:264–65.

had misled them about the prospects for a peaceful resolution of the Franco-American differences. Not only would divulgence thwart the Federalists, the Republicans believed, but they were certain that time was on their side. Gen. Napoleon Bonaparte had scored sensational victories late in 1797, knocking Austria out of the war and increasing the chances of a French invasion of England. Moreover, if Great Britain was defeated, the ardor for war in Federalist circles was certain to cool. Thus, for once the Republicans joined with the High Federalists to demand that Adams release the dispatches of his envoys to France.[41]

Adams complied with Congress's demand for disclosure, and it was in this manner that the nation learned of the XYZ Affair. The result was like manna from heaven for the most extreme Federalists, but a nightmare for the Republicans. A tidal wave of militancy washed over the land, seeping into the presidential mansion along the way. Adams promptly pledged never to send another minister to France "without assurances that he will be received, respected, and honored" as the representative of a sovereign nation. He also adopted a belligerent persona. Not only did he begin to appear in public dressed in a military uniform and sword, but between April and August he authored seventy-one pugnacious public addresses to militia units, political clubs, and local governments. In these messages he repeatedly urged Americans to adopt a "warlike Character" and told them that the "Character of Warriors" is "highly honorable." He additionally warned his countrymen that submission to French threats would be the basest cowardice, whereas to fight for love of country was the most noble of human virtues. He played on the theme that hostilities were "less Evil than national Dishonour," and he warned that if the nation did not arm, it would signal that corruption and debasement had overtaken the country.[42]

---

[41]Jefferson to James Madison, Mar. 21, 1798, Ford, *Writings of Jefferson,* 7:219; Elkins and McKitrick, *Age of Federalism,* p. 187.

[42]Adams, Address to Congress, June 21, 1798, Richardson, *Messages and Papers of the Presidents,* 1:256; Adams to Plymouth and Kingston, Massachusetts, June 8, 1798, Adams Family Papers, reel 389; Adams to the McPherson [Philadelphia] Blues, June 18, 1798, ibid., reel 389; Adams to Commander-in-Chief of the New Jersey Militia, June 20, 1798, ibid., reel 389; Adams to Wilmington, North Carolina, May 31, 1798, ibid., reel 388; Adams to New York Society of Cincinnati, July 9, 1798, Myers Collection, New

alists in order to hold his party together and maintain support for his administration during the national emergency. However, from the outset he was deeply troubled by their calls for a provisional army and the new taxes that such a military force would require. Adams feared that heavy taxation would cause political problems. Taxes "suggest a vexation to me," he remarked. Others recognized the danger as well. High taxes, Jefferson remarked, would sweep the "witches" out of power. Yet many High Federalists ignored the political danger; Senator Cabot, for instance, thought the citizenry so bellicose that it would accept any measure the administration recommended.[47] Adams worried about a provisional army for other reasons. Not only did he think it unnecessary, but like many eighteenth-century Americans he feared standing armies; he worried that the provisional army might grow into "a many headed and many bellied Monster of an Army to tyrannize over Us." Adams had still another worry. The Federalist party was not a monolith. The moderate wing of the party, like the president, was concerned about the implications of the High Federalist program. Adams could not ignore this element; it comprised up to one-third of the Federalist congressmen. Thus, Adams proposed a patchwork program, embracing only a portion of that desired by the High Federalists. He refused to support their demand that the regular army be expanded to a twenty-thousand-man force supplemented by a provisional army of an additional twenty to thirty thousand men. Instead, he asked only for the creation of a provisional army, and one that was one-third smaller than that desired by many extreme Federalists. Furthermore, Adams declined to assent to the radical Federalists' calls for the immediate licensing of privateers, a step tantamount to a declaration of war, and turned a deaf ear to Pickering and the attorney general, Charles Lee, ordinarily the most moderate member of his cabinet, who proposed that he ask Congress to declare war.[48]

[47]Adams to Oliver Wolcott, Oct. 20, 1797, Adams, *Works*, 8:555; Miller, *Federalist Era*, pp. 246–47; Cabot to Wolcott, May 15, 1797, Henry Cabot Lodge, *Life and Letters of George Cabot* (Boston, 1878), p. 138.

[48]Brown, *Presidency of John Adams*, p. 53; Dauer, *Adams Federalists*, pp. 297, 303; Adams to Jefferson, May 11, 1794, Cappon, *Adams-Jefferson Correspondence*, 1:255; Adams, Annual Address to Congress, Nov. 22, 1797, Richardson, *Messages and Papers of the Presidents*, 1:250–51; Hamilton to Wolcott, June 6, 8, 1797, *PAH*, 21:99–100, 103–4; Hamilton to Pickering, Mar. 17, 1798, ibid., 21:364–66; Richard E. Welch, Jr., *Theodore*

Between April and July, Congress gave Adams everything he had requested. For the first time since Adams had taken office the Federalist party enjoyed a working majority in both houses. The "XYZ dish cooked up by Marshall," as Jefferson put it, had accomplished electoral wonders for the Federalists. The party scored numerous triumphs throughout 1798. In addition, many Republicans, hitherto foes of military preparedness, now supported Adams's program; some Republicans who could not vote for the proposed defense measures, but dared not vote against them, absented themselves under the pretense of consulting with constituents at home. By year's end the Federalist party had doubled its numbers in the House of Representatives and could outvote the Republicans by roughly a twenty-vote margin on most issues.[49]

The Federalist Congress quickly established the Navy Department, made the Marine Corps a distinct body, and increased its numbers. Congress authorized the construction of six ships of the line — carrying seventy-four guns each — as well as several sloops, schooners, and galleys, bringing the fleet to a total of forty-five vessels of varying size. Money was appropriated to fortify harbors, all treaties with France were abrogated, naval vessels were authorized to attack and seize French ships that endangered American property, and merchantmen were permitted to arm and resist attack. But what Congress did not do was equally significant. Following the lead of the president, Congress refused to license privateers and a Federalist party caucus rebuffed a move by its most bellicose members to have Congress declare war.[50]

In one area only did Congress move in an unanticipated direction. It adopted the Alien and Sedition Acts that curtailed free speech and free press and authorized the president to deport dangerous aliens. Adams subsequently offered varied and contradictory explanations for his role in the passage of this legislation. At times he attempted

---

Sedgwick, Federalist: A Political Portrait (Middletown, Conn., 1965), pp. 166, 172; Elkins and McKitrick, *Age of Federalism,* pp. 583, 585.

[49]Sharp, *American Politics in the Early Republic,* p. 223; Brown, *Presidency of John Adams,* p. 52; Elkins and McKitrick, *Age of Federalism,* pp. 588–89; Donald Stewart, *The Opposition Press of the Federalist Period* (Albany, 1969), pp. 295–323.

[50]Gardner W. Allen, *Our Naval War with France* (New York, 1909), pp. 56–57, 61, 84–85; Elkins and McKitrick, *Age of Federalism,* pp. 588–90; DeConde, *Quasi-War,* pp. 90–91; Brown, *Presidency of John Adams,* pp. 57–58.

to absolve himself of any complicity. At other times he defended the acts as necessary for the expulsion of the "French spies [who] swarmed in our Cities and in the Country." On still other occasions he claimed that he had not enforced the laws. In reality, Adams's bellicose rhetoric had helped create the environment in which such acts could pass Congress. In addition, he not only made no attempt to prevent their passage, he acknowledged that he was "ready and willing" to exile troublesome aliens, and his Department of Justice zealously enforced the Sedition Act.[51]

Adams had acted astutely throughout the yearlong crisis. He had successfully fashioned a national posture calculated to convince France of the wisdom of rapprochement. Moreover, he had preserved the integrity of his office and remained firmly in control of the nation's foreign policy. In fact, his newfound popularity with the citizenry and the support he enjoyed with moderates in both parties left Adams with the strength and flexibility to exercise virtually any policy option that he chose. But Adams's seminal achievement had been to buy time. He had managed the militant firestorm so successfully that a tenuous peace — but peace nonetheless — prevailed, and time remained for France to change its course.

Within a few months Adams glimpsed the first signs that his policies might pay dividends. In October the president met in Quincy with Elbridge Gerry, only recently returned from his abortive mission to France. Gerry's report brimmed with optimism. The French foreign ministry had grown more solicitous during the spring, Gerry said; after learning in the summer of the American response to the XYZ Affair, France seemed ready to negotiate an end to the crisis it had created. Gerry was a problematic source, but soon thereafter Adams learned that Richard Codman, a Boston merchant who lived in Paris, Joel Barlow, an American poet who resided in France and had been American consul to Algiers, and Dr. George Logan, a Philadelphia Quaker who

---

[51]"Correspondence Originally Published in *The Boston Patriot*," Adams, *Works*, 9:291; Adams to Jefferson, June 14, 1813, Cappon, *Adams-Jefferson Letters*, 2:239; Sharp, *American Politics in the Early Republic*, p. 181; Elkins and McKitrick, *Age of Federalism*, pp. 590–93; Brown, *Presidency of John Adams*, pp. 121–26. On the Alien and Sedition Acts, see James Morton Smith, *Freedom's Fetters: The Alien and Sedition Laws and American Civil Liberties* (Ithaca, N.Y., 1966), and John C. Miller, *Crisis in Freedom: The Alien and Sedition Acts* (Boston, 1951).

had undertaken a private peace mission to France, had drawn similar conclusions about a Gallic change of heart. Word from American diplomats was of even greater import. Adams's sons—Thomas Boylston, who returned to America in January 1799 after serving a stint as secretary to his brother, John Quincy, now minister to Prussia—likewise sensed the shift in French policy. However, the reports of William Vans Murray, a Maryland Federalist who had become the U.S. minister to The Hague, were the most persuasive. Murray wrote that France feared war with the United States. Among the papers Murray sent home was a letter from the French foreign minister that promised that any future American plenipotentiary would "be received with the respect due to the representative of a free, independent, and powerful country." Adams was still sorting through Murray's packet when word reached Philadelphia that the French fleet had been decimated by the British Royal Navy in the Battle of the Nile. The president believed this drubbing gave France an even more urgent reason to settle its differences with the United States.[52]

Adams found these ruminations and reports to be interesting, but he had not received official word from the French government. If he should send off another team of envoys without adequate assurances from Paris, and if those diplomats should be humiliated, Adams would

---

[52]Gerry to Pickering, Oct. 1, 1798, *American State Papers: Foreign Relations,* 38 vols. (Washington, D.C., 1832–61), 2:204–8; Washington to Adams, Feb. 1, 1799, in John C. Fitzpatrick, ed., *The Writings of Washington,* 39 vols. (Washington, D.C., 1931–44), 37:119–20; Adams to Francis Dana, Nov. 7, 1798, Adams Family Papers, reel 119; Adams to Gerry, Dec. 15, 1798, Adams, *Works,* 8:617; Murray to Adams, July 1, 17, 22, Aug. 3, 20, Oct. 7, 1798, ibid., 8:677–91; Adams, "Correspondence Originally Published in *The Boston Patriot,*" in ibid., 9:245–46; Stephen G. Kurtz, *The Presidency of John Adams: The Collapse of Federalism, 1795–1800* (Philadelphia, 1957), p. 341; Worthington C. Ford, ed., "Letters of William Vans Murray to John Quincy Adams, 1797–1803," *Annual Report of the American Historical Association* (1912), pp. 347–715; Samuel Flagg Bemis, *John Quincy Adams and the Foundations of American Foreign Policy* (New York, 1956), pp. 99–101; Elkins and McKitrick, *Age of Federalism,* pp. 607–10; DeConde, *Quasi-War,* pp. 147–48. See also Eugene F. Kramer, "John Adams, Elbridge Gerry, and the XYZ Affair," *Essex Institute Historical Collections* 94 (1958):57–68; Eugene F. Kramer, "Some New Light on the XYZ Affair: Elbridge Gerry's Reasons for Opposing War with France," *New England Quarterly* 29 (1956):509–13; Robert Durden, "Joel Barlow in the French Revolution," *William and Mary Quarterly,* 3d ser. 8 (1951):327–54; Frederick A. Tolles, "Unofficial Ambassador: George Logan's Mission to France, 1798," *William and Mary Quarterly,* 3d ser. 7 (1970):3–25; Alexander De Conde, "William Vans Murray and the Diplomacy of Peace, 1797–1800," *Maryland Historical Magazine* 48 (1953):3–18.

succeed only in embarrassing the United States and destroying his presidency. However, Adams knew that he could not wait forever. In fact, before the end of 1798 evidence had mounted that America's warlike mood was vanishing like snow under a warm sun. Resentment of the new property taxes, detestation of the Alien and Sedition Acts, and apprehension of the provisional army had transformed the national mood. By year's end the Republicans had scored electoral victories in previously safe Federalist districts. The gathering climate of opinion augured a loss of leverage against France, but it also held the promise of greater public support for the dispatch of another commission to Paris.[53]

By the late fall of 1798, Adams's actions suggest that he was moving toward a decision to dispatch another mission to France. He ended his practice of issuing truculent patriotic addresses and sought to prepare public opinion by releasing Gerry's notes and reports. However, he did not make up his mind to act until February 1799. Several occurrences during the first two weeks of that month led him to his final decision. He received another optimistic report from Murray at the beginning of the month. Later during the same week he learned not only that Washington thought France wished to avoid war, but that the patriarch strongly believed that peace was in the best interests of the United States; Adams knew that Washington's concurrence would be an important political asset. A week later, on February 15, Adams received confirmation that France had restored some trade with the United States.[54]

Washington's tacit endorsement of the peace process and a host of diplomatic revelations had provided the president with the opening to take bold diplomatic action, but it was Adams's growing fear of members of his own party that led him to believe that his momentous step could not be delayed. By February 1799 Adams had reached the unalterable conclusion that a radical wing of the Federalist party posed a grave danger to the new nation and its constitutional structure. He

---

[53]Elkins and McKitrick, *Age of Federalism*, p. 615; DeConde, *Quasi-War*, pp. 177, 182–83; Dauer, *Adams Federalists*, pp. 334–35.

[54]Murray to Adams, Oct. 7, 1798, Adams, *Works*, 8:688–90; Washington to Adams, Feb. 1, 1799, Fitzpatrick, *Writings of Washington*, 37:119–20; DeConde, *Quasi-War*, p. 178.

had come to believe that the High Federalists and their undisputed leader, Hamilton, sought nothing less than a counterrevolution. In January or February Adams was shown one or more letters from Hamilton to High Federalists in Congress in which the congressmen were urged to contemplate declaring war on France if negotiations had not commenced within six months. In addition, the congressmen were lobbied to use the army, ostensibly created for defensive purposes, to invade French Louisiana or Spanish Florida. Furthermore, Hamilton urged his correspondents to stand ready to demand that the president use the provisional army to "attack and arraign" enemies in Republican Virginia, a state allegedly under the sway of French dupes who sought to destroy the U.S. Constitution.[55]

Adams had long suspected that a hidden agenda lay behind the policy recommendations of some members of his party. Prior to his inauguration he had speculated that Hamilton was an ambitious, conniving sort who would stop at nothing to elevate himself. Hamilton's conduct in the creation of the provisional army confirmed the president's suspicions. Adams had never believed that a French invasion was even remotely likely. He remembered Paris's reluctance to dispatch a small army to America during the War of Independence; a French invasion in the 1790s would require the commitment of an army many times the size of the force it had sent to the United States in 1780. Adams knew that even if France wished to send such an army across the Atlantic, it would not hazard such an undertaking while it fought the British navy. "There is no more prospect of seeing a french Army here, than there is in Heaven," the president once remarked. Nevertheless, in 1797 and 1798 Adams had urged a small army in an effort to demonstrate American resolve; Hamilton, in contrast, had sought to put up to fifty thousand men under arms.[56]

That aroused Adams's suspicions, but Hamilton's behavior in securing control of the provisional army that had been created in mid-1798 provoked rage in the president. Not only was Adams prevented by

[55]Hamilton to Harrison Gray Otis, Dec. 27, 1798, Jan. 26, 1799, *PAH,* 22:394, 440–41; Hamilton to Sedgwick, Feb. 2, 1799, ibid., 22:452–53; Adams to Otis, May 9, 1823, Adams Family Papers, reel 124.

[56]Adams to Abigail Adams, Dec. 12, 1796, Adams, *Works,* 1:495; Adams to McHenry, Oct. 22, 1798, ibid., 8:612–13.

party pressure from appointing several meritorious Republicans to the rank of general officer, but he was outmaneuvered politically and compelled to name Hamilton as second in command to General Washington. As Washington was old and not inclined to leave Mount Vernon except in the gravest emergency, Hamilton was in reality the army's commander. Adams was furious. His power had been usurped. He suspected that he had been the victim of a plot — he called it a "combined effort" — carried out by Hamilton and his satraps in the cabinet and Congress to "appoint him [Hamilton] general over the President." Thereafter, Adams called Hamilton "the most restless, impatient, artful, indefatigable and unprincipled Intriguer" in the United States. The First Lady, whose views usually coincided with those of her husband, labeled Hamilton "a second Buonaparty."[57] Adams now was convinced that Hamilton and his sycophants in the cabinet "intended to close the avenues to peace, and to ensure a war with France" that would enable Hamilton to utilize his army.[58]

Republicans in Congress had long since denounced the "unprincipled" Hamiltonians and accused them of plotting to invade the South as a means of destroying American republicanism. Sen. Stevens Mason of Virginia charged that it was the Federalists' "intention . . . to arm one half of the people, for the purpose of keeping the other half in awe." Long before Adams read the private letters that confirmed his worst fears, the Republican press had alleged that the Federalists had created the provisional army in order to solidify their national hegemony and to pave the way for the establishment of a monarchy in America. Adams had reached the same conclusion by early 1799, prompting him to surmise that what he had most feared when he

---

[57]Adams to McHenry, July 6, 1798, ibid., 8:574; Adams to Gerry, May 3, 1797, Adams Family Papers, reel 117; Adams to James Lloyd, Feb. 19, 1815, ibid., reel 122; Adams to Abigail Adams, Jan. 9, 1797, ibid., reel 383; Sedgwick to Hamilton, Feb. 7, 1799, *PAH,* 22:471; Abigail Adams to Smith, July 23, 1798, Smith Townsend Collection, Massachusetts Historical Society, Boston, Mass. On the appointment of officers in the provisional army, see William J. Murphy, "John Adams: The Politics of the Additional Army," *New England Quarterly* 52 (1979):234–49; Bernhard Knollenberg, "John Adams, Knox, and Washington," American Antiquarian Society, *Proceedings,* 56, Part 2 (1946):207–38; Robert Grough, "Officering the Army, 1798," *William and Mary Quarterly,* 3d ser. 43 (1986):461–71.

[58]Adams, "Correspondence Originally Published in *The Boston Patriot,*" Adams, *Works,* 9:305–6.

wrote the *Defence* a decade earlier was coming true. He believed that Hamilton and his satraps in Congress plotted to elevate the army commander above the president; he additionally thought this was to be their first step in extirpating republicanism and establishing an aristocratic oligarchy. In the *Defence* Adams had insisted that the executive must be the savior of the public, its protector against aristocratic tyranny. Convinced that Hamilton's "mad" design had to be thwarted before it produced an "instantaneous insurrection" by the republican citizenry, Adams believed he had to act. He possessed both the power and the popular support to defuse the French crisis. Furthermore, he was convinced that peace not only would shield the nation from a potentially disastrous war, but that it was the one sure antidote against the provisional army.[59]

On February 18, 1799, without prior notification of his cabinet or the party's congressional leaders, Adams acted. He sent Congress a terse statement: "Always disposed and ready to embrace every plausible appearance of probability of restoring tranquility, I nominate William Vans Murray . . . to be minister plenipotentiary of the United States to the French Republic." The messenger bearing Adams's stunning announcement arrived while Congress was in session. Vice President Jefferson, the president of the Senate, happily interrupted business to read the announcement. Harrison Gray Otis, a High Federalist from Massachusetts, was speaking on behalf of a bill to further increase the army when a senator brought Adams's message to the House chamber. Otis, visibly shaken by the news, sank into his seat. Jefferson later remarked that the Federalists' morose reaction to Adams's peace initiative proved that all along "war had been their object." The British minister to the United States wrote home that the "federal party were thunderstruck," the very term that had been used by Secretary Pickering to describe his reaction to the president's message.[60]

---

[59]Dauer, *Adams Federalists*, p. 215; Stewart, *Opposition Press*, p. 284; Sedgwick to Hamilton, Feb. 7, 25, 1799, *PAH*, 22:471, 503; Sedgwick to Rufus King, Sept. 26, 1800, ibid., 25:198 n.; Adams to Otis, May 9, 1823, Adams Family Papers, reel 124; Samuel Eliot Morison, *Life and Letters of Harrison Gray Otis*, 2 vols. (Boston, 1913), 1:162.

[60]Adams to the Senate, Feb. 18, 1799, Richardson, *Messages and Papers of the Presidents*, 1:282–83; Pickering to George Cabot, Feb. 21, 1799, Lodge, *Life and Letters of George Cabot*, p. 221; Wolcott to Cabot, Nov. 4, 1799, ibid., p. 253; Jefferson to Madison, Feb. 19, 26, 1800, Ford, *Writings of Jefferson*, 7:361–67, 370; Elkins and McKitrick, *Age of*

Adams's surprise announcement "stirred the Passions of some," the president remarked in a classic understatement. He knew that his message would provoke a furor, probably even cost him reelection in 1800, he told his wife. Later he charged that the "squibs, scoffs, and sarcasms" hurled at him by the extreme Federalists had been orchestrated in "secrecy and darkness" by Hamilton. In fact, Federalist newspapers denounced Adams in vituperative editorials, and anonymous party members sent him assassination threats. "Every decided Federalist is outrageously angry," one High Federalist stormed. Pickering, vitriolic as always, privately called his chief a "wrong-headed president" and declared that he was "wholly destitute" of the qualities of greatness. A Massachusetts senator portrayed Adams as insane, attributing his behavior, including his refusal to consult with his cabinet, to the "wild & irregular starts of a . . . half frantic mind." High Federalists who had praised Adams's independence only six months before now decried his resolute action. For instance, in private Sen. Theodore Sedgwick of Massachusetts sarcastically referred to the president as "the great man." He complained that Adams had isolated himself from his advisers and made crucial decisions unilaterally.[61]

Adams's behavior was not that of a madman. In fact, his actions were far more savvy than scholars have understood. Adams knew there

---

Federalism, pp. 618–19. On Adams's decision to send another mission to France, also see Jacob E. Cooke, "Country above Party: John Adams and the 1799 Mission to France," in Edward P. Willis, *Fame and the Founding Fathers* (Bethlehem, Pa., 1967), pp. 52–69, and Stephen G. Kurtz, "The French Mission of 1799–1800: Concluding Chapter in the Statecraft of John Adams," *Political Science Quarterly* 80 (1965):543–57. On the moderation of French policy in 1798, see Frances S. Childs, "French Opinion of Anglo-American Relations, 1795–1805," *French American Review* 1 (1948):21–35; James A. James, "French Opinion as a Factor in Preventing War between France and the United States, 1795–1800," *American Historical Review* 30 (1924):44–55; Wilson E. Lyon, "The French Directory and the United States," *American Historical Review* 43 (1938):514–32; William Stinchcombe, "Talleyrand and the American Negotiations of 1797–1798," *Journal of American History* 62 (1975):575–90; William Stinchcombe, "The Diplomacy of the XYZ Affair," *William and Mary Quarterly,* 3d ser. 34 (1977):590–617; Bowman, *Struggle for Neutrality,* pp. 334–59.

[61]Adams to Abigail Adams, Feb. 22, 1799, Adams, *Works,* 1:544–45; Adams, "Correspondence Originally Published in *The Boston Patriot,*" ibid., 9:272–73; Brown, *Presidency of John Adams,* p. 99; Pickering to McHenry, Feb. 3, 1799, Steiner, *McHenry,* p. 568; Sedgwick to Hamilton, Feb. 22, 25, 1799, *PAH,* 22:494, 503; DeConde, *Quasi-War,* p. 182; "Benjamin Goodhue," Sibley et al., *Biographical Sketches of Those Who Attended Harvard,* 16:364; Sedgwick to Henry Van Schaack, Jan. 4, 1800, Sedgwick Papers.

would be opposition to a diplomatic mission, as well as angry divisions over the diplomats entrusted with the undertaking. By naming only one envoy, Murray, he successfully channeled High Federalist dudgeon away from the central issue — the mission itself — and into a frantic attempt to enlarge the negotiating team, packing it with men they could trust. In fact, Senator Sedgwick remarked at the time that the Senate dared only challenge the president "on the fitness of the man nominated." Moreover, it is likely that Adams favored a multimember team all along. This was the manner in which the United States had responded to virtually every extraordinary diplomatic problem. In 1776 Congress had sent a team of three diplomats to Canada and another three-member commission to France. Congress appointed a team to negotiate the peace settlement at the conclusion of the War of Independence and a multimember commission to conclude postwar commercial treaties with the nations of Europe. Adams had been a member of three multimember diplomatic missions and he had appointed a three-member commission to carry out his initial probe to France in 1797. The lone exception to the practice of using teams of diplomats to cope with extraordinary problems had been when Washington appointed John Jay as the sole plenipotentiary to negotiate differences with Great Britain, and the treaty he brought home had resulted in a tempest.

Adams hinted to his wife in 1799 that he had expected his party to demand that Murray be accompanied by additional envoys. When the High Federalists in fact made that demand, President Adams immediately acquiesced and nominated two additional Federalists, Chief Justice Oliver Ellsworth and Gov. William Davie of North Carolina, to join Murray in Europe. Later Adams remembered that the High Federalists in the Senate interpreted his supposed concession as an "enlightened" move. Senator Sedgwick even boasted that the inclusion of Ellsworth and Davie had amounted to a congressional triumph that would save the country from the "vile scrape" brought on by Adams.[62]

---

[62]Adams to Abigail Adams, Feb. 22, 1799, Adams Family Papers, reel 393; Adams, Address to Congress, Feb. 25, 1799, Richardson, *Messages and Papers of the Presidents,* 1:284; Adams, "Correspondence Originally Published in *The Boston Patriot,*" in Adams, *Works,* 9:250; Sedgwick to John Rutherford, Mar. 1, 1799, Sedgwick Papers; Sedgwick to Henry Van Schaack, Feb. 26, 1799, ibid.; Elkins and McKitrick, *Age of Federalism,* p. 365.

Adams further defused the opposition by letting eight months pass before he ordered the diplomats to sail for Europe. He waited for the completion of the men-of-war that Congress had authorized the previous summer, and he hesitated until he received still more assurances that the envoys would be received in Paris.[63] When confirmation arrived from France on July 30, the president immediately ordered the preparation of the final instructions for his diplomats. A foot-dragging secretary of state and one final effort by some members of the cabinet to delay or destroy the mission hindered matters, but by late November America's three envoys were on European soil.

The gamble that Adams took was successful. Fourteen months after the envoys sailed, and just days after Jefferson had defeated Adams in the election of 1800, the president learned that his diplomats had concluded a treaty with France. The Convention of 1800 did not secure every concession that Adams had sought. For example, France refused to pay compensation for the damages caused by its commerce raiders. Nevertheless, even High Federalist senators were willing to ratify with reservations a treaty with flaws rather "than leave it to a Jacobin Administration to do much worse," as Hamilton remarked. Besides, Hamilton added hypocritically, the Federalists in future elections could claim credit for securing the treaty that had prevented war with France. If anyone deserved credit for preserving the peace, it was President Adams, and he was not above taking credit. With peace assured, he told his son that he had sailed the ship of state through stormy seas and into a safe port, and he added again that his actions had been prompted by the threat of the "old tories," who hoped to force "on the people a change of some sort in the constitution."[64]

Adams experienced a troubled, and in some ways unique, presidency. He held the post in an extraordinarily tempestuous time. His presidency was consumed with a lone issue, a foreign policy crisis. The

---

[63]Brown, *Presidency of John Adams*, p. 102.

[64]Hamilton to Sedgwick, Dec. 22, 1800, *PAH*, 25:270; Hamilton to Gouverneur Morris, Jan. 10, 1801, ibid., 25:307; Adams to Thomas B. Adams, Jan. 14, 16, 24, 1801, Adams Family Papers, reel 400. Also see E. Wilson Lyon, "The Franco-American Convention of 1800," *Journal of Modern History* 12 (1940):305–33, and Richard C. Rohr, "The Federalist Party and the Convention of 1800," *Diplomatic History* 12 (1988):237–60; Bowman, *Struggle for Neutrality*, pp. 386–413.

national government was new. The roles of the executive and legislature were often ill-defined. Political parties were embryonic. Furthermore, unlike modern presidents, Adams came to office uncommitted to a specific domestic program. His private utterances suggest that he hoped to make reforms in the nation's currency system and the functions of the Bank of the United States, and he publicly spoke in vague terms of patronizing education and revising the judiciary system. However, these aspirations were initially subsumed by the foreign policy crisis and later fell victim to the deep fissures within the Federalist party. Only the Judiciary Act of 1801, a law popular with lame-duck Federalists who hoped to pack the courts before the Jeffersonians took office, passed in Adams's last two years in office.[65]

In such a fluid and passionate atmosphere, virtually any president would have faced difficulties, but Adams's temperament and habits contributed to his woes. He was irritable, tactless, and indiscreet, and he had long since habituated himself to working alone. His manner and style, as well as his inexperience in an executive capacity, inhibited his ability to act as the intermediator who might have brought the two wings of his party, together even with an occasional sympathetic Republican, into a more harmonious and efficacious coalition. Furthermore, had Adams surrounded himself with loyal lieutenants, he and his cabinet might have succeeded in bonding together the diverse elements within his party. Had Adams eschewed his protracted vacations and remained in the capital, he might have had a better feel for public opinion and sentiment within both parties. But his choices and habits left him terribly isolated, too much so to succeed politically.

In 1800, as he neared the end of his term and faced reelection, Adams was not without friends. Although some Federalists who backed him did so more out of fear of Jefferson, his opponent, than out of love for Adams, the president's courageous effort to save the peace had "endeared him to the great body of federalists," one Federalist senator remarked. Even most Republicans had come to see that he was not the war hawk they had imagined at the height of the French crisis.[66]

---

[65]Adams, Inaugural Address, Mar. 4, 1797, Richardson, *Messages and Papers of the Presidents,* 1:231; Adams, Annual Address, Nov. 22, 1800, ibid., 1:306; Dauer, *Adams Federalists,* pp. 241, 242–43, 258, 303; Brown, *Presidency of John Adams,* pp. 198–200.

[66]Fisher Ames to Wolcott, June 12, 1800, George Gibbs, ed., *Memoirs of the Admin-*

But Adams's actions had provoked considerable enmity as well, particularly within his own party. Some Federalists questioned his character—Hamilton spoke of his "unfortunate foibles of a vanity without bounds"—and portrayed him as a man of reckless, even irrational, judgment. McHenry, his secretary of war, regarded him as "actually insane."[67]

Yet Adams was not entirely culpable for the cleavages within his party. The Federalist party was always divided. From the outset of Adams's presidency, about 20 percent of Federalist congressmen broke with High Federalists on substantive issues. The party was "uncemented," as Sen. George Cabot of Massachusetts once put it. It was divided between moderates and radicals, as well as between Southerners—whom a Massachusetts senator called "appeasing men"—and Northerners. President Adams would have been confronted with divisiveness and bitter opposition within his party regardless of the diplomatic choice he made.[68]

Adams ultimately believed, as have some scholars, that his presidency was destroyed and he lost his bid for reelection in 1800 because of the fissures that burst open within his own party in response to his foreign policy initiatives in 1799.[69] It is true that the Federalists failed egregiously in elections during late 1799 and 1800, until by early 1801 the Republican party controlled both houses of Congress. But Adams's diplomacy was not entirely—or perhaps even largely—to blame for the party's electoral woes. The Federalist party, originally thought of as the party of Washington and the embodiment of the spirit that

---

istrations of Washington and John Adams, 2 vols. (New York, 1846), 2:368; Ferling, *John Adams*, p. 393; Brown, *Presidency of John Adams*, p. 177; James Madison to Jefferson, Nov. 5, 1800, *PAH*, 25:181–82 n.; Jefferson to Madison, May 12, 1800, Ford, *Writings of Jefferson*, 7:446.

[67]Alexander Hamilton, Letter from Alexander Hamilton, Concerning the Public Conduct and Character of John Adams, Esq., President of the United States, *PAH*, 25:190; McHenry to John McHenry, Jr., May 20, 1799, ibid., 24:509.

[68]Dauer, *Adams Federalists*, pp. 245, 303, 316, 321; Cabot to Christopher Gore, Jan. 21, 1800, Lodge, *Life and Letters of George Cabot*, p. 268; Welch, *Theodore Sedgwick*, p. 168; Brown, *Presidency of John Adams*, p. 98.

[69]Adams to Mercy Otis Warren, July 20, 1807, Adams Family Papers, reel 118; Adams to James Lloyd, Feb. 6, 1815, Adams, *Works*, 10:15; Shaw, *Character of John Adams*, pp. 259–60; Smith, *John Adams*, 2:1058; Kurtz, *Presidency of John Adams*, pp. 374–404; Gilbert Chinnard, *Honest John Adams* (Boston, 1933), pp. 284–315.

had produced the new U.S. Constitution, largely suffered a backlash of popular resentment against its military, civil rights, and taxation policies.[70]

Adams in fact remained about as popular as he had been at the outset of his presidency. Even Hamilton had to admit on the eve of the election that "in the body of [the] people there is a strong personal attachment" to Adams. Ultimately, Adams made a better showing than his party during the election of 1800. Indeed, had he won in New York, a state he had carried four years earlier, he would have had a second term. But Adams's fate in New York was sealed early on. Although the Federalists were deeply divided in New York in 1800 and Hamilton openly vilified Adams as irrational and emotionally unstable and urged his defeat, the party's self-immolation did not cause Adams's failure in this key state. The Republicans had gained control of the New York legislature — which selected the state's presidential electors — in 1797 and never thereafter lost their majority, not even during the high tide of Adams's stature in 1798. The Federalist party's strength had eroded in New York even before the Quasi-War crisis, a fatal harvest brought on by political ineptitude, an endemic distrust of the people, and a popular identity as a pro-British, pro-aristocratic faction.[71]

Few chief executives have suffered through as stormy a term in office as that experienced by Adams. It is likely that anyone who was elected in 1796, save perhaps Washington, would have experienced similar difficulties, for public opinion was deeply divided in a crisis-laden environment. Adams made mistakes, but under the circumstances he performed well. He pursued a coherent foreign policy

---

[70]Noble Cunningham, "Election of 1800," in Arthur M. Schlesinger, Jr., *The Coming to Power: Critical Presidential Elections in American History* (New York, 1971), pp. 61–63; Brown, *Presidency of John Adams*, p. 193; John C. Miller, *Alexander Hamilton: Portrait in Paradox* (New York, 1959), p. 510; Elkins and McKitrick, *Age of Federalism*, pp. 726–43.

[71]Hamilton to Charles Carroll of Carrollton, July 1, 1800, *PAH*, 25:2; Hamilton, *Letter from Alexander Hamilton, Concerning . . . John Adams*, ibid., 25:186–234; Dauer, *Adams Federalists*, pp. 258, 303; Sharp, *American Politics in the Early Republic*, pp. 247–48; John C. Miller, *The Federalist Era, 1789–1801* (New York, 1960), p. 276. On the election of 1800, see Cunningham, "Election of 1800," in Schlesinger, *History of American Presidential Elections*, 1:101–58, and Morton Borden, "Election of 1800: Charge and Countercharge," *Delaware History* 5 (1952):42–62.

throughout his presidency. He exhibited an extraordinary feel for public opinion. He sensed the threats to the safety of the union posed by those capable of formidable treachery.

Adams assumed the office guided by the belief that the president must be the "father and protector" of the many against the malevolence of the few. In the great crisis of his presidency, a perilous time for an uncertain union, President Adams exercised the powers of the presidency to stanch what he believed to be an oligarchic plot to substantively alter American politics and society. Thereafter, he never wavered in the conviction that his resolute, defiant, statesmanlike quest for peace on honorable terms had been his greatest act in a public career that spanned a quarter century, "the most splendid diamond in my crown," as he subsequently remarked.[72] Not all of Adams's successors could boast of such selfless, sacrificial service to the national interest.

---

[72]Adams to James Lloyd, Feb. 6, 1815, Adams, *Works,* 10:115.

Contributors

Kenneth R. Bowling is coeditor of the Documentary History of the First Federal Congress, 1789–91, and associate adjunct professor of history at The George Washington University. He is the author of *The Creation of Washington, D.C.: The Idea and Location of the American Capital* (1991) as well as several articles on the politics of the American Revolution. Since 1994 he has been the moderator of the United States Capitol Historical Society's annual conference on the history of Congress, 1789–1801.

William R. Casto is the Allison Professor of Law at Texas Tech University and author of the award-winning book *The Supreme Court in the Early Republic*. He is currently at work on a book dealing with the allocation of foreign affairs powers under the Constitution.

William C. diGiacomantonio is associate editor of the Documentary History of the First Federal Congress, 1789–1791, a project of the National Historical Publications and Records Commission of the National Archives and The George Washington University in Washington, D.C. His publications include articles on Quakers' antislavery lobbying, President George Washington's federal city commissioners, and federal support for the arts and sciences in the First Federal Congress.

John Ferling is professor of history at the State University of West Georgia. He is author of *The First of Men: A Life of George Washington* (1988) and *John Adams: A Life* (1992), as well as several books and articles on early American warfare. His most recent study, *Setting the World Ablaze: Washington, Adams, and Jefferson in the American Revolution*, was published by Oxford University Press in July 2000.

Joanne B. Freeman is assistant professor of history at Yale University. She is the author of "The Election of 1800: A Study in the Logic of Political Change," *Yale Law Journal* (1999); "Dueling as Politics: Reinterpreting the Burr-Hamilton Duel," *William and Mary Quarterly* (1996); and "Slander, Poison, Whispers, and Fame: Jefferson's 'Anas' and Political Gossip in the Early Republic," *Journal of the Early Republic* (1995). She is currently completing *Affairs of Honor: Political Combat and Character in the Early Republic*, a study of the logic and culture of national politics before the establishment of formal political parties.

Mary A. Giunta is a historian with the National Historical Publications and Records Commission. She served as project director and editor in chief of the commission's three-volume documentary project, *The Emerging Nation: A Documentary History of the Foreign Relations of the United States, 1780–1789* (1996), and the accompanying reader, *Documents of the Emerging Nation: U.S. Foreign Relations, 1775–1789* (1998). Dr. Giunta holds a doctorate in history from The Catholic University of America. Her interests include early American history and the development of the first party system in the U.S. Congress.

John D. Gordan III is a partner in the New York office of Morgan, Lewis and Bockius LLP. His previous publications include "United States v. Joseph Ravara," in *Origins of the Federal Judiciary Act of 1789,* ed. Maeva Marcus (1992) and *Authorized by No Law: The San Francisco Committee of Vigilance of 1856 and the United States Circuit Court for the Districts of California* (1987).

Wythe Holt is University Research Professor of Law at the University of Alabama. He has authored several articles from his research project on the origins of our national court system and its functioning in the first fifteen years of its existence, including the article in this volume; " 'To Establish Justice': Politics, the Judiciary Act of 1789, and the Invention of the Federal Courts," *Duke Law Journal* (1989); and "John Blair: 'A Safe and Conscientious Judge,' " in *Seriatim: The Supreme Court before John Marshall,* ed. Scott Douglas Gerber (1998).

Elizabeth M. Nuxoll is project director and coeditor of the Papers of Robert Morris, 1781–1784, at Queens College of the City University of New York. She is the author of *Congress and the Munitions Merchants: The Secret Committee of Trade during the American Revolution, 1775–1777* (1985). She is currently working on a biography of Robert Morris.

Anna Coxe Toogood is a career historian with the National Park Service at Independence National Historical Park. She is coauthor of the introduction to the 1993 reprint of *Bring Out Your Dead* by John Harvey Powell, as well as "The Philadelphia Yellow Fever Epidemic of 1793," *Scientific American* (1988). As park historian she has completed cultural landscape reports for Independence Square and Independence Mall. She is now researching and writing about the eighteenth-century history and development of the three city blocks forming Independence Mall.

Jack D. Warren, Jr., served as assistant editor of the Presidential Series of *The Papers of George Washington* at the University of Virginia from 1993 to 1998. He is the editor or coeditor of four volumes in that series. He also is the coauthor, with Donald S. Lutz, of *A Covenanted People: The Religious Tradition and the Origins of American Constitutionalism* (1987). Most recently, he is the author of *The Presidency of George Washington,* published in 1999 by the Mount Vernon Ladies Association in commemoration of the 200th anniversary of Washington's death.

Index

Page numbers in italics refer to illustrations.